THE DIVINE
ORDER

THE DIVINE ORDER

WESTERN CULTURE in the
MIDDLE AGES
and the RENAISSANCE

by HENRY BAMFORD PARKES

New York: Alfred · A · Knopf

1 9 6 9

THIS IS A BORZOI BOOK

PUBLISHED BY ALFRED A. KNOPF, INC.

FIRST EDITION

Contents

Illustrations

following page 244

vii

INTRODUCTION

Western civilization originated during the period of Western history popularly known as the Dark Ages. This period began with the dissolution of Roman authority in the western provinces of the Empire during the fifth century of our era and its replacement by new kingdoms controlled by barbarian invaders from northern Europe. In the course of the next half-dozen centuries the barbarians began to assimilate the classical and Judeo-Christian heritage, to fuse this heritage with what was still viable in their own social and artistic traditions, and to exhibit new creative powers. This union of diverse cultures produced the new civilization.

Before the Protestant Reformation of the sixteenth century the main bond of cultural unity in the West was the teaching of the Roman Church, and the area covered by the new civilization was coterminous with that of Latin Christianity. This area included Italy, France, Britain, and much of the Spanish peninsula, all of which had formerly been part of the Roman Empire. It also comprised a number of northern peoples—Irish, Germans, Scandinavians, and Poles and other Slavic groups—who had never submitted to Roman rule but who were gradually incorporated into the west-European culture area by the efforts of Catholic missionaries during the Dark and early Middle Ages. Despite the primacy of the Pope at Rome, the main centers of cultural innovation were not in the Mediterranean provinces but farther north, in the areas where the Greco-Roman civilization had never established deep roots. Independent creative powers first began to manifest themselves in the British Isles fairly early in the Dark Ages, but the West's real coming of age took place in the eleventh and twelfth centuries and had its center in northern France, which retained cultural leadership until the Italian Renaissance in the fourteenth and following centuries.

Classical civilization had been located in the Mediterranean countries, which had been unified, politically and culturally, by Roman imperialism. But during the Dark Ages the Mediterranean world was split into three sections. While the northwest became part of the new culture area, the northeast, dominated by

Greek Christianity and the Byzantine Empire, preserved much of the classical civilization, though with a strong admixture of Oriental elements; and the southern provinces were conquered in the seventh and eighth centuries by the Mohammedan Arabs. This threefold division of the countries bordering on the great inland sea has persisted with few territorial changes down to our own day. And despite a common intellectual indebtedness to the Hellenic aspects of the classical culture, these three different civilizations have had relatively little influence on each other and have generally regarded each other with hostility. Even the profession of common religious beliefs by the Westerners and the Byzantines, and considerable scientific and philosophical borrowing by the West from the Arabic civilization, did not promote mutual understanding and cooperation. The cultural and institutional differences made these three civilizations sharply hostile to each other. In fact, the most important debt owed by the West to the two neighboring civilizations was negative rather than positive. Close contact, especially through the Crusades, stimulated the new Western society to an awareness of cultural antagonisms which hastened the process of self-definition. Without such a process no civilization can achieve greatness.

In making use of the word "civilization" to describe Western society and its Mediterranean neighbors, I do not wish to imply that a civilization is an organic entity destined to go through preordained processes of youth, maturity, and final dissolution, as argued by exponents of the cyclic theory of history, such as Spengler and Toynbee. By "civilization" I mean simply a group of peoples who have similar institutions, moral and political values, and general views of life, and who, often in spite of frequent and intense conflicts, are able to exert a continuing influence on each other. In analyzing cultural history it is necessary to regard the whole civilization as the basic unit of study, as one cannot otherwise find continuous lines of development. The cultural growth of the different peoples who belong to the same civilization is constantly affected by trends that are common to all of them and cannot be explained without continuing reference to the whole civilization. It is impossible to understand the development of any one country if it is studied in isolation from its neighbors. Since its origins in the Dark Ages, Western civilization has exhibited this kind of unity, and it continues to do so today despite its extension to other parts of the world.

When two different civilizations are in contact with each other, on the other hand, their borrowings are not continuous and are mostly of minor importance. If the civilization is deeply affected by its neighbors, it is likely to lose much of its own essential character and sense of values, and its citizens are always obscurely aware of the dangers of total subversion. The normal attitude of different civilizations toward each other is therefore marked by misunderstanding and antagonism, and this often has some justification. It is, of course, true that during the early Middle Ages, Western civilization borrowed extensively from its two competitors, but it took only what it could readily assimilate, which consisted mainly of specific scientific and philosophical formulations—many of them originally derived from Hellenic sources. There was no continuous interchange, and the West remained unaffected by the general spirit of both Byzantine and Arabic society. In more recent times, Western borrowings from other societies have been of minimal importance, while the Asiatic civilizations, on the other hand, have been so deeply influenced by the West that they have lost much of their traditional character.

But while it is generally necessary, in writing cultural history, to think in terms of different civilizations as the only comprehensible units of study, it should not be supposed that all civilizations pass through the same phases of development or that all societies are to be regarded as necessarily parts of civilizations. It is possible to trace certain parallelisms in the development of different civilizations, but their importance can easily be overestimated. They have been grossly exaggerated in the work of Toynbee, who seems to have generalized largely from a single example, that of the classical civilization which preceded the civilization of the West. None, however, of the twenty-odd civilizations that he discusses can be regarded without considerable distortion as going through the same sequence of phases. In some parts of the world, especially in the Near and Middle East, so many different societies have been so intermingled over so long a period that it becomes impossible to identify any specific civilizations. Both the classical and the Western civilizations were able to develop such clearly marked qualities because they were largely isolated from other peoples during their formative periods. And in certain important qualities Western civilization has enjoyed a unique development. It is unique, in particular, because although it began as an independent growth, originating among northern peoples who had hitherto been barbaric, it adopted much of the intellectual and the aesthetic heritage of its classical predecessor. This combination of independence and affiliation is not paralleled by any other civilization in history; and because Western civilization had novel beginnings, we may suppose that its future history may be similarly unpredictable. The major Asiatic civilizations, by contrast, have had a continuous history since very early times, passing periodically through phases of decline and renewal, but—at least until the late nineteenth century—never undergoing any total transformation.

Perhaps the central theme in the history of the West—how far this has been true of other civilizations is a debatable question—has been the interplay between the forces that maintain social unity and order and the movement toward individual freedom and rational thought. Creativity depends on freedom; individuals must be at liberty to affirm new hypotheses and to explore new ways of thinking and new modes of sensibility. But the growth of freedom may lead to a denial of the premises upon which unity and order depend. This disturbs the equilibrium of society and may result in the threat of disintegration and anarchy and in an acceptance of a government based solely on brute force as necessary for the maintenance of order. But the balance of freedom and order can be maintained as long as there is general agreement about the meaning of human life and about values and standards of behavior. The basic hope of Western man—a hope derived from both Hellenic and Jewish sources—is that such an agreement is in accord with the underlying realities of human life, freedom and order being ultimately in harmony with each other. If this is true, then the individual who seeks self-fulfillment and the realization of his own potentialities is at the same time contributing to the welfare of society. A civilization acquires its cultural qualities from the affirmation of a general view of life and from the specific beliefs and values associated with it; but these always transcend rationality and cannot be fully justified in intellectual terms, and they may therefore be described as constituting an ideology.[1]

Every society accepts certain values as self-evident postulates that are not usually subject to question. Thus, for example, in the Western civilization of today, and more especially in the United

---

[1] In the Introduction to *Gods and Men* I spoke of these nonrational elements in the view of life of the society as myths. But "ideology" is a more accurate, though less attractive, word for what I have in mind. In its narrowest meaning a myth is a story in which imaginary characters enact experiences which society regards as of a special significance in the development of its individual members. Through the enactment, these experiences acquire form and meaning, and their destructive potentialities are brought under control by a kind of catharsis. Most myths deal, directly or implicitly, with the processes of growth from childhood to maturity and the dangers of such a growth, and hence include some kind of rebellion against parental figures and the appropriate punishment for it. The stories of Adam and Eve and of the Crucifixion and Resurrection of Jesus are the most important myths in Christian society. Similar attitudes are conveyed in a number of Greek myths, notably those of Prometheus and Orestes. In Western civilization certain widely known stories have expressed basic experiences on such a profound level that they can be described as myths. Notable examples are the stories of Faust and of Hamlet—the subject of Hamlet, as of the Orestes story, is the struggle of a young man to achieve maturity by assuming his father's role. See p. 462.

To avoid confusion, I am using the word "ideology" to describe the general concepts which make up a view of life, and am restricting the use of myth to stories that have a special social significance, whether or not they are believed to be true. Some myths (like those of Christianity) are, of course, generally regarded as having a basis in historical fact, while with others the question of truth is irrelevant. (I am indebted to Professor Warren Susman for pointing out to me the importance of the distinction between ideology and myth.)

States, the values of freedom and democracy and of economic growth are usually taken for granted, and almost all serious political discussion takes place on the basis of these premises. Yet they originated in the process of moral affirmation which transcends reason and logic; and when they are called in question, there is no way by which their validity can be conclusively established. A society's general conception of the nature of reality is even less capable of rational justification. It makes a considerable difference to a society's view of life whether time and space are regarded as finite or infinite. One of the basic changes in the sensibility of Western society at the end of the Middle Ages was the shift from belief in an enclosed and finite universe to acceptance of the universe as infinite; this shift was reflected in political and moral thinking and in the arts, and preceded the formulation of the appropriate astronomical concepts. Yet a finite and an infinite universe are equally beyond the scope of a human mind and imagination. Normally, of course, it has been the function of organized religion to inculcate society's general view of life and to give it support by means of appropriate beliefs and symbolisms. Western society since the sixteenth century has been unique in the generally secular tone of its intellectual and aesthetic creations, but these have not actually been as rational as is frequently supposed. An insistence that the Western ideology is rational, in fact, is a part of that ideology; the assumption of its rationality is an affirmation incapable of proof.

The happy and productive periods in the history of the West have been characterized by implicit faith in some general "frame of acceptance" (a phrase coined by Kenneth Burke). The most obvious examples of a frame of acceptance have been the feudalism of the early Middle Ages, the monarchical state of the sixteenth and seventeenth centuries, and the capitalism and representative government of the nineteenth century. At such periods the whole social order appears to its individual members as just and rational. They believe that they can achieve self-fulfillment by conforming with the established mores and institutions, and there is little serious sense of conflict between individual drives and social organization. There is general agreement about principles of justice, and individuals are willing to support these principles even when such principles conflict with their own interests, in spite of the fact that they must inevitably appear as arbitrary and merely conventional in some of their practical applications. At such times the social order is felt to be legitimate and hence the proper focus of individual loyalties. And its basic institutions are regarded as endowed with sovereignty (sovereignty is essentially a psychological concept; it belongs to whatever form of authority, whether secular or ecclesiastical, ecumenical or local, that people of any particular epoch think it ought to belong to), but a social order is accepted as legitimate only when there is a general belief that it is in accord with objective standards and values, and these cannot be based on reason alone. The frame of acceptance needs the support of a whole view of life, including an appropriate cosmology. Man's view of the universe always reflects social trends. Thus, for example, the shift from a Ptolemaic to a Copernican universe during the Renaissance was a response to the growth of an individualism which manifested itself also in the voyages of discovery.

The causes of cultural change have been both economic and ideological. Twentieth-century Western historians have mostly been accustomed to regard economic developments as basic and to interpret intellectual and aesthetic trends as reflections of economic and political conditions. But economic progress does not come about automatically. It is the result of favoring social and intellectual conditions, and its causes are therefore partly ideological. Western civilization has been unique in the encouragement it has given to technological advances. In other parts of the world there has been relatively little economic progress since the third millennium B.C., except insofar as their peoples have come under the influence of the West. Some Asiatic civilizations, such as the Chinese and the Arabic, have made important technological innovations, but these have not been applied in such a way as to promote continued economic advance. In the whole history of humanity, such advances have been the exception rather than the rule. The emphasis on technological progress in Western civilization has resulted from a number of different noneconomic factors, including particularly a view of life which regarded nature as orderly and capable of being understood and controlled by human beings, and which affirmed the possibility of progress. Thus cultural change was caused not by any single factor but by the interplay of both material and spiritual forces.

Western civilization has remained dynamic and has never become frozen at any particular stage of development, and each of its successive frames of acceptance has been relatively short-lived. Epochs of creative harmony have alternated with epochs of social and cultural disintegration. Under the impact of economic and institutional change, of new ideas calling into question the accepted view of life, and of individual demands for greater freedom, an established order ceases to be regarded as legitimate. Individuals no longer give it an unquestioning loyalty or accept it as the fulfillment of ideals of justice. Thus men and women develop a sense of alienation from the society to which they belong, and feel that they can achieve self-realization only in opposition to the established modes of social discipline, not in harmony with them. This might lead finally both to the acceptance of despotic government based frankly on force as the only remedy for the disintegration of society and to a permanent loss of creativity.[2]

But in Western society, so far at least, the breakdown of a

---

[2] Such a situation is exemplified in the writings of Machiavelli. The Italian city-state society had completely lost all sense of legitimacy, so that any government had to be based frankly on force and fraud. Machiavelli realized what had happened, but he could not find a solution to the problem, which was, in fact, insoluble. There can be no political order unless some kind of authority is recognized as legitimate, and legitimacy always transcends rationalism. The Italian cities eventually accepted an order imposed by Spain. Since Machiavelli was attempting to find remedies for a disintegration which has fortunately been a rare occurrence in Western history, and since the terms in which he stated the problem made any solution impossible, his work is much less important than has often been supposed. See pp. 381–7.

frame of acceptance has not meant any complete abandonment of the basic Western beliefs and values. After a prolonged and often painful period of transition, the sense of legitimacy and the loyalties of individuals become attached to new institutions, and the belief that the social order is just and rational is re-established. Thus during the later Middle Ages there was a transfer of allegiance from the feudal aristocracy and the Catholic Church to the monarchical state, and in subsequent centuries from the king to the nation. Meanwhile the fundamental affirmations of Western society—natural law and ethical monotheism—have continued to command general assent, though they have been given new interpretations and have served to justify different institutions.

Thus the subject matter of Western cultural history consists especially in the rise, disintegration, and reformation of the frames of acceptance which give support to established institutions and promote a harmony of individual freedom with social order. And each frame of acceptance is supported by the affirmation of a general view of life with the appropriate values and mores, and includes ideological elements which transcend and sometimes contradict rational thinking. This view of life is reflected in religious beliefs and philosophical speculations, in literary and artistic creations, and even in scientific hypotheses.[3]

Philosophy, literature, and the arts are therefore prime materials for the study of past societies, not because they necessarily influence social development but because they reflect and express it. One can gauge the general character of society more fully and directly from its philosophical trends and its art forms than from works of political history or sociology. In political or economic history one is always handicapped by the incompleteness of the

---

[3] There are, for example, obvious parallels between the Newtonian universe and the monarchical state, Darwinian evolution and nineteenth-century capitalism, Einstein's theory of relativity and twentieth-century thought in general. It would seem that scientific theories (as distinct from the observations which they purport to explain) are more subjective than is usually supposed.

record and the unreliability of its recorders; but a philosophical treatise or a work of art is a direct communication from a past society to its living students.

Socially accepted values and beliefs find expression in both popular and serious literature and art, though at different levels of discernment. The popular arts generally reflect these values at the level of wish-fulfillment and thus indicate the hopes and expectations of the mass of the population. Particularly significant is the hero whom the audience is expected to admire and identify with. Much of the development of Western civilization is reflected in the transition from the feudal warrior and the saint of the early popular literature of the Middle Ages to the cultivated young nobleman of the Renaissance and subsequently to the social climber of the bourgeois novel and to the alienated escapist, unable to conform with a corrupt society, of twentieth-century American popular fiction. Each major change in Western society is accompanied by the adoption of a new kind of model for imitation, and this is reflected in the new type of success story. The more serious writers and artists, on the other hand, while presenting the same values and beliefs, are aware of their limitations and inconsistencies and of the costs and penalties of social success. Attuned to the more subtle changes of feeling and sensitivity, they are able to record the secret emotional history of the community to which they belong and to present psychological trends which are beyond the scope of more intellectual observers. This often makes them prophetic of future developments. Social significance is especially manifested in painting and sculpture, which (whether representational or abstract) always endeavor to present what society regards as ultimate reality and which frequently reflect social attitudes more fully and directly than do literature and music.

The early cultural history of the West consisted primarily of the gradual fusion of barbaric and classical traditions, a process which was not substantially completed until the Renaissance. While the West derived its mores and institutions largely from the barbaric background, its official values and general view of life are products of the classical heritage. Throughout the early Middle Ages these conflicting traditions existed side by side with relatively little mutual penetration, and the emergence of a new civilization in which both elements were fully incorporated took place only after several centuries of gradual mingling.

The most important elements in the classical heritage were certain basic concepts affirming the ultimate harmony of freedom and order and thus presenting a view of life which promoted optimism and the belief in progress. The major Greek contribution was the doctrine of natural law. This was not only descriptive of natural processes but was also normative for human behavior, thus combining the scientific understanding of natural processes with ethical affirmation. The ideal society was the society that followed the guidance of nature, and what was good for the state was good also for the individual, so that there was no distinction between political and ethical values. The doctrine of natural law liberated man from the duty of obedience to the irrational powers of religious superstition and made him the master of his own destiny. The detailed applications varied. There were sharp differences between the democratic ideals of fifth-century-B.C. Athens, as voiced in the funeral speech of Pericles, and the authoritarianism of Plato, and to a considerable extent all Western political history has been a continuing debate between these two points of view. But both of them believed that man should be guided by reason and could find his moral and political values in the study of nature. The Jews added the belief in ethical monotheism, declaring that the universe was ruled by a single deity who was righteous as well as all-powerful and that goodness meant conformity with his will. Thus, unlike the Greek philosophers, who had conceived of God as an impersonal being unconcerned with human affairs, the Jews continued to envisage him in personal terms as their own peculiar deity. Although Jehovah retained much of his original tribalistic quality, he was universalized and moralized through the teaching of the prophets. The affirmations of the prophetic movement could easily be fused with the Hellenic doctrine of natural law, and were, in fact, so fused by early Christianity, beginning with St. Paul's epistle to the Romans. According to Christian doctrine the law of nature was identical with the will of God, and its ethical standards were known to the conscience of every individual even without the aid of divine revelation.

The Jewish prophets looked forward to a time when any form of coercive authority would become unnecessary because all men would know and voluntarily perform the divine will, so that all conflict between freedom and order would be transcended. In the words which the prophet Jeremiah put into the mouth of Jehovah, "They shall teach no more every man his labor, and every man his brother, saying, know the Lord, for they shall all know me." The Lord would "put his law in their inward parts and light it in their hearts." [4] This promise of the coming harmony was incorporated into Christianity in the form of belief in the kingdom of heaven, which would become a reality after the second coming of the Messiah. And in its original form the kingdom of heaven was to be achieved not only in a heavenly afterlife but also on earth. Judaism repudiated the cyclic view of history held by all other ancient peoples and affirmed that it was a meaningful process leading to the gradual regeneration of humanity. This was the origin of the Western belief in progress, which has gradually been secularized and become a kind of substitute religion, but retains elements of its prophetic origin. Both the liberalism of the eighteenth-century enlightenment and the Marxism of the nineteenth and twentieth centuries looked forward to a kingdom of freedom still recognizably derived from the promises of Jeremiah.

Natural law, ethical monotheism, and the coming of the heavenly kingdom have been the basic elements of the Western view of life, and have been incorporated into each successive frame of acceptance. They were, of course, transmitted to Western civilization by the Church, which, by the fourth century, had

---

[4] Jeremiah, xxxi, 33–4.

largely forgotten its initial antagonism to the classical culture and had adopted theological doctrines in which much of classicism was fused with Judaism. The Church of the later Roman Empire, however, was also deeply affected by the decadence of classical society and had acquired a strongly ascetic tendency which had been absent from the Christianity of the gospels and the Pauline epistles. This became predominant during the fourth century, and was particularly exemplified in the monastic movement. Another new tendency, exemplified most fully in Neo-Platonism but exerting a deep influence on Christianity, was the mystical emphasis on oneness. The material world was regarded as an emanation from God which was aspiring to return to its divine matrix. Salvation meant being swallowed up in the divine One-All, with no preservation of personal identity. God was the first cause of all phenomena and the final consummation to which everything would return. This mystical cosmology, which denied value and significance to the whole sensuous world, was, in part, a reflection of the trend toward autocratic government in the later Roman Empire, the oneness attributed to the universe being an echo of the political oneness of the imperial government; but it continued to be a characteristic of the Western view of life until the Renaissance, in spite of its total lack of relationship to actual social conditions during the Middle Ages. These elements of the classical and Christian heritage were originally transmitted to the new Western society in the form of dogmas which were accepted without any appreciation of their real meaning or of their relevance to human life. Much of the cultural history of the Middle Ages consisted of the gradual rediscovery and revivification of the spiritual experiences which these dogmas conveyed and reflected. The West incorporated its heritage by a slow process of working backward from the attitudes of the last age of Roman imperialism to those of the Hellenic efflorescence in which classical civilization originated. This process was completed in the Renaissance.

Throughout the Dark and early Middle Ages there was little connection between these ways of thinking and actual living conditions. Official beliefs were almost completely divorced from the practical problems confronting a barbaric society which was struggling to acquire the rudiments of culture. Western civilization did not begin in the Mediterranean countries, which still retained remnants of the old classical order, but among the barbarian peoples who had taken possession of Britain and northern France. These peoples had a social organization which had remained largely tribalistic, with little sense of individualism, and an ethic which glorified slaughter and destruction. Before they could develop a new civilization, they had to learn the rudiments of self-control and to build institutions which could hold tribalistic attitudes in check and give some degree of security to the individual. In performing these tasks they received little effective guidance from the classical and Christian heritage. The early institutions of the new civilization were mostly of barbarian origin, as were also their early art forms, which were superficially classical but northern in their underlying tone and spirit.

Thus the early cultural history of the West consisted of two different movements, a fact which gave it a uniquely complex and even paradoxical character. While one movement consisted of the gradual rediscovery of the ancient heritage by a process of working backward, there was at the same time a forward movement from barbarism to a new kind of order. In the early Middle Ages there was remarkably little connection between these two movements, which proceeded side by side with little awareness of discrepancies between them. The twelfth century, which marked the apex of medieval creativity, was the century of the *chansons de geste* and of the poems of the troubadours. These displayed no understanding or appreciation of the Christian ethic, warfare being glorified, but in their emphasis on the necessity of self-control they had a profoundly civilizing effect. They were thus important influences in the movement forward from barbarism. But the twelfth century was also the age of Abelard, who began the process of rationalizing Christian dogma, and of St. Bernard, who gave it new life by transforming it into deeply felt personal experience. Not until the Renaissance did the two movements reach some kind of completion, barbarism having given place to effective political order imposed by strong monarchs ruling national states, while the major experiences of the classical civilization had been made available to Western man. Thenceforth one can speak of a single Western view of life.

This fusion of traditions was unique in history, and has given to Western civilization its unrivaled spiritual richness and complexity. The classical and Christian heritage endowed the West with a vast storehouse of achievements and experiences which served as models for imitation and individual self-understanding. No other civilization has been endowed with such a rich supply of memories. Until recent times every educated Westerner was intellectually a citizen of two different societies: his own and that of the ancient Mediterranean world. He could draw on the ancient experience for giving shape and meaning to his mental and emotional processes and for guidance in political action. This was true of Western man even in the early Middle Ages; the Renaissance gave a new emphasis and new interpretations to the study of the classics, but by no means initiated it.[5]

Yet although the West could make use of whatever elements in the classical civilization were relevant to its own development, it was not condemned to repeat the tragic history of that civilization but was able to evolve in new directions, make new experiments, and seek new solutions for the problems that its predecessor had failed to solve. This plasticity was especially important in its political evolution. Classical civilization had failed to find any lasting harmony between freedom and order and ended in an

---

[5] One should not forget, however, that one of the main reasons for the continuance of classical education was that it served to justify aristocratic government. Only members of the upper class could afford to have their children given this wholly nonutilitarian type of education, which was supposed to provide invaluable political and ethical wisdom. This class emphasis began with the schoolmasters of the Renaissance, and did not end until the twentieth century. The association of the study of the classics with class privilege was perhaps most conspicuous in the English public school system of the nineteenth and early twentieth centuries.

autocracy maintained mainly by force and imperfectly legitimized by the religious mysticism of Plotinus and the Church Fathers. This process was apparently irreversible, as was indicated by the continuance of autocratic government during the final eastern-Mediterranean phase of the old civilization in the Byzantine Empire. Only a new civilization whose political institutions were still flexible could make a new attempt to combine individual freedom and initiative with order and unity.

Is some degree of conflict between freedom and order an inherent element in human life, condemning all civilization to a perpetual oscillation between an individualism which may end in anarchy and an imposed order and unity which limit creativity? Or is there some validity to the Western hope that by adhering to "the laws of nature and of nature's God" man can create a society in which freedom and order will be found to be ultimately identical and the conflict between them capable of being transcended? It is permissible to speculate about the possibility of such a society. The prophecy of Jeremiah would be expressed by modern man in different terminology, but the hope of a coming "kingdom of freedom" has not lost its appeal, and still serves to give meaning to historic processes. It is not sufficiently recognized, however, that it requires a deepening of the human consciousness and cannot be achieved merely by new political and economic arrangements. Any attempts to realize such a society through institutional changes alone necessarily ends in some kind of totalitarian dictatorship, as the history of Marxism has abundantly demonstrated.

Certain modes of human experience suggest that man is capable of finding within himself a moral and spiritual authority which supersedes the external authority of dogmas and institutions. The saint and the mystic usually express their insights in the theological vocabulary available in their own particular society, and hence appear as giving support to the established religious system. But as they progress in sanctity they become less dependent on any system of dogmas and encounter spiritual realities which are common to all the different higher religions.

Introduction

The validity of such modes of experience is demonstrated by their practical results. Much human history bears witness to the numinous and charismatic power which may be exercised on human beings by the beneficent and saintly individual who has undergone a process of spiritual and moral self-discipline. Unless we understand the authority exercised by such individuals, the history of an epoch like the Middle Ages becomes unintelligible.

All forms of creativity testify similarly to man's capacity for spiritual autonomy. Creativity, whether in the arts or in the sciences, cannot be imposed from without, and requires freedom as a necessary condition. It resembles the mystical experience of religion in that it is felt as coming from the deeper levels of the human psyche. The creative individual does not produce innovations by an effort of the will. On the contrary, new creations present themselves to his consciousness with a compulsiveness which was formerly ascribed to divine inspiration. Modern man no longer attributes inventive genius to external spiritual powers; but the experience of creativity remains the same, although interpretations have become psychological rather than theological.

The vast majority of mankind, however, are neither saints nor artists, and need the guidance of dogmas and institutions. Mystical and creative insights have been limited in their appeal and application; and most men have been guided by moral and political dogmas rather than by movements of the spirit. It is permissible to hope for an ideal kingdom of freedom, but no such society is known to history. And certain qualities of Western civilization may perhaps be regarded as directly impeding the achievement of such a society. Whereas the civilizations of India and China have tended to emphasize the achievement of inner peace by processes of self-examination and self-discipline, the civilization of the West has promoted the mastery of natural forces and the constant reformation of social institutions, hoping that the growth of material production and of democratic liberty would in itself bring about the kingdom of freedom. There are dangers in this extroverted approach to nature and society, especially if Western man should become so intent on changing the world around him as to lose contact with the world within. Possibly both East and West are in possession of half-truths which must be combined in some world civilization of the future. But in the twentieth century, after almost a thousand years of continuous growth and achievement, the limits of the Western endeavor are still not yet apparent.

PART I

THE DARK AGES

I

The End of the
Western Empire

Comprehensive social changes never come quickly, and the dissolution of the Western Empire was no exception. Historians have generally emphasized the barbarian invasions of the fifth century and the establishment of the Germanic kingdoms as marking the end of Roman authority in the western provinces. These were indeed the most spectacular events in the process of social transformation; but it is easy to exaggerate their importance. In reality, the decline of the classical civilization was a much more gradual process, initiated as early as the second century and continuing until it was checked by the emergence of new constructive forces which cannot be dated earlier than the eighth century. The main features of this process were the weakening of Roman authority and Roman institutions and the consequent growth of the power of non-Roman barbarian peoples. But these peoples were not explicitly hostile to Rome. On the contrary, they hoped to share in the benefits of Roman civilization. If their rise to power brought that civilization to a slow and inglorious end, it was because they lacked the moral and intellectual discipline needed to maintain it.

We know little of the earlier history of the peoples of northern Europe who were responsible for the invasions. For thousands of years different groups of warrior tribesmen had occupied the plains of Germany and provinces farther east, remaining partially nomadic and keeping no written records. At long intervals some of them were impelled by population pressures, economic need, or the hope of plunder to migrate westward or southward and take possession of warmer regions. This had been the case with the ancestors of both the ancient Greeks and the Romans, who had settled in Mediterranean areas in the second millennium B.C. All of these northern peoples lived partly by agriculture and partly by hunting, had a tribal rather than a fully political method of organization (loyalties being attached to extended family groups rather than to an established government), maintained religious institutions which—unlike those of the Mediterranean peoples—strongly emphasized masculine predominance, and cultivated art forms which were abstract rather than representational.

For the early history of the West, two of these peoples are of special importance: the Celts and the Germans. There were deep differences between them, at least as they have been represented in popular tradition. The Celts have been credited with a greater capacity for poetry and art, with significant consequences in early medieval culture, while the Germans have been regarded as more materialistic and more practical. How far such differences actually existed, and whether they were due to ethnic, institutional, or environmental factors, are debatable questions. Certainly the resemblances between the northern peoples were more fundamental and more significant than the differences.

We first hear of the Celts about halfway through the first millennium B.C., when they emerged from somewhere in eastern Europe and overran the western provinces of Gaul, Spain, Britain, and northern Italy. Most of the area they had conquered was subsequently absorbed into the Roman Empire; and though the mass of the population retained a strongly Celtic character— some Gallic peasants were still speaking Celtic rather than Latin in the fourth century after Christ—the aristocracy was thoroughly Romanized. Some nationalistic historians have wishfully traced a continuing Celtic influence on the development of France, but concrete examples of any persistence of Celtic institutions are hard to find. In another area, however—Ireland and northern Britain—the Celtic tribes remained independent of the Empire, while even in southern Britain the Roman influence was thin and easily eradicated. Converted to Christianity during the fifth century, the Irish tribesmen were the first people to demonstrate the creative potentialities of the fusion of barbarian institutions and ways of living with the intellectual heritage of classicism.

The Germanic tribes had apparently moved into western Germany after the departure of the Celts, and were already threatening the northern borders of the Roman Empire by the beginning of the first century B.C. For the next three centuries Rome was strong enough to hold them at bay, but for a variety of reasons—political, economic, and cultural—the empire failed to maintain its capacity to defend itself. During the third-century civil wars between rival emperors, trade, industry, and city life began to decline; Celtic peoples in Gaul and Britain began to revert to their pre-Roman institutions and art forms; and groups of German warriors were permitted to settle within the boundaries of the empire, especially in the Rhineland and northern Gaul. The later empire adopted the fatal policy of recruiting German barbarians into its army and permitting them to remain, only thinly assimilated, after their period of service ended. Thus the Germans learned the weaknesses of the empire, and its native inhabitants became accustomed to barbaric German neighbors.

Drastically reorganized and given new institutions and a new religion by the emperors of the early fourth century, Rome was able to hold its own for another hundred years. The reorganization was more effective in the Eastern Empire, known to historians as Byzantine; but in the western provinces German tribesmen could not permanently be held in check. In the fifth century, German war bands carved out kingdoms for themselves, though most of them still professed obedience to Roman authority. The invaders were more numerous than their Germanic predecessors, but the peoples among whom they settled do not seem to have regarded them as essentially different. In this fashion the Vandals took possession of North Africa, the Visigoths of Spain, the Ostrogoths of Italy, the Franks and the Burgundians of France, and the Angles and Saxons of southern Britain. Only the Frankish and Anglo-Saxon dominions proved to be permanent; the other Germanic kingdoms were overthrown by the revived power of Byzantium in the sixth century or by the Arabs in the eighth century.

For the German tribesmen the age of the invasions was a heroic epoch. Men of valor had limitless opportunities for glory, plunder, and destruction. Tribal bards celebrated the bloody exploits of the conquerors, and some of their compositions appear to have been handed down by word of mouth for many generations, eventually supplying some of the subject matter of such medieval German epic poems as the *Nibelungenlied*. But since we see the Germanic chieftains mostly through the eyes of their victims, it is difficult for the modern reader to regard them as in any way glorious. During the conquests and for long afterward many of them behaved like delinquent children, indulging in indiscriminate murder, robbery, and rape with no visible hesitation or pangs of conscience.

Yet in actuality the invasions were less cataclysmic in their immediate results than has often been supposed. It was a fact of immense importance that most of the invaders wished not to overthrow Roman civilization but to take possession of it and enjoy it. Many of the Germanic tribes had been in contact with the Romans for centuries, and regarded Roman society with awe and envy rather than total hostility. During the fourth century many of them had even been converted, at least nominally, to Christianity, though by an unfortunate accident they had encountered it in its heretical Arian form and hence were regarded by western Catholics as little better than infidels. Once their conquests had been completed, the Germans regarded themselves as now belonging to the Greco-Roman world and wished to become Romanized. This facilitated the preservation and transmission of Greco-Roman culture and was therefore of decisive importance for the whole future development of Western civilization.

In Britain the barbarian conquests made a sharp break with the Greco-Roman tradition. In this province Roman civilization had never been deeply rooted, and had apparently almost disappeared even before the invasions, being replaced by a resurgent Celtic tribalism. Its Anglo-Saxon invaders, moreover, came from northern Germany and had had little previous contact with Roman civilization. Britain was reintegrated into the Western culture area by the efforts of Catholic missionaries in the seventh and eighth centuries. But in the continental provinces the old civilization survived the invasions, and for a long time there was no awareness that it was moribund.

The dissolution of the Roman order was a protracted process, initiated by the decay of its creative vitality and its capacity to adjust itself to meet new conditions, and completed during centuries of barbarian misgovernment. For in spite of the admiration which the barbarians felt for the old civilization, they continued to delight in war and plunder and lacked any real comprehension of the values and institutions on which that civilization depended. The early centuries of the Dark Ages were therefore marked by a slow deterioration of cultural standards and a descent of Western society into barbarism. Yet the generations that witnessed the establishment of the Germanic kingdoms displayed no recognition that traditional ways of living were coming to an end. The material conditions of human life are always much more flexible than established habits and attitudes, and men may live through a major social transformation without any awareness of the need for new codes of behavior and views of life. In the sixth century, as in the fourth, it was generally assumed that the old Roman *imperium* was still in being and would eventually be fully reestablished. No alternative form of order was even imagined. And since the Western world had recently come to know and worship the one true God, it was believed that it could rely on divine protection against its enemies. Christianity promised its adherents not only salvation in the afterlife but also greater peace and security in this world. If this peace was not achieved, it was because God wished to rebuke mankind for its sins; but if men repented, they could rely on God to give them victory over their enemies. The most effective form of self-defense—and, indeed, the only form which would certainly prove efficacious—was therefore prayer. This faith in God was expressed by numerous Dark Age statesmen from whom one would have expected some degree of realism about God's methods of ruling the world. Possibly they recognized that fervent prayer might be good for the morale of their troops.

And indeed conditions in western Europe during the sixth century did not seem radically different from those of the fourth. In theory the empire still existed, the supreme authority remaining vested in the emperor, who continued to reign at Constantinople. Most of the Germanic kings affected to consider themselves as his allies and representatives; they adopted Roman titles, such as consul and patrician, and tried to make use of the old Roman machinery of administration. Although the invaders appropriated estates for themselves, much of the land was still held by the old aristocratic families of the empire, and these tried to maintain the elegant style of living and the cultural pursuits of their ancestors, sinking to the level of their German neighbors only in the course of several generations. Nor was there any abrupt economic change. During the early Dark Ages the gold coinage of the empire continued to circulate in most of the western provinces, and trade with the East was not yet permanently interrupted. Caravans of Syrian and Jewish merchants still distributed African oil and papyrus and Oriental textiles and spices through Gaul and Spain. It was not until the eighth and ninth centuries, perhaps because the Mediterranean was controlled by Arab sea power, that regular commercial relations between the eastern and western provinces ceased and the West was thrown back on its own resources.[1]

---

[1] This is the argument of Henri Pirenne in his *Mohammed and Charlemagne,* translated by Bernard Miall (New York, 1939). Most other historians feel that Pirenne attaches too much importance to the rise of Arab power.

1 · The End of the Western Empire

The cultural traditions of the classical civilization came to no sudden end. The Catholic Church, which had become the main residuary legatee of the Roman *imperium* in both its political and its cultural aspects, now assumed increased powers in order to promote law and order and protect the conquered populations; but since the conversion of Constantine its bishops had become virtually a part of the Roman bureaucracy and few of them continued to represent any new social ideals. Nor did the cultivation of literature and the arts immediately disappear. For several generations after the invasions, poets continued to study rhetoric, imitate the traditional Latin models, and seek patronage by composing complimentary or obscene verses for the edification of Vandal, Gothic, and Frankish chieftains. New Christian basilicas adorned with mosaics and wall paintings were built in Gallic and Italian cities. Under the Ostrogothic kings of Italy, as we learn from the letters of Cassiodorus, the Roman populace could even enjoy their traditional chariot races, wild-animal combats, and theatrical spectacles. These no longer included gladiator shows and the slaughter of criminals by wild animals, but the Church had not succeeded in its efforts to abolish the public games wholly.

The assumption that the Roman Empire was still essentially in being and that it would eventually be fully restored continued to pervade Western thought through the whole Dark Ages and even longer. The empire was the only form of authority which thinking persons could recognize as legitimate—the barbarian kingdoms were based on force and worthy of allegiance only insofar as they could claim somehow to be linked with Rome or with the Roman successor state at Constantinople.

The human race, it was affirmed, was an organic whole, and peace and order required a union of authority. All legitimate power came from God, who had decreed that the Roman *imperium* should extend throughout the whole world and that it should be governed by a single emperor. For the third-century Neo-Platonic philosopher Plotinus, the rule of the emperor on earth paralleled the mystical supremacy of the divine One-All, while the Christian Church, relying on promises made by St. Paul in the Epistle to the Thessalonians, declared that the empire would endure until the final time of troubles heralding the day of final judgment. Its sway was universal, and its mission was to establish peace, repress human wickedness, and protect the true religion. These doctrines were repeatedly reaffirmed through the Dark Ages, in spite of their total lack of practical application. While society in the western provinces became increasingly barbaric, thinking men continued to hope for the re-establishment of Roman rule, and any constructive efforts were therefore devoted to the restoration of the old order rather than to the building of something new, the result being the so-called Holy Roman Empire of Charlemagne and his German successors. In Italy, where memories of the Roman past were especially vital and tenacious and gave support to the claim that persons of Italian origin had special virtues equipping them for government, belief in the empire lasted even longer. Its permanence and universality were still being maintained in the fifteenth century by the humanist scholar and future Pope, Aeneas Sylvius.

Nothing illustrates more forcibly the total divorce of theory from practice which characterized almost all the formal thinking of the Dark Ages. Even by the limited geographical knowledge of the time, it was apparent that Rome had never united the human race or ruled the whole world, or even the major part of it; and the empire that Charlemagne founded was at best a feeble echo of its Roman predecessor. But the view of life and the modes of thinking which early Western civilization inherited from the classical decadence made it necessary for the myth of Roman universality to be maintained in defiance of the most obvious factual discrepancies.

Although the intention of the German invaders was to take possession of Roman civilization rather than to destroy it, the delicate mechanisms of a complex society could not survive generations of mishandling by illiterate warrior chieftains. Thus through the early centuries of the Dark Ages, order enforced by an effective government was gradually disappearing and being replaced by the institutions of German tribalism. But this process of dissolution may be regarded as a necessary preliminary to the emergence of a new civilization. Only by making a new beginning from primitive attitudes could men recapture the sharpened perceptions and fresh eyes, the sense of adventure, and the pleasure in aesthetic and intellectual exploration which were necessary for the release of a new impulse of creativity. And while the most conspicuous aspects of cultural history before the Carolingian renascence of the eighth century were the lack of creativity and the continued shrinking of the classical inheritance, the period can be viewed in more positive terms. What survived of the classical inheritance, both in secular learning and in religious beliefs and institutions, was transmitted to the new Western culture area and in due course became the starting point of new intellectual developments.

2

The Classical Inheritance

The cultural heritage of classicism had a continuous existence in Italy and the West until the sixth century. Despite the barbarian invasions, men of letters had continued, in imitation of their predecessors, to write for a literate audience of Latin-speaking nobility, some of Roman and some of German descent. This group, however, was rapidly shrinking. By the end of the century, literacy was almost restricted to the inmates of monasteries, and these were, of course, not inclined to extend patronage to secular litterateurs. The seventh and eighth centuries formed the great hiatus separating classical from Western civilization. Nor was the literature produced during the sixth century of such value as to make one regret this change: most of it was drearily conventional and lacking in any trace of originality.

Men of learning were aware, however, that the classical tradition could not survive unless it was effectively transmitted to the new barbarian ruling class, and this required a conscious effort of summation. The most significant cultural products of this period were textbooks, some of which were to retain their authority for nearly a thousand years. This was the last epoch in which the cultural achievement of Greece and Rome was still accessible to Western scholars, before the darkness set in, and their interpretations of the ancient culture were the main links between the classical civilization and its Western successor. As intermediaries between the classical and the Western minds, the writers of this epoch have, in fact, a historical importance out of all proportion to their intrinsic merits. W. P. Ker declared that "almost everything that is common to the Middle Ages, and much that lasts beyond the Renaissance, is to be found in the authors of the sixth century." [1] Ker was, of course, referring not to the sensibility of the Middle Ages as conveyed in its works of art, which were totally different from those of the classical world, but to its stock of intellectual formulations.

Between the classical and the Christian heritage there were no longer any sharp distinctions. The two intellectual traditions had largely become amalgamated, and both of them acquired honor and prestige among the barbarians through association with the political and material achievements of the Roman *imperium*. Long before the triumph of Christianity the old pagan gods had lost their reality and faded into mere allegorical figures, and this enabled professing Christians to continue reading Virgil and Ovid and speaking of Jupiter and Venus with no apparent sense of incongruity. It is true that early Christians had often been sharply hostile to pagan culture; for St. Paul the pagan gods had been not poetic conventions but actual demons seeking to corrupt human beings, and according to many later theologians any merits in the Greek philosophers were to be attributed to borrowings from Moses which they had kept secret in order to avoid persecution. Some later churchmen remained suspicious of classical learning. But after prolonged controversies about the value of the classical heritage so much of it had been incorporated into Christianity that even the severest of theologians could not wholly repudiate it. The second-century apologist Justin Martyr had declared that "whatever things were rightly said among all men are the property of us Christians. For next to God we acknowledge and love the Word who is from the unbegotten and ineffable God . . . For all the writers were able to see realities

---

[1] W. P. Ker: *The Dark Ages,* p. 100.

darkly through the sowing of the implanted Word that was in them . . .";[2] and this had become the accepted Christian attitude. Western learning remained both classical and Christian, and any unacceptable elements in pagan literature, as in the Bible, were disposed of by the convenient device of allegorical interpretation. A medieval saint as austere as Bernard of Clairvaux could quote a poet as immoral as Ovid with no expression of disapproval.

In historical retrospect one can see that the fusion of the two traditions was not so complete as Dark Age scholars supposed, and that in absorbing so much of the classical heritage Christianity had adopted beliefs and ethical standards that were significantly different from the original teachings of Jesus and Paul. The suspicion of classical learning that had been manifested by the more radical Christian spokesmen had considerable justification. After Christianity had become the official religion of the Roman Empire, it had lost much of its original quality, and both its theological doctrines and its ethical rules were closer to Neo-Platonism than to the gospels. The cultural heritage which scholars sought to transmit to the barbarians had, therefore, more of late classicism than of Christianity.

Yet the tradition which sixth-century scholars set out to summarize and conserve was in the last stages of decadence, and one can fairly ask whether it did not prove to be more an encumbrance than a stimulus to the growth of a new life in the Western world. The main importance of the sixth-century summation was that it maintained lines of communication between the civilizations and hence made it possible for the Western mind in later centuries to work back to the earlier and more creative phases of classicism. Beginning with sixth-century writers like Boethius and Cassiodorus, the West gradually became equipped for understanding Virgil and Cicero. But through most of the Dark Ages

---

[2] Justin: *Second Apology*, translated by A. Roberts and J. Donaldson (Buffalo, 1885), p. 13.

34

the ideas, beliefs, and aesthetic forms with which men sought to interpret their experience had virtually no relationship with actual ways of living. While social conditions were becoming increasingly disorderly and barbaric, men of learning continued to reiterate classical and Christian formulas which did not correspond with anything in their emotional experience and were totally lacking in practical efficacy and applicability. One can find almost anything in the writings of the Dark Ages, even including bawdy stories, as in the memoirs of Bishop Liudprand of Cremona. But what chiefly characterized the higher culture of this period was its imitativeness, incoherence, and lack of real creativity. What passed for literature and philosophy was mostly the mechanical and undiscriminating copying of the works of earlier writers.

The visual arts continued to display vitality, at least in Italy and in the eastern provinces, reflecting the decline of humanist views of life and the growth of a mystical consciousness. The sculpture of the great classical period had been representational but not strictly realistic; it had portrayed human figures in idealized forms. The art of the decadence, particularly in its reliefs and its mosaics, continued to present human figures, but sought to give them transcendental meaning by showing them frontally and without any sense of motion. Art ceased to be fully three-dimensional, presenting its figures in a kind of stage-space with little sense of depth or vista. In both late-pagan and early-Christian art, rows of figures confronted the spectator with a solemnity of expression and a lack of plastic solidity that suggested concentration on eternal rather than temporal realities. In the course of time the art of the classical decadence became fused with the wholly abstract art that had developed among the northern barbarians, and their union produced the art of the early Middle Ages.

In literature and learning, on the other hand, the decadence had little of value to contribute and much that was obstructive. The main content of late Roman culture consisted of rhetorical studies which stifled all originality and had totally lost all rela-

35

tionship to genuine human emotions and aspirations. The Romans had been great builders, yet they had never displayed any interest in the advancement of science, and their philosophical studies had been borrowed wholly from Greece. Education consisted primarily of training in rhetoric, students being taught how to organize words and devise appropriate metaphors and other figures of speech according to the conventional rules, with an exclusive concentration on the means of expression, not on what was expressed. After contemplating a few typical specimens of late Roman literature, the modern reader begins to feel that Pope Gregory's contempt for grammatical and rhetorical studies was an expression not of clerical obscurantism but of a healthy common sense. Nor did the later Greek literature offer much more that was valuable. The knowledge of Greek, moreover, had never been widespread in the western provinces, and in the course of the Dark Ages (except in Ireland) it became virtually nonexistent.

The great Christian theologians, especially Augustine, were, of course, the most influential agents in the transmission of culture; but alongside the devaluation of the material world which they acquired from the pagan decadence, they also affirmed new and more optimistic doctrines that were specifically Christian. For the summation of classical learning, one must turn to various minor figures of the period of transition: for example, to Martianus Capella, whose dreary and uninspired allegory *The Nuptials of Mercury and Philology* served for many centuries as a textbook of grammar and rhetoric; to Orosius, who at the suggestion of St. Augustine compiled a survey of history intended to show the misery of human life before the adoption of Christianity; and to Isidore of Seville, whose *Etymologies* was a kind of encyclopedia. Of greater intrinsic merit were three sixth-century Italians: Cassiodorus, Venantius Fortunatus, and Boethius.

Of the various Germanic kingdoms, that of the Ostrogoths in Italy was perhaps the most sympathetic to ancient traditions. Its founder, Theodoric, who reigned at Ravenna from 489 until 526, had spent much of his boyhood at the imperial court in

Constantinople; and after inheriting the kingship of the Ostrogoths from his father and leading them to the conquest of new homes in Italy, he did not forget his Byzantine education. Endeavoring to govern in the interests of both Germans and Romans, he gave high official positions to representatives of the old Roman aristocracy, among whom were Cassiodorus and Boethius. Serving Theodoric and his successors for thirty years, Cassiodorus consciously tried to conserve and transmit the heritage of classical culture. His greatest services to civilization, however, were performed after he had retired from his official duties. In middle life he returned to his ancestral estates at Squillace in Calabria, where he founded a monastery, wrote a summary of what he thought all educated persons should know entitled *Institutions of Divine and Human Study,* and set his monks to work in a program of copying ancient manuscripts. These activities were of vast and prolonged importance. The course of studies outlined in the *Institutions* was a major influence in shaping the basic curriculum of medieval schools and universities, while the labors of his monks were responsible for the preservation of much of the corpus of classical literature. The role of the monasteries in the transmission of culture has often been exaggerated; most Western monasteries, following the rule of St. Benedict, were unconcerned with secular learning. But Cassiodorus represented a more humanistic attitude. In this belated and unexpected Indian summer of the old civilization, he undertook to preserve through the coming winter the essentials of a cultural tradition that had now lasted for a thousand years, trying to educate his barbarian masters and making little distinction between classicism and Christianity.

Yet in spite of Cassiodorus's services to posterity, his own writings make all too plain the ossification of the tradition that he sought to preserve. The culture that he tried to transmit to the barbarians had come to consist chiefly of a kind of elaborate verbal play which served no practical purpose and could convey no genuine experience. Virtuosity in using the traditional rules of grammar and rhetoric, making recondite literary and mythological allusions, and devising interesting metaphors had become an end in itself. No documents of late classicism illuminate the decadence more clearly than Cassiodorus's *Letters*. These were mostly official letters and state papers written during his public career, many of them signed by King Theodoric. In accordance with a long-established Roman practice, they were afterward collected and published by their author for the edification of posterity, with conventional expressions of modesty. They combined the most commonplace thoughts with the most fantastic hypertrophy of expression. Cassiodorus was unable to convey the simplest royal command without swathing it in an inflated mass of learned allusions. An order to send a harpist to the King of the Franks was accompanied by a treatise about the history of music, with numerous references both to the pagan gods and to the Psalms. Instructions to put a famous charioteer on the government payroll provided an excuse for some lengthy meditations about chariot-racing. When Theodoric issued a proclamation summoning his army for defense against the Franks, Cassiodorus made him describe how young hawks were trained for war by their mothers; in reprimanding an official for delay in the dispatch of vessels carrying foodstuffs, he engaged in picturesque and highly unscientific speculations about various species of fish that were alleged to interfere with shipping; and he was unable to complain about negligence in the manufacture of purple dye without including a poetic rhapsody about the shellfish from which the dye was extracted. Thus did this Roman aristocrat seek to maintain a respect for classical values in the new Gothic kingdom.

Cassiodorus's *Letters* were typical of the culture of the decadence; and the indurated conventionality of almost all late Roman writing except that of some Christian theologians typifies the whole Roman decline. Minds trained in this fashion were insulated against any apprehension either of the realities of human experience or of objective facts. After wandering through some of the verbal labyrinths which the late Roman world had come to regard as the essence of culture and learning, the modern reader begins to see more clearly why the barbarian invasions were necessary if the Western world was to regain its cultural vitality.

Venantius Fortunatus, another Italian litterateur, born a generation later than Cassiodorus, illustrates other aspects of this age of transition. Devoted to rhetorical conventions and comfortable living, Fortunatus was able to support himself by poetry even in the sixth century. Moving from Italy to France, he obtained patronage from Frankish kings and noblemen by writing Latin verses in praise of their virtues. As we know from other sources, some of his barbarian patrons were guilty of numerous murders and adulteries, but Fortunatus was not concerned with realities. Eventually he found a congenial supporter in a former Frankish queen, Radegund by name, who had left her husband to devote herself to good works in a convent at Poitiers. Yet although most of his work represented only the final running-to-seed of the Latin tradition of belles-lettres, he belonged to the future as well as to the past. When Radegund obtained a portion of the cross of Christ as a gift from the Byzantine emperor, Fortunatus composed hymns to be sung in honor of the occasion, *Vexilla Regis* and *Pange Lingua,* which had a new and strange power foreshadowing the religious poetry of the Middle Ages. In his secular poems he had followed the classical models and displayed only ingenuity in verbal play, but the hymns were written in the meter of Latin popular songs, with some use of rhyme.

While Cassiodorus and Fortunatus illuminate in their writings different aspects of the decline, Boethius succeeded in conveying something of the spirit of an earlier and more vigorous era. His *Consolation of Philosophy* was the last great book of the ancient civilization and remained for the next thousand years the most important agent in the transmission of classicism to the Western mind.

Like Cassiodorus, Boethius set out to provide illumination for the coming Dark Ages, while holding various positions at the court of Theodoric. He wrote surveys of logic, mathematics, and music which were still being used many centuries later as texts in medieval schools, and he planned to provide Latin translations of all the works of Plato and Aristotle, though he was able to complete only a small part of this ambitious program. It is an extraordinary example of the intellectual inertia of Roman civilization that such a task was not accomplished earlier. The Romans had been students of Greek philosophy for some seven hundred years; yet it cannot be affirmed that learned men knew enough Greek to make translation unnecessary. Knowledge of Greek was by no means universal (even St. Augustine had only a smattering of it). The Greek classics had—for seven hundred years—been studied largely in Latin surveys and abridgments.

Less fortunate than Cassiodorus, Boethius was put to death in 525, at the age of forty-four, on charges of conspiring against his Ostrogothic master, and his *Consolation of Philosophy* was written in prison while awaiting execution. The book can best be regarded as a summation of the central philosophical tradition of classicism. There has been much controversy about Boethius' attitude to Christianity; but as his authorship of several theological treatises is now established, it appears that he regarded himself as a believer. Yet the *Consolation* is a pagan book, presenting the essence of a thousand years of pagan thinking about the fundamentals of human life, with especial indebtedness to Plato and the Stoics. Its strong emphasis on divine providence perhaps shows some Christian influence, but there is not a trace of the new modes of feeling introduced by Christianity—of the Christian sense of human sinfulness and of goodness as an obligation owed by man to his divine Father. For Boethius, as for Socrates and Zeno, man had a natural desire for blessedness (*beatitudo*—a word that implies both happiness and goodness) and could attain it through a knowledge of philosophy rather than through an ethical and emotional transformation of his personality. Boethius' classicism was apparently more deeply ingrained than his Christianity, so that when awaiting execution he turned for consolation to Athens rather than to Calvary.

The *Consolation* was largely a reaffirmation of the old paradox, first propounded by Socrates, that nothing evil could happen to a good man. It was man's nature to desire blessedness, but he must learn to look for it not in external circumstances, which were subject to the apparent caprices of fortune, but in resignation to the cosmic order in the knowledge that whatever happened was ultimately for the best. "All men's thoughts, which are turmoiled with manifold cares, take indeed divers courses, but yet endeavor to attain the same end of blessedness, which is that good which, being once obtained, nothing can be further desired . . . For there is naturally ingrafted in man's minds an earnest desire of that which is truly good." Philosophy taught that the world was a unity pervaded by a divine providence, of which fortune was merely the instrument. "This world could never have been compacted of so many divers and contrary parts, unless there were One that holdeth together that which be united." Once man had come to understand the divine oneness, he would be reconciled to whatever might happen to him. "Since that all fortune, be it pleasing or unpleasing, is directed to the reward of exercise of the good, and to the punishment and direction of the wicked, it is manifest that it is all good, since all is just or profitable." "All their fortune, whatsoever it be, who are either in the possession of or increase or entrance of virtue is good; and theirs, which remain in vices, the worst that may be." [3] Thus Boethius told himself that he should cheerfully accept as providential the onset of bad fortune, the ruin of his career and his family, and the imminence of torture and execution.

For western Europeans the *Consolation* remained the most important source of the thought of classicism for the next thousand years. No book was read more widely and continuously or attracted a more distinguished list of translators into the vernacular languages. [4] It provided the standard statement of the belief in

---

[3] Boethius: *Consolation of Philosophy,* revised by H. F. Stewart (London: Loeb Classical Library; 1846), pp. 229, 287, 357, 359.

[4] They included two English monarchs, Alfred and Elizabeth I.

a divine order and unity which the medieval mind inherited from late classicism, and its philosophical *obiter dicta* precipitated some of the major controversies of medieval scholasticism, particularly the debate between nominalism and realism. Yet a complete understanding of Boethius' meaning depended on the recognition of certain implicit assumptions which belonged to the classical tradition but which Boethius did not succeed in fully communicating. Despite the emphasis on divine providence, the book was too alien to Christianity in its spirit and deeper meaning to be fully comprehensible to the Middle Ages.

The modern reader is likely to feel that despite the book's nobility of tone, it fails to carry conviction. Too much of the argument depends on apparent non sequiturs and verbal ambiguities, particularly on the illegitimate assumption that the belief in the spiritual unity of the world implies a belief in divine providence, and on the use of the word "blessedness," meaning both happiness and goodness, to describe man's basic desire. But what Boethius is really talking about is not the nature of the universe but a process of emotional development by which man can achieve blessedness, and his system of intellectual doctrines is derived from this process. Ever since the end of the great age of Hellenism, the highest wisdom of the classical world had found expression in ethical philosophies (such as Stoicism and Epicureanism) which taught their adherents to resign themselves to destiny and liberate themselves from all disturbing emotions. This emphasis on the acceptance of the world and on emotional detachment was associated with several different systems of thought, the attitude being basic and the doctrines that served to justify it being derivative. In their practical applications to human experience there was relatively little difference among the philosophical systems, despite wide variations in their metaphysical doctrines. In preaching detachment and offering examples of wise men who had achieved it, they strongly resembled Buddhism.

The basic function of all religious and philosophical systems is, of course, to assist men in overcoming their aloneness, becoming reconciled to life, and feeling at home in the universe; but this theodicy may assume many different forms. For the mind of the classical decadence, and for Boethius as its final representative, wisdom meant submission to whatever happened and freedom from sorrow and desire. But in the new world-view of Christianity, human existence had a new positive meaning through the hope of a kingdom of heaven, and sorrow and desire were means by which man might be led to seek salvation and become united with God and with other human beings. Man could achieve regeneration not by making himself free of emotion but by the active practice of love and charity, and in regenerating himself he could hope for the regeneration of the material world.

3

Dark Age Christianity

To a civilization that had achieved political order and unity but had lost its sense of spiritual meaning and direction, Christianity had brought a new gospel of divine fatherhood and human brotherhood. Its teachings were in part a reflection of the development of secular society and in part a response to the feeling of frustration and futility that was spreading through that society. In unifying the Mediterranean world, the Roman *imperium* had undermined belief in the traditional tribal and civic deities, thus leaving a gap that only a new universal religion could fill. But it offered no goals or purposes higher than material order and prosperity, and the benefits of its rule went mostly to a small landowning upper class and to the army and the bureaucracy. Christianity appealed primarily to the urban middle and laboring classes, affirming (in accord with the universalism of Roman rule) that all men were the children of one divine father and promising that inequality and oppression would be brought to an end by the second coming of Jesus and the establishment of the kingdom of heaven.

The original affirmations of Christianity, embodied in the person of Jesus and made explicit in the writings of Paul and other theologians, had revolutionized man's views of God, of nature, and of himself. According to most late classical philosophies, especially that of the Neo-Platonists, man's soul was a spark of divinity imprisoned in matter. The material world, being

44

only partially shaped and molded by the divine forms, was necessarily evil and irrational; man should endeavor to achieve impassivity in this world, and could hope to be swallowed up in divinity after death. For Christianity, on the other hand, the world had been created by an omnipotent and righteous creator, and was therefore initially good. The original source of evil was not matter but human pride and egoism. Man had misused the power of free choice with which God had endowed him, and hence both human nature and the whole natural order had been partially corrupted. But God himself, becoming incarnate in Jesus, had paid the necessary penalty for human sins by death on the cross; and by uniting themselves with Jesus through faith and following his example in love and charity, men could hope for the regeneration of both the world and themselves. These were the essentials of the Christian myth, and none of the world's religions has offered a more exalted view of man's nature and destiny. For the classical civilization, the teaching of the gospel meant an almost total transvaluation of accepted values. *Agape* (benevolent love) replaced *gnosis* (knowledge) as the means of salvation, and pain and deprivation, no longer regarded as accidents of fortune which man must stoically endure, acquired a new positive significance as a means by which man could imitate Jesus and unite himself with his fellow men.

In considering the reasons for the spread of Christianity, we should never forget that the core of the new religion was not doctrine or belief but personal experience. The process by which the convert acquired his faith in Christ consisted primarily of self-surrender, resulting in a sense of absorption into the Christian community, in freedom from anxiety and insecurity, and in absolute trust in God. This experience was, of course, partially incommunicable to those persons who had not actually lived through it, though all Christian apologists, beginning with St. Paul, endeavored to find words for it. But since true believers felt that they knew the meaning and truth of Christianity by direct personal revelation, superior to all merely intellectual argument, the doctrines of the new religion could never be fully rationalized. This process of conversion was often preceded by acute inner conflicts, the individual feeling himself unable to resist sinful desires or to obey the rules of morality, and consequently regarding himself as a miserable and helpless sinner. This state of mind was, of course, especially frequent while the individual was struggling with the most difficult and most important of all man's psychic tasks: the acceptance of his maturity and of the responsibilities of adulthood and the realization of his own identity.

In the process of becoming the official religion of the Roman Empire, however, Christianity had undergone a drastic change of character. Its promised kingdom of heaven, in which mankind would be unified not by rules of justice but by love and charity, had originally been both a standard for judging earthly society and the ultimate goal of history, though Christians expected it to be realized not by human effort but by a divine intervention outside the historic process. By the fourth century, however, the kingdom had been transferred from this world to the afterlife, becoming a promise of eternal happiness in heaven for Christian believers, and the gospel ethic was henceforth applied to society in this life only in a very attenuated form. After the conversion of Constantine, the Roman *imperium* was accepted as a divinely appointed means of maintaining order and repressing human wickedness, but the Church did not ask the emperors to govern in accord with the gospel ethic, although its leaders occasionally reprimanded them if they flagrantly misbehaved. But for the average Roman official or citizen, who lacked all knowledge of the spiritual meaning of the new faith, the chief functions of the Church were now to promote the security and prosperity of the secular state by assuring it of divine favor and protection, and to guide its members to heaven in the afterlife. The carpenter of Galilee had replaced Romulus and Mars as the guardian of the empire, and the revolutionary implications of his teaching had been rendered innocuous.

Meanwhile Christianity had incorporated much of the pagan philosophies, leading to a darkening of its views of man and nature and to egocentric interpretations of the new ethic. The

46

early Church had believed in the regeneration of the whole of nature, and had inculcated an ethic of positive love rather than of ascetic self-repression. But by the fourth century the Church had been deeply affected by the attitudes of late classicism, and had come to regard the whole natural world as too corrupt for any redemption to be possible. One natural impulse, in particular, now seemed to be sinful in essence. By the fourth century, theologians were beginning to declare that all men were corrupt from birth because all men were conceived in lust. And although sexual relations in marriage for the purpose of propagating children were permissible, the necessary element of carnal desire being pardoned, celibacy was a higher state than marriage. St. Jerome declared that "marriage peoples the earth, but virginity peoples heaven." The individual who wrestled with his sexual impulses was closer to salvation than his brother who followed St. Paul's advice that it was better to marry than to burn.

The influence of Neo-Platonic mysticism led, moreover, to a most significant transformation of the gospel ethic. This began with Greek theologians of the third century, but it reached the West chiefly through the works of an unknown mystic who assumed the name of Dionysius the Areopagite (mentioned in the New Testament as an Athenian convert of Paul) and who was writing sometime between the years 485 and 515. In early Christianity the essence of the new ethic was conveyed in the Greek word *agape*, which meant an active benevolence toward other people. For those Christian mystics who had come under Neo-Platonic influence, however, *agape* was subordinated to *eros*, which meant desire and was applied to the desire of human beings for union with God. While *agape* was philanthropic, and could be fully achieved only by the annihilation of selfish desire, *eros* was egocentric and had no regard for the welfare of other people. Since desire was properly directed only toward the good, in fact, the love for one's sinful fellow creatures might be positively wrong. One should love only God, while God's primary quality was his love for himself. As the Dark Age Irish theologian John Scotus Erigena declared, "If then the Holy Trinity loves

47

itself in us and in itself, it is assuredly loved by itself in a glorious manner unknown to all created beings."[1] *Eros,* moreover, was regarded as the main unifying and cohesive force in the universe, all things being bound together and held in order by their desire for God. Thus there were two totally different conceptions of love in the teaching of Dark Age and medieval Christianity, and for most mystically inclined writers *eros* was, on the whole, regarded as superior to *agape,* the result being a fundamental distortion of the teaching of the gospel. Western thinkers remained largely unaware of the confusion because in Latin (as also in English) the same word, *amor,* was used for both conceptions. And although some Latin-speaking theologians, such as Augustine, had tried to preserve the distinction by translating *eros* as *dilectio* and *agape* as *caritas,* there was no clear recognition of all that was involved until the Protestant Reformation of the sixteenth century.

This new view of human nature found expression in the monastic movement, which had originated in Egypt about the beginning of the fourth century and spread rapidly to all areas where Christianity was dominant. An important factor in its growth was the disillusionment that followed the elevation of Christianity into the official religion of the empire. Coming under the control of the secular government, the Church no longer represented a new way of life. Its bishops were henceforth chosen mainly from the aristocratic and bureaucratic classes, and their chief concern seemed to be the maintenance of orthodox beliefs, the definition of which was accompanied by the most bitter conflicts and schisms, rather than the practice of the gospel ethic. Monasticism reflected in a new form the original Christian protest against the corruption of society. Like the early Church, the monastery was a community of believers, set aside from secular society by faith in the imminence of the kingdom of heaven and free from social and economic inequalities. But it

---

[1] Quoted in Anders Nygren: *Agape and Eros,* p. 608.

differed from the early Church in stressing personal salvation, to be achieved by celibacy and other ascetic disciplines, rather than the regeneration of the whole social order.

In the Greek-speaking eastern provinces, the Church retained the close association with the state that had originated with the first Christian emperor, Constantine. In practice the Church was largely controlled by the secular authorities, and only on very rare occasions did its leading spokesman, the Patriarch of Constantinople, venture to rebuke the emperor or express an independent opinion on any controversial question. The main preoccupations of the Greek church were mystical and metaphysical rather than ethical or political. In the Latin western provinces, on the other hand, the Church had always displayed much of the old Roman concern for ethical standards and practical efficiency. With the disappearance of the Western Empire in the fifth century the Church was left independent of all secular authority except the emperor in far-away Constantinople. Though its power depended on spiritual and psychological factors, not on material force, it was the only authority left in western Europe that stood consistently for unity and order. How much responsibility it assumed varied according to the personality of the Pope.[2] But the activities of Christian missionaries in the conversion of barbarian peoples was the most important factor in the development and unification of the new culture area which produced Western civilization and in the dissemination of the elementals of classical culture. These missions, often planned and

---

[2] Augustine's *City of God* was the most influential book of the Dark and Middle Ages; and Augustine's explicit point of view was that all earthly institutions were too deeply corrupted by human sin to be capable of regeneration. Salvation in the next life was what man should hope for, but this could be achieved only by divine grace, not by human effort. But Augustine also— with visible inconsistency—glorified Rome as the protector of peace and order. The empire would continue to protect human beings until a final time of troubles followed by the end of the world and the establishment of the millennium. This beneficent view of Rome was originally derived from St. Paul's Second Epistle to the Thessalonians. See II Thessalonians, ii, 7–8.

organized by the Pope, were mostly conducted by monks, and their first action in moving into a new area was usually to found a monastery, to provide headquarters for missionary activity.

By universal agreement the outstanding figure among the Dark Age Popes was Gregory the Great, who served from 590 to 604. He is also ranked as one of the four doctors of the Latin Church. Born into a wealthy Roman family, he had embarked on a political career and had risen to be prefect of the city of Rome, abandoning worldly ambitions and entering a monastery only in middle life. His elevation to the papacy followed sixteen years of intense religious activity. It is impossible to read his letters without feeling a deep respect for his efficiency, his good intentions, and his common sense; whether conveying God's will to a Germanic king, negotiating with the emperor at Constantinople, or administering the estates and other properties of the Church, he showed that the old Roman capacity for statesmanship had not yet wholly disappeared. The vigor with which he asserted papal leadership throughout western Europe and organized missions to unconverted peoples seems the more remarkable if one remembers that through most of his pontificate he was in sickness and acute bodily pain, apparently because of an excess of asceticism. But the intellectual level of his Christianity was far lower than that of St. Augustine or St. Jerome. His *Pastoral Rule* was a useful guide to the functions of a priest. But his longest work, a commentary on the Book of Job known as the *Moralia,* was drearily mechanical and uninspired, each passage being lengthily examined for its literal, its allegorical, and its moral meaning. In his *Dialogues* he presented a collection of miracles that had occurred in recent years in Italy. Recounting stories of how floods and fires had been suddenly brought under control, shortages of oil and wine had been abruptly ended, diseases had been cured, and evil spirits had been prevented from playing tricks on good Christians, they had all the credulity and the banality that so generally characterize this category of literature.

Another member of the Roman aristocracy of the sixth century, Benedict of Nursia, set the standards for Western monasticism for many centuries to come. After spending four years as a hermit in a cave on Mount Subiaco, close to the ruins of one of Nero's palaces, he became a founder of monasteries, ending his life as the abbot of Monte Cassino. His *Rule,* which was eventually adopted by most of the Western monasteries, was important chiefly because of its provisions for efficient organization; the duties of the abbot and the daily routine to be followed by the monks were prescribed with great care and realism. The virtues of obedience and humility were especially stressed. The main purposes of the monastic life, as Benedict defined them, were to provide for the worship of God and to enable the monks "to escape the pains of hell and reach eternal life." Hard work, including not only labor in the fields but also the reading of religious books, was obligatory, but chiefly because "idleness is the enemy of the soul" rather than because of any value in the fruits of industry. The monk was supposed to spend two hours a day in reading, but that he would normally read very slowly seems to be indicated by another passage in which it was stipulated that he must borrow at least one book from the library during Lent. In later years the Benedictine monasteries performed most useful services in improving agricultural methods and preserving learning, but Benedict himself evinced little interest in such practical achievements. Monasticism existed in order to save the souls of its monks, not to raise the level of civilization. This was Christianity stripped to its barest essentials, in the form best suited for its survival through the ages of barbarism that were to come.

Many of the Germanic tribes had been converted to Christianity in the fourth century, though this had had little effect on their ethical standards; but since they had encountered the new religion in its Arian rather than its orthodox form, they were regarded by the papacy as dangerous heretics. Other groups, like the Franks in northern France and the Anglo-Saxons in Britain, were won over to Catholic Christianity after the invasions; and during the later Dark Ages, missionaries were actively at work in Germany and Scandinavia. The success with which Christianity was propagated was due partly to its association with Roman civilization, which the barbarians wanted to absorb rather than to destroy, and partly to the vigorous support given by tribes already converted; but it is impossible to explain the rapid growth of the new religion without emphasizing more personal and intangible factors. Its great apostles had a spiritual force and conviction acquired through long years of ascetic discipline. This gave them an immense personal influence over barbarian converts.

Yet relatively little of the Christian doctrine could be effectively transmitted to the Europe of the Dark Ages. The level of Christian teaching, which had sharply dropped with the conversion of Constantine, plummeted again when the new religion was adopted by the barbarians. How could a faith in universal brotherhood be imparted to the members of a war band delighting in slaughter, loot, and destruction? Only a much more elemental religion, stressing the fear of divine anger against wrongdoers, could promote those habits of self-control which must be the first step in the growth of a new civilization. The Church of the Dark Ages did not wholly forget the original gospel promise, but it appealed chiefly to much more primitive attitudes and motivations, sanctifying tribal warfare if the cause could be made to seem good, and promising success in battle and happiness in heaven to chieftains who obeyed its dictates. After the emergence of the new Western civilization, the full meaning of Christianity, as of the classical heritage, could be recaptured only by a slow process of working backward from Dark Age tribalism to earlier and more spiritual modes of belief. Much of the spiritual history of the West can be interpreted as a gradual unfolding of meanings which were always potential in Christian doctrine but which could not all become explicit at the same time.

The barbarian chieftain had little interest in anything so visionary and intangible as eternal salvation, at least as long as he retained his health and vigor. He wanted to be assured of divine favor in governing his kingdom and doing battle with his enemies, and the chief function of the priests of the Church, as of their predecessors who had served the old tribal war-gods, was to make sure that Jesus was sufficiently propitiated. The chief means of accomplishing this necessary objective were constant prayer and the celebration of the prescribed rituals of worship. The Christian deity (like the chieftain who hoped for his assistance) was regarded as sensitive about his reputation and susceptible to flattery, and to sing psalms in his honor was as effective in winning his approval as was conformity with the moral law, and required considerably less moral effort and emotional transformation. One of the commonplaces of Dark Age thinking was the threefold division of the population into those who fought, those who labored, and those who prayed. These three occupations were all regarded as directly necessary for the welfare of society. The cleric who spent his time in prayer was performing a service quite as indispensable as the tasks of the soldier and the peasant. The most valuable members of the clergy, moreover, were not the parish priests or the bishops, who had to spend part of their time in mundane activities, but the monks, who could devote themselves almost exclusively to prayer and worship. The numerous kings and noblemen who founded or endowed monasteries were primarily motivated by a desire to increase the volume of praise that rose every day to heaven in order to avert divine anger. The economic and cultural activities of the monks were mere by-products to which Dark Age thinking attributed only secondary importance.[3]

---

[3] It is astonishing to what degree even the most realistic religious leaders of the Dark Ages continued to insist on the efficacy of prayer in persuading God not to allow the barbarians to triumph. Pope Gregory the Great declared that the main protection of Rome from Lombard invaders was the tears and the sexual abstinence of the three thousand nuns who belonged to Roman convents. When the Viking raids began in western Europe, the intellectual spokesman of the Carolingian Empire, Alcuin of York, repeated the usual magical assurances. The raids were successful because their Frankish victims had not won God's approval by sufficiently fervent prayer.

Throughout the Crusades the clergy continued to affirm that they were in accord with God's will and therefore could not fail. Clerical attitudes, however,

To this primeval conception of religion as a means for ensuring welfare in this life, Christianity had added the hope of individual redemption after death and the threat of eternal punishment for the wicked. This conception of the afterlife had been affirmed in the gospels, but had not been given much emphasis in early Christian preaching. The persecutions had given it more vividness and emphasis, because the martyrs had felt an understandable desire to know that they would be vindicated after death; and the expectation that the blessed would be able to watch the damned in torment was supported by Christian theologians. The doctrine of purgatory had been added in the fourth century. Throughout the Dark and Middle Ages, the horrors of eternal punishment remained one of the main themes of Christian preaching. As Isidore of Seville declared, "Let every convert begin with fear for his sins; . . . it is necessary that he should first turn to God in fear, that through dread of future torments his fleshly temptations may be conquered." [4] Preachers were especially fond of insisting on the small number who would be saved —the vast majority of mankind, including many professing Christians, being destined to be damned. But although the doctrine of eternal punishment undoubtedly increased the influence of the clergy, who were generally held responsible for the salvation of their parishioners, it had remarkable little effect on moral standards. The concept of hell, so wholly inconsistent with the gospel doctrine of divine fatherhood, was so far beyond the grasp

---

were slowly acquiring a more realistic recognition of hard fact. Bernard of Clairvaux was the main preacher of the so-called Second Crusade, and it was even suggested that he might assume military leadership. The total and rapid failure of the expedition caused him to put the blame on the sins of the participants, but he seems to have been a little puzzled by God's behavior, as well he might. The deity's wishes were apparently more complex than his earthly supporters recognized. It is an illustration of Bernard's real greatness that he was not content with an easy answer. "All my works frighten me," he declared, "and what I do is incomprehensible to me" (quoted in J. Pieper: *Scholasticism*, p. 89).

[4] Quoted in G. G. Coulton: *Life in the Middle Ages*, I, 33.

of the human imagination that it defeated its own purposes. Some individuals, for whom the fear of eternal damnation provided objective confirmation of inner anxieties and feelings of guilt, were driven to extremes of asceticism, usually without achieving any lasting sense of spiritual security. But for the average layman, one's destiny in the afterlife would be determined by magical rather than moral prerequisites. The rite of baptism, for example, by which the infant became a member of the Christian community, was one of the necessary means of salvation. Even St. Augustine, whose conceptions of religion were far more spiritual than those of the average believer, affirmed that infants so unfortunate as to die without being baptized would go infallibly to hell. Most people probably felt that they could be assured of entry into purgatory, and ultimately into heaven, by attendance at church ceremonials, the physical incorporation of Christ's body through the Mass, the intercession of the Virgin and the saints, and, if necessary, a deathbed repentance accompanied by the rituals of Extreme Unction. The notion that a lifetime of sin would be blotted out if one felt sincerely religious at the last moment, or even if one merely received Extreme Unction from a priest, was, of course, especially reassuring. It was confirmed by the gospel story of Christ assuring one of the thieves between whom he was crucified that they would meet that same day in paradise. It was unfortunate if the sinner died abruptly, still in a state of sin and with no priest available, but medieval warriors found ways of reducing even this risk. According to the French epic poems, knights customarily swallowed three blades of grass before going into battle, and this was considered the equivalent of a final Holy Communion.

Many of the attitudes that had become associated with Christianity belonged to even more primitive levels of thinking. In becoming the official religion of the Roman Empire it had assimilated a vast mass of long-established beliefs and rituals that were wholly alien to its true character. These had gained new strength during the Roman decadence; as Greco-Roman civilization lost the energy needed for the maintenance of order, there had been a reversion to more primitive methods of seeking security. Christian missionaries, moreover, had learned that they were more likely to achieve successful results if they did not insist on any total transformation of religious habits. As can be seen in the instructions given by Gregory the Great to the missionaries whom he dispatched to convert the Anglo-Saxons, Christian churches were built on the same sites as pagan temples, and pagan rituals were, as far as possible, assimilated into Christianity rather than abolished. The result was the survival of innumerable pagan customs and superstitions. Christian saints and martyrs replaced the traditional local deities of the peasants, inheriting the same holy places and the same miraculous powers; and festivals and ceremonies perhaps many thousands of years old continued, with only minor changes and with the blessings of the Church. Popular Christianity became virtually polytheistic, while the Virgin Mary replaced the great goddess of fertility, both spouse and mother of the dying and reviving vegetation deity, whose worship had been established among the peasants since long before the beginning of civilization.

Practices which Christianity failed to assimilate were condemned as forms of devil-worship, but the lines between what was sanctified and what was condemned were not always drawn with much clarity or logic, and there were many borderline cases. Peculiar rituals which were clearly of pagan origin, and which had acquired little or no Christian significance, continued to be performed by clerical functionaries in different parts of Europe. A well-known example was the Feast of Fools, celebrated annually in a dozen French cities until the sixteenth century. This was clearly a survival of the old Roman Saturnalia. The lower clergy attached to a cathedral would conduct the ceremonials, singing ribald hymns, wearing peculiar clothes, preaching hilarious sermons, and conducting a kind of parody of the Christian Mass. In some instances it remained uncertain whether a ceremony of pagan origin was to be accepted or condemned. Parish priests occasionally incurred episcopal censure by participating in pagan rituals, such as dances in churchyards, which the higher ecclesiastical authorities refused to tolerate.

Much the most persistent and pervasive of these survivals of the old religion was the cult of the dead. The belief that the corpses of heroes retained a numinous power which could be both beneficent and destructive was deeply rooted among the peasants of southern Europe, both preceding and outliving the worship of the Olympian deities. The tombs of such men, it was supposed, promoted the fertility of the earth and gave protection against catastrophes, though, like all sacred objects, they had to be approached with caution. This hero-worship acquired a new vitality when it was adopted by Christianity and applied to Christian saints. As early as the fourth century, the belief that the tombs of martyrs were endowed with magical qualities, especially for the cure of diseases, was well established. Visitors to the sacred spots could share in their health-giving and beneficent powers—an attitude that made pilgrimages one of the favorite occupations of the Middle Ages.[5] Rome, which contained the tombs of both St. Peter and St. Paul, was a favorite pilgrim resort, but the country richest in numinous power was obviously Palestine, a conception that was to be one of the causes of the Crusades.

From this primeval reverence for the dead there quickly developed a cult of relics. Any part of the body of a saint, or any object that had been closely associated with him, retained a portion of the same life-giving quality. A community lacking an authentic saint's tomb could therefore be assured of health and prosperity for its citizens by securing possession of sacred bones or articles of clothing or of portions of something that had been used by Jesus or the apostles, the most prized of such articles being a fragment of the cross. This extension of magical power

---

[5] According to the eighth-century British missionary leader, St. Boniface, almost every town between Rome and the English Channel contained an Anglo-Saxon prostitute who had set off to make a pilgrimage to Palestine but had been unable to reach it and had been compelled to resort to this method of supporting herself. Nothing could better illustrate the extraordinary confusion of values in Dark Age Christianity. See Boniface's *Letters,* edited by E. Emerton (New York, 1940), p. 140.

from the actual corpse in its tomb to transportable objects associated with it seems to have been purely Christian, not a pagan survival. Throughout the Dark and Middle Ages the demand for these fetishistic objects reached fantastic proportions. To what extent it was carried is illustrated by a number of occasions when communities went to war to secure possession of the corpse of a saint who had recently died. Of St. Romuald, an Italian holy man of the eleventh century, it is even recorded that he was in grave danger of being killed by a peasant community which wanted to make sure of retaining his body. There is little exaggeration in the verdict of the French historian Achille Luchaire that the true religion of the Middle Ages was the worship of relics.[6]

Thus popular Christianity became largely a series of magical devices for avoiding material ills, with little concern for ethical values. The healing power of a relic exerted its influence directly, regardless of the moral merits of the individual who invoked it. For the laity, Christianity had come to consist of a series of rituals, correct performance of which would bring good fortune. Respect for such duties as attendance at the Mass, fasting during Lent, and not eating meat on Fridays would normally ensure divine protection and counted for more than obedience to moral rules. As for the gospel ethic, it survived, if at all, only in the attenuated form of charity to the poor. And though the clergy and the monks were expected to conform to much stricter standards than the laity, and by so doing would acquire merits that would benefit society as well as themselves, these standards were often derived from the attitudes of the pagan decadence rather than from the teaching of the gospel.

The full meaning of the gospel ethic could not be recaptured

---

[6] Roland was a mighty warrior; but this did not prevent him from seeking magical aid and assurance, just as Achilles' prowess was compatible with immunity from all possible wounds except in his heel. Roland's sword, Durandal, contained a tooth of St. Peter, blood of St. Basil, hair of St. Denis, and a piece of cloth that had been worn by the Virgin. What skilled blacksmith actually forged the implement we are not informed.

until the Dark Ages had ended and some progress had been achieved in the building of a new civilization. In the early stages of that progress it is possible that secular literature played a more significant role than the teaching of the Church, because its moral standards were more applicable to actual ways of living. When in the course of time the ruling class in medieval feudal society began to recognize the need for the control of their sensuous and murderous appetites, they could find appropriate models of conduct in the *chansons de geste* with their emphasis on the virtue of moderation (*mesure*) and in the troubadour exaltation of love from a mere appetite into an idealized emotion promoting courtesy and humility. The ethic of the Christian Church, on the other hand, was in principle too elevated, and in actuality often too lax, to be a fully effective instrument in the advance of Dark Age society from barbarism.

The general view of life of Dark Age and early medieval man was, however, derived from Christian theology, in spite of its lack of practical application, though Dark Age versions of that theology perhaps owed more to Plotinus than to the Bible. Christianity retained the monistic conceptions of ultimate reality that had characterized the thinking of the classical decadence. Insofar as it believed in the existence of the devil, it was also dualistic; and many Christian ascetics had a very vivid sense of being constantly tempted or tormented by diabolical agencies. But this dualism remained a psychological rather than a metaphysical reality. For the Dark Age thinker, the world was a unity, created and governed by the divine will, and all things began with God and led back to God. This Dark Age view of life was supported by the Ptolemaic cosmology inherited from Hellenism, which portrayed the universe as a finite and orderly system, the sun, the planets, and the stars moving around the earth in a series of concentric circles. This geocentric hypothesis both exalted man by considering him as the center of the created universe and at the same time debased him by insisting that corruption was possible only in the sublunar sphere, in contrast with the divine perfection of the stars and planets and the empyrean. This whole cosmology depended on the existence of God, and it was there-fore impossible not to believe in him. Because the world was finite, there had to be a final cause; and because all objects were static unless they were put in motion by some external force, there had to be a first mover. Various proofs of God's existence were worked out, but these were valid and carried conviction only in terms of the prevalent intellectual attitudes. In the late Middle Ages, on the other hand, when new ways of thinking began to develop (most notably the change from a finite to an infinite universe, and the new view of motion as not requiring a mover), the reality of God suddenly became problematic.

From the oneness of the universe it followed that the same laws were to be found in every part of it. This assumption, accepted implicitly and without critical examination until the late Middle Ages, pervaded medieval thought. In consequence, a plausible concrete analogy was immediately accepted as a suffi-cient proof of any theoretical proposition. This was particularly evident in thinking about human society. Since God was the ruler of the universe and since the sun was lord of the sky, it followed that the king must be the master of the state. To the medieval mind this argument from analogy was wholly convincing. This kind of thinking retained much of its force as late as the early seventeenth century, as is witnessed by the speech of Ulysses in defense of monarchy in Shakespeare's *Troilus and Cressida*.

Every visible object could therefore be interpreted as an expression of a divine truth. In the course of time, this view of the universe would lead to a recognition of natural beauty and to the belief that the universe was rational and therefore capable of being understood by the mind of man; but the Dark Ages were concerned only with the creator, not with his creation. Material things were of significance only because of what they reflected of God's mind and purpose, not because they had any intrinsic beauty or utility. This was perhaps the most striking and perva-sive characteristic of almost all early Western thought. Only with extreme reluctance could an early medieval mind be brought to regard a visible object as having value in itself. As John Scotus

Erigena declared, "There is nothing in visible and corporeal things that does not signify something invisible and incorporeal." [7] The whole material world was therefore regarded as a storehouse not of objects worthy of study in themselves but of analogies for the incarnation, the crucifixion, the resurrection, and other Christian dogmas. The natural world was a system of allegories, and this was the sole reason why human beings should be interested in it—an attitude which was, of course, wholly incompatible with any development of the physical sciences.

The habit of searching for allegories had originally been cultivated in the interpretation of the Bible. Every passage was regarded as having both a moral and an allegorical, as well as a literal, meaning, to which was sometimes added an anagogical (or mystical) meaning. By this method, theologians could dispose of passages in which the literal meaning was embarrassing or immoral. The story of David, Bathsheba, and Uriah, for example, was explained by St. Augustine as an allegorical foreshadowing of the relations between Jesus, the Church, and the Jewish synagogue. Once the habit of looking for hidden meanings had been established, it was extended to virtually everything. Medieval notions of zoology, for example, were derived mainly from the *Physiologus,* a collection of fantastic animal stories that had originated in Egypt or Asia Minor during the Roman period; these tales of unicorns, phoenixes, and other zoological prodigies were taken seriously for nearly a thousand years, and were constantly cited as exemplifications of theological truths.

Thus for the mind of the Dark Ages what was ultimately real was Christian dogma, and visible things acquired reality only insofar as they reflected and expressed spiritual truths. But a nobler view of life was always present in Christianity, although it remained latent as long as Western society remained barbaric. The ages of highest creativity are those in which spiritual and aesthetic values are believed to be capable of realization and

---

[7] Quoted in Henry Osborne Taylor: *The Medieval Mind,* I, 552.

embodiment in temporal and material forms, and the whole
material universe is seen as the expression of a divine reason and
beauty. This sense of epiphany was always implicit in Christian
doctrine and ceremony. It was the inner meaning of the doctrine
of the incarnation, by which God had put on human flesh; it was
extended to the whole human race in the myth of the bodily
resurrection, which had replaced the Greek belief in the immortality of the soul; and it was given visible and concrete expression
in the regular rituals of the Church. In every Christian church
Christ again became miraculously incarnate in the simplest
human foods, and his worshippers were permitted to assimilate
the "medicine of immortality." [8] For most Christians, the sacri-
fice of the Mass was a promise of eternal salvation after they had
been released from the ills of earthly life. But this incessantly
repeated reincarnation of divinity in the most homely material
forms had deeper meanings. It was a symbolic statement of the
belief that spiritual values were to be found not merely in heaven
but here and now, and that the whole material world was capable
of deification.

---

[8] So called by St. Ignatius early in the second century. Quoted in A. C.
McGiffert: *History of Christian Thought* (New York, 1932), I, 43.

4

Decline and Renewal

in the West

While the formal thinking of the new Western civilization was derived from classical and Christian sources,
the civilization itself developed among northern peoples who had
hitherto been barbaric. It began when these peoples were stimulated to creative innovation by the adoption of Christian beliefs
and by contact, through the medium of the Roman Church, with
what survived of the Helleno-Roman cultural heritage. Their
traditional institutions, ways of living, and aesthetic sensibilities
were carried over into the new civilization and underwent no
sudden transformation.

Such a development was possible only in areas of northern
Europe where society was still primitive and had not been affected by the decadence of classicism. The peoples of Italy,
southern France, and Spain, despite the advent of Germanic
conquerors, retained too much of the old civilization to be
immediately capable of innovation. They had adopted Christianity in a spirit of world-weariness and disillusionment; and when
their religion was more than a superstitious demand for material
security, it was likely to take the form of a gloomy and morose
pursuit of personal salvation in monastic retirement. But the less
sophisticated northern peoples adopted Christianity in enthu-

siasm rather than despair, associating it with the whole heritage of Roman civilization and trying to practice it with a naïve confidence in its truth, without conscious awareness of many inconsistencies and incongruities.

Like most warrior and hunting peoples (a group's political characteristics can generally be attributed to its phase of economic development, not to special ethnic traits), the Germans of the period of the invasions had little organized government. The power of the kings was strictly limited, and individual heads of families were largely independent of any central authority. But German society cannot be called democratic; there were sharp hereditary distinctions between the chief families and the rank and file of the tribesmen. It was essentially prepolitical, and any of the words normally used to describe political institutions are likely to be misleading.

The most important feature of this prepolitical society was the dependence of the individual for his security on familial and personal ties. He lacked the protection of an organized territorial state enforcing uniform rules of justice. Loyalties were still personal rather than political. The basic social unit was the extended family, which was obligated to exact recompense for murders or other injuries suffered by any of its members. The individual was therefore fortunate if he had numerous relatives. In an effort to limit feuding, scales of wergild (blood-money) payments had been worked out, varying according to the rank of the victim; and the relatives might accept the appropriate sum in lieu of retaliatory killings. But they were not obliged to forgo vengeance, and incidents in the annals of the Dark Ages show that men were likely to develop uneasy consciences if they failed to exact a life for a life, feeling that to accept wergild was a mark of cowardice.

The loyalties that maintained social cohesion might also be determined by individual choice. Every chieftain had his war band (*comitatus*), consisting of warriors who had attached themselves to him and who were pledged, if necessary, to die in his defense. This primeval quality of personal devotion was idealized as the highest kind of virtue and regarded as a peculiarly German trait. Long after German tribalism had given place to organized territorial states, German writers continued to insist that their compatriots were especially distinguished by their fidelity (*treue*).

Germanic conceptions of justice were, of course, wholly incompatible with the judicial institutions of the Roman Empire. Most of the new kingdoms tried at first to maintain two different legal systems, Germanic for the invaders (this being largely concerned with fixing wergild payments) and Roman for the conquered populations. In the long run the continuance of Germanic family loyalties was both a main cause and a consequence of the gradual breakdown of organized law and order in the Western kingdoms. When finally the dissolution of the social order had reached its limits and a new society with new institutions began to emerge, its initial mode of integration was derived mainly from Germanic sources. The personal loyalty binding the vassal to his lord was the essential cohesive element in feudalism. Through the early Middle Ages, men continued to seek security by attachment to the extended family or to the village community or the local lord, not through membership in the state, which existed only in theory, or in the nation, which had not yet been born. The French *chansons de geste,* which tell us more about social attitudes than any chronicle or public document, are pervaded with a sense of the binding obligation of individual loyalties and of the possible tragic consequences of any conflict of loyalties. The attitude is largely prefeudal in that the loyalties are usually personal and not associated with the holding of land. It is surprising, and not easily explicable, to find strong traces still surviving of the matrilineal descent upon which the Germanic family must originally have been based, most notably in the fact that the closest attachments of the young warrior are not to his father (who is rarely even mentioned) but always to his maternal uncle.

Equally important for the development of the West was the Germanic conception of kingship. A king was normally chosen from a hereditary ruling family, which was supposed to be of divine descent; but he owed his position to election by the chief men of the tribe, and virtually his only functions were to provide leadership in war and to preside over tribal assemblies in peace-time. He was expected to consult with the chief men before reaching any important decision and had, at least in theory, no legislative powers. The tribal laws were generally regarded as immutable, and although the king might sometimes exercise broad powers of interpretation, he was not permitted to change or violate them.

The Achaean conquerors of Greece had originally had similar attitudes, as is shown in the Homeric poems, but classical civilization had passed through a long and ultimately disastrous political evolution and had ended in the surrender of all liberties to a despotic government. According to Roman political theory, sovereignty originated in the popular will, but once it had been transferred to an individual emperor, the grant was unlimited and irrevocable. The will of the ruler had the force of law. But the new Western civilization was not condemned to repeat the classical experience. The formation of the Germanic kingdoms was followed by a considerable enlargement of royal power, owing mainly to the influence of Roman methods of administration and legal traditions; but the Germanic aristocracies insisted on maintaining the practice of consultation and never permitted their kings to become wholly autocratic.

In the course of the Dark Ages the Germanic tradition of the supremacy of tribal law became fused with the classical concept of normative laws of nature and with the Christian belief in immutable laws of God. Thus Germanic practice combined with Greek and Christian theory to produce the Western concept of limited rather than absolute government. All these different elements can be discerned in a statement made in the ninth century by Archbishop Hincmar of Rheims. "Monarchs and ministers of state," he declared, "have laws by which it is their duty to govern the inhabitants of every province; they have the capitularies of Christian kings and of their forebears, which these proclaimed with the general consent of their faithful subjects that they would observe in accordance with law." [1] No such affirmation could have been made by any citizen of the late Roman or the Byzantine Empire, and the Germanic belief in the supremacy of law and in the need for popular consent was never wholly lost by Western society, in spite of the continuing influence of Roman jurisprudence, with its emphasis on autocratic sovereignty. Even the absolute monarchs of the sixteenth and seventeenth centuries recognized that they were responsible to God and God's law, though if they violated divine law they could not be called to account by their subjects; only God could remove a tyrannous ruler.

In culture and the arts the barbarian contribution to the new civilization is less easy to trace, chiefly because little has survived. We know that the Germanic tribes had poems of an epic quality, handed down orally; these presumably were forerunners of the *chansons de geste*. But the surviving examples are few and probably untypical. In art, on the other hand, the importance of the northern tradition is clearly apparent. Art for all the northern peoples was decorative rather than pictorial, consisting not of pictures but of abstract designs on brooches, bowls, sword handles, and other implements. Such designs were believed to have magical qualities. The notion of representationalist or illusionist art, conceived of as a kind of window looking out on physical realities, was altogether lacking. This kind of abstract art prevailed from Ireland to southern Russia, with minor geographical variations.

The special quality of northern art was its dynamism. Abstract art elsewhere has mostly conveyed a sense of religious submission to transcendental realities, and has therefore emphasized rest and peace. But the art of the northern barbarians, consisting mostly of lines organized into complex patterns, suggested motion, restlessness, and disharmony. The art of the Celtic

---

[1] Quoted in A. J. and R. W. Carlyle: *History of Medieval Political Theory in the West*, I, 230.

peoples consisted mostly of curving lines interlaced in patterns of extraordinary intricacy. Seeming to move from the center outward rather than to have been planned to fill a given space, these designs conveyed chiefly an impression of intense vigor and movement. Germanic art, which was less highly developed, had a liking for animal shapes (which seems to have been originally acquired from peoples in eastern Europe), but the shapes were used as elements in designs and were not realistic portrayals.

This was the art of peoples who believed in the constant need for struggle against an unfriendly nature, and it had none of that sense of harmony between man and his natural environment which has mostly characterized the art of the Mediterranean regions. Whether this northern attitude was the result of geographic or ethnic factors or of some accident of cultural transmission is, of course, an unanswerable question. But it was this northern tendency which prevailed in the art of the early Middle Ages, despite a considerable copying of southern representationalism. At a later period, the northern sense of dynamism and of the natural world as something to be transcended, not accepted, became especially evident in Gothic architecture, which originated in northern France and never took deep root in the Mediterranean countries. Similar tendencies can be traced in much of the art of northern Europe down to the present day. They reflect a continuing difference in the approach to nature of northern and southern peoples.

. . .

Much the most important of the political units set up during the era of the Germanic invasions was the kingdom of the Franks. It was the strongest of the barbarian dominions and eventually became the chief center of the new civilization. In its history can be traced the whole process of dissolution and reintegration that made the division between the classical and the Western civilizations. All the other barbarian kingdoms except those in Britain proved to be relatively short-lived.

The Frankish dominion was able to endure largely because of a firm alliance between its rulers and the Catholic Church. By the sixth century it covered most of what is now France and western Germany; and though this expansion was followed by a long period of decay, it revived in the later Dark Ages, achieving its greatest extent under the Carolingian rulers of the eighth and ninth centuries. We are fortunate in being able to watch the earlier stages of its development in the *History of the Franks* written at the end of the sixth century by Bishop Gregory of Tours. Both in his superstitions and intellectual deficiencies and in his positive values, Bishop Gregory, unlike other writers of the sixth century, points forward to the Middle Ages rather than backward to the classical past.

Much of Gregory's *History* has the flavor of a police gazette, and the strongest impression to be derived from it is that Gallic society was becoming increasingly barbarized as a result of the misdeeds of its Merovingian dynasty of rulers. Early Merovingian France was still essentially Roman, but the remnants of the old civilization diminished with each generation. Clovis, who reigned from 481 to 511, was the founder of the Frankish kingdom. He had Gregory's general approval because of his conversion to the Catholic faith and support of the Church. Yet this blond and blue-eyed savage, belonging to a family who claimed descent from a Germanic sea-god and marked their royal status by never cutting their hair, was guilty of more numerous and heinous crimes than the worst of the Roman emperors. Becoming chieftain of one of the Frankish tribes which had hitherto remained settled in parts of the Rhineland and the Netherlands, Clovis made himself the master of much of the modern France by an unremitting reliance on treachery and murder. Yet because the Franks had turned to orthodox Catholicism, while their Visigothic and Burgundian competitors were Arian heretics, Gregory regarded the misdeeds of Clovis as serving divine purposes, correct theological beliefs being more important than a multitude of crimes.

Clovis adopted Christianity after winning a battle against the

Alemanni in which he had prayed to Jesus for victory, and was then baptized with three thousand of his warriors in a mass ceremony at Rheims. Subsequently he received the title of Consul from the emperor at Constantinople and was invested with the traditional purple tunic and mantle of Roman officials in the church of St. Martin at Tours. Thenceforth he claimed clerical and even divine support in his wars with the other Germanic tribes. When he invaded the territories of the Visigothic king, with whom he had recently sworn oaths of eternal friendship, he was aided by miracles and encouraged by a fiery beacon issuing from a church and shining above his head. While building the Frankish kingdom, Clovis was also engaged in consolidating his own power by murdering all his Frankish competitors, including both the chieftains of other tribes and his own Merovingian relatives. After disposing of all his known rivals, often with his own hands (cleaving the victim's skull with an ax was the preferred Merovingian mode of slaughter), he bemoaned his lack of kinsmen who could come to his aid in a time of crisis, though not from grief, as Gregory explains, "but craftily, to see if he could bring to light some new relative to kill." Yet while recounting this sanguinary record, Gregory abruptly pauses to remark, in an echo of the Book of Kings, that "daily the Lord laid his enemies low under his hand, and increased his kingdom, because he walked before him with an upright heart, and did that which was pleasing in his sight." [2] So deeply had moral values been confused and perverted by ecclesiastical insistence on theological orthodoxy.

Clovis's descendants did not acquire any more profound understanding of the civilization they had appropriated and the religion they had adopted. France continued to suffer under the misrule of the Merovingian kings for more than two hundred years. On the death of each ruler, the kingdom was invariably

---

[2] Gregory: *History of the Franks,* translated by O. H. M. Dalton (Oxford, 1927), II, 31–42, 29–40.

divided among his sons, and this was usually followed by civil wars until all but one of them had been poisoned, assassinated, or slain in battle and the kingdom had been reunited by the winner in this fratricidal competition. Their women had to be equally adept in the conflict for survival, almost all the Merovingians being unrestrainedly polygamous. The most extraordinary of the characters portrayed in Gregory's *History* was Queen Fredegund, originally a palace servant, who rose by dexterity and sexual attraction to be the wife of King Chilperic, murdered or otherwise eliminated several rival wives and their children, fought long wars against her husband's brothers and nephews, and eventually died peacefully in her bed after seeing her son established as king. Fredegund's great antagonist Brunhild, wife of Chilperic's brother Sigebert, who had equal vigor but displayed some glimmerings of moral feeling, ended less fortunately: in her old age she was captured by enemies and put to death by being dragged across rocky ground by an untamed horse. Carnage and debauchery were so habitual among the Merovingians that anybody who seemed relatively restrained was regarded as a man of extraordinary virtue. The brother of Chilperic and Sigebert, Guntram, who was only moderately murderous and polygamous, became known as the good king and even attained the honor of canonization.

During generations of misrule, the lights of the old civilization grew steadily dimmer. Under the earlier Merovingians much of it still survived. France still had rich cornfields and vineyards, and old Gallo-Roman aristocratic families continued to gather substantial revenues from the labors of their dependents and to live in considerable luxury. Urban life, fine craftsmanship, and trade with the East did not immediately disappear. Much of the administration in both state and church was still exercised by members of the old families, and wealthy individuals, including some Frankish as well as Gallo-Roman nobles, patronized the arts and letters. But as the country sank into barbarism, trade and communication decreased and society was atomized into smaller units. Literacy disappeared except among some of the monks, and there was no longer any written language that was generally accepted and understood. Speaking various Germanic dialects or forms of popular Latin, men from different districts could no longer communicate with each other. The central government, unable to collect taxes and no longer served by a trained bureaucracy, became increasingly ineffective, and political authority in local areas was assumed by the landowning aristocracy. Different provinces, even different villages, became isolated from each other and were left dependent on their own resources for economic necessities and the maintenance of order. Nor was the Church able to maintain civilized standards; it had largely come under the control of the kings, who endowed it with large estates but assumed the power of nominating bishops and abbots.

The dissolution of the old civilization is vividly mirrored in its earlier stages in Bishop Gregory's *History*. A member of an old Gallo-Roman aristocratic family, he was well aware that he lived in an era of cultural decline, as is shown by his apologies for his ignorance of correct grammatical Latin. A more significant indication is his inability to organize his material into any kind of unity. He belonged to an anarchical society which was no longer pervaded by any general view of life giving meaning and value to individual experiences. He was a conscientious and firmly orthodox Christian, but his Christianity meant chiefly a belief in supernatural powers expressing themselves not in the regular process of nature and society but in miraculous interventions. His *History* is thus a confused mixture of major political events, anecdotes about the sanctity or immorality of obscure individuals, miraculous cures performed by the relics of saints, acts of God and prodigies of nature, and autobiographical reminiscences, all thrown together with no recognition of their relative importance.

The loss of all sense of order is manifested not only in Gregory's narrative methods but also in his style and grammar. The complex sentence structure of classical Latin, with its logical deployment of numerous subordinate clauses which had seemed expressive of the whole Roman capacity for organization, has disappeared. Strings of factual statements are loosely tied together with meaningless or incorrectly used connectives, and the relationship between them frequently remains obscure. As Erich Auerbach has pointed out, "Gregory's language . . . is but imperfectly equipped to organize facts; as soon as a complex of events ceases to be very simple, he is no longer able to present it as a coherent whole. His language organizes badly or not at all." [3]

But the change is not all loss, for while Gregory cannot see life as a whole, he can record the actions and experiences of individuals with a sensory vividness that had long since disappeared from the literature of late classicism. Except in such religious documents as the *Confessions* of St. Augustine and the *Letters* of Jerome, late Latin writers could portray men and women only in terms of long-established clichés and conventions; they were not interested in real individuals. But Gregory's narrative is filled with anecdotes illustrative of human idiosyncrasies, told with a simple recognition of what human beings are like, that often recall the Old Testament. His language, says Auerbach, "lives in the concrete side of events, it speaks with and in the people who figure in them. And it can give forceful and varied expression to their pleasure, their pain, their scorn and anger, or whatever other passions may chance to be raging in them. . . . His style is wholly different from that of the authors of late antiquity, even the Christians among them. . . . It is a decadence, a decline in culture and verbal disposition; but it is not only that. It is a reawakening of the directly sensible." [4] With the breakdown of the classical order, the individual was coming alive again. It would be a long time before there was any intellectual recognition of the uniqueness of every individual. Early medieval writing, like that of the classical decadence, lacked the vocabulary needed to define individual traits and tended to deal solely with classes and categories, as though all noblemen and all

---

[3] Erich Auerbach: *Mimesis* (Anchor Books), p. 80.
[4] Auerbach: op. cit., p. 82.

peasants were merely representatives of general qualities and always acted in keeping with what was expected of them. But medieval man from the beginning was, in practice, an individualist, as can be seen if one considers his actual behavior rather than the formulas used to describe it.

Meanwhile, ignored by the contemporary chroniclers and unnoticed by most historians, the civilization of the later Dark Ages was making technological advances that were probably more important than any achieved by Greece or Rome. Unlike the classical civilization, that of the West promoted technical progress from the beginning. How far this was due to certain specific factors—the virtual disappearance of slave labor and its replacement by a partially independent peasantry, and the establishment of monasteries whose inmates had strong inducements to make technical innovations—is an unanswerable question. Northern peoples had always been inclined to the domination rather than the acceptance of natural forces and were therefore predisposed to technical changes.

The later Dark Ages saw a revolution in agricultural methods that gradually spread through western Europe, in spite of the lack of regular communications. The main ingredients were a heavier plow, the substitution of horses for oxen, and three-field crop rotation. In place of the traditional scratch-plow, suitable only for dry uplands, peasants had begun to use a heavy iron plow which made it possible to cultivate the more fertile bottom-lands. Its inventors are unknown, but it was in use in eastern Europe by the end of the sixth century and was spreading to the West before the end of the seventh. Since it required a team of eight oxen, it was beyond the resources of individual peasants, but it could be adopted where the open-field system was in operation; it may have caused an expansion of this system. The use of horses for heavy traction had been impossible with the traditional type of harness, which tended to constrict their windpipes. But an improved horse collar, invented somewhere in the East, became known in western Europe in the eighth or ninth century. It was accompanied by the use of nailed horseshoes. Thenceforth horses began to replace oxen, being quicker, more easily fed, and capable of pulling heavier loads. The third major innovation, by which only one third of the land instead of half remained fallow at any one time, the other two thirds being planted with wheat and with oats or legumes, seems to have been established in the eighth century.

Thus the Dark Ages, so barren in political and cultural achievement, assume a different aspect when one turns to technological innovation. During the Dark Ages, new devices were adopted which would eventually make the civilization of the West materially much more productive than its classical predecessor. While formal thinking continued to be concerned with traditional doctrines that had no relevance to actual ways of living, less visible but more dynamic forces were preparing the way for a new advance.

· · ·

The first signs of a new cultural beginning can be found relatively early in the Dark Ages, not in France but among the Celtic and Anglo-Saxon inhabitants of the British Isles, though these were afterward overshadowed by more substantial developments in northern France and the Rhineland. Although southern Britain had belonged to the empire for more than three centuries, Roman civilization had exerted only a superficial influence there. As we know from archaeological evidence, the disorders of the third century caused a decline of the cities, which had been the main centers of Romanization, and a growth of big estates owned by a native aristocracy. Early in the fifth century the last Roman officials and legions were withdrawn from the island, and Britain again became wholly Celtic, government being assumed by various tribal chieftains who seem to have engaged in wars with each other whenever they were not trying to repel barbarian raids from abroad. Apart from the introduction of Christianity, the whole Roman occupation seems to have left remarkably few permanent traces. After the departure of the legions there was even a revival of the original Celtic tradition of abstract decorative art, which had been partially displaced and driven underground by Roman representationalism.

Anglo-Saxon invaders from northern Germany began to take possession of southeastern Britain halfway through the fifth century, but they encountered vigorous Celtic resistance and did not win control of the major part of England for nearly two hundred years. Memories of a successful Celtic leader of the sixth century, apparently preserved in Wales and by Celtic refugees who fled to Brittany, seem to have given birth to the Arthurian legend, though this was quickly intermingled with traditional Celtic legends that had no connection with the conflict with the Anglo-Saxons. After prolonged struggles, most of England and southern Scotland were divided among a number of small Germanic kingdoms, which were not united under a single government until the eighth century, while Celtic tribesmen, nominally Christian but still barbaric, continued to hold Wales and other western provinces. Thus the history of Britain during the early Dark Ages was wholly different from that of continental Europe. In Italy, Gaul, and Spain the Germanic invaders met with little opposition and were able to take possession of the Roman machinery of administration and make themselves masters of a Romanized and largely submissive population. In Anglo-Saxon England nothing survived of Roman civilization, apart from ruined cities, and there seems to have been little mingling of races.

Meanwhile, Celtic institutions in their full vigor were preserved in the more remote sections of the British Isles, especially in Ireland, which had never been conquered by Rome. This remote and ocean-bound outpost of the Western world was inhabited by tribal groups whose values and ways of living strongly resembled those portrayed in the poems of Homer. Warrior chieftains, dominated by a heroic compulsion to win immortal glory, engaged in incessant wars, mostly caused by thefts of cattle or competition for the possession of beautiful women, and their feats of valor and numerous love affairs were commemorated by a hereditary class of bards. The tales of Cuchulain, Conchobar, Deirdre of the Sorrows, and other legendary heroes and heroines displayed at their best some of the Greek capacity for the simple and tragic recognition of the realities of human experience, though they were often overlaid with meaningless rhetorical embellishments. The tales apparently date from early in the first millennium of our era, though they were not recorded in writing until the ninth century or later.

There has been much controversy about the Celtic contribution to Western literature and culture. Probably emphasis should be placed on the primitive level of Celtic society rather than on any special ethnic qualities it may have had. Yet it is undeniable that the romantic strain in early Western literature was largely of Celtic provenance, though its chief immediate sources seem to have been Welsh and Breton rather than Irish. In particular, the Celtic peoples developed the Arthurian legend, with its attendant stories of the Grail and of Tristram and Iseult. The pagan Irish legends convey a similar sense of wonder and an easy acceptance of the supernatural, with little recognition of any barriers between the miraculous and the commonplace. One has the impression of a twilight world in which all forms and limits are elusive and indeterminate and anything is possible. Mysterious powers, sometimes maleficent but more often playful, constantly intervene in human affairs. Strange and sudden delights and *frissons* of terror are always equally imminent. A stranger met on a road proves to be a supernatural visitor, a pathway across the hills or through the woods leads to fairyland, and an ocean voyage may start on the Atlantic and end in the afterlife.

The most novel feature of Celtic literature was its capacity for regarding nature with fresh eyes. Non-Celtic writers through the Dark and early Middle Ages may generally be said to have taken nature for granted, borrowing conventional epithets from their classical models and never looking at natural objects for themselves. Only the Irish and the Welsh, it has been remarked, could "make poetry out of mere Nature and nothing else, or at any rate nothing else besides the spirit of the poet, and his pleasure in what he sees, hears, and lives among." [5]

---

[5] W. P. Ker: *The Dark Ages,* p. 329.

The Irish were converted by St. Patrick and other missionaries in the fifth century, and thus for the first time acquired cultural links with Mediterranean civilization. Irish Christian art shows some Coptic influence. Apparently Coptic missionaries had come to Ireland from Egypt, though we do not know when, why, or how the linkage between the two extremities of the Christian world took place. But in the primitive society of Ireland, Christianity acquired a new un-Roman quality, particularly after the Anglo-Saxon conquest of southern Britain prevented regular communications with the continent. The Irish Church was predominantly monastic; its bishops had little authority. The monasteries were supported and controlled by the different tribes; the abbots were normally chosen from the same ruling families, and intertribal warfare, though less prevalent than in the pagan past, was never wholly ended. It was not until the ninth century that ecclesiastics were exempted from the duty of accompanying the tribal armies into battle and assisting them to win victories by the intensity of their prayers. The monks practiced an extreme asceticism unequaled elsewhere in western Europe and carried over from the pagan background an easy acceptance of the supernatural. They generally chose the most desolate spots to establish monasteries and had a strong inclination to a more mobile and footloose mode of ascetic living than was customary among Christian monks. Possibly this was the result of Coptic influences. Coptic monasticism was both more ascetic and more individualized than other branches of the institution, as the career of St. Anthony shows. The lives of the Irish saints have a curiously dreamlike quality. No other branch of Christian hagiology is so replete with marvels and miracles and examples of divine guidance and intervention.

In spite of their asceticism, however, the Irish saints did not feel that the world was wholly corrupted by sin. Irish Christian literature displayed a childlike pleasure in natural phenomena, a sense of gaiety and of adventure, and an ability to see spiritual potentialities in the most commonplace objects. Its capacity for enjoyment had been absent from the world-weary Mediterranean cultures for many centuries. Some examples of this Celtic sense of wonder were a little grotesque. Only an Irish Christian could have written a poem beginning: "I should like to have a great pool of ale for the King of Kings; I should like the Heavenly Host to be drinking it for all eternity." [6] Only in Irish literature could one encounter a legend like that of St. Ide, to whom Christ appeared in the form of a baby so that she could nurse him in her hermitage.

But the most refreshing quality of the Irish religious poets was their awareness of nature, as exemplified in poems like the soliloquy of a tenth-century Irish hermit enumerating with simple and loving precision all the sights and sounds of his forest home. While continental writers were still culling conventional epithets from Virgil and Prudentius, the Irish were taking note of the colors of apple blossoms and rowan berries, the sounds of bees and of the wind in the pines, the flight of geese and cranes, the movements of salmon and trout in the rivers, and—with special frequency—the "heavy waves over the glittering ocean" [7] by which Ireland was surrounded.

The most distinctive literary expressions of the Celtic spirit were written in the vernacular and influenced development in other countries only slowly and indirectly. But the Irish made a more immediate contribution to Western culture in their Latin poetry. Throughout the Dark and early Middle Ages, writing in Latin continued to represent the mainstream of Western literature, and new techniques appeared first in Latin before they were adopted into the new vernacular languages. The use of rhyme and accent, originating in Roman popular songs and afterward developed in Christian hymns, was checked throughout the whole Dark Ages by the superior prestige of the quantitative verse of the Latin classics. But writings in classical Latin could not possibly achieve any originality, and they remained purely

---

[6] Quoted in K. H. Jackson: *A Celtic Miscellany,* pp. 312–13.
[7] Jackson: op. cit., p. 307.

imitative. Only new poetic techniques could give expression to new human attitudes and experiences. It is significant that Irish monks were the first to develop the full potentialities of rhyme, presumably because they were freer than any continental people from the inhibiting influences of the classical tradition. Among the hymns composed at the monastery of Bangor as early as the seventh century one can find verses such as:

> Navis nunquam turbata,
> Quamvis fluctibus tonsa,
> Nuptiis quoque parata
> Regi domino sponsa [8]

This is not yet accentual, though it is no longer quantitative; it has a rhythm based on the simple principle of giving each line the same number of syllables. But the complete and obviously quite deliberate rhyme scheme antedates anything comparable written on the European continent by several centuries.

Apart from the Latin hymns, little of the Irish Dark Age learning has survived; but we know that some of the Irish monasteries were centers of classical scholarship, Greek as well as Latin, for several centuries. During the later Dark Ages the wandering Irish scholar was a familiar figure at continental courts and monasteries. The greatest of them, John Scotus Erigena, who lived at the court of the Frankish king in the ninth century, made a number of translations from Greek and wrote a philosophical reinterpretation of Christian Neo-Platonism, *De Divisione Naturae,* which can fairly be regarded as the only work of original thought produced anywhere in western Europe during the seven hundred years between St. Augustine and St. Anselm.

Through much of the Dark Ages, in fact, Ireland was the most dynamic center of spiritual energy in western Europe. Irish missionaries were active in expanding and revitalizing Christianity in Britain and on the continent, and it is plain from their

---

[8] Quoted in F. J. E. Raby: *History of Secular Latin Poetry in the Middle Ages,* I, 136.

surviving poems that, in spite of their severely ascetic practices, they were motivated by an enjoyment of exploration and adventure and an appreciation of natural beauty as well as by a more narrowly religious fervor. The best known of them was St. Columba (Colum Cille), the apostle of much of northern Britain. Born of an Irish royal family and trained as a poet, he founded several monasteries in Ireland, but was impelled to go into exile by an episode which shows to what extent Irish society was still barbaric in spite of its Christian convictions. While staying with another abbot, Columba secretly copied out a part of the Book of Psalms. His angry host wished to keep the precious book all to himself and his monastery, and appealed to the high king of Ireland, who delivered the famous verdict, "To every cow her calf, to every book its copy." Columba refused to accept this interpretation of copyright law, and the dispute led to warfare between the tribes and to the bloody battle of Culdremna, fought in the year 561. In order to understand all the implications of this story, one must realize that the Irish—despite their conversion to Christianity—continued to believe that sacred books had magical powers, especially in warfare. It was in penance for inciting his tribal kinsmen to violence that Columba moved to the island of Iona, off the west coast of Scotland. This became a center of missionary activities throughout Scotland and northern England.

Other Irish missionaries were active much farther afield. They were responsible for founding in different parts of western Europe nearly one hundred monasteries, many of which became important centers of learning as well as of the extreme asceticism that continued to characterize Irish Christianity. The greatest of the Irish itinerants was St. Columban, who left home with twelve companions at about the same time as Columba's move to Iona. Columban founded the monasteries of Luxeuil and Fontanes in France and Bobbio in the mountains of northern Italy. Despite the severity of his religious practices, he wrote Latin poems displaying a refreshing gaiety and sense of humor.

· · ·

Meanwhile, the Anglo-Saxon kingdoms were being added to the community of Western Christendom. Their conversion began with a mission dispatched by Pope Gregory the Great and headed by the Roman monk Augustine, which reached England in 597. As has already been remarked, it is illustrative of the technique of conversion adopted by the Roman Church that Augustine was instructed to reconsecrate pagan temples instead of destroying them and to adapt animal sacrifices and other pagan rituals to Christian purposes. It is also of interest, as an indication of the magical emphasis of much Dark Age Christianity, that the questions about which he subsequently wrote to Pope Gregory for advice were largely concerned not with the moral behavior of his converts but with ritualistic rules of sexual purity.[9] Augustine's mission was partially successful, but the full conversion of the Anglo-Saxon kingdoms was not completed for a century, and much of the work, especially in the north, was done by Irish missionaries from Iona and its daughter monasteries. There were some differences of practice between the Irish Church and Roman Church, but at the Synod of Whitby in 664 the Church in northern England agreed to conform to Roman usages. The Pope responded by sending a new mission, headed by a Greek and a North African (who was possibly a Negro), to organize all the English churches and promote education, for which purpose they were well supplied with books.

Thus another barbaric society never exposed to civilization had been brought in contact with Christian and Helleno-Roman culture. Like the Irish, the Anglo-Saxons were stimulated to a display of creative initiative not paralleled anywhere on the west European continent until a much later period. The main centers of cultural activity were in northern England, in areas where

---

[9] May a menstruating woman attend church? May a man who has had sexual relations attend church without first washing himself? May a priest celebrate mass after he has had a nocturnal emission? And so on, "of all the which the rude nation of the English hath need to be informed." See Bede: *Ecclesiastical History,* translated by J. E. King (London, 1944), I, 27.

there had been a strong Celtic influence and an invigorating conflict between Celtic and Roman traditions. It is indicative of superior vitality that Anglo-Saxon writers used the vernacular from the beginning instead of writing in Latin, like all the early writers of the continental kingdoms.

Anglo-Saxon poetry remained largely pagan in spirit despite some Christian coloration. The highest achievements were a few works, the longest being the famous *Beowulf,* that retained much of the epic flavor that must have characterized the compositions of the tribal bards during the migrations. Despite Christian editing, such poems still displayed the delight in the prowess by which men win immortal glory, combined with a gloomy recognition of the imminence of death and destruction, that is typical of all heroic ages. More specifically Christian was the growth of learning in the monasteries of northern England. The greatest of the Anglo-Saxon scholars was the Venerable Bede, who spent his life in the monastery of Jarrow, in the county of Durham, and died there in 735. Bede was the most learned man of the whole Dark Ages, and his voluminous writings covered the whole range of existing knowledge. But what most impresses the modern reader, especially in his most famous work, *The Ecclesiastical History of the English Nation,* is the refreshing common sense and sobriety of tone, which seems already to differentiate the English from the more fanciful and inventive Irish. Bede's *History* is primarily a record of God's dealings with the Anglo-Saxons, and there is no lack of miracles or of theological animus against Celtic deviations from the practices of the Roman Church; but it displays more respect for objective standards of verification than any other Dark Age chronicle, and the materials are organized with an admirable clarity and coherence.

The Anglo-Saxons seem to have been less prone to wanderlust than the Irish, but they were equally active in missionary enterprises and played a leading part in the conversion of their Germanic kinsmen. In this activity they were assisted by the Frankish kings, who had their own political motives for wanting these peoples to be Christianized and pacified. The greatest of the

Anglo-Saxon missionaries was Wynfrith, better known by his later name of Boniface, who led a party of monks to Germany in 716, did more than any other man to establish and organize Christianity among the pagan peoples living between the Rhine and the Elbe, retired in old age to a monastery at Fulda, and finally at the age of seventy-nine, having apparently become bored with inactivity, resumed his travels into northern Germany and was martyred by the heathen Frisians.

The most interesting aspects of these cultural beginnings, both Irish and Anglo-Saxon, are to be found in art. British Dark Age art clearly represents a fusion of barbaric and Helleno-Roman traditions, and can fairly be regarded as the first convincing indication that a new civilization, itself neither barbaric nor classical, was beginning to emerge. This art was both Celtic and Anglo-Saxon, and it seems to be impossible to make any sharp distinction between the contributions of the two ethnic groups. Its initial development seems to have taken place not in Ireland, as was formerly supposed, but in areas of northern England that had been converted mainly by Irish missionaries. The stimulus leading to artistic innovation was contact with Helleno-Roman representationalism through the medium of illustrated manuscripts of the gospels brought to England by Roman missionaries.

The most impressive of the early specimens of British Christian art seems to be the Lindisfarne gospel book, which dates from late in the seventh century. In addition to the text, this contains a number of pages of pure decoration and portraits of the four evangelists. The decorative pages, exquisitely colored, are covered with intricate spirals and interlacings in the Celtic manner, while occasional heads of birds and other animals suggest a Germanic influence. The portraits are copied from figures in books imported from Rome, but while adhering to the same forms and postures as the Mediterranean originals, this northern artist has deprived them of all spatiality and reduced them to linear calligrams. Here for the first time we find a use of the human figure which was to remain characteristic of Western art through the early Middle Ages and to become an appropriate

means of expressing the medieval sense of visual objects as symbolizing transcendental truths outside of space and time. The
tendency of such art, it has been said, is "to destroy the Mediterranean concept of the body existing in space and to substitute for
it the symbol lying on a surface. But this symbol is no longer the
pure calligram of the Celtic miniaturist; it is the skillful reduction
for medieval purposes of the humanist image invented in antiquity—man himself, with all his functions fully developed. The
humanism of antique art is taken over by the medieval artist for
its expressive value, not for its power of creating an illusion." [1]

Some other works of art of the same period show a more
sympathetic response to Mediterranean traditions. The great
stone crosses erected at Bewcastle, Ruthwell, and other places in
Scotland and northern England are decorated with reliefs of
Biblical figures which are three-dimensional and fully representational, and they have a strength and simplicity generally lacking
in the crowded and overemotional reliefs of the Helleno-Roman
decadence. These are the finest surviving works of sculpture
produced anywhere in western Euope during the Dark Ages. But
illuminated manuscripts remained the chief media of artistic
expression, and one can trace a continuing tendency for Mediterranean forms to become absorbed and assimilated into northern
abstractionism. The balance was best preserved in the figure
paintings of the English Winchester school of the tenth and
eleventh centuries. In Irish art, on the other hand, as exemplified
in the gospel books preserved in the monasteries of Kells and
Durrow and probably dating from the eighth century, the Celtic
ornamental tradition remained wholly dominant. These books
are extraordinary *tours de force* of decorative industry and dexterity, and the display of calligraphic skill seems almost to have
become an end in itself. The pages filled with multicolored rec-
tangles, circles, and interlacings, within which by careful observation one can identify numbers of human heads and shapes of

---

[1] Roger Hinks: *Carolingian Art,* p. 210.

small animals, have an almost inexhaustible complexity, though they have lost much of the intellectual and emotional meaning they probably held for the original craftsmen, who believed in the magical powers of books. It is not surprising that the Book of Kells should have been reputed in later generations to be the work of angels.[2]

For Dark Age Ireland, decorated manuscripts were, in fact, regarded quite explicitly as sources of magical power. To carry one of them three times around an army preparing for battle was a guarantee of victory. This was done at the battle of Culdremna, presumably with the approval of St. Columba, thus demonstrating that the conflict about ownership of the book had much deeper causes than a mere interest in enlarging a monastic library.[3] Fifteen of these Irish gospel books have survived, and until modern times magical powers continued to be attributed to them, though often in peculiar ways. In the seventeenth century, for example, the Book of Durrow was owned by an illiterate farmer who would dip it in water and give the water to ailing cattle in the belief that it had acquired curative powers.

These cultural developments in Ireland and northern England were abruptly cut short by the raids of the Vikings, beginning in 787 and continuing through most of the ninth century.

---

[2] A love of complexity seems to have become a permanent tendency of Irish culture. Anything said in praise or blame of the Book of Kells might be repeated, *mutatis mutandis,* for the later writings of James Joyce. Irish art was, however, not wholly abstract. According to Françoise Henry (*Irish Art in the Early Christian Period, to 800 A.D.,* p. 206), "Celtic art throughout its history is dominated by a constant desire to escape from two threatening dangers; it shrinks as violently from the exact and literal imitation of living shapes as from the complete assimilation of an ornament to the rigidity of an obvious geometric figure. Between these two pit-falls it proceeds in a sort of zigzag course, recoiling from one only to be frightened by the other. These perpetual oscillations are the essential cause of its fluidity and elusiveness."

[3] The actual psalter of St. Columba seems to have been in use for its magical powers in intertribal warfare as late as 1497. It remained in private hands for the next three and a half centuries, and finally reached the Royal Irish Academy, which still holds it. See Henry: op. cit., *passim.*

4 · Decline and Renewal in the West

For a long period Ireland was partially under Viking control, and Irish culture never fully recovered. England did not suffer so acutely, and during the reign of Alfred the Great (871–99) peace was restored and culture began to revive. It is interesting that Alfred followed earlier writers in promoting the use of the vernacular Anglo-Saxon, himself translating Boethius and other Latin works into Anglo-Saxon at a time when in all other parts of western Europe, Latin was still the only language regarded as respectable. But England was not strong enough to develop into a major cultural center, and in 1066, with the Norman Conquest, Anglo-Saxon was replaced by French as the language of all English literature, law, and learning. The vernacular did not regain any official status until the fourteenth century.

This whole British efflorescence was like a premature spring, producing blossoms that were too fragile and delicate to withstand new blasts from the barbarian north. Yet it was by no means wholly fruitless, since some of its creations had been transplanted into the Frankish mainland, where they made a direct contribution to the growth of the new civilization.

· · ·

By the end of the seventh century the Merovingian dynasty in France had ceased to produce vigorous leadership, and its kings, worn out by debauchery and mostly dying young, had faded into mere figureheads, the *rois fainéants* of the chroniclers. Later generations (according to Charlemagne's biographer, Einhard) remembered the occasional spectacle of some long-haired and effete descendant of Clovis, dressed almost like a peasant and being transported in an ox cart to give his sanction to decisions taken by the nobility he was supposed to govern. Effective political authority, so far as it existed at all and was not usurped by the landowning class, had been assumed in the different Frankish provinces by hereditary officials known as mayors of the palace. Meanwhile, Islamic imperialism, which invaded Spain in 712, would soon be threatening southern France; and partly because of economic decay and partly because of Arab control of the western Mediterranean, all regular trade and communication between the Western countries and the civilizations of the East had come to an end. This was the darkest period of the Dark Ages, dark both in the breakdown of order and authority and in the paucity of historical records.

Out of this darkness there emerged, in the eighth century, a new movement of order and cultural revival. It derived its strength from the union of German traditions and Christian beliefs, and it was given form and direction by a new dynasty, the Carolingian, which by a fortunate biological accident produced a sequence of three rulers of outstanding energy, ability, and statesmanship.

The Carolingians were originally mayors of the palace in Austrasia, which comprised northeastern France and the Rhineland. Its population was mostly Germanic rather than Gallo-Roman, but the Carolingians themselves were of mixed descent. Charles Martel, the first Carolingian to become ruler of the whole empire (in the year 714), enforced order, adopted a new system of requiring military service from landowners which proved to be an important step in the development of feudalism, defended France against the Mohammedans, and extended Frankish power and Christian beliefs among the barbarian peoples in Germany, not from any love of empire for its own sake but as a necessary safeguard against further raids and invasions. His son Pepin intervened in Italy to protect the papacy from the Lombards, thus continuing the traditional Frankish policy of alliance with the Pope, and with papal sanction ousted the last of the Merovingians and assumed the title of King. Pepin's son Charlemagne, in a long life of almost unbelievable activity, pursued the Mohammedans into Spain, conquered the Lombards and made himself king of northern Italy, subdued and Christianized the Saxons and other pagan tribes in a large part of Germany, fostered the arts and letters, and on Christmas Day, 800, was crowned emperor by the Pope in the basilica of St. Peter's in Rome. This union of all the Christian West except the British

Isles under a single ruler did not endure through the ninth century, but it had most important effects on the whole subsequent development of medieval civilization.

Charlemagne's immense and varied achievements quickly made him a legendary figure, but the historical records of his career and personality suggest that the man was even more remarkable than the myth. He was a warrior king, but the long series of wars that filled most of his life were plainly motivated not by a love of fighting for its own sake but by concern for the security and order of Western Christendom. Although he could be merciless when the situation seemed to require it—he was guilty of massacring thousands of rebellious Saxon tribesmen—his imperial glory never destroyed his capacity for friendship and generosity. In the writings of men who knew him he appears as a warmhearted and gregarious patriarch, devoted to his wives and children, willing to treat his counselors almost as equals, and living with a most refreshing simplicity and lack of ceremony. We see him, always in the company of his family and friends, riding out to hunt in the parklands around his palace at Aachen, disporting himself in swimming parties in the big palace pool, dealing out huge portions of meat to his guests at dinner,[4] and engaging eagerly with his high-pitched voice in philosophical and theological discussions. Nothing could be more different from the god-kings of the Mediterranean and Oriental empires.

Charles, in fact, remained a Germanic chieftain, although he displayed a quite unbarbarian devotion to order and culture. In accordance with tribal practice, all the leading men of the kingdom were summoned to council twice a year; and in spite of Charles's assumption of imperial dignity, it was still recognized that new laws could not be adopted without at least some kind of

---

[4] It seems most unlikely that Charlemagne himself should have carved the beef, but Bishop Theodilfus describes him as *"largas disponens epulas ordine pacifico."* Quoted in M. L. W. Laistner: *Thought and Letters in Western Europe, A.D. 500–900,* p. 340.

show of popular consent. That Charles esteemed the barbaric heritage is suggested by his interest in preserving the poems of the old tribal bards (these seem to have been destroyed by his more narrow-minded successors). He still belonged to the barbaric background in his easygoing sexual mores, which were by no means in conformity with the ethics of Christianity and which the ecclesiastical authorities apparently thought it politic to condone. Although he did not have more than one wife at a time, he married a total of four wives, in addition to keeping a series of five mistresses; and he permitted his daughters to have lovers, apparently because he wanted to keep them by him and regarded this as preferable to giving them away to husbands. Yet while Charles's methods of ruling and style of life were German, his ideals and beliefs were Christian and Roman. His favorite book was *The City of God,* which had a deep influence on his whole political program. In this combination of Germanic ways of behaving and Greco-Roman ways of thinking, Charles was representative of the whole early Middle Ages.

His coronation as emperor, which marked the beginning of the so-called Holy Roman Empire, was an event of the deepest psychological significance, although modern historians are by no means in agreement about the motivations either of Charles or of the Pope who crowned him. According to his friend and biographer Einhard, he was surprised and displeased by the Pope's action, but this was probably because he did not wish to seem to owe the crown to any power except God. There can be little doubt that he regarded himself with complete seriousness as the restorer of the Western Empire of Rome and the legitimate successor of Augustus and Constantine. This was a declaration of independence from Byzantium, which had been regarded since the fifth century as the repository of the whole traditional authority of imperial Rome. The Latin West now had its own emperor again, and this may fairly be taken as the beginning, at least in a symbolic sense, of the new Western civilization. Yet in the act of asserting its spiritual and political autonomy, the West reverted to the forms and institutions of the past. Christendom had to be united, and the maintenance of peace and order was identified with the continuance of the Roman Empire. This was the teaching of Christian theology, and no alternative political ideal was conceivable.

Charlemagne, moreover, like Constantine and like his Byzantine contemporaries, assumed clerical as well as secular powers. He was the vicar of Christ, endowed with authority from God to reform clerical practices and even to decide questions of doctrine. One of his functions was to defend and propagate Christian belief, if necessary by the use of force, as he had done among the pagan Saxons. Unlike the Merovingian dynasty, which had been considered as wholly secular, the Carolingians claimed that they owed their power to God, who entrusted them with religious responsibilities. The Pope expressed in his letters some resentment against these assumptions, but he could not successfully dispute them, the more so because he needed Charles's protection both against the Lombards and against opposing factions among the Roman aristocracy. (Shortly before the coronation he had been assaulted in the streets of Rome by rival ecclesiastics, who had apparently attempted to gouge out his eyes and tongue. His recovery of sight and speech was rumored to be miraculous.)

An analogous reverence for Greco-Roman models characterized Charles's cultural program, which was essentially a process of going to school with the classics. Its most important immediate sources were British. Charles's main educational advisor, Alcuin, was an Anglo-Saxon from northern England, and his chief director of art and architecture, Einhard, was an alumnus of Boniface's monastic foundation at Fulda. In promoting education and organizing such activities as the copying of manuscripts, Alcuin and his associates did work of inestimable value. Probably their most important single contribution was the adoption of a new script, the Carolingian minuscule, which did much to facilitate both copying and reading and which, after being abandoned temporarily during the Middle Ages, became standard for most of the Western world after the invention of printing in the fifteenth century. But the intellectual interests of the group around

Charlemagne, to judge from their writings, did not rise much above the study of grammar and the most elementary forms of logic, and nothing of real originality was produced. As with so many other aspects of Dark Age culture, what was borrowed from the classics consisted of forms and conventions which were not fully apprehended emotionally and hence could not stimulate new creation. A considerable quantity of Latin verse was written at the courts of Charlemagne and his immediate successors; for two or three generations, in fact, skill in verse composition seems to have been expected of educated ecclesiastics and public servants, and some of their products show real ability for natural and social description. But the standards were largely set by writers of the classical decadence, such as Prudentius and Venantius Fortunatus, all of whom were accepted as masters without any recognition of their inferiority to Virgil and Ovid. Even Einhard's biography of Charlemagne, the liveliest product of the Carolingian Renaissance, is partly a mosaic of phrases culled from Suetonius's *Lives of the Caesars*. The modern student would gladly exchange all these imitations of the classics for a little of the Germanic tribal epic poetry which Charlemagne's successors failed to preserve.

No vital literature could be produced because there was neither an established language nor an educated or recognized audience. The French vernacular had not yet acquired sufficient uniformity or standards of shape and form, and classical Latin, according to Erich Auerbach, was "simply incapable of expressing the life of the times." Auerbach refers to "the blurred lifeless quality of the figures we encounter in the Latin literature of the Carolingian and post-Carolingian periods" and points out that this was in no sense due to primitivism.[5] The Carolingian scholars would have done better if they had written in the vernacular and sought to refine and amplify it, as King Alfred was to do in

---

[5] Erich Auerbach: *The Literary Language and Its Public in Late Latin Antiquity and the Middle Ages,* p. 123.

England a century later. Their attempt to resuscitate the Latin of the classics led them down a blind alley, though it should be added that in subsequent generations medieval Latin acquired an unexpected vitality both for religious writing and for secular poetry. It took a second "Renaissance" of the classics—in Italy in the fifteenth century—to bring about the final death of the language in which they had been written.

In the visual arts, on the other hand, the Carolingian program produced more interesting results. Here also the intention was to imitate classical models; but, as previously in Britain, the northern craftsmen could not easily forget their own long-established aesthetic practices, and the result was a fusion of styles which largely set the standards for the early medieval period in western Europe.

Charlemagne's attitude to art was strictly utilitarian. Adopting a middle ground between the image-breakers then in power at Constantinople and the Roman image-worshippers, he affirmed that pictures in churches were useful as aids to religious knowledge but (to the distress of the Pope) that they were not to be regarded as, in themselves, sources of spiritual power. The "Libri Carolini," drawn up either by the emperor himself or by his advisors and stating his attitude toward religious images, quoted the dictum of Pope Gregory the Great: "Painting is admissible in churches, in order that those who are unlettered may, by gazing at the walls, read what they cannot read in books." [6] Art was therefore not considered as an independent expression of spiritual truth, and its proper function was to portray scenes from the Bible and figures of saints, adopting the Greco-Roman tradition of representationalist figure-painting. But as previously in Britain, Carolingian craftsmen adopted the outward forms of classical art without assimilating its underlying spirit, and the final result was that classical representationalism was gradually absorbed into the northern decorative tradition.

---

[6] Quoted in Hinks: op. cit., p. 97.

The wall paintings of the Carolingian period have not survived, but we have a considerable number of illustrated manuscripts from the ninth century, many of them displaying exquisite colors and designs. Scenes and figures seem to have been mostly copied from Byzantine or Roman originals, but, as in Britain, there was a constant tendency, which became stronger in the later ninth century, to deprive them of spatial solidity and reduce them to surface decoration. The practice of purely abstract design continued, moreover, especially in the elaborate treatment of initial letters, some of the earlier examples being clearly modeled after British originals; but craftsmen learned to pay their respects to their classical models by substituting vine and acanthus leaves for the spirals and interlacings of Celtic tradition.

The most interesting trend in Carolingian art is the incorporation into figure drawing of the dynamism that had characterized Celtic abstractionism. In this blend of Mediterranean and northern traditions, artists found it possible to convey the Christian Dark Age view of man as directed and inspired by a divine power outside of space and time. It is particularly exemplified in the line drawings of the Utrecht psalter. These portray multitudes of tiny figures, with craning necks, goggling eyes, and fluttering robes, who seem to one commentator to be dancing a perpetual tarantella.[7] More effectively expressive of spiritual forces are the vibrant and swirling draperies enveloping the four evangelists in the Gospel Book of Archbishop Ebo. "This painter," it has been remarked of the creator of the Ebo evangelists, "was seeking to convey not so much the outward aspect as the psychic essence of the persons he portrayed and in so doing he initiated a new mode of expression that was to prevail in all subsequent medieval art."[8]

The reign of Charlemagne marks the great divide in the early history of the West. The impetus he had given to education and

---

[7] Hinks: op. cit., p. 194.

[8] John Beckwith: *Early Medieval Art* (New York, 1964), p. 144.

94

cultural activity did not lost its momentum in spite of another breakdown of law and order. The intellectual scene was never again so black as in the seventh and eighth centuries. Thinking and the arts, moreover, now began to assume new forms expressive of the gradual emergence of a new sensibility. Before Charlemagne we are still in the final stages of the Greco-Roman decadence, and outside the British Isles it is difficult to find anything that points clearly to the future. After Charlemagne the Western mind is recognizably medieval.

Charles's political achievement proved, however, to be ephemeral, except insofar as the idea of restoring the Roman Empire continued to be taken seriously until the later Middle Ages. After four centuries of administrative and economic disintegration, the unification of so large an area under one government was, of course, an unrealistic objective, and Charles's successors were unable to hold his vast dominion together. The disintegration of the empire was initially the work of the Carolingians themselves. Charlemagne's son, Louis the Pious, governed the empire as a single unit, though with much less vigor and effectiveness, but in the year 843, by the Treaty of Verdun, Charlemagne's three grandsons divided it into three kingdoms, and further subdivisions were made in later generations.

Before the end of the ninth century the kingdoms of the West and East Franks, later to be known as France and Germany, were emerging as separate units, distinguished, in part, by linguistic differences. Italy and the area of southwestern France then known as Burgundy also had governments of their own, though these did not prove to be viable. The conflict between France and Germany for control of the Rhineland borderlands lying between them, which began with the division of Charlemagne's empire, remained one of the central factors in European political history for more than a thousand years. All these kingdoms were originally governed by descendants of Charlemagne, but during the tenth century the family became extinct and new dynasties were then elected to succeed them. In 919 the German nobility gave their kingship to the Duke of Saxony, and in 987

Hugh Capet, Count of Paris, the ancestor of all later French kings, became titular King of France.

The disorders of the ninth and tenth centuries were due mainly to new waves of barbarian invaders, which the later Carolingians were wholly unable to repel. This danger had been the main reason for Charlemagne's military and missionary activities in Germany; but while he had subdued the Saxons, he had failed to extend his empire northward into Denmark and Scandinavia. These countries had little effective central government and were inhabited by peoples accustomed to warfare and impelled by economic need to plundering and expansion overseas. In 814, the year of Charlemagne's death, Viking raiders from Denmark, who had already begun to attack England, burned a monastery at the mouth of the Loire. This marked the start of a hundred years of almost incessant plundering and destruction. Initially the Vikings arrived every spring and returned home for the winters, but after the middle of the century they began to establish permanent bases with a view to conquest as well as plunder.

During the same period, western Europe was suffering also from raids by the heathen Magyars, who had left their Asiatic home and settled in the plains of the Danube in what is now Hungary; and there was almost incessant border warfare between Christians and Mohammedans in Spain and southern France. For the French people, especially those who lived on navigable rivers or close to the seas, this was unquestionably the most frightful period in their entire history, filled with horrors far surpassing those of the fifth century. All over the north and west the rich cornfields and vineyards were laid waste, vast regions were depopulated, trade and industry ceased, and the survivors fled for refuge to the mountains or the forests. Virtually every town in France was destroyed. Thus society was reduced to its barest and most elemental components, and the whole process of establishing economic and political foundations for the building of civilization had to be undertaken all over again.

5

The Eastern Civilizations

W hile civilization in the Western countries was dying and being reborn, the other two segments into which the Mediterranean world had been divided—the Byzantine Empire and the Arab Caliphate—were preserving, and even enriching, the ancient heritage. The term "Dark Ages" belongs only to the West, and its indiscriminate use by historians, to mark a period in the history of Europe as a whole, betrays the provinciality of the Western mind. The Byzantine Empire and the Arab Caliphate were not a part of Western history, and it is unnecessary in this volume to describe them in detail. But the West owed them an immense debt for knowledge and cultural stimulation, so they cannot be ignored.

Early Western civilization borrowed from them extensively in philosophy, science, and the arts. It was especially indebted to them for serving as intermediaries in re-establishing contacts with the classical Greek heritage of science and philosophy, to which the Arabs also added significant contributions of their own. Possibly even more important was that the West was stimulated to self-consciousness and self-awareness as a result of contacts with the East. The contrasts in attitudes and institutions made Westerners more sharply aware of their own character and cultural unity. The West acquired a vast mass of theory and information from the Eastern civilizations; but in developing its own views of life and forms of expression it reacted against them rather than incorporating them. Contact with an alien culture is often an important factor in arousing a people to creative activities of their own. It was no accident that the French cultural efflorescence of the early twelfth century coincided in time with the beginnings of the Crusades.

In theory the Byzantines and the Westerners upheld the same Christian values and standards against their common opponents, the Mohammedans. But in actuality the two Near Eastern civilizations had more in common with each other than either had with the West. Despite the religious antagonisms between the empire and the caliphate, and the centuries of almost incessant warfare between them, their institutions and beliefs in many ways paralleled each other. They resembled each other closely enough for mutual stimulation, and their peak periods coincided, both of them achieving their greatest prosperity and cultural productivity in the tenth and eleventh centuries. But because both of them (despite the new energy temporarily imparted by the Arabs) were essentially continuations of long-established and largely decadent cultures rather than new beginnings, they had only a limited capacity for growth and creative innovation. The Western kingdoms remained technologically, intellectually, and morally inferior until the later Middle Ages, but they had a primitive flexibility and capacity for growth.

The scene of conflict between rival imperialisms for thousands of years, the whole eastern Mediterranean region was strewn with the wreckage of ancient civilizations and tribal groups, the living representatives of which maintained divers cultural traditions and memories of departed glories. Both the empire and the caliphate attempted to legitimize order by means of a religious universalism, affirming the brotherhood of all believers. Both of them included many different ethnic groups and made little or no discrimination between them; religion rather than race was the main bond of unity. And in both of them the ruler was supposedly chosen by God, who expressed his will through some process of election by the community, though once the ruler had been appointed only God could call him to account.

5 · The Eastern Civilizations

The ruler had religious as well as secular functions, and the caliphate was actually the supreme religious authority; no distinction was made between church and state. In the empire the ruler was, in practice if not wholly in theory, superior to the Patriarch, who supposedly headed the Church.

Thus both the caliph and the emperor resembled, in theory at least, the divinely appointed autocrats of the ancient theocracies. Belief in the divine origin of political power, which had originated in the Near East several thousand years earlier, had never disappeared among the mass of the population and had been revived by the later Roman emperors. But neither the religious universalism of the Greek Church nor that of Islam was fully effective in promoting a sense of political order and inculcating loyalty. In practice, autocracy in both the empire and the caliphate was tempered by frequent rebellions and coups d'état, and adventurers from any social background could sometimes rise to supreme power. The sense of society as an organic whole to which individuals owed loyal service had long since disappeared in this part of the world and could not be recaptured. In consequence, the most important element in the Greco-Roman-Christian tradition as it was handed down to the Western peoples —the belief in standards of justice by which order could be reconciled with freedom in earthly society—was never an effective reality in either Byzantine or Mohammedan society.

In theory, life in this world was supposed to be directed by religiously sanctioned ethical standards, as affirmed in the Bible and the Koran. But in both societies the most vital form of religious belief was a transcendental mysticism, derived partly from the Neo-Platonism of Plotinus and partly from earlier Near Eastern cults, which looked for consummation not in an ideal order in this world but in union with God in the next life. The Near Eastern peoples had a strong sense of divine transcendence, God being regarded as wholly above the world he had made, and hence as incapable of being represented in any material form. This religious attitude was expressed fully and uncompromisingly both in the Old Testament of the Bible and in the Koran. According to Christian doctrine, God was immanent as well as transcendent, and had actually been united with man in the person of Jesus. But this conception was rejected by a number of heretical groups in the Near East, such as the Monophysites and Monothelites, who mostly preferred the rule of Mohammedanism to that of orthodox Christianity. And even in the Byzantine Church there were strong tendencies toward the emphasis on divine transcendence rather than on divine immanence. Early in the eighth century the iconoclastic movement for the destruction of all religious images was introduced by a new dynasty of Asiatic origin, and this was accompanied by a sharp devaluation of the whole Hellenic heritage. Only after more than a century of bitter conflict was the use of pictures and images representing God, Jesus, and the Virgin once again introduced into religious worship. Byzantine religion always tended to be mystical rather than practical, showing little concern for the regeneration of earthly society.

. . .

After losing Syria and Egypt to the Arabs in the seventh century, the Byzantine Empire regained much of its strength in the eighth. It survived partly through its control of Asia Minor, whose land-owning and peasant families supplied its ablest generals and most reliable soldiers, and partly through the military strength of Constantinople. Built on a line of hills in the triangle formed by the Sea of Marmora and the Golden Horn and shielded from land assault by its massive five-mile line of ramparts, guarded (as its inhabitants proudly affirmed) by divine providence and by its special patroness, the Virgin Mary, the city seemed for many centuries to be inviolable. On the landward side, a long series of Slavic and Finno-Ugrian invaders from eastern Europe overran the Balkans but failed to penetrate the walls of the city; from the south and east, Moslem armies and navies several times assaulted the city by water. But until the loss of most of Asia Minor to the Turks in the late eleventh century, each period of crisis was successfully surmounted. Constantinople itself remained impregnable until it was seized by Westerners in the so-called Fourth Crusade of 1204, and it did not permanently come under alien rule until the Turkish conquest of 1453.

This vast city was a storehouse of the Greco-Roman heritage. Its libraries preserved the corpus of Greek literature, and its streets were adorned with masterpieces of the great age, many of them removed from pagan temples by the early Christian emperors. Even its amusements retained a classical quality; the Hippodrome was always the chief center of popular entertainment, though by the ninth century races by professional charioteers seem to have given place to equestrian competitions by amateurs. With the architectural splendor of its churches, monasteries, and imperial palaces, with the immense wealth it derived from trade with the Orient and from its own metallurgical, textile, and silk industries, with its traditions of learning, art, and fine craftsmanship, and with the sophisticated and disillusioned attitudes of its upper-class inhabitants, Constantinople was always an overpowering experience to barbarian visitors from the Germanic kingdoms. Legends of the great magical city became a part of Western fairy tales and folklore.

In theory, the political institutions of the empire were both Roman and Asiatic. Sovereignty belonged to the people and was, according to a doctrine inherited from Roman sources, merely delegated to the emperor by the affirmation of the senate, the army, or the citizens of Constantinople, though the grant of power could be ended only by violent revolution. Although strong emperors were usually succeeded by their sons, the succession never became officially hereditary. This lack of system justified itself by generally providing competent rulers; the Byzantine emperors included more men of high ability than have ever been produced by any strictly hereditary line of succession or, indeed, by most systems of popular election. But in spite of the republican origins of the imperial authority, that authority itself was—in theory—absolute and all-embracing, as in ancient Asiatic kingdoms. The emperor was God's lieutenant and was officially described as the equal of the apostles. A heretical or erring ruler sometimes evoked clerical opposition, but as long as the emperor remained orthodox he was supreme over both state and church. With the aid of a large and remarkably efficient bureaucracy, he also exercised most extensive powers over economic life; Byzantium, like ancient Egypt, was a semisocialist state, and commerce and industry were elaborately regulated and partially owned by the government in order to maintain full employment, limit private profits, and fill the imperial treasury. In his powers and position the emperor, in fact, was more obviously the successor of the pharaohs than of the republican magistrates of Greece and Rome. As in ancient Egypt, the daily life of the ruler was conducted with the utmost splendor, and every detail was elaborately ritualized in order to evoke reverence for his semidivine powers. On important occasions, especially when it was necessary to impress a foreign ambassador, he was made to appear almost supernatural by means of mechanical devices. When the visitor was conducted into the great hall of the palace, gilded birds would sing and gilded lions would roar; and while he was bowing before the throne, it would suddenly be elevated almost to the ceiling; and by a sudden change of robes, the emperor would appear even more dazzling and resplendent than before.

Yet neither religion nor play-acting could make the imperial authority genuinely legitimate. In the last resort power depended on force and skill, not on any spontaneous sense of loyalty. Out of a total of 107 emperors, no less than 65 were either compelled to abdicate or removed by poison, stabbing, strangulation, or some other violent means. Some lost their lives in popular uprisings of the utmost ferocity. In 1185, for example, the Emperor Andronicus was seized by a mob who showered him with excrement, tore out his beard, broke his teeth, cut away an eye and a hand, and finally hacked him to pieces in the Hippodrome. Such outbreaks against the lieutenant of God and the equal of the apostles suggested that the turbulent republicanism of the ancient city-states was not yet dead. They showed also that Byzantine institutions had failed to create an organic sense of order and voluntary obedience to authority.

Byzantine religion was a similar mixture of Greek and Asiatic attitudes. Greek Christianity had always differed from that of the Latin West, though the definitive break between the two churches did not come until the eleventh century. Latin Christianity retained a Roman emphasis on ethical and practical values and a Roman sense of history as a dynamic and meaningful expression of the divine will. The religion of Byzantium was Greek in its metaphysical preoccupations and its more static conception of reality, and Asiatic in its tendency to consider God as a transcendent being rather than a power whose will was immanent in material processes. It tended to regard salvation as a mystical *gnosis,* dependent on the knowledge of theological truths and resulting in a mystical submersion of the individual soul in the divine essence. For four and a half centuries, beginning with the First Ecumenical Council, held at Nicaea in 325, and ending with the Seventh Council, also held at Nicaea, in 787, Greek-speaking theologians were largely concerned with defining the nature of Christ and the interrelationships of the Holy Trinity, displaying a logical subtlety and virtuosity and an argumentative exuberance that were characteristic of the Greek mind. The formulas worked out by this series of councils affirmed the unity of God and man in the person of Jesus, and hence preserved the essential Christian belief in the potential regeneration of every part of human nature. But the practical implications of this Christology were always somewhat alien to the spirit of the Greek Church. As the tempestuous and often sordid political history of the Byzantine Empire bears witness, it did relatively little to maintain high ethical standards or promote social reform, though it never forgot the duty of charity to the poor. Its characteristic institution was always monasticism; and whereas the monks of the West often displayed a practical bent, those of the East were almost exclusively devoted to the pursuit of mystical communion with the divine. The Byzantine monastery with its surrounding gardens and orchards, whether located within the city of Constantinople or removed to the almost inaccessible promontories of Mount Athos or the mountaintops of the Meteora, gave its inmates a life of peaceful contemplation while they waited for the death that would unite them finally with God. But by immobilizing much of the manpower and wealth of the empire, it contributed to the final decline of its power.

Meanwhile the fetishism of relics was as deeply entrenched in the civilized East as in the barbarian West. Constantinople became an unrivaled storehouse not only of classical literature and the arts but also of numinous bones and other magical objects. Helena, the mother of Constantine, had visited Jerusalem and, under a divine guidance not customarily given to archaeologists, had unearthed the true cross, the crown of thorns, and other relics of the crucifixion. This precious collection was removed to Constantinople to protect it from the invading Persians early in the seventh century. The city also acquired a long series of saintly corpses, including those of well-known New Testament characters like Lazarus, Mary Magdalene, Andrew the apostle, and Luke the evangelist. To these were added the mantle of Elijah, the sandles of Jesus, and a variety of articles associated with the Virgin Mary, including a phial of the milk with which the infant Jesus had been suckled. This primeval fetishism was combined with a trust in the powers of individual saints that was directly derived from the worship of the pagan gods. Shrines of the Archangel Michael and of Sts. Damian and Cosmas had medicinal properties resembling those formerly attributed to the temples of Asclepius. Some saints were especially gifted for the curing of specific diseases; men and women with sexual problems, for example, could seek aid from Sts. Artemius and Febonia. To others was delegated the patronage of particular cities. Salonika, the second largest city of the empire, was guarded by St. Demetrius, who on two occasions appeared in person to aid its inhabitants in repelling foreign invaders.

Relatively uncreative in literature and philosophy, the spirit of Byzantine civilization found expression in the visual arts. Greek art had always represented natural forms, though during its great period it had been concerned with the expression in human figures of an ideal and divine reality, not with realistic portraiture. Much of the art of the Near East, on the other hand, sought to convey a belief in divine powers that transcended nature. In some areas, notably in Syria, this led to the portrayal of figures conveying intense religious emotion, in sharp contrast with the idealizing tendencies of Hellenism. More often the Near Eastern religious sense was expressed in two-dimensional, static and frontal renderings of human beings or in abstract decorative patterns. The union of these diverse artistic traditions began in the later Roman Empire and had produced a distinctive style by the sixth century, as exemplified in the churches at Ravenna.

The greatest period of Byzantine religious art came in the tenth and eleventh centuries, after the image-breaking movement of the eighth and ninth centuries had been ended. Presumably the secular arts also flourished, but few examples have survived. The extant art consists mainly of mosaics and frescoes decorating churches, and generally it conforms to a prescribed pattern, Christ in the role of ruler of the universe (the "Pantocrator") being portrayed on the inside of the dome, the Virgin Mary in blue robes behind the altar, and scenes from the gospels around the walls. Art remained faithful to the Hellenic tradition in concentrating on the human figure, and there was, in fact, more of the Hellenic sense of movement in three-dimensional space in the art of the tenth century than in that of the sixth. A second major efflorescence in the fourteenth and fifteenth centuries displayed Hellenic tendencies even more strongly, although this may have been partially an influence of the Italian Renaissance. But the primary purpose of Byzantine art was always to convey a sense of divine majesty and omnipotence very different from the graceful and smiling humanism of classical Greece. In spirit it was more Middle Eastern than Greek. Yet despite its mixed heritage it conveyed no feeling of disharmony. In the broad expanses of its blue and gold backgrounds, in its brilliantly garbed emperors and empresses portrayed in attitudes of obeisance to God, and above all in the somber and brooding intensity of its blue-robed Virgins and great bearded Pantocrators, Byzantine mosaic affirmed the reality of transcendental divine powers more convincingly than any other art in human history.

It was especially through its art that Byzantium contributed to the civilization of the West. From the Dark Ages onward, the emergent artistic tradition of the West was almost continuously indebted to Byzantine models, transmitted partly through illuminated manuscripts and partly through the emigration of Greek craftsmen. Much of the history of medieval art, especially in Italy, consisted of the interplay between Byzantine styles and techniques and the growth of a new humanistic sensibility requiring new models of expression. The West developed its own view of life and forms of expression by reacting against the Byzantine models rather than by incorporating them.

Although Byzantine and Latin Christians professed to worship the same God and to believe the same theological and ethical doctrines, they were utterly different from each other in spirit and sensibility, as they discovered whenever they tried to cooperate against their common Moslem opponents. Byzantine civilization was old and disillusioned, concentrating its energies on the preservation of its glorious heritage rather than on the creation of anything new. Its rulers, inheriting age-old techniques and lessons of statesmanship, sought primarily to conserve the resources of the empire, preferring diplomacy to force and the expenditure of money rather than of manpower, and knowing by long experience how to manipulate barbarian peoples by bribery and intrigue and by dazzling them with the riches of the empire. To the Westerners, with their simple-minded belief that divine providence would always give them victory, they seemed subtle, crafty, treacherous, and insincere. Liudprand of Cremona, visiting Constantinople on a diplomatic mission in the tenth century, described its inhabitants as liars and eunuchs devoid of the heroism that could be expected of Western warriors; the twelfth-century historian of the Crusades William of Tyre declared that the Byzantines lacked "sincerity and good faith" and were guilty of trickery and treachery, in contrast to the "single-hearted confidence and trust" displayed by the crusaders from the West.[1]

But the Byzantines did not count on any easy victory against the infidels, and they saw no value in heroism for its own sake. The mere survival of the empire was itself a miracle of divine providence, and this miracle would not be indefinitely repeated. Of the many legends and prophecies associated with the early history of Constantinople, the best remembered were those that fixed the day of its final downfall. Its citizens were willing to enjoy wealth and splendor while they lasted; but their ultimate hopes were attached to the life of eternity under the rule of the Pantocrator, not to the processes of time.[2]

. . .

Emerging from the deserts of Arabia early in the seventh century, Islam was carried by force of arms through the whole of the Near East as far as the borders of India, absorbing the Sassanid kingdom of the Persians and the Byzantine provinces of Syria and Egypt. Westward it spread across northern Africa as far as the Atlantic and into Spain. The period of expansion ended halfway through the eighth century, and the Arab empire quickly began to split into different provinces governed by local chieftains. This was followed by a cultural efflorescence, which for several centuries made the Arab dominions the most highly civilized parts of the Western world. Yet in the long run Islam was lacking in the cultural and humanitarian potentialities of Christianity. Its main strength lay in its unrivaled capacity to maintain a sense of unity

---

[1] R. W. Southern: *The Making of the Middle Ages,* p. 33; William of Tyre: *A History of Deeds Done Beyond the Sea* (New York, 1933), II, 12, 19, 20.

[2] The citizens of a complex and long-established society always seem to less sophisticated visitors to be corrupt and insincere. The complaints of the Crusaders against their Byzantine hosts strongly resemble those of the more simple-minded American tourists against Europeans. Sincerity is the favorite American virtue, and Americans are inclined to forget that all societies, their own included, need forms and rules of politeness of some kind.

among diverse peoples over a wide area, thereby making possible a remarkable cross-fertilization of cultural traditions already in existence; but unlike Christianity it propounded no new principles capable of stimulating new forms of political and intellectual creativity. Its main intellectual function was conservation rather than creation.

The least complex of all the world's major religions both in doctrine and in quality of emotional experience, Islam began as a reassertion of the Semitic sense of divine transcendence and human abasement. Its God was an omnipotent and inscrutable will, beyond all question and understanding, and man, by contrast, was nothing. Mankind was offered, however, a simple and easy way of salvation, free from the doctrinal subtleties and pessimistic soul-searching of Christianity. Submission to the divine will, acceptance of Mohammed as God's prophet, performance of the requisite prayers, fasts, and pilgrimages, obedience to a virile moral code, charity to the poor, and recognition of the brotherhood of all true believers: these would ensure divine protection in this life and eternal happiness in the hereafter after the day of judgment. Since Mohammed was regarded as wholly human, his religion led to nothing comparable to the Christological controversies that plagued Christianity, while a salvation dependent on obedience to the rules prescribed in the Koran rather than on any complex process of emotional transformation promoted a sense of inner security. Mohammedanism, moreover, was more tolerant toward nonbelievers than the Christianity of the Greek and Latin churches, and was refreshingly free from the grosser superstitions that had been incorporated into Christian theology. Mohammed was not a miracle-worker—he declared that the composition of the Koran was the only miracle necessary to validate his mission—and his followers did not attribute magical powers to the bones of saints.

But while the new religion had a simplicity that promoted rapid expansion, it was also inflexible, with little capacity for development, and always preserved much of the quality of the primitive Arab tribalism in which it had originated. The Koran was an encumbrance from which Islam could never free itself. This repetitious, arid, and forbidding book consists largely of reminiscences of the Bible and of Jewish legend, mingled with monotonous assertions of God's mercy toward the righteous and his coming punishment of nonbelievers, moral injunctions applicable only to the simple patriarchal society of the Arab tribesmen, veiled allusions to crises in Mohammed's personal life, and special injunctions designed to end quarrels among his various wives and buttress his domestic authority. Yet every word of the Koran was supposed to have been revealed to Mohammed by God, and his followers, unlike Christians, could not dispose of the more embarrassing sections of their sacred book by interpreting them allegorically. There can be no doubt that Mohammed felt an overpowering conviction of the reality of God, of the nothingness of man, and of his own divine mission; like Moses and the Jewish prophets, he proclaimed moral imperatives which seemed to him to be dictated by an external spiritual power. By the standards of Arab tribalism his teachings were relatively enlightened, especially in their emphasis on charity to the poor and on respect for women, although they appeared barbaric when contrasted with the practices of a civilized society. But the Koran was far inferior to most parts of the Bible in both spiritual insight and aesthetic quality, having none of the vivid concrete imagery with which the Jewish prophets could communicate their apprehensions of the moral law. Vague adjectival epithets, endlessly repeated, were applied to God; with equal monotony true believers were promised the lasting enjoyment of "gardens beneath which rivers flow"—a description of paradise with an obvious appeal to natives of the desert—and the wicked were threatened with eternal fire.

Islam began as a union of Arab tribesmen who retained the sense of brotherhood, the simple patriarchal institutions, and the feeling of intimate relationship with their God and dependence on his guidance that had always characterized the seminomadic pastoral society of the desert. Similar attitudes had been attributed in the Book of Genesis to the legendary ancestors of the

Israelites. The chief change brought about by Mohammed, apart from the preaching of monotheistic beliefs and of a more humane morality, was to unify the Arab peoples by making religion instead of blood relationship the source of social cohesion and thereby to launch them on a career of imperialist expansion. It was recognized that men needed a leader, an Imam, but in accordance with Arab tradition his powers were limited and were derived from the people, though obedience to a legitimate leader was regarded as a divine command. The caliphs who exercised leadership after the death of the prophet owed their position to informal election by the chief men of the community. Since everything requisite for worldly prosperity and eternal salvation had already been revealed in the Koran, no new laws were needed, and the caliph was limited to the simple functions of enforcing the divine will and spreading the knowledge and practice of the true religion. The Christians, Jews, and Zoroastrians of the conquered provinces were not forcibly converted but were compelled to pay tribute for the support of their Moslem masters. Thus the empire in its early period remained a conglomeration of diverse ethnic and religious groups dominated by a master race of primitive Arab warriors.

The conquered peoples, however, quickly began to adopt the new religion. They were attracted by its simplicity and its efficacy in bringing victory, while a more potent cause was financial pressure, since conversion meant exemption from taxes. The ironic result of the expansion of their religion was that the Arabs ceased to be a privileged ruling race and a great variety of non-Arab peoples were admitted to the brotherhood of the faith. But the simple institutions of Arab tribalism could not be adapted to these new conditions, nor were Arab warriors qualified for the complex tasks of imperial administration. The Koran set forth no principles of political order applicable to a world empire. In consequence, the Mohammedan world failed to develop institutions by which authority could be legitimized and the practice of election by the community effectively maintained. The later caliphs continued to claim that they were appointed by

God, but in actuality their rule was based on force, not on popular choice.

Only the first four caliphs could truly be regarded as legitimate successors of Mohammed. The last of them, Mohammed's cousin and son-in-law Ali, was murdered in 661, and the caliphate was then seized by the Omayyad family, who established their capital at Damascus and, despite their own Arab origin, relied largely on Syrians and Greeks for administrative services. In 750 the Omayyads were overthrown by the Abbasids, who moved the capital to Baghdad. Persian influences now became predominant, to such an extent that the Abbasid caliphate can almost be regarded as a continuation of the Sassanid kingdom. The next three hundred years were the greatest period of Islamic culture, and similar intellectual and aesthetic activities were pursued through the whole vast area from Bokhara and Samarkand in central Asia to Cordova in Spain. But political conditions became increasingly chaotic. The empire gradually split up into a number of different political units with shifting boundaries, and adventurers from any ethnic and social origin could sometimes carve out new kingdoms for themselves and found new dynasties, which usually became effete and disappeared within three or four generations. Finally, in the eleventh century, Turkish warriors from central Asia took control of Mesopotamia, and the Abbasids ceased to be even the nominal rulers of the empire. Much of the Mohammedan world remained thereafter in a state of incessant flux, with a consequent decline in its cultural levels. Lacking the sense of law and order as immanent in social processes, it failed to develop the organic political life which led in western Europe to the growth of enduring national states with governments representing the popular will. Like the Byzantine Empire, the caliphate was, in theory, theocratic, and in actuality close to a condition of anomia.

Mohammedan thinkers could offer no solution to the problems of political order, and could merely advise obedience to anybody strong enough to enforce it. The ruler capable of holding power was the instrument of God, until he was overthrown by some rival adventurer even better qualified to hold power. It was a Moslem principle that "whoever rebels against the Imam rebels against God." The dilemma was stated frankly in the eleventh century by the greatest of Mohammedan theologians, the Persian Ghazali. "The concessions made by us are not spontaneous," he declared, "but necessity makes lawful what is forbidden. We know it is not allowed to feed on a dead animal: still, it would be worse to die of hunger. Of those that contend that the caliphate is dead for ever and irreplaceable, we should like to ask: which is to be preferred, anarchy and the stoppage of social life for lack of a properly constituted authority, or acknowledgement of the existing power, whatever it be? Of these two alternatives, the jurist cannot but choose the latter." Two hundred years later the Qadi Ibn Jama'ah of Damascus spoke even more plainly: "The sovereign has a right to govern until another and stronger one shall oust him from power and rule in his state. The latter will rule by the same title and will have to be acknowledged on the same grounds; for any government, however objectionable, is better than none at all; and between two evils we must choose the lesser." [3]

The doctrine of submission to a transcendental and inscrutable deity led easily to attitudes of fatalistic passivity, and obedience to any authority, however arbitrary, continued to be upheld by orthodox "Sunni" Moslems. Not all Mohammedans were willing to accept this legitimation of naked power, but revolutionary sentiment could find expression only in mystical and irrational forms. The chief disturbing element in the Islamic world was the Shiite movement, which denied the legitimacy of the Omayyad and Abbasid caliphates and declared that leadership was hereditary in the family of Ali. Ali's claims had been transmitted to his son Hosayn, who was killed in 680, and to a line of descendants which seems to have become extinct in the ninth century. But

---

[3] Sir Thomas Walker Arnold and Alfred Guillaum, eds.: *Legacy of Islam* (Oxford, 1931), pp. 300, 302.

according to the Shiites the true Imamate would never be allowed by God to die out; the heirs of Ali remained the secret lords of the world, and one of them would eventually manifest his presence and establish the millennium. This was a complex and many-sided movement which incorporated elements from many of the ancient religious traditions of the Near East. Primarily, it was a revival of the mystical salvation cults that had been widespread in Syria and Egypt for thousands of years. Its emphasis on the principle of sacred hereditary leadership, in opposition to the Arab belief that the caliph should be chosen by the community, recalled the theocratic monarchy of early Egypt, while the mourning for the death of Hosayn, which became the chief annual ritual of the Shiites, resembled both the Christian mourning for the crucifixion and the mourning for the death of Tammuz among the peasants of early Mesopotamia.

Shiism was always a minority movement, but in spite of its lack of all rational content it won some political successes and did not disintegrate when its millennial fantasies were thereby proved to have no realistic basis. The strongest branch of the movement professed a special reverence for Ismael, an Alid who had died in 762. In 968 the Ismaeli organization won control of Egypt and set up the Fatimid caliphate, which lasted for two hundred years and made Egypt into the most brilliant center of Moslem culture and prosperity. According to William of Tyre, the Egyptians were accustomed to "cherish and revere as a supreme divinity" [4] the reigning caliph of the Fatimid family: an attitude obviously transmitted from the time of the early pharaohs and illustrative of the extraordinary persistence of religious traditions among Near Eastern peoples. Another branch of the Ismaeli, the so-called Assassins, set up a secret society with headquarters on a mountain in Persia, which carried on the systematic murdering of opponents of the Shiite cause. Some branches of the Shiite movement have lasted down to the present day, the most

---

[4] William of Tyre: op. cit., XVIII, 9.

important being the group whose hereditary leader is the Aga Khan.

The chief gift of Islam to its adherents was the sense of inner peace that came from total resignation to divine providence. In its original form it gave no encouragement to scientific investigation or philosophical thought. According to the Koran, the universe is governed not by laws of nature and reason which man can hope to decipher but by an inscrutable divine power, and it is therefore, by human standards, basically irrational and incomprehensible. The renaissance that occurred under the Abbasid caliphate resulted from the establishment of peace, unity, and a common language throughout the whole Near Eastern area, which had been the scene of conflicts between rival civilizations for several thousand years, and to the consequent renewal and integration of earlier traditions of culture and learning; it owed little to the Mohammedan religion itself. And since the mind of the Islamic world was not animated by any new principle capable of leading to new views of life and new hypotheses and discoveries, it did not make any significant advance beyond the achievement of earlier societies. Its essential function may be summarized as conservation rather than innovation. Along with the Byzantine Empire, it served as a medium for transmitting Hellenic and Near Eastern science and philosophy to the new Western civilization, but it made no major contributions of its own.

During the resurgence of Oriental cultures that had occurred under the late Roman and early Byzantine empires, Greek scientific and philosophical works had been translated into Aramaic, the language of Syria, chiefly by clergy belonging to the unorthodox Near Eastern Christian sects. Under the Abbasids some of these works, especially those of Aristotle, were retranslated into Arabic. Mohammedan science was based mainly on these Greek sources, with some contributions from areas farther east. Original work was done in some fields, such as optics and some forms of mathematics, and in almost all branches of science many new observations were added to the corpus of knowledge. But significant scientific progress depends on the capacity to make fruitful new generalizations and hypotheses, and this capacity was largely lacking. Perhaps the most useful single contribution of the Mohammedans was the adoption of the Indian system of numerals and its introduction to the Western world, where it superseded the clumsy Greek and Roman alphabetical systems, with which rapid calculation had been impossible.

Mohammedan philosophy, which flourished especially at the two extremities of the Arab-speaking world, in Persia and in Spain, was similarly derived from Greek influences. Thinkers generally regarded Aristotle as infallible and devoted themselves primarily to commenting on his doctrines and trying to reconcile them with the dogmas of their religion. But they interpreted him largely in Neo-Platonic terms and were more concerned with his views of God and the human soul than with the empirical aspects of his thinking. Probably the most influential of the works attributed to Aristotle was a Neo-Platonic treatise, the *Theology,* which had actually been written in the fourth century of our era by Porphyry of Tyre. Neo-Platonism, in fact, with its belief in the mystical unity of God and the soul of man and in the emanation of the world from God, pervaded the thinking of Islam no less than that of Byzantium. This philosophy of the Helleno-Roman decadence remained the main intellectual influence throughout the whole eastern Mediterranean world, becoming fused with Near Eastern traditions of religious ecstasy that had been handed down from primitive times. There was a fundamental contradiction between the Neo-Platonic sense of cosmic oneness and the concepts of human freedom and individuality that were taught by Christianity as well as by Mohammedanism, and this set the main problems of philosophical speculation. Mohammedan thinkers, especially Avicenna and Averroës, analyzed these problems with a logical subtlety which had a vast influence on the scholasticism of medieval Europe, but they did not move beyond the categories of thought that had been formulated by their Hellenic predecessors.

The same contradiction, worked out in terms of emotional

autobiography rather than of metaphysical argument, pervaded the writings of the Sufis. The spirit of Islam led more easily to mystical than to conceptual thinking, and Sufism, which seems to have begun in Mesopotamia early in the ninth century, was perhaps the most vital and original of its cultural expressions. Many of the Sufis, however, affirmed a sense of direct personal union with God which conflicted with the orthodox theology of divine transcendence and appeared to lead to a repudiation of all external moral and religious authority. Hallaj, for example, who was put to death on charges of heresy at Baghdad in 922, declared: "I am He whom I love, and He whom I love is I; we are two spirits dwelling in one body. If thou seest me, thou seest Him, and if thou seest Him, thou seest us both." The belief that the human soul could achieve unity with God may have been partially derived from Neo-Platonism and the mystery cults, but for the Sufis it was primarily an interpretation of their inner experience. All forms of mysticism represent a threat to authoritarian concepts of religion, especially when the official theology, as in both Mohammedanism and Christianity, emphasizes the separate identity and indestructibility of the human soul and insists on obedience to a rigid ethical code. In Mohammedanism a partial reconciliation was worked out in the eleventh century in the theology of Ghazali, though mystical poets, who flourished chiefly in Persia, continued to describe ecstatic emotional states in terms that hovered on the edge of pantheism and antinomianism. Essentially the same problem confronted the theologians of medieval Christianity.

Islamic dogma, like that of Judaism, affirmed that divinity could not be given material representation. This was an obstacle to the development of painting, which can achieve major importance only in a society that believes ultimate spiritual reality to be immanent in sensuous forms. Forbidden to give visual embodiment to religious truths, the arts of the Mohammedan world became decorative rather than expressive, and hence must be classified as minor. But the fusion of Hellenic and Persian traditions of fine craftsmanship produced a great mass of exquisite work in ceramics, textiles, metalware, and similar fields. Few civilizations in all history have displayed a more finely developed aesthetic sense in articles of daily use, possibly because the artistic impulse was inhibited from more ambitious objectives. It was fitting that a society that could express its conceptions of God only in words should have used the Arabic script, the most beautiful ever devised.

Islam's greatest and most characteristic aesthetic creations were in architecture. The original mosques were simple and unadorned structures, in conformity with the desert puritanism of the Koran; but in the course of time it became permissible to employ the greatest architectural skill and ingenuity and to decorate with the most brilliant colors and the most exquisite abstract designs. In their external appearance, the Mosques often resembled Byzantine churches, with the addition of minarets—some notable examples seem, in fact, to have been planned by Hellenic architects—but there was a wide variety of structural forms. The dome, native to the Near East, became almost as characteristic of Mohammedan as of Byzantine architecture, though it was used with more emphasis on the external effect, in contrast with such buildings as the Hagia Sophia, where it was scarcely visible except from a considerable distance. Externally, the mosque often gave an impression of an overwhelming material power and magnificence, though the minarets flanking the dome served as a reminder that this was made possible by the will of God. But internally the mosque remained faithful to the desert origins of Islam and continued to represent a totally different view of life from that conveyed in the Christian church. The church was an organization of inner space planned to express the belief in divine immanence in nature. The altar where God became incarnate in the Eucharist was the center on which the eyes and attention of the congregation were irresistibly concentrated, each individual member feeling himself to be part of an organic collectivity engaged in the worship of a manifest divinity. But the mosque had no center. It remained merely a section of ground and air set aside for communion with a transcendent spirit. Instead of feeling his thoughts and emotions to be guided and directed toward a concrete object by the organization of the building, the worshipper was left free for personal prayer and meditation; withdrawal from the sensuous world was further aided by the color harmonies and decorative patterns of the carpets and walls. Whereas the Christian church promoted moral effort and aspiration, the mood of the mosque was the peace and relaxation that came from total submission to the divine will.

PART II

THE MIDDLE AGES

6

Feudalism

In the material organization of life the early tenth century probably marked the lowest point in Western history. A hundred years of barbarian raiding had wiped out whatever advances had been made under the early Carolingians. Most village communities were isolated from the outside world and wholly dependent on their own economic resources. The area under cultivation had sharply declined, and immense forests covered much of the countryside. Organized commerce had almost disappeared, so that there was little to maintain urban life; and those cities that still survived were compelled to support themselves largely by agriculture. With the breakdown in communications, the central governments of the various kingdoms had become increasingly ineffectual. The most significant feature of tenth-century Western society, especially in France, was the assumption of political power by innumerable petty lords, who offered the peasants their only means of protection against Viking, Magyar, and Saracen attacks. For most practical purposes sovereignty had been atomized into small units that were not effectively related to each other or to any higher authority. The anarchical consequences of this development became apparent as soon as the foreign raiding ended and the lords were free to exploit their peasant dependents and to wage war against each other.

The Viking invasions ended early in the tenth century, chiefly because of political changes in the Scandinavian countries where they had originated. Strong kings enforced order in Denmark and Norway, adopting Christianity and ending the anarchical conditions that had made these plundering expeditions possible. Groups of Vikings who had made permanent settlements in northern England and in the area of northern France thereafter known as Normandy were gradually assimilated and Christianized. Later in the century the Magyars were brought under control, being decisively defeated by the King of the Germans in the battle of Augsburg in 955. Adopting Latin Christianity and thus becoming integrated into the Western culture area, they remained confined to their settlements in Hungary. And while there was no peace with the Mohammedans, Western society gradually became strong enough to assume the offensive against them. The West was now able to enjoy a long immunity from foreign invasions. Later invaders from Asia, such as the Mongols in the thirteenth century and the Turks in the fifteenth, overran much of eastern Europe but never penetrated into the Atlantic provinces. This security has been rare in the history of civilizations and was a most important factor in the West's rapid development.

The eleventh and twelfth centuries were a time of rapid progress in all areas of human life, material, institutional, and cultural; and while all sections of the West shared in it and contributed to it, northern France remained the most dynamic center of creativity. There was a rapid increase in agricultural production, made possible both by improved techniques and by an immense expansion of the land under cultivation. This made the threat of famine less imminent, brought about a substantial growth of population, and made possible a revival of city life and of trade and manufacturing. Royal government became gradually more effective in the maintenance of peace and order, and the private wars engaged in by the aristocracy were partially brought under control.

As the West became stronger, it began to take the offensive against its external enemies, expanding into eastern Germany at the expense of its Slavic barbarian inhabitants and taking the initiative against the Mohammedans in the Mediterranean. This material growth was accompanied by a cultural efflorescence. In the course of the twelfth century, France produced the *chansons de geste,* the troubadour lyrics, and the romances; Gothic architecture, art, and sculpture; scholastic philosophy; and polyphonic choral music. This was the most widely and variously creative period in all Western history. It can be compared only with the efflorescence of classical Greece in the sixth and fifth centuries B.C.

The poet Chrétien de Troyes, writing about 1170, justifiably took pride in the cultural achievement of France.

> Our books have informed us that the pre-eminence in chivalry and learning once belonged to Greece. Then chivalry passed to Rome, together with that highest learning which now has come to France. God grant that it may be cherished here, that the honour which has taken refuge with us may never depart from France. God had awarded it as another's share, but of Greeks and Romans no more is heard; their fame is passed, and their glowing ash is dead.[1]

. . .

Such a display of creative energy needs favoring material conditions, but it cannot be explained by material factors alone. It becomes possible only when men feel that they live in a rational society, with standards of justice and rules of behavior that are believed to be in conformity with the will of God or with the structure of the universe. Institutions endowed with authority for the maintenance of order must appear to be based on legitimate principles, and thus entitled to loyal obedience and support, rather than on force and fraud. Otherwise the individual will feel alienated from the society in which he lives, with no sense of duty or obligation to defend it. Such a legitimization of the established

---

[1] Quoted in R. W. Southern: *The Making of the Middle Ages,* p. 14.

order is possible only by means of a general acceptance of an ideology that transcends reason.

How is a new ideology formulated and diffused throughout society? How do human beings lose the sense of alienation and begin to feel that the society in which they live is just and rational? These questions are not easily answered. The whole process of legitimization is mysterious, since it is not usually achieved by any process of conscious and deliberate planning and indoctrination. At certain major turning points of history, man's need to live in a society which he believes to be just and orderly begins to find new realizations. From feeling himself to be the helpless victim of irrational and unpredictable forces, he changes to loyal acceptance of an order that has become meaningful. These spiritual transformations mark the beginning of new epochs and constitute revolutions much more fundamental than the changes of government that result from them.

Throughout the Dark Ages, as we have seen, thinking men in western Europe had clung to concepts of order derived from memories of the Roman Empire. Only the restoration of that empire, they supposed, could restore the sense of security; no alternative political system was even conceivable. The principle of unity, both in the universe as a whole and in terrestrial society, was, moreover, emphasized in formal philosophical and theological thinking, which was derived partly from Greco-Roman traditions and partly from Christianity in its late-classical phase. All legitimate authority, it was believed, originated with God and was transmitted downward to his earthly representatives. Individuals were expected to conform with the divine order, which was the source of all political and ethical standards. During the early Middle Ages this belief in unity guided the policies of the papacy, leading to assertions of clerical omnipotence. But except insofar as the concept of a divine order led to conflicts between the Church and the secular authorities, it remained a theory with little practical relevance or efficacy. The way in which most people actually lived was wholly alien to the ideals in which they professed to believe.

During the tenth century the German kings attempted to revive the Carolingian program. Otto the Great, the second ruler of the Saxon dynasty, added northern Italy to the areas under his control and in 962 was crowned emperor by the Pope. His successors continued for several centuries to claim authority over both Germany and Italy. But these German emperors never held any power in France; and their program was always too ambitious to be realistic, ending finally in the breakdown of all effective central government in both the countries they had tried to rule. In the later Middle Ages, both Germany and Italy remained congeries of small provinces and city-states, which for all practical purposes were autonomous. The real line of advance was not the restoration of the empire but the emergence of nation-states governed by strong kings. The earliest example of a modern state governed by a king with the aid of a bureaucracy was the Norman kingdom of Naples and Sicily, though this had no ethnic basis and could not be considered a nation-state. Three such states were emerging in the later Middle Ages—France, Spain, and England—though it was everywhere a slow process.

In the early Middle Ages, the most urgent immediate need was to find principles by which the small units into which society had been atomized could be effectively related to each other. After the dissolution of the Carolingian Empire, Western man began to find such principles embodied in the institutional framework which is known to modern historians as the feudal system. The material conditions of feudal society had already been in existence for a long time, but not until the tenth and eleventh centuries did they begin to be regarded as infused with positive principles of order and justice. Originating on the level of actual living and never undergoing much theoretical elaboration, feudalism provided a system of obligations for the regulation of human relationships; and these obligations were actually applicable and meaningful in the disintegrated society of the post-Carolingian epoch. Their chief sources were Germanic rather than classical, and they were never deeply affected by the doctrines of Christianity. In practice, of course, these feudal obligations were rarely respected by the warrior aristocracy, and actual social conditions continued to be largely anarchical; but it was immensely important that feudal society was now seen as embodying ideal norms and standards. This change occurred especially in northern France—in Germany the Carolingian influence, with its emphasis on monarchy, lasted longer and went deeper—but in some degree it permeated the whole of the Western culture area. It was an essential preliminary to the outburst of creativity that began in the eleventh and twelfth centuries.

In Merovingian times, Gallic society was already sharply divided between a warrior ruling class and their peasant dependents. Some members of the ruling class may have been descended from the Roman landowning aristocracy that had dominated Gaul before the barbarian conquests; others were of Germanic descent and owed their position to royal appointment which gradually became hereditary. Through the Dark Ages there was a general tendency for the peasants to lose whatever freedom they had managed to preserve and to become more dependent on the aristocracy. The local lords gained power and responsibility at the expense of the central royal authority. In theory the king still reigned, but after the dissolution of the Carolingian Empire he had effective control only over the communities belonging to his personal domain. Accompanied by the officers of his household, which was in no way distinguished from the machinery of government, he spent much of his time in travel among his different personal estates. On a smaller scale the same was true of the high officials who were supposedly entrusted with the government of provinces. The supremacy of the warrior lords was due also to a technological innovation. The stirrup, invented in Asia, reached western Europe in the eighth century, and by enabling the horseman to stay in the saddle while engaged in active combat, it made him the master of the battlefield. This mastery lasted until the development first of improved methods of archery and then of gunpowder in the late Middle Ages. Feudalism was associated with the dominance of the armed knight on horseback, as is indicated in the derivation of the word "chivalry."

The origins of most of these lords were obscure. In later

generations some of them claimed noble descent from Germanic or Gallo-Roman forebears, in some instances correctly, but genealogies did not generally go back beyond the late Carolingian era. In that time of total anarchy, anybody with the requisite audacity and material resources could often acquire a lordship and found a noble family. Ownership of a horse and a suit of armor was the essential initial requirement. And while the peasants turned to the lord for protection, they were for all practical purposes at his mercy. The lords had powers of life and death over their dependents; their main social justification was to provide security against foreign raiders, but they abused their powers by fighting little wars against neighboring lords in which they delighted chiefly in slaughtering peasants and burning houses, orchards, and fields of grain. Their privileges were based originally on brute force, with scarcely a pretense of legality; and their primary and specialized function was to make war. Necessary during the period of the Viking raids, their warrior proclivities, continued through later epochs, made the maintenance of peace and order impossible. The glorification of war as a noble activity by which all kings and aristocrats were expected to win fame continued in Western civilization until very recent times.

Under such conditions any family that displayed strength and ambition for several generations could steadily rise in the social scale. This was true, for example, of the Angevins, ancestors of the Plantagenet kings of England. The first of them acquired a lordship in the Loire valley, by means that history has not recorded, late in the ninth century. His descendants, all of them ruthless men with driving energy and volcanic passions, gradually enlarged their domain by successful wars and marriages and favors to the Church until they had become counts of Anjou and ranked among the greatest of the French nobility. Later members of the family liked to claim descent from a Roman aristocrat. Its enemies, awed by the recurrence of hereditary traits that seemed demonic, repeated a legend that the first of the Angevins had married a creature from hell who, when taken forcibly to church, had flown out the window and never been seen again.

In the social dissolution of the ninth and tenth centuries it was only elemental personal ties that provided any kind of integration. Legal government was powerless, and legal contracts could give no security since there was nobody to enforce them. Christianity survived, at least for the warrior lords, only as a series of magical devices for ensuring good fortune. But as in the Germanic tribes of earlier periods, the direct relationship of man to man was considered binding, though the constant emphasis on the sinfulness of disloyalty proved that it must often have occurred. The strongest of such ties were those that bound the family together. Despite the efforts of the Church and the Carolingian monarchs to end the duty of private vengeance, all members of a family group still felt obligated to protect each other, and a man's effective power was largely measured by the number and importance of his relatives. Society, moreover, thought in terms of family groups, so that a man's relatives, in addition to being expected to exact vengeance if he were murdered, were also considered as sharing in his guilt if he committed a crime. The *chansons* are filled with examples of this primitive sense of family, recalling the clan system of early Greece and other early societies. When the traitor Ganelon in the *Chanson de Roland* is put to death, it is considered proper that forty of his relatives should be hanged with him.

It was by the extension and refinement of such personal loyalties and by their association with the ownership of land that a new kind of social order slowly began to take shape. Western man began to see personal ties, and especially the tie between the lord and his dependent vassals, as rationalizing and legitimizing the exercise of power and privilege. The essential element of the new view of society was the belief that all obligations were mutual. In the words of the twelfth-century French lawyer Beaumanoir, "the man owed his lord by reason of his homage as much faith and loyalty as the lord owes the man." [2] Mutual bonds held together the lord and the peasants, the lord being expected to

---

[2] Marc Bloch: *La Société Féodale,* I, 351.

give protection and the peasants owing agricultural services and a variety of dues. Similarly, the lesser lords were required to perform military service and other duties for the greater lords who governed provinces, and these, in turn, had obligations to the king, so that society was conceived as a kind of pyramid in which the king was the apex and the peasants were the base.

The obligations were at first regarded largely as personal, binding man and man; and this Germanic sense of personal ties did not wholly disappear until the late Middle Ages. But such loyalties gradually became associated with the holding of land, whoever held any particular estate being considered as owing certain services to some higher individual in the feudal pyramid. There was no conception of private ownership of land, since the occupancy of any piece of land was always conditional on the payment of dues and services to some kind of overlord. This principle seems to have originated during the Carolingian period, especially with the policy adopted by Charles Martel for maintaining forces of armed cavalry useful for defense against the Mohammedan raiders. Warriors had been endowed with lands (many of them being appropriated by Charles from the Church, which never forgave him) on condition that they do military service and maintain the necessary horses. But the association of landholding with services was considerably expanded during the period of the Carolingian breakdown. And once this system of services and obligations had become established, it virtually took the place of the state. Individuals owed services to their lord and to the king, not as citizens but as holders of the lands from which these services were due; and the king acquired revenues, not through taxation but partly through feudal dues and partly from the estates that remained under his personal and direct control.

In the early feudal period, the transmission of land was not yet fully hereditary. The kings still remembered that the rulers of provinces had originally been officials owing their powers to royal appointment, not to birth (the conflict between the two conceptions was a frequent theme of the *chansons*). But the nobility gradually established its claim to hereditary succession, and this was accompanied by the growth of a corresponding ideology serving to justify the sharp class distinctions between the nobility and the peasantry.

Plato, seeking means of preserving the class inequalities of his republic, had suggested the propagation of a myth that God had made some men out of gold and silver and others out of brass and iron, the species being generally preserved in the children. Such a myth won general acceptance in early medieval Europe, though it was not invented by anybody in particular. That most noblemen inherited the virtues of courage, generosity, courtesy, and capacity for leadership, and that most peasants were born devoid of these qualities, gradually became a commonplace of medieval thinking. Writers of fiction were especially fond of illustrating the myth by telling stories about the offspring of noble families who were lost or abandoned in early childhood and brought up in peasant or bourgeois families, but who insisted on behaving like noblemen and were finally reinstated in their true social positions. The consequent fusion of class and moral characteristics is illustrated in the double use of such words as "noble" and *"vilain"* (or—in English—"villain"), which refer both to social categories and to the qualities supposedly associated with them, and in the idealistic connotations acquired by the word "chivalry," which originally meant simply horsemanship. This ascription of class divisions to a kind of law of nature, not to social convention, could not, of course, be supported by historical fact. As we have seen, most noble families seem to have owed their superior status to successful climbing during the Carolingian period, despite their claims to descent from Roman aristocrats or Germanic chieftains. Class lines, moreover, always retained some fluidity. Even after the ideology of feudalism had become well established, parvenu families could sometimes enter the ranks of the nobility, most often through services to the king, though it might be several generations before their plebeian origins were no longer held against them. That a medieval king relied on low-born counselors and administrators was one of the most frequent complaints made by feudal aristocrats against him. The mythical belief in the virtues of noble blood proved to be extraordinarily pertinacious; even today it has not wholly disappeared.

To regard the myth as merely a device employed by the nobility to protect its privileges would be a very superficial interpretation. The adoption of an ideology is never effective if it is only a conscious and deliberate process. Deeper and more complex motivations are involved. A society cannot flourish unless the principles by which it operates are accepted as intrinsically just and rational, and the myth of noble lineage was therefore a necessary instrument for achieving some degree of stability and diminishing the reliance on outright force. Any exposure of the truth about the myth would immediately have made it ineffectual. Its main importance, moreover, was not in promoting the obedience of the peasants but in prescribing models of conduct for the ruling class and thus inculcating some degree of self-discipline and self-control. The young lord was expected to prove himself worthy of his lineage by displaying the qualities of the ideal nobleman; he must not act like a peasant. He had a code of values for his guidance. The code, of course, was applicable only to feudal society and emphasized chiefly the warrior virtues. The nobleman was expected chiefly to show himself *preux,* a portmanteau word which can be roughly translated as "valiant" and which covered most of the qualities needed for success in battle. He was also required to be generous, distributing his wealth in largesse to his dependents and to the Church and the poor, not saving it or investing it in economic improvements. This emphasis given to generosity was characteristic of a society that had no thought of economic progress, and the efforts of noblemen to show themselves suitably extravagant meant that they were constantly in danger of total impoverishment and constantly under the necessity of refilling their treasure chests by means of successful war. Yet by idealizing the personal loyalties that cemented the system of mutual obligations, the feudal code gave support to the whole social structure and promoted a discipline of egoistic impulses that had been largely absent from Frankish society through much of the Dark Ages.

Thus during the early Middle Ages there were two wholly

different principles of order in western Europe: that of the Church, which emphasized unity and preached ethical doctrines that were far too elevated for practical application in secular society; and that of feudalism, which began in actual social conditions and provided relevant norms and ideals, though these did not rise far above a barbaric level. The feudal view of life was static, offering no higher goals or aspirations beyond the maintenance of the feudal order; it had little sense of individuality, men and women being identified by their roles in the class structure rather than by any personal qualities; and (as with most ideologies) the beliefs and attitudes by which the structure was supported remained effective only as long as they were not exposed to rational examination.

· · ·

The feudal code, at least in its earlier forms, had no real relationship to Christian ethics. It developed mainly out of the Germanic background, and the Church seems to have made no significant contributions to its development until a relatively late period. The mutual loyalties of lord and vassal and the act of homage in which they were sealed, consisting of a clasping of hands and a kiss, were of Germanic origin, and the dubbing by which the young man was made a knight, and thus became entitled to the privileges of nobility, seems to have been derived from Germanic puberty rituals. These rituals were not brought under clerical sponsorship until the thirteenth century. Despite the professed adherence to Christianity, the popular religious beliefs of feudal society remained essentially pagan. The clergy was expected to do what was necessary to secure divine favor (its main function being to propitiate God by spending as much time as possible in praying and singing hymns), but the feudal lords seem to have felt contempt for everybody who did not display the warrior virtues, at least if the *chansons* are a true reflection of their attitude. Bishop Turpin was one of the heroes of the *Chanson de Roland,* and was praised for his effective sermons, but he was admired chiefly because he was also a valiant warrior. According to a proverb of the Carolingian period, "whoever, without mounting a horse, has remained at school up to the age of twelve is no longer good for anything except making a priest." [3] The attitude reflected in this saying recurs frequently in the *chansons*.

The feudal nobles believed that God would give protection in this life and salvation in the next to those who complied with his wishes, but his wishes were represented as mostly ritualistic. The good nobleman reverenced God, respected the properties of the clergy, was the enemy of all non-Christians, refrained from eating meat on Fridays or in Lent, did not marry more than one wife at a time,[4] and took the Eucharist regularly, especially (if possible) before going into battle. The *chansons* repeatedly illustrate total incomprehension of the true meaning of Christianity. The Pope, for example, seeking the aid of William of Orange in the protection of Rome against its enemies, is represented as offering him the privileges of marrying as many wives as he wishes and of eating meat every day of the week. When Raoul of Cambrai first burns a town and all its inhabitants, including a convent containing a hundred nuns, and then, ignoring the fact that it is both Lent and Friday, orders a meal of roast peacocks and deviled swans and venison, it is the second of these acts of blasphemy that more especially horrifies his servants and makes them fearful of divine vengeance.

It must be admitted that the feudal code was for a long time not very effective in curbing the animal impulses of the warrior class. The description of feudalism in practice as organized anarchy is true, though not the whole truth. After the cessation of

---

[3] Bloch: op. cit., II, 17.

[4] While prohibiting divorce, the Church was usually willing to annul a marriage if the participants were too closely related to each other. In the early Middle Ages a relationship was considered too close if it could be traced back for seven generations. Practically all royal and aristocratic marriages were subject to annulment on this ground. Many medieval kings were permitted on these principles to have a whole series of marriages.

the Viking raids which had been mainly responsible for the emergence of the feudal lords, western Europe continued to suffer from the domination of this class of men who were trained and habituated to war and to nothing else. Any detailed analysis of affairs in any segment of France during the early Middle Ages reveals a frightful picture. Private war between different lords was chronic, both because fighting was their favorite occupation and because they needed plunder; and while the lords respected each other and observed certain rules of war, they had no compunction whatever about slaughtering peasants, burning cottages and crops, and plundering monasteries. When a town was captured, the victorious army claimed the right to sack it, doing what they pleased with the unfortunate inhabitants and appropriating their possessions. The sacking of a city was an orgiastic performance, the most pleasurable available to medieval man, offering a release from all moral inhibitions that was quite as complete as the most savage of primitive fertility rituals and much more bloody and destructive.

Yet in spite of the barbaric elements in feudalism, the concept of feudal society as an order became slowly more effective. One can watch part of this process in the *chansons*. These celebrations of the warrior virtues were profoundly moral, though their morality had only the most superficial relationship to Christianity and was, in fact, close to that of ancient Greece during the heroic period, as described in the Homeric poems. The mutual obligations binding lord and vassal, which formed the main integrative principle in feudal society, were regarded as morally compulsive, while any conflict of loyalties constituted a problem which might have tragic consequences. The quality which most often brought a hero to destruction was a lack of moderation and self-control, of *mesure,* and was closely akin to the Greek sin of *hybris.* A further stage in the movement toward civilization was registered in the lyric poetry which originated with the troubadours of southern France early in the twelfth century. Troubadour poetry was totally non-Christian; it glorified adultery, and denied any possibility of love between husband and wife. But it transformed the whole meaning of sexuality, changing it from an animal appetite to an instrument for promoting self-control, respect for women, and appreciation for cultural values. Thenceforth the warrior nobleman was expected to be not only *preux* but also *courtois* and endowed with a "gentle heart."

The feudal aristocracy of the twelfth century, like that of the tenth and eleventh, still regarded warfare as the main purpose of its existence. But its warrior impulses were increasingly channeled into socially acceptable activities. Beginning with Pope Urban's call for the reconquest of Palestine from the Mohammedans in 1096, crusading provided an outlet by which bellicose and impoverished noblemen could win glory and plunder. Another means for the expression of aggression, which the Church vigorously condemned with no visible effect, was the growth of mock battles known as tournaments. Penniless members of the warrior class, whom the practice of primogeniture was making increasingly numerous, could not only win glory and attract the favorable attention of wellborn ladies by showing prowess in a tournament; since they were permitted to collect ransoms from defeated opponents, they could also hope to reduce their economic difficulties. Late in the twelfth century it was calculated that in northern France there was a tournament every two weeks, and a considerable body of unattached knights seem to have treated tournament-going as a regular way of life.[5]

Meanwhile the whole profession of knighthood was being idealized and associated with higher standards of behavior. To an increasing extent it was now a privilege available only to those born into the right families, whereas a couple of centuries earlier men of low birth could sometimes become knights by showing the right kind of prowess. But a knight was now expected to be *courtois* as well as *preux,* winning feminine approval by good manners and social grace; and—at least in theory—he was sup-

---

[5] These victims of economic pressure, not the idealized warriors of the Arthurian legend, were the original "knights errant."

posed to protect the weak and use force only on the side of justice. The process of assuming the rights and responsibilities of knighthood was becoming an elaborate ritual, designed both to inculcate the appropriate virtues in the young candidate and to demonstrate to all *vilains* that knighthood was a high privilege reserved for those of noble birth. The ceremonies began with a bath, a vigil in church, and attendance at Mass; and on the following morning the young man was solemnly robed in a cloak of squirrel fur (known as the *vair* and the gray, which became a general symbol of knighthood), equipped with arms, and smitten on the nape of the neck by his sponsor. Despite the vigil and Mass in church, no clergyman took part in the actual ceremony, which was derived from pagan rituals. When in 1213 the son of a high French nobleman, Simon de Montfort, was dubbed by two bishops, there was much comment on this break with tradition.

The barbaric elements in feudalism were too deeply ingrained ever to be eradicated wholly. A real political order could be achieved not by any idealization of feudalism but by its subordination to royal power. As noted, the feudal nobility was driven to almost incessant warfare not only by its own training and code of values but also by the pressure of economic need. The knight could obtain the money needed to show a properly aristocratic generosity and hospitality only by exploiting his peasants or by robbing his neighbors. The whole feudal ethos was expressed with a frank brutality that was essentially true by the twelfth-century Limousin troubadour Bertran de Born, who thoroughly deserved the place in hell among those guilty of violence that was assigned to him by Dante. Bertran glorified violence both because he loved it and also because of the opportunities for robbery and plunder. He could fairly be called not only a poet of genius but also a man of criminal propensities but for the fact that he was expressing the attitudes of a whole social group, though with a disconcerting frankness.

> The joyous season approaches when our ships shall land, when King Richard, wanton and valiant as he never was before, shall

come. Now shall we see gold and silver spent; newly built foundation shall break with envy, walls shall crumble, towers shall sub-
side and fall to pieces, and his enemies shall taste the prison and
its chains. I love the melee of shields with blue and vermilion tints,
flags and pennons of different colors, tents and rich pavilions
spread over the plain, the breaking of lances, the riddling of
shields, the splitting of gleaming helmets, and the giving and taking
of blows.[6]

If one judges a historical phenomenon by its contribution to
economic and political progress, then feudalism must be regarded as a necessary means of maintaining some kind of security during the anarchy following the collapse of the Carolingian
Empire, and subsequently as an obstacle to all further progress.
But in the cultural history of the Western world it has a lasting
importance. The conception of feudalism as an order based on
rational and moral principles, not as a chaos dependent solely on
force (though never effective in practice), was the first step in the
growth of a new civilization in which men could feel themselves
members of a rational and just society. The feudal ideal, moreover, found expression in legends, like that of King Arthur,
which have been enduring elements in the culture of the West
and which have continued to express social values and influence
individual conduct down almost to the present day. If the Western hero differs from that of ancient Greece, with its emphasis on
an individualism that is frankly self-seeking and often tricky, or
from that of Rome, which glorified obedience to civic duty, that
is mainly because he was largely shaped by feudalism. Compelled
to justify himself against a hostile bourgeoisie and basing his
claims to pre-eminence not on wealth or ability but on the fictitious virtues of noble lineage, seeking to legitimize his position of
privilege by assuming the role of protector of the weak and of the
true religion, the feudal aristocrat claimed for himself the quali-

---

[6] Quoted in Achille Luchaire: *Social France at the Time of Philip Augustus,*
translated by E. B. Krehbiel (New York, 1912), p. 257.

ties of courage, generosity, and respect for women and for all who needed protection, and the capacity to assume the responsibilities of leadership. This was not the nobleman of history, who was generally brutal, sensuous, and greedy. But the nobleman of myth continued to support an ideal of good conduct, with far-reaching and partially desirable results, long after the feudal nobleman of history had become extinct.[7]

Meanwhile the future was represented by the rising bourgeoisie, whose way of living promoted individual enterprise and a rationalistic calculation of profits and losses, means and ends. With the growth of agricultural production and the achievement of a greater degree of law and order during the tenth century, urban life began to revive, usually with the encouragement and practical support of the monarchy, which found the bourgeoisie a useful ally against the feudal lords.[8]

---

[7] The world of chivalry, so sordid and destructive in many of its manifestations, has continued to be favorably regarded in popular speech. Words especially associated with feudal society have mostly retained favorable connotations. A crusade, for example, is generally viewed as a noble enterprise, to such an extent that political movements often present themselves to the electorate as crusades. As a weapon customarily used by medieval warriors, a sword generally has eulogistic connotations and is often referred to by political speakers as a weapon for the defense of right. Thus pro-feudal propaganda continues to be reflected in popular speech, with astonishing success.

[8] Some historians still refer to the bourgeoisie as a "middle class," presumably regarding it as in the middle between the landowning aristocracy and the peasantry. This is a misleading conception of the social structure. The bourgeoisie is not to be regarded as lying between the nobility and the peasantry but rather as constituting a wholly separate group. Among the most important factors in Western economic history since the early Middle Ages have been the growth of the bourgeois occupations of industry and trade and the emergence of a new wealthy class whose wealth consisted primarily of money rather than of land. In the course of time the upper bourgeoisie rivaled the landed aristocracy in wealth and political power. Most of the bourgeoisie did not reach such levels and can be regarded as a middle class lying between the upper bourgeoisie and the urban working class. But this middle class never rose to political power, nor did its fortunes have any special importance. In some countries a middle-class citizen who rose to wealth generally bought his way into the aristocracy (as in Tudor England). In some other countries (Italy

Commerce increased, much of it involving the transportation of luxury articles over long distances by caravans of merchants; and conveniently located places became permanent centers of marketing. The village communities had always included craftsmen, and these began to settle in the new urban centers and to expand their activities, developing new forms of industry and hiring assistants. The urban population gradually separated itself from the peasants in the surrounding villages and developed new institutions and new views of life. The land upon which the cities grew originally belonged to a local lord, to the Church, or to the king. As their populations expanded, cities became aware of their common interests and needs, and began to bargain for, and sometimes to fight for, the essential rights of self-government, wanting both immunity from oppressive taxation and other forms of interference and the power to draft regulations governing commercial and industrial practices. "Communes" were formed for the protection of bourgeois interests, leading sometimes to bitter and bloody struggles with feudal lords or with bishops or abbots.

Yet although the bourgeoisie represented new social forces with new interests and ideals, it did not, during the early Middle Ages, make these fully explicit. Once it had achieved the necessary degree of self-government, it mostly accepted traditional beliefs and values. A growth of individualism was inherent in the ethics and views of life of craftsmen and merchants. Unlike the peasant class, they were not bound by traditional ways of doing things. Wealth—for the bourgeoisie—consisted primarily of money rather than of land, and money was a great liberating force, opening infinite possibilities of choice. But the bourgeois themselves were frightened by the dangers of individualism, and

---

is an example) the aristocracy moved into the cities and became amalgamated with the bourgeoisie. Thus the lines between the middle class and the upper class were not drawn tightly, and there was considerable class fluidity. The peasant, on the other hand, rarely rose to a higher status.

during the early Middle Ages they maintained the guild system, which strictly regulated economic activities, allegedly in accordance with ethical considerations, limiting competition and controlling prices, wages, and methods of workmanship. There was more freedom in the cities than in the villages, but city economic practices were still very far from anything that could be described as free enterprise or economic individualism.

Early medieval culture reflected partly the doctrines of the Church and partly the values of the warrior aristocracy, and was little influenced by the rise of the bourgeoisie. The chief contributions of the bourgeoisie were not ideological but financial. Bourgeois wealth made possible the building of the cathedrals and the growth of the schools attached to them. Not until the fourteenth century did thinking and the arts begin to reflect specifically bourgeois points of view.

. . .

The most spectacular exhibition of feudal qualities and ideals was the crusading movement. It was initiated by the papacy, which wished to divert the energies of the feudal nobility into conflict with the Mohammedans, not only in order to re-establish Christian rule over Palestine but also to limit private warfare in the Western countries. Palestine, it was believed, was peculiarly the domain of the Christian God (his rights over it were regularly defined in feudal terms),[9] and it was therefore the duty of Chris-

---

[9] "God has brought before you his suit against the Turks and Saracens, who have done him great despite. They have seized his fiefs, where God was first served and recognized as Lord."

"God has ordained a tournament between Heaven and Hell, and sends to all his friends who wish to defend him, that they fail him not."

"God has fixed a day for you to be at Edessa: there the sinners will be saved who hit hard and who serve him in his need."

From a song of the Second Crusade of unknown authorship; quoted in J. Bedier and P. Aubry: *Les Chansons de Croisade* (Paris, 1909), pp. 8–11.

tian warriors to recapture it from the infidels. According to the standards of Christianity or of any other system of beliefs, the whole movement was, of course, utterly unjustifiable, and even in terms of self-interest Europe had nothing substantial to gain by it. Nevertheless, from the original appeal of Pope Urban in 1096 down to the fifteenth century, virtually all spokesmen of Christianity continued to speak of crusading as a religious duty, and apart from a protest by St. Anselm at the time of the First Crusade [1] no reputable religious leader seems to have doubted the assumption that Palestine must be brought by force under Christian control.

From any rational viewpoint the Crusades can be regarded only as an expression of mass insanity, though on an epic scale. They exhibited at their worst the barbaric elements that were still so conspicuous in the new civilization. From beginning to end, over a period of nearly two centuries, their history was filled with examples of Christian hysteria, intolerance, blood lust, sensuality, and superstitition. And from beginning to end the Mohammedans showed themselves notably superior in humanity, courtesy, respect for promises and agreements, and all other qualities except brute force. Nevertheless, the movement had most important psychological results for the development of the West.

Intermittent warfare between Christians and Mohammedans had been occurring in Spain and along the coasts of Italy and southern France for several centuries; but it had not evoked any major Christian response. The initial suggestion of an expedition to the eastern Mediterranean came from the Byzantine emperor,

---

[1] " 'I advise you'—Anselm wrote to a young man—'I counsel you, I pray and beseech you as one who is dear to me, to abandon that Jerusalem which is now not a vision of peace but of tribulation, to leave aside the treasures of Constantinople and Babylon which are to be seized on with hands steeped in blood, and to set out on the road to the heavenly Jerusalem which is a vision of peace, where you will find treasures which only those who despise these (earthly) ones can receive.' " Southern: op. cit., p. 50.

who was in dire need of reinforcements for his troops in Anatolia. Much of this wealthy and well-inhabited province had been lost after the disastrous battle of Manzikert in 1071, in which the Turks had inflicted a blow from which the Byzantine Empire never fully recovered. But Pope Urban II expanded the proposal far beyond Byzantine expectations, launching what quickly developed into a mass movement. Rational considerations had some weight with the crusaders. Adventurous and impoverished noblemen hoped to acquire estates in the Holy Land. Palestine, moreover, was filled with relics of saints and apostles, which could be profitably sold to churches and monasteries in Western countries. The Pope himself was partially motivated by a desire to assert his leadership of Western Christendom. But the rank and file of the crusaders were moved by less tangible expectations. They were promised forgiveness of their sins and immediate entry into heaven if they died for their religion. It was remarked at the time by St. Anselm and other observers that men of notoriously bad character were especially attracted to the enterprise. A Crusade, in fact, offered unrivaled opportunities for making the best of both worlds. Crusaders could enjoy unlimited possibilities for slaughter, plunder, and rape, with the assurance that as long as the victims were infidels, their hopes of eternal salvation would in no way be impaired. Some of them actually anticipated the delights of slaughtering Mohammedans by attacking Jewish communities in western Germany. One of the many ill effects of the Crusades was that (contrary to the exhortations of all reputable religious leaders) they inaugurated a long series of anti-Semitic outbreaks.

The effective element among the crusaders consisted of feudal nobility, largely from France, along with attendant men-at-arms. But long before these warrior groups were ready to move, a crowd of peasants and townspeople, some of them accompanied by wives and children, were on their way to Palestine under the leadership of two ignorant fanatics, Peter the Hermit and Walter Sans-Avoir. Many of them perished in Hungary and the Balkans, either succumbing to hunger and exhaustion or being killed by natives whose property they were guilty of seizing; those who actually reached Constantinople were hastily transported across the Bosporus by the Byzantine authorities (who were profoundly surprised and embarrassed by this response to their appeal for aid) and were mostly slaughtered by the Turks.

Medieval Europe was always prone to such manifestations of mass hysteria, evoked by ignorance and by unreal fantasies of a glory which had no rational basis. What did the participants expect to find in Palestine? Certainly they counted on divine assistance in their enterprise, and perhaps they confused Palestine with paradise. Christianity, with its hope of a millennium and its uncertainty as to whether this is to be realized in this world or the next, has always been especially prone to produce movements of this kind. An even more extraordinary case of mass delusion was the Children's Crusade early in the thirteenth century. An ignorant shepherd boy proclaimed that innocent children would succeed where adult warriors had failed, and led a large party to the coasts of southern France. Deceived by shipowners, most of them ended in slave markets in North Africa.

The effective elements in the First Crusade made rendezvous at Constantinople in the spring of 1097. They then made their way by land across Anatolia, spent more than eight months in the siege of Antioch, and completed their capture of Jerusalem in July 1099. In their behavior one can see, written large, the worst aspects of feudal society. Especially characteristic was their insistence on their right to spend several days in the sack of any city they captured. For this reason they much preferred to take a city by storm rather than to allow it to surrender. They felt entitled to their share of massacre and rape, in addition to recouping their expenses by wholesale plunder. They were highly indignant with the Byzantine emperor for arranging the surrender of Nicaea, the first Turkish city they besieged, thus depriving them of their expected rewards. This was an example of what William of Tyre, the historian of the movement, described as the Greek "lack of sincerity and good faith," by contrast with the "single-hearted confidence and trust" of the crusaders.[2] When they captured Antioch they enjoyed all the pleasures of the sack; while after the capture of Jerusalem, in one of the most revolting episodes in all Christian history, they slaughtered every inhabitant before going up to the Church of the Holy Sepulcher for holy tears and kisses and thanksgivings to God.[3] It was considered appropriate that the capture of the city had occurred on a Friday at the ninth hour, the same hour as the crucifixion.

Miracles were not wholly absent, though the most important of them was finally shown to be fraudulent. The lance which had pierced the side of Jesus at the crucifixion was discovered at Antioch by an ignorant peasant, Peter Bartholomew, who

---

[2] William of Tyre: op. cit., II, 12, 19.

[3] "Among the first to enter was Tancred and the Duke of Lotharingia (Godfrey), who on that day shed quantities of blood almost beyond belief. After them the host mounted the walls, and now the Saracens suffered. Yet although the city was all but in the hands of the Franks, the Saracens resisted the party of Count Raymond as if they were never going to be taken. But when our men had mastered the walls of the city and the towers, then wonderful things were to be seen. Numbers of the Saracens were beheaded— which was the easiest for them; others were shot with arrows, or forced to jump from the towers; others were slowly tortured and were burned in flames. In the streets and open places of the town were seen piles of heads and hands and feet. One rode about everywhere amid the corpses of men and horses. But these were small matters! Let us go to Solomon's temple, where they were wont to chant their rites and solemnities. What had been done there? If we speak the truth we exceed belief: let this suffice. In the temple and porch of Solomon one rode in blood up to the knees and even to the horses' bridles by the just and marvellous Judgment of God, in order that the same place which so long had endured their blasphemies against Him should receive their blood. . . . When the city was taken it was worth the whole long labour to witness the devotion of the pilgrims to the sepulchre of the Lord, how they clapped their hands, exulted, and sang a new song unto the Lord. For their hearts presented to God, victor and triumphant, vows of praise which they were unable to explain. A new day, new joy and exultation, new and perpetual gladness, the consummation of toil and devotion drew forth from all new words, new songs. This day, I say, glorious in every age to come, turned all our griefs and toils into joy and exultation." From the narrative of Raymond of Aguiles, a young priest; quoted in H. O. Taylor: *The Medieval Mind,* I, 552.

claimed that he had been guided by a vision of St. Andrew. The lance was then taken into battle as a promise of victory, but when Peter began to develop a habit of seeing visions in which instructions were given to the whole crusader army, skepticism began to develop. Peter was required to submit to ordeal by fire, running between two burning piles of logs. When he died of his burns twelve days later, the lance was discredited.

The kingdom of Jerusalem maintained a precarious existence for nearly two centuries. The Mohammedan world was now split into a number of small units with fluctuating boundaries and a lack of legitimate authority, though skillful adventurers would occasionally build formidable, but transitory, dominions. The Christians who settled permanently in Palestine gradually adopted ways of living appropriate to the climate, intermarried with Palestinian women, and acquired tolerant feelings toward their Moslem neighbors. But there was never any lasting peace between the two religions, and any tendencies toward toleration among the Christian population were checked by new arrivals from western Europe, who came to Palestine eager for warfare and anticipating the delights of slaughtering and plundering the enemies of the true faith. There was little cultural interchange, since the Christians were mostly too barbaric to take any interest in intellectual matters. The effects of contact with the Mohammedan world were mostly limited to ways of living and of sensuous enjoyment. The creative encounters between the two civilizations took place mostly in Spain and in Sicily, not in Palestine.

The kingdom held most of what had been conquered in the First Crusade until the rise of an able Moslem chieftain of Kurdish descent, the famous Saladin, who became ruler of Egypt in 1071 and subsequently succeeded in uniting the Moslems of Syria and Egypt under his own able and chivalrous leadership. At this point the kingdom of Jerusalem was inherited by a young woman who married a young French nobleman, Guy of Lusignan, thereby making him king. Weak and foolish, Guy led the Christians to total disaster in the battle of the Horns of Hattin in 1187. Trying to take the offensive against Saladin's army, they were compelled to camp for the night in a spot in the Galilean hills totally devoid of water. Here they were surrounded by the Moslems, who added to their misery by starting brushfires whose smoke was blown into the Christian camp. Next morning the entire Christian army, gasping from thirst and heat, was slaughtered or taken prisoner. This was followed by the capture of Jerusalem, though the surviving Christians still held a series of fortresses along the coast of the Mediterranean. A series of subsequent crusading movements bringing reinforcements enabled the Christians to retain some of the footholds in Palestine until the final capture of their last stronghold in 1291.

Meanwhile a long series of disputes between Westerners and Byzantines had culminated in another display of Western barbarism. From the beginning the Westerners had chafed at Byzantine subtleties and Byzantine assumptions of superiority. Preferring to rely, where possible, on intelligence rather than on brute force, diplomacy rather than warfare, the Byzantines seemed to the crusaders to be lacking in true Christian fervor. Most of the crusaders passed through Constantinople and were impressed by its immense riches. Finally, in 1204 a crusading expedition, known as the Fourth Crusade, was induced to begin its activities by imposing an exiled Byzantine prince on the imperial throne. When the Byzantines resisted, the city was seized by the crusaders and subjected to all the horrors of a three-day sack. The riches accumulated during nine centuries were seized by brutal Western soldiers, and an immense quantity of manuscripts and works of art, the heritage of the classical tradition, was destroyed. Neither monasteries nor churches nor libraries were spared. In the great cathedral dedicated to the Hagia Sophia, drunken soldiers tore the great silver iconostasis to pieces and trampled books and images underfoot, while a prostitute seated on the patriarch's throne sang a ribald French song. As the historian of the expedition, Villehardouin, truthfully declared, never in all history had such a quantity of plunder been amassed in the taking of a city. The crusaders then set up one of their own leaders, Baldwin of Flanders, as emperor, beginning the Latin Empire, which endured until 1261. Greece was scattered with "Frankish" fortifications, thus adding another element to its Mycenean, Greek, Roman, and Byzantine remains; but the Latin Empire had no deep roots, and princes of native stock regained control of the empire in 1261. The last period of Byzantine civilization was not unproductive, art in particular undergoing another revival; but the crusaders had fatally weakened it, preparing the way for its conquest by the Turks in 1453. Thus one of the most important results of the Crusades was to lay open eastern Europe to Mohammedan conquest.

With the loss of Palestine the crusading movement was brought to an end, though individual kings and clerics and noblemen continued to speak of recapturing the Holy Land until as late as the end of the fifteenth century. Even Columbus hoped to redeem the holy places with the gold that he expected to find in the Indies. The humanist pope Aeneas Sylvius, who assumed the papal title of Pius II, died in 1464 at Ancona in Italy while trying to organize a crusading expedition, though his attendants concealed from him how few persons had responded to his appeals. Crusading movements were actually launched against Mohammedans elsewhere. In 1396 a large crusading army of knights and nobility, who had come to the Balkans to fight the Turks, was slaughtered at Nicopolis in a debacle almost as complete as that at the Horns of Hattin.

A full verdict on any historical episode, however, must take account of spiritual results which cannot be weighed and measured. The crusading movement was of immense psychological importance. Spreading to every part of western Europe and bringing it into close contact with an alien civilization, it evoked an effort of self-affirmation and self-definition. It helped to make the West aware of its own essential character at a time when this was still in the process of formulation. Some such encounter often has fruitful consequences in the development of a new society, though it does not necessarily take a warlike form. The Crusades played an essential role in the efflorescence of culture which marked the twelfth century, as can be seen in the *chansons,* which dealt primarily with wars between Christians and Saracens. Positive influences of the East, moreover, can be traced in troubadour poetry, in architecture, and in the other arts, though what the West borrowed was transmuted and made into expressions of the Western spirit. The Crusades played in Western cultural development a role similar to that of the Persian wars in promoting the golden age of Greece.

7

The Development of

Christianity

While feudal society was evolving its own concepts of order, along with the appropriate values and ideals, wholly different principles were being asserted by the reformers of the Church. The Church of the later Dark Ages ignored the ethical doctrines that it was supposed to represent and had become, at best, an instrument of the secular state. Morality and learning had largely been forgotten, and even the papacy, involved in sordid conflicts between different factions of Roman aristocratic families, rarely provided spiritual leadership. Reform in the Church meant a revivification of Christian ethics and the Christian experience and a successful assertion of its independence of the secular state.

The problem was complicated by the deep ambiguity in the nature and purpose of religion in the new Western civilization. Christianity was, on the one hand, the official religion of society, inheriting from its pagan predecessors the function of propitiating God. Yet at the same time it was the repository of moral and spiritual values which had never been realized in social institutions and must always remain incapable of complete fulfillment. If the belief in these values was to be revitalized, the Church had to be disentangled from secular institutions and endowed with independent spiritual authority. But the belief in the unity of Christian society made it impossible to consider church and state as wholly separate bodies. The Church, in fact, could become independent of the state only by dominating it. The reform of the Church thus led to bitter conflicts which ended by discrediting the claims made by the Pope and the clergy to the spiritual and moral leadership of Western man.

Belief in the unity of church and state had originated in the later Roman Empire, with the state, on the whole, exercising the dominant role in practical affairs, while the ideals of the Church could be fully realized only in the afterlife. But because both were guided by the same Christian principles, it was unnecessary to specify which powers belonged to which institution. If the emperor erred, the Church could call him to account (as St. Ambrose had done with the Emperor Theodosius, when he was guilty of a wanton massacre of the people of Salonica); and if the Church became corrupt, the emperor could reform it. The disappearance of the Western Empire had left the Pope as the only representative of unity in the Western world, but with Charlemagne came a return to the attitudes of the Constantinean empire. Charlemagne regarded himself as the vicar of Christ, and was not willing to concede more than coordinate authority to the Pope. In practice the Church was largely absorbed into the imperial government. Similar policies were adopted in tenth-century Germany by Otto I and the other Saxon emperors. They leaned heavily on the bishops for political support against the rebellious feudal aristocracy, and on several occasions claimed the power to remove erring popes. Thus the Church seemed to be regarded as a mere instrument of the secular order. And since large estates had become attached to bishoprics and monasteries, it was virtually a part of the feudal system. In all western European countries the monarchy had acquired the power to appoint bishops and abbots and normally expected from them the same services as were owed by its secular vassals.

All religious reformers wanted the clergy to free themselves from these secular tasks and to assume their duties of spiritual leadership. The clergy gradually began to claim not merely independence of the state but supremacy over it, on the ground that they alone could interpret the will of God. The apostle Peter was supposed to have been made head of the Church and to have transmitted his powers to the Popes, who had succeeded him as Bishops of Rome. The full implications of this doctrine of papal supremacy became apparent late in the eleventh century when it was asserted by the Roman priest Hildebrand, who became Pope Gregory VII. This was followed by more than two hundred years of intermittent conflict between the papacy and the emperor and other secular rulers, which degenerated in its later phases from a conflict about spiritual principles into one about political power and thereby destroyed most of the popular support on which the papacy depended. The history of medieval Christianity does not, however, consist merely of struggles for power and wealth. The main line of development was the rediscovery of the Christian experience, at first by men who accepted papal leadership, and afterward, as that leadership became more and more self-seeking, by independent mystical groups who paid little attention to clerical institutions.

In the earlier stages of the religious reawakening the main appeal was to fear, and the main emphasis was on the corruption of the whole natural world. Christianity was presented as a series of dogmas to which man must submit rather than as a way of life which he could rediscover in his inner emotional experience. Its validation was external, in the spectacle of a world of suffering and insecurity, rather than internal, in providing positive fulfillments for emotional drives and aspirations. Man could save himself only by renouncing the world and the flesh and adopting severe ascetic disciplines.

A religion on this elemental level was appropriate to Western civilization in the early medieval period, both because fear alone was strong enough as an emotional force to repress the barbaric attitudes still prevalent in secular society and because most people had indeed good reason to feel fear. Living in a chaotic and uncertain world, always in imminent danger of natural or man-made catastrophes, medieval people were never far from hysteria, and outbreaks of mass panic or mass savagery were frequent phenomena.

Men who saw life in these terms could escape from the world and the flesh only by seeking refuge in monasteries, and the revitalization of Christian belief therefore began with monastic reforms. In 910 a new monastery was founded at Cluny in the Burgundian hills, with endowments supplied by the Count of Aquitaine. The count presumably hoped that by providing for the praise and worship of God he could assure himself of divine protection in this world and the next. Cluny differed from earlier foundations in emphasizing worship more than labor and in giving high value to architectural and artistic beauty. It was fortunate in its early abbots, several of whom were endowed with remarkable powers of leadership, combined with a broad humanity, and served for long periods. Responsible only to the papacy, not to the local bishop, Cluny became the parent house of a large number of affiliated establishments scattered over western Europe, and the whole Cluniac congregation came to stand for high moral standards and for clerical supremacy.

The growth of monasticism, combined with the assertion of clerical supremacy over secular authority, continued to be the central factor in religious development until the twelfth century, and the more extreme ascetics found the life of the Cluniac order too easygoing and too tolerant of worldly comfort. Several new orders with stricter practices were founded, notably the Carthusians and the Cistercians. The deep corruption of human nature in all its aspects remained the main theme of Christian preaching.

The evils of sexual desire continued to obsess clerical reformers, since it was believed that the inability of human beings to procreate without feeling lust was the instrument for the transmission of original sin. Preachers delighted in impressing upon their hearers a revulsion against carnal pleasure by elaborating in crude detail the more unsavory features of the human body. As Odo of Cluny declared, "bodily beauty is but skin deep . . . If a man consider that which is hidden within the nose, the throat, and the belly, he will find filth everywhere; and if we cannot bring ourselves even with the tips of our fingers to touch such phlegm or dung, wherefore do we desire to embrace this bag of filth itself?" [1] One of the most intense haters of the human body was the eleventh-century Italian monk Peter Damian, whose catalogue of the sins to which men were addicted, the *Liber Gomorrianus,* goes into details which make it unprintable. Toward the end of his life he declared: "I, who am now an old man, may safely look upon the seared and wrinkled visage of a bleareyed crone. Yet from sight of the more comely and adorned I guard my eyes like boys from fire. Alas, my wretched heart!—which cannot hold scriptural mysteries read through a hundred times, and will not lose the memory of a form seen but once." [2]

The spirit of early medieval Christianity survives most fully in its abbey churches, especially in their sculptured portals. Here the emphasis is all on Jesus as lord and judge, condemning the sins of mankind and not sharing their sufferings. He is the transcendent power of divinity, not the human figure who died on the cross. Thus, for example, the south portal of the abbey church of Moissac (built about 1130) shows Christ as a solemn and awe-inspiring figure, crowned and long-bearded and larger than life, altogether dwarfing the eighty-four elders who surround him, as described in the Book of Revelation. It became customary to portray the last judgment on the tympanum of the west door, with Christ sitting aloft and sternly enforcing the irrevocable decisions, while mankind is represented by a multitude of tiny figures divided into the saved and damned.

As society became less anarchical and more deeply permeated with Christian belief, the Church gradually began to appeal to more positive emotions and its doctrines were confirmed in the experience of religious believers instead of being set forth as dogmas which one must obey but should not attempt to

---

[1] Quoted in G. G. Coulton: *Five Centuries of Religion,* I, 327, 443.
[2] Quoted in Will Durant: *The Age of Faith* (New York, 1950), p. 787.

understand. Fear of hell was replaced, at least for the more pious of the clergy, by the hope of spiritual fulfillment, in both this world and the next. Religion ceased to be legalistic and became mystical.

Man's spiritual history, unlike the history of his political and economic development and even that of his cultural achievement, has been largely a history of remarkable individuals who have reaffirmed religious doctrines on a basis of personal experience and transmitted them directly to their disciples through personal contact. The doctrines preached by such men may often appear unoriginal and even trite. Their influence is due to a personal force derived from a sense of total integrity. Having achieved an inner harmony and certainty in their personal experience, they speak with a compelling authority that inspires confidence in their disciples; and their ways of living are in accord with their beliefs. Medieval Christianity produced a number of such characters, who formed a sharp contrast with the type of human being glorified by feudalism. The two religious leaders who best exemplified this kind of spiritual leadership were Bernard of Clairvaux and Francis of Assisi.

Bernard of Clairvaux was the first great medieval exponent of a mysticism that was practical as well as transcendental. Solely through his strength of personality, and without holding any official position except that of abbot of his monastery, he exercised a spiritual supremacy throughout western Europe to which history has no parallels. Bernard's own experience was in accord with the classic mystical pattern, but he interpreted it as justification of the extreme asceticism of Christianity in its monastic phase.

Born in 1091 of a French noble family, Bernard became a monk in the abbey of Citeaux at the age of twenty-two, bringing with him twenty-nine relatives and friends who exemplified his powers of persuasion. Two years later he was sent out with twelve companions to establish a new monastery, and the group decided to settle in a deep, gloomy valley in the Burgundian hills, uninhabited and known as the valley of wormwood. Here, practicing

154

most extreme austerities and supporting themselves on nuts and soup made of beech leaves, they began to build the abbey of Clairvaux. This remained Bernard's home for the rest of his life. For thirty-eight years—except when he was employed on clerical business elsewhere—he lived in a single cramped cell, with a bed of straw and no seat except a cut in the wall; and during his numerous travels in the service of the Church his constant wish was to return to Clairvaux "that my eyes may be closed by the hands of my children, and that my body may be laid at Clairvaux side by side with the bodies of the poor." [3] Meanwhile his spiritual force had become widely known, and during the last two decades of his life his help and advice were being sought all over western Europe. He seems to have spent a third of his time away from Clairvaux. He made and unmade popes and dictated the policies of kings, and the common people flocked around him whenever he appeared in public because of the miracles of healing which his mere presence brought about.

In his overt attitudes Bernard appears as a complete reactionary, opposed to all the creative and liberalizing movements in medieval culture. Convinced of the total sinfulness of the natural man, he was an extreme ascetic. His early austerities, in fact, ruined his health, so that through his later life he had difficulty in holding food and was frequently close to complete collapse. Sensitive to the beauty of nature, he preferred to cover his eyes while passing the lakes of Switzerland lest he should be distracted from religious contemplation. He vehemently opposed any departure from apostolic simplicity, either in ways of living or in worship. "Do soft and warm tunics, expensive cloths, large sleeves, an ample hood, a thick, soft covering and fine linen make a saint?" he asked a young relative who had deserted Clairvaux for the easier life of Cluny. "These are the comforts of the sick, not the weapons of the army. Wine and fine flavor and fat things fight for the body, not for the soul. Broiled meats fatten the flesh, not the

---

[3] Coulton: op. cit., I, 138.

spirit. . . . Cabbage, beans, and coarse bread are unappetizing to an idle person, but are delicacies to the laborer, for idleness produces distaste, but exercise, hunger. . . . Watchings, fastings, and manual labor are tiring, certainly, but compared with eternal burnings, are mere trifles; and solitude is far easier to bear than outer darkness. Nor is silence a trial when one considers the punishment meted throughout eternity to him who used vain words or dealt in lies. A couch of boards is as nothing when compared with weeping and gnashing of teeth; and he who keeps the night watch conscientiously knows not if his bed be hard or soft." [4]

Basing his religious beliefs on the direct personal experience of sin and grace, Bernard was deeply suspicious of any trust in human reason and was therefore hostile to any attempt to rationalize theology. He was the enemy not only of Abelard but also of the whole new trend toward scholastic philosophy. "The human intelligence" he complained, "usurps all for itself, leaving nothing to faith; it wishes to go too high in researches that are beyond its strength; what is well closed and sealed, it does not open but breaks; what it does not find easy of access it thinks to be nothing and disdains to believe." But this hostility to reason was not mere obscurantism; it was derived from a conviction that the truth could be grasped only by living it, not by processes of logic. Bernard's attitude can fairly be described as existentialist. "What do the holy apostles teach us?" he asked. "Not to read Plato or to turn and re-turn the subtleties of Aristotle, not to be always learning and never reaching the knowledge of truth. They have taught me to live. Do you think that to know how to live is a small thing? It is great, and even the greatest." [5]

He was similarly opposed to the other major cultural achievement of twelfth-century Christianity, the evolution of Gothic art and architecture. Churches, he insisted, at least those built for the

---

[4] Quoted in Davison: *Bernard of Clairvaux,* p. 64.
[5] Quoted in Emile Brehier: *The Philosophy of the Middle Ages,* pp. 164, 165.

monastic orders, should be plain and unadorned, decoration being a distraction from true religious worship and a misuse of money which should be given to the poor. He bitterly denounced the elaborate ornamentation of the church at Cluny and the beginnings of the Gothic style, as exemplified in the abbey of St. Denis. "I will not speak of the immense height of their churches, nor their immoderate length, nor superfluous breadth. Is not this avarice rather than piety? By the sight of wonderful and costly vanities men are prompted to give rather than to pray. . . . If we cannot spare sacred figures, can we not spare at least beautiful colors? Is the object of such things to promote penitence of the contrite or the admiration of the beholder? . . . They show, indeed, far more admiration of what is beautiful than veneration for what is sacred. . . . On the walls of the cloisters where the brethren read, what place have these absurd monsters, these odd and beautiful deformities, so striking and varied that the brethren are attracted to gaze at them rather than read their books. The statues of stone are splendidly adorned but the poor are left naked and bare." [6]

Nor did Bernard's mystical conception of religion prevent him from supporting the most barbaric of medieval religious enterprises. God could be worshipped not only by prayer and mystical ecstasy but also by slaughtering infidels. Bernard's last major activity was to impel the French king and the German emperor to embark in 1149 on the Second Crusade; in fact, there was even some discussion of Bernard himself leading the movement, though it should be added that he had enough humanity to denounce the massacres of the Jews that had resulted from the crusading hysteria. The rapid and total failure of the crusade seems to have left Bernard completely stunned and perplexed, almost to the point of questioning the ways of God, though he continued to assert that the cause of the catastrophe must somehow have been human sin.

---

[6] Davison: op. cit., p. 65.

Yet in spite of all Bernard's narrowness and intolerance, on a deeper level he was on the side of life and growth. He made, perhaps, a more important contribution to the growth of Western culture than any of the philosophers and artists whose work he so distrusted. For he spoke and wrote of religion not as a system of dogmas but as a personal emotion. Its essence was not obedience but love. This shift from external authority to subjective experience was potentially more revolutionary than all the intellectual theorizing of Abelard and the philosophers.

The core of Bernard's religion was his sense of mystic unity with God. In the mystic ecstasy he felt that his soul was swallowed up in divinity, like a drop of water lost in wine, an incandescent coal absorbed into a fire, or air becoming transparent when the sun's rays passed through it. But he was able to interpret this experience as a validation of Christian dogma. The soul was at first separated from God, on account of original sin. It could achieve salvation only by learning to love God. Man "must love with all his being the One to whom he knows he owes everything." [7] And in the love of God he regained the freedom and the integrity which had been lost by the sin of Adam, thus realizing his true nature. Yet the "deification" of the soul could never be complete; the human substance would remain, though in a new form and glory and power.[8] This mystic process was possible only because man, in spite of sin, retained a natural desire for God and for the recovery of his own true likeness to the divine image. "While still confounded by your ugliness," declared Bernard to his auditors, "do not forget your beauty." [9] It was the intensity with which Bernard felt the truth of Christian dogma in his own inner life that gave him his extraordinary personal influence.

One may deplore Bernard's antagonism to human reason, his

---

[7] Quoted in Paul Vignaux: *Philosophy in the Middle Ages*, p. 61.
[8] Maurice de Wulf: *History of Medieval Philosophy*, I, 251.
[9] Quoted in Vignaux: op. cit., p. 63.

contempt for art and science, his belief that the God whom he knew as love was at the same time a God who wished his worshippers to slaughter Mohammedans; but it is impossible to read his letters and sermons without coming to recognize his greatness. The guiding principle of his life was actually love, a love for God's creatures as well as for God himself. One feels his deep concern and his tenderness and charity for the monks under his charge, for the peasants and shepherds of his Burgundian homeland, and indeed for every human being he encountered, even for men like Abelard whom he felt to be grievously in error. One can even understand why Clairvaux, in spite of all its ascetic severity, was actually a place of happiness, so that its inmates were always reluctant to leave it and glad to return. And what is most important is that Bernard's love was expressed in personal terms, not by the repetition of established formulas, in a symbolism that was often vividly erotic (as in his sermons on the Song of Songs). It was himself that Bernard was expressing, with a frankly autobiographical impetus which seems almost egotistical. Latin, as used by Bernard, was again a living language in which the most personal emotions could be conveyed with a force and a sense of sincerity which nobody else had displayed since St. Augustine had written his *Confessions* more than seven hundred years earlier. In internalizing Christian doctrine and making it a vital experience rather than a series of dogmas, Bernard performed an essential service to the development of the West, indirectly even to tendencies that ran counter to all his own ideals and beliefs.

In spite of Bernard's emphasis on the peril of eternal damnation, the main tendency of his sermons and letters was to make Christianity a religion of love rather than of fear. This was in accord with the spirit of the twelfth century, as illustrated in its art. Gothic painting and sculpture moved away from the representation of transcendent powers and values which had characterized Romanesque; artists found an increasing beauty in natural objects, and their depiction of human figures became an idealization of reality. Christ was more often a deity who had become incarnate in order to share human suffering, less often the stern judge of the last day. Prophets and saints ceased to be elongated and ascetic, and acquired more natural proportions. Gothic sculptors, moreover, liked to portray leaves and flowers that were closely copied from nature, while their animal carvings were often exuberantly fanciful. This whole artistic development showed an increasing confidence and an increasing love for natural objects.

The religion of the Church was still far removed from the religion of the people, which was chiefly concerned with miracles of healing and protection performed by saints who had taken the places of the deities of paganism. But the gap was being bridged. This was the special function of the cult of the Virgin Mary, which perhaps reached its peak during the twelfth century. Mary had become an object of worship during the late Roman period, and had always been particularly honored in the Byzantine Empire. But it was not until the twelfth century that she was elevated to a position which made her almost equal to the persons of the Trinity. St. Bernard was one of her most ardent admirers, though he disappointed more extreme devotees by refusing to accept the new doctrine of her immaculate conception. The growth of Mariolatry had obvious parallels with the exaltation of womanhood by the troubadours, but one cannot say how far it may have been deliberately promoted by the Church in order to counteract the idealization of earthly and sexual love and how far it was simply an expression of the same psychic tendencies. The numerous stories which were told about Mary on the popular level suggested that an element of feminine irrationality had been added to the government of the cosmos. She was the universal mother whose intercession could save sinners from punishments which, by masculine standards, they richly deserved. Some of the acts of forgiveness that were attributed to Mary were in complete negation to accepted moral values. A nun left her convent and lived for fifteen years as a prostitute; finally repenting and creeping back to the convent, she found that the Virgin had assumed her form, so that her absence had remained unnoticed. A woman whose husband had taken a mistress complained to the Virgin, but received the reply: "I cannot avenge you on the woman, because she bows before me a hundred times a day and says Ave." The mistress, however, heard what had happened and promised to renounce her love.

Such stories, which verged on blasphemy, indicated an increasing boldness on the part of popular storytellers, a growing protest against the masculine severity of Christian ethics. But Mary also occupied a more central position in twelfth-century religious attitudes. The masculine image of the deity which Christianity had inherited from Judaism evoked fear rather than love. Even Jesus was viewed as the judge of the last day as well as the sufferer on the cross who had given his life for the salvation of human beings. The mystic might experience God as love, but his feelings were incommunicable and restricted to a few ascetics. But by adding a feminine element to the Trinity, medieval Christianity created a figure for whom it was easy to feel positive love. In theory Mary remained human, though her immaculate conception and her assumption into heaven without knowing death set her apart from all other women. To some degree she inherited the functions of the great goddess, both spouse and mother of the dying and reviving vegetation deity, who had been the chief object of worship of peasant communities for many thousands of years. But essentially she was a new creation, and for many of her worshippers she seemed almost a member of the Trinity, replacing the shadowy and unrealizable figure of the Holy Ghost. For twelfth-century Christians she was the queen of heaven, fastidious in her tastes as a queen should be, a lover of beauty and courtesy and decorum, not lacking in a sense of humor, and glad to give her protection to those who sought her patronage. Many of the great Gothic cathedrals were built in honor of Mary, and men would not have toiled so industriously to give beauty to every part if they had not believed themselves to be erecting monuments for the pleasure of a queen.

Mariolatry provided means by which normal and universal human emotions could be sanctified and sublimated into the service of the Church. But as long as monasticism was regarded as the highest form of Christian life, important aspects of the Christian attitude were necessarily forgotten. Monasticism had appeared at a relatively late date in the development of Christianity, being almost unknown before the fourth century. The original Christianity of the gospels had been imbued with a spirit of love for all mankind and of human brotherhood which could be fully expressed and practiced only by men and women who continued to live in society. This spirit was rediscovered and reasserted early in the thirteenth century by Francis of Assisi, who may be regarded as completing the process by which medieval man rediscovered the emotional meaning of Christianity.

It has often been said that of all the Christian saints, Francis came closest to modeling his life on that of Jesus. It is true that in the imitation of his master, Francis achieved through the intensity of his desire a kind of incandescence which has few, if any, parallels. Unlike those saints who spent their lives in cloisters or in study or administration, he lived the same kind of life as Jesus, wandering without any settled home and preaching wherever he found a responsive audience. He resembled Jesus also in the kind of influence he exerted. He attracted men and women primarily because of his distinctive qualities of personality, manifest not so much in words as in symbolic gestures. He had a style which, like that of Jesus, was unmistakable and inimitable. This personal touch, rather than any doctrine or moral exhortation, was what his disciples chiefly liked to remember.

Between Jesus and Francis, however, there were differences of emphasis, attributable partly to the differences in their social environment. Jesus belonged to a nation that had suffered foreign conquest and was looking forward to messianic redemption from oppression. The main theme of his preaching was that the day of redemption was indeed approaching but that its realization demanded brotherly love and mutual forgiveness rather than nationalistic violence. Francis was born into the rapidly expanding bourgeois society of the northern and central Italian cities. Concerned largely with material gains, it was in danger of being wholly torn apart by conflicts between different cities and be-

tween the rich merchants and the mass of the working population. The son of a wealthy cloth merchant, Francis participated
as a young man in warfare between Assisi and its neighbor and
rival Perugia, and in intense political conflicts among his fellow
citizens. It is therefore understandable that the central concern of
Francis's mission was the question of property. He had, in fact,
remarkably little to say about anything else.

From the symbolic action which marked the real beginning
of his mission, his stripping himself of all his clothes and giving
them back to his father, down to his deathbed exhortations to his
disciples, the dangers of owning property were his main theme.
True Christian holiness was impossible without poverty. And by
poverty Francis did not mean owning a little; associated with the
struggle for existence of a peasant or a laborer, the word has
acquired somewhat sordid and squalid connotations. He meant
owning nothing, not from necessity but by a deliberate choice
which would produce new positive values. Unlike the monks, he
and his followers were to live wandering lives, preaching to
whoever would listen to them, supporting themselves, where possible, by manual labor and, if necessary, by begging, and literally
taking no thought for the morrow. Such possessions as they did
acquire, such as clothing and buildings, they must never regard
as their own but must always be willing to share with others.
Numerous anecdotes illustrate how literally and completely
Francis applied this belief. On one occasion, for example, when
he was asked by an old woman for alms and could find nothing
else to give her, he parted with the only copy of the New Testament available to the brotherhood, being convinced that making
a gift of it was more pleasing to God than reading it. Poverty was
allegorized as a beautiful lady, to be celebrated with praises like
those the troubadours gave to their mistresses (Francis had always loved the troubadour poetry, and did not forget it after he
had turned from worldly glory to the service of God). This
reverence for poverty is most charmingly illustrated in an allegory written by an anonymous later Franciscan. The lady Poverty is invited by some of the brethren to share their scanty and

unappetizing food, after which she sleeps on the bare ground with a stone for a pillow. The next morning she asks the brothers to show her their monastery, upon which they lead her up a hill and show her the world lying at her feet, saying to her, "This is our monastery, lady."

Francis did not explain his reasons for pursuing poverty as a positive ideal; he acted in direct response to intuition, not on the basis of doctrinal analysis. Obviously he was not concerned with economic justice, the aim of which would be not the abolition of property but its redistribution, nor did he idealize the lives of the poor. He saw freedom from ownership as necessary for salvation, and apparently several different motives were involved, though Francis himself made no attempt to distinguish them. According to his own statements he welcomed deprivation and suffering as a means of ascetic self-discipline and of identifying himself with Christ. Toward the end of his life he seems to have felt that he had carried asceticism to excess, unduly depriving himself of physical strength. "Rejoice, brother body," he is said to have declared, "and forgive me, for behold now I gladly fulfill thy desires, and gladly hasten to attend to thy complaints." [1] But he remained always on guard against temptations to unchastity, and declared that he knew only two women by sight, though unlike most other Christian saints he showed reverence and respect for women in general—were they not all potential brides of Christ? His relations with St. Clare and with his Roman friend the Lady Jacqueline were full of tenderness.

Francis's asceticism, however, had a new positive quality which differentiated it from that of earlier medieval saints. He did not spend his life bemoaning his sins and punishing his body because of the wickedness of carnal desire. His special contribution to the Christian attitude was to give asceticism a new positive quality. He welcomed suffering and deprivation not only because he felt that he deserved them but because they were a

---

[1] Quoted in Thomas of Celano: *Life of St. Francis,* II, 210.

means to higher spiritual qualities, and hence should be received with joy. And while he recognized that the disciplining of the lower self made possible a mystical union with God, the most characteristic emphasis of his preaching was on the sense of freedom to be derived from the acceptance of the severest forms of suffering. Poverty was essential because it meant getting rid of all the anxieties resulting from material insecurity and competitiveness. Once one had repudiated all worldly desires and ambitions and had learned to accept the worst sufferings as a valuable means of self-discipline, one had achieved a spiritual independence and inner strength which nothing could disturb. A well-known story tells of Francis explaining to a disciple that the most joyous thing that could happen to anybody was to suffer the worst possible hardships. But this delight in suffering was as far removed from the morbid masochism of so many earlier saints as it was from the emotional apathy recommended by classical philosophies. It was a new spiritual discovery, and hence was constantly reaffirmed by Francis, with an emphasis on its paradoxical qualities.

The sense of freedom derived from the ability to accept suffering with joy could never appeal to more than a few spiritually sensitive individuals, but it was associated with a new attitude toward nature, which was perhaps the most important of the spiritual revolutions explicit in Francis's teaching. For nearly a thousand years most Christian saints, while recognizing that nature was originally God's creation, had regarded it as too corrupted by human sinfulness and too full of carnal temptations to be worthy of human enjoyment. The sense of natural beauty which had been expressed in some of the sayings of Jesus and by some early theologians (Tertullian, for example) had been almost lost. But for Francis all natural things were full of joy and wonder. Many of the stories told about him illustrate his reverence for nature, often in whimsical and fantastic ways. Everybody knows that he preached to the birds, converted the wolf of Gubbio who had been raiding hen roosts, and was sometimes so disturbed by the sight of animals led to slaughter that he would beg or buy them from their owners and set them free. Some of the symbolic gestures with which he expressed his reverence for natural objects verge on a kind of holy simpletonry. He would touch water tenderly, in reverence for its cleansing powers, and was even so respectful of "brother fire" that he refused to extinguish a flame that was consuming his gown. This side of his teaching produced the *Canticle of the Sun,* though this was not written down until after his death and we probably have only a faint approximation of the original composition. The new attitude to nature led quickly to new developments in philosophy and the arts, though these were utterly alien to the concerns of Francis himself. As many stories and sayings indicate, Francis was deeply suspicious of intellectuality. For him, religion was a matter of direct spiritual experience and direct contact between human beings, not of book learning, even the learning of the Bible.

During Francis's lifetime the revolutionary implications of his mission were more apparent in ecclesiastical practice than in intellectual development. His doctrine of holy poverty was a direct rebuke to churchmen who enjoyed power and prestige and lived in luxury. The corruptions of the Church had already provoked a long series of protests, some of which, especially in the cities of northern Italy, were voiced by heretical sects appealing primarily to the working class. Francis began his mission during the pontificate of Innocent III, when the western Church reached the peak of its strength and its claims to universal domination had not yet evoked successful opposition. Francis was well aware of the wide discrepancies between the ideals of the gospel and the practices of the clergy, and his remarks about the behavior of bishops were often decidedly sardonic. A story which carries the authentic Franciscan flavor and quality represents him as rebuking a young novice who wanted to own a Psalter. "My son," declared Francis, "once you have got the Psalter, then you will want a Breviary; when you have got a Breviary, you will want to sit in the high seat like a great prelate and say to thy brothers, 'Bring me my Breviary.' "

Francis, however, always insisted on the duty of submitting to ecclesiastical authority and on the reverence due the clergy who performed the daily miracle of the Eucharist. He preached obedience not because the authorities to whom the obedience was due were worthy of it but because it was conducive to humility and the abnegation of the self. If he was denied permission to do something that he felt would be pleasing to God, he usually continued asking for it until the prohibition was revoked, but he never openly violated clerical commands. Yet his behavior was a constant embarrassment to the hierarchy of the Church, and it was only through the exercise of considerable skill and tact on the part of a series of popes and cardinals that Franciscanism was successfully incorporated into the Church instead of being forced into open rebellion. In this conflict of ideals one should not cast all the blame on the authorities, though the final victory was regarded by Francis's most loyal disciples as catastrophic. Francis's advocacy of total poverty was too extreme to remain a permanent program, once Francis's own leadership and the enthusiasm he had initially aroused had disappeared. Francis, moreover, had no talents for organization, as he himself recognized.

Francis obtained papal sanction for his order in 1210, three years after the beginning of his mission. The Pope suggested that the rules of the order were too strict to be permanently effective, but did not insist on immediate modification. During the following decade several thousand converts joined the order, and missions to preach the gospel of holy poverty were dispatched to most of the countries of western Europe. Francis himself worked mainly in Italy, though he visited the camp of the crusaders at Damietta in Egypt in the hope of converting the Mohammedan leaders by peaceful methods. But as the order grew, some relaxation of the initial doctrine of total poverty became necessary if it was to continue working effectively. It had to be permitted to acquire property, especially in the form of buildings, and to cultivate secular learning. In 1220, Francis recognized that the order had grown beyond his capacity for leadership and resigned from his position as minister-general, Brother Elias being elected to succeed him. His subsequent attempts to preserve the purity of the original rule were unsuccessful. His last years, until his death in 1226, at the age of forty-four, were devoted mainly to solitary prayer and contemplation; the most famous experience of this period was his reception of the stigmata while staying in a lonely hut near the summit of Mount Verna. His corpse became the possession of the people of Assisi, who had to protect it from capture by the Perugians, and was housed a few years later in the magnificent Gothic church that was built under the direction of Brother Elias. Aesthetically, this was one of the finest monuments of medieval Italian Christendom, but Francis himself would have regarded such an edifice as contrary to the whole gospel of poverty that he had given his life to preach.

Within a generation of Francis's death the order had largely forgotten its original ideals. It acquired monastery buildings and churches all over western Europe, and some of its members were making important contributions to science and philosophy, with no apparent sense that they were violating their master's principles. St. Bonaventura, who served from 1257 to 1274 as minister-general of the order and wrote what may be described as Francis's official biography, was also one of the greatest of medieval philosophers. The characteristic qualities of Franciscan learning were a trust in nature and a willingness to be guided by experience, which distinguished it from the more dogmatic and intellectualized approach of the rival Dominican order, formed in 1215 with the conversion of heretics as its main purpose. This made the Franciscans the most progressive of medieval philosophers and enabled them to become pioneers in the growth of the natural sciences. Thus Francis's attitude to life continued to influence his followers, though in ways Francis himself would have disapproved. A similar contribution was made by Franciscanism to the development of art. Giotto, the most important early figure in the revolt against Byzantine abstractionism and the development of three-dimensional realism, was strongly attracted to the memory of St. Francis, as he showed in the numerous murals depicting episodes in his life.

Meanwhile a number of brethren remained faithful to the original austerity of the order. They continued to preach in the villages of Italy, especially in the hill country of the March of Ancona, where social conditions were more primitive than in the cities. Brother Elias, who remained minister-general until 1239, was regarded as the Judas who had betrayed his master's teaching, though the trust and affection Francis had shown him suggest that he was condemned unfairly. These so-called Spiritual Franciscans preserved a number of biographical writings which conveyed the flavor of Francis's personality much more vividly than the official life by Bonaventura. They were strongly influenced by the apocalyptic writings of the Abbot Joachim of Flora, a twelfth-century Calabrian mystic who had predicted the advent of a new era in the near future, probably in the year 1260. Restating a utopian fantasy which had originated with the prophet Jeremiah and had been reaffirmed in the Dark Ages by John Scotus Erigena, Joachim looked forward to an Age of the Holy Spirit when all men would be guided by divine inspiration and ecclesiastical and political institutions would become unnecessary. Under such influences the Spiritual Franciscans became increasingly hostile to the organized Church, and were finally condemned as heretics. Early in the fourteenth century more than two hundred of them, having been examined by the Inquisition, were burned at the stake. Francis would not have approved of their disobedience to the clerical authorities; but in their insistence on total poverty and their closeness to the poor, they undoubtedly were closer to the original teachings of Francis than were the members of the official order which bore his name.

With Francis the full meaning of the early Christian tradition had been recaptured and integrated into the organization of the Church. The later decades of the thirteenth century were a period of consolidation, in which the greater scholastics sought to organize and synthesize the different elements in the Christian view of life. The fourteenth and following centuries were to see the breakdown of the synthesis and a growth of conflict between its component parts, while individuals turned either to skepticism or to a private mysticism.

8

Medieval Thought

In his formal thinking, as in his religious beliefs, medieval man began with a system of dogmas inherited from the classical decadence which had virtually no relationship to reality. Repeating formulas sanctioned by the authority of the Church, he gave himself the illusion of understanding the world in which he found himself and hence acquired the confidence and courage needed to cope with practical problems. But his thinking gave him no useful insight into such problems, no guidance in learning to handle them. Dogma had no vital relationship with experience, and did not explain either the material world or the nature and motivations of man. If we are to judge medieval thinking by its recorded manifestations, medieval man was incapable of looking directly at real objects and describing what he saw. Every concrete object was considered only as an example of some spiritual generalization. The process of linking formal thought with the concrete world of human action was even slower than the corresponding process in religious experience.

What was believed to be ultimately real was Christian dogma, and visible objects acquired reality only insofar as they reflected and expressed these spiritual truths. Medieval thinkers and artists were generally too intent on the search for spiritual meanings to form any clear conceptions of the spatial and temporal universe, so that their creations often had a curiously dreamlike quality. They did not locate persons and objects in any kind of realistic space and time. Allegorical significance was the main organizing principle, objects being juxtaposed without regard for realistic spatial and chronological possibilities. The two most important medieval works of literature, *The Romance of the Rose* and *The Divine Comedy,* were avowedly allegorical; but even in works that had no such intent, like the *chansons* and the Arthurian romances, there was no realistic presentation of space or time. Even in architecture, the one art form that has to take account of spatial realities, the whole drive and impetus of medieval builders was to present an appearance of transcending these realities by erecting structures that soared into the heavens, released from terrestrial limitations. Not until the fourteenth and fifteenth centuries did thinkers, writers, and artists begin to consider space and time realistically, and this was the beginning of a whole cultural revolution.

How could a society whose formal thinking was so infused with fantasy and allegory learn to cope successfully with practical problems? How could beliefs so far removed from concrete actualities exert any practical influence? If one relies only on the surviving writings and art objects for knowledge of medieval life, one has the impression of a society wholly unconcerned with economic and technical progress. Yet somehow the warriors of the *chansons de geste* were equipped with sharp swords and coats of mail, though the *chansons* nowhere make mention of any skilled craftsmen. Cathedral towers were planted so firmly (though not often at the first attempt) that they have survived for nearly a thousand years. And in spite of the vagueness of all geographical references in medieval literature, the crusaders were able to find their way to Palestine. In actuality, as we have seen, the early Middle Ages made important advances in agricultural techniques and in various forms of craftsmanship. But none of its practical achievements was recognized in the formal thinking of the period or given any stimulus or guidance by it, nor was the importance of those achievements recognized in medieval literature or art.

There was a similar lack of relationship between the theology and philosophy of the early Middle Ages and its institutional and moral development. The basic concept of the feudal system, by which the warrior class came to accept certain rudimentary notions of law and order and self-control, was a great constructive achievement, the more so in that it was solidly based on actual social conditions. But feudalism developed by a kind of spontaneous growth, unaided by formal political theory. Theorists continued to affirm the continued existence of the Roman Empire as the only possible basis of political and social order and concerned themselves with the rights and obligations of the emperors and their subjects and the division of authority between the empire and the Church. There was little or no discussion of the concrete realities of feudalism in medieval thought. Thus in the field of politics, as in that of technology, theory and practice were divorced from each other. Theory restated and expounded concepts derived from the classical decadence, while practice exhibited the slow emergence of a new society from barbarian beginnings. Both the movement backward from decadence and the movement forward from barbarism had to proceed for several generations before they could effectively interact upon each other. Not until the warrior ruling class had learned certain elementary forms of self-control and had begun to find values in other things beside slaughter and sensuality and not until the monk or hermit endeavoring to live in total repudiation of terrestrial existence had given place to the active Christian scholar or preacher as the highest exemplar of religious faith and practice did the culture of the new Western society begin to acquire coherence, congruity, and practical efficacy. But until the later Middle Ages, Western man continued to live on two different planes of thought and action, and his most significant concrete achievements had little relationship to his general view of life.

Most of the direct sources of early Western thought date from the fifth and sixth centuries. The most important was, of course, Christian dogma as expressed in the creeds of the Church and expounded by the early Fathers, especially St. Augustine. Medieval thinkers also inherited fragments of classical learning transmitted by Boethius and other late Roman writers, including treatises on grammar, rhetoric, and other literary studies, and some elementary information—or misinformation, not very helpful—about mathematics and science. Of the earlier classical writers, the more important Roman poets were available, and a few fragments of the works of Plato and Aristotle. Much Platonic doctrine was inherited indirectly through the works of St. Augustine. It was important that these elements of the classical heritage had never been fully integrated into Christian learning and represented, however inadequately, a very different tradition, thus stimulating medieval thinkers to search for syntheses. But there was little disposition to condemn any classical author, however overtly pagan or sensual, as an enemy of Christianity. The whole classical heritage was endowed with authority, and little distinction was made between pagan and Christian traditions.

A more significantly discordant element in the inheritance was the mystical thought of Neo-Platonism, as restated by the unknown sixth-century Greek who assumed the name of Dionysius the Areopagite. The writings of Dionysius became known in the West in the ninth century through the translations of John Scotus Erigena, and acquired almost scriptural authority through the identification of the author both with the convert of St. Paul mentioned in the Acts of the Apostles and with the early Christian martyr, generally known as St. Denis, who was alleged to have walked after decapitation and who became the patron saint of France. Superficially Christianized by the pseudo-Dionysius, Neo-Platonic mysticism was actually an alien element in Christian thought. Defining Christian love as *eros* rather than as *agape,* it found the essence of the Christian experience not in the practice of benevolence but in the satisfaction of man's inner desire. This had its ultimate fulfillment in the mystical union of the soul with God, in sharp contrast with the Christian doctrine that man had been created by God as a separate being and must always retain his individuality. In other respects most medieval mysticism conformed with the Neo-Platonic patterns, leading to an emphasis on the private salvation of the individual soul and a devaluation of the altruistic elements in the original gospel ethic.

Another important element of diversification was Arabic science and philosophy, which began to percolate into western Europe by way of Spain as early as the tenth century. But it was not until the later years of the twelfth century that the Western mind became acquainted with any large body of Arabic writings. While Arabic learning was mostly based on that of Greece, it had been filtered through different intellectual traditions, Greek philosophical treatises having been translated into Syriac and thence into Arabic before being Latinized by Western translators.

Yet in spite of these conflicting intellectual tendencies, the West inherited from its classical and Christian sources certain basic concepts about which there was no fundamental disagreement and which have remained as essential premises of almost all later Western thinking. The most important contribution of the classical mind was the doctrine of natural law. Insofar as this was descriptive of the material world, it led to the growth of the sciences, though there was relatively little scientific development until the fourteenth century. Even more important was the sense of natural law as normative for human behavior and institutions. Nature supplied certain universal and immutable standards by which moral and political activities could be guided and judged. Natural law was identified with the law of God and regarded as known intuitively by the human mind. According to the usual Christian view, the laws of God, of nature, and of reason had been fully realized in the Garden of Eden before the fall. But the advent of sin made it impossible for man to follow natural law completely. On account of sin man needed authoritative government to repress wickedness, and he needed the institution of private property, in contrast with the communism which would have prevailed if he had never sinned. These post-fall institutions thus had a rather anomalous status in Christian thought. They were good insofar as they were in accord with natural law, but prior to the coming day of judgment and the millennium any complete harmony with natural law was impossible. This left a wide field open to controversy, but it was agreed that no merely human authority could be regarded as absolute and beyond question. Natural law, despite variant interpretations of its content, continued to provide sanctions for individual freedom. Tyrannical governments which violated natural law might be, and in fact should be, overthrown, although there was no universal agreement as to what constituted tyranny. But as long as the belief in some kind of natural law was preserved, there was intellectual justification for individual liberty. Men could judge by objective standards the authorities set over them instead of blindly submitting to them.

All human thought oscillates between the poles of absolute monism and absolute diversification. When reflective thinking first emerges, in the early stages of the growth of a new civilization, it usually seeks some simple and unitary explanation for the apparently chaotic phenomena by which man is confronted (this tendency was particularly prominent in the Ionian thinkers of the sixth century B.C. who founded Greek philosophy). This is followed by a growing awareness of diversity, and in the great period of a philosophical tradition there is a recognition both of oneness and of multiplicity, which are felt as ultimately harmonious. The harmony, however, is not maintained, and thought finally arrives at a conviction of total multiplicity, with no unifying explanation. This necessarily puts an end to the development of philosophy, being followed either by a reaction back to monism or by a new beginning in human thought based on the assertion of new premises. This interplay between the sense of unity and the sense of diversity parallels the general movement of society, of which it is both a reflection and—in some degree—a cause.

The monism which characterized the beginnings of Western philosophy was particularly comprehensive, since it originated in the heritage of the classical decadence rather than in the first fumbling attempts of a new society to explain the world in which it found itself. This view of life was accepted by early medieval thought as a fundamental premise, not to be subjected to doubt or criticism. As long as men thought in these terms, it was impossible not to believe in God. But it was only by a leap of faith that the abstract deity of Greek philosophy, engaged solely in the leisurely contemplation of his own perfections, was endowed with the wisdom and benevolence and the other personal qualities of the Jewish Jehovah. This affirmation of unity characterized medieval thinking about human society as well as about the universe. The actual existence of many different political units and of two churches, the Roman and the Greek, was a discrepancy which the medieval mind could never assimilate. A similar monistic tendency was evident in medieval thinking about classes and categories. Abstract generals were more real than concrete particulars. In practical terms, this meant that the human being was defined by his social rank and functions rather than by his individual qualities. A man was to be considered primarily as a nobleman, a peasant, or a cleric, and was expected to exhibit the appropriate qualities; there was little awareness of his more personal and individual traits.

The general development of the West, as of other, earlier civilizations in their early stages, was toward rationalism and individualism. This was both a social and an intellectual movement, the changes in social institutions and ways of living being closely intertwined with the evolution of new ways of thinking. Medieval philosophy began with the assertion of religious dogmas, reason being employed simply for the exposition of truths already known by faith. In the great period of scholasticism, reason was regarded as providing an independent access to truth, but faith and reason were believed to be in harmony with each other. Finally, the sense of harmony was lost, and reason and faith appeared to be in conflict, which brought to an end the whole scholastic attempt to rationalize Christian belief. There was little further philosophical development until a new beginning with new premises was made by Descartes in the seventeenth century.

The trend toward individualism followed a similar course. In early medieval thinking, the Platonic idea was more real than its concrete exemplifications; in the great age of scholasticism, both the general and the individual were regarded as equally real; and in the final stages of medieval thought, individuals alone were seen as real, the general category being a mere word invented by men for purposes of description. This marked the end of scholasticism, just as in medieval society the growth of political and economic individualism put an end to the effectiveness of medieval institutions, particularly of feudalism, and made necessary the formation of new loyalties and new concepts of law and order.

Medieval thought may be regarded as beginning in the late tenth and early eleventh centuries with the foundation of schools attached to cathedrals. It had been mainly the monasteries that had preserved learning during the Dark Ages, but monastic life was not conducive to mental originality. Monks were primarily concerned with the worship of God and with physical labor, and intellectual activity (such as reading and copying manuscripts) was engaged in chiefly for the sake of discipline rather than for intrinsic desirability. Monastic intellectual production was always scanty and usually consisted either of anthologies of extracts from the Church Fathers or of chronicles of events. But the cathedral schools, being located in cities, were in direct contact with the most vital elements of medieval life. The students who attended these schools, moreover, were interested not in becoming monks but in preparing themselves for active careers either in the ecclesiastical hierarchy or—after the growth of royal power —in the king's service, so that they had a direct incentive to learning, of a kind that is always necessary if education is to retain vitality. The more successful cathedral schools gradually developed into universities. Much the greatest of medieval institutions of learning was the University of Paris, which began as a cathedral school late in the eleventh century and acquired university organization and established itself on the Left Bank about a century later.

Despite the Viking invasions, the impetus that Charlemagne had given to learning had never been wholly lost, and there had been no relapse into the intellectual darkness of the seventh and eighth centuries. But until the twelfth century, learning continued to emphasize the classical literary tradition as represented by the study of rhetoric and of the leading Latin authors, rather than undertaking the more rigorous tasks of logical and philosophical analysis. Although this recapture of the classics was a necessary preliminary to original work, it meant that there was no movement beyond the classical decadence. Education remained a mere adornment to human life rather than a search for new truths.

These strictures are not wholly true of Gerbert, the most extraordinary figure of the tenth century. The son of a French peasant, he had a monastic education, spent three years studying Arabic learning in Spain, taught in Rheims and Paris, playing a leading role in the establishment of the Capetian dynasty in France, became the chief adviser of the Emperor Otto III, served as Abbot of Bobbio and as Archbishop first of Rheims and then of Ravenna, and ended his life as Pope Sylvester II. Because of his scientific knowledge he was popularly regarded as a magician. Such a figure eludes all conventional categorizations and refutes all traditional conceptions of the Dark Ages. Yet in spite of Gerbert's varied interests, he gave rhetoric the main place in his educational activities, and it was through his teaching of rhetoric that he mainly influenced his age. "Since the ordering of morality and self-expression are both inseparable from philosophy," he declared, "in my study I have always joined the art of living well with the art of expressing myself well." [1] This emphasis on the correct use of language as the basic element in education echoed the educational attitudes of the classical decadence, which had set the knowledge of words above the knowledge of things. Gerbert's best-known pupil was Fulbert, who founded the school of Chartres in 990 and made rhetoric the central subject of study. Fulbert was remembered by several generations of students for his broad learning and warm humanity, but he made no original contribution to thought.

---

[1] Quoted in Paul Vignaux: *Philosophy in the Middle Ages,* p. 24.

The school of Chartres continued to be an important center of learning for some two centuries, representing attitudes which a later age would call humanistic rather than philosophical or narrowly religious. Like the scholars of the Carolingian Renaissance, the masters of Chartres regarded the recapture of the Latin classical tradition as the main objective of learning. Broad-minded, tolerant, and steeped in the study of the classics, the school makes an attractive contrast with those medieval universities that were periodically ravaged by theological hatreds. Its students became acquainted with a wide range of ancient authors, emphasized the study of classical Latin and classical rhetoric, and presented interpretations of the natural world which more narrow-minded Christians might have condemned as partially pagan. In philosophy they mostly remained faithful to Platonism as known through fragments of the most mystical and antiscientific of Plato's dialogues, the *Timaeus*. These attitudes were represented by a series of masters: Bernard of Chartres, Theodoric of Chartres, Clarembald of Arras, Bernard of Tours, William of Conches, and John of Salisbury.

The last of these was perhaps the most attractive figure of the twelfth century. Educated in France, he returned to his native England for nearly thirty years of administrative activity in the English church, but ended his life in 1180 as Bishop of Chartres. His numerous writings, philosophical and political, show liberality, good sense, and a knowledge of Latin literature that would have done credit to a humanist of the Italian Renaissance. He wore his learning easily, as was to be expected from a man of such wide practical experience; and though he supported the beliefs of orthodox Catholicism in both theology and political theory, he was free from any taint of fanaticism. His younger contemporary, the Cistercian monk Alan of Lisle, showed a similarly tolerant spirit in the allegorical poems in which he defended Catholicism against the Albigensian heretics. Alan, who died in 1202, was the last important figure to be strongly influenced by the spirit of Chartres.

Yet in spite of the liberal qualities of Chartres, its students could make no significant new contributions to thought or culture. Neither in their allegorical poems nor in their philosophical treatises did they add to medieval man's efforts to understand himself and his intellectual heritage. Their thinking was a kind of daydreaming around accepted beliefs, lacking in both the logical rigor and the exact observation that were needed for new discoveries; and their literary works were too imitative to give expression to the new Western spirit.

Excepting the isolated Dark Age figure of John Scotus Erigena, the first original Western thinker was St. Anselm, who was born in Italy in 1033, spent many years as a monk in the Norman Abbey of Bec, and served as Archbishop of Canterbury from 1093 until his death in 1109. He stands out not only as a thinker but also as a singularly humane and saintly person, his moral sensitivity being illustrated in his protest against the First Crusade and—in an age when beating was supposed to have real therapeutic values—in his plea for the teaching of children by kindness.

Anselm was the first medieval scholar to grapple in serious terms with the relationship of religion and reason, but since he made reason definitely subordinate to faith, he cannot be regarded as a founder of scholasticism, the main purpose of which was to present reason not as subordinate to faith but as in harmony with it. Anselm presented a faith in search of reason rather than a reason moving toward faith. What one knew by faith one knew certainly and directly, not as a result of logical processes. "He who has not believed cannot understand; for he who has not believed has not experienced, and he who has not experienced cannot understand, for just as the experience of a thing surpasses the fact of hearing it spoken of, so the knowledge of one who experiences outweighs the understanding of one who only hears." [2] Thus there could be no real conflict between faith and reason, the truths of faith being known by direct experience.

In a series of philosophical meditations, with a strong ele-

---

[2] Quoted in Vignaux: op. cit., p. 50.

ment of personal confession, Anselm presented rational interpretations of the existence of God and of the atonement and other Christian dogmas. These carry conviction only if one accepts the general premises of Anselm's view of life—his belief in the spiritual unity of the universe and in its hierarchical order. By these assumptions it was, of course, impossible not to believe in God.

A similar emphasis on the direct knowledge of religious truths was displayed by several members of the Abbey of Saint-Victor in Paris, which became an important center of thought early in the twelfth century. Two of its priors, Hugh and Richard, wrote mystical treatises, while another Victorine, Adam, was one of the greatest of the medieval Latin poets. The Victorines were not hostile to secular learning; on the contrary, they believed in the values of a liberal education along lines similar to that represented by the school of Chartres. But reason was inferior to faith, which perhaps explains their preference for rhetorical studies rather than logic and philosophy. The highest experience available to man was the contemplation of God, though—unlike some other mystics—the Victorines believed in an intellectual rather than an emotional conception of mystical experience. Man had lost the faculty of direct knowledge of God through original sin, but he could regain it through the gift of divine grace manifested in faith. The Victorines traced the stages in the discovery of God, who could finally be found in the depths of the human soul. The soul was a mirror in which one could see God; and it was "by the knowledge of self that one mounts to the knowledge of God," moving by the practice of contemplation from the creature to the creator.[3] Once one had achieved the knowledge of God, one could see the entire universe as animated by a spiritual order. "The spirit was created for God's sake; the body for the spirit's sake, and the world for the body's sake, so that the spirit might be subject to God, the body to the spirit, and the world to the body. . . . All the natural arts serve divine science, and the lower

---

[3] Emile Brehier: *The Philosophy of the Middle Ages,* pp. 189, 190.

knowledge rightly ordered leads to the higher." [4] Thus all natural things were sacramental, material and external objects being infused with spiritual significance. This view of the material world was markedly more liberal and optimistic than that of most early medieval clerics. Nature, commonly depicted as wholly corrupted by sin, was regarded by the Victorines as the expression of spiritual principles. The Victorine attitude was not yet scientific; the function of the "lower knowledge" was not the understanding of the "higher knowledge." But it promoted the development of a more realistic art, for all natural objects were regarded as expressions of spiritual values.

As long as religious dogmas were considered as known to the individual believer by direct experience (in accordance with the Augustinian formula "Unless you believe, you will not understand"), reason remained subordinate to faith, and there could be no conflict between them. But medieval thinkers had inherited from their classical forerunners certain problems that appeared to be purely philosophical and could be answered only by rational inquiry. Thus there were areas of thought where reason had to function independently without the guidance of belief. Yet it soon became apparent that the solutions reached by reason had important religious implications, from which it followed that in order to demonstrate the harmony of faith and reason, further inquiry was needed, and this inquiry could use only the methods of rationalism. This situation led to the growth of scholasticism, which began in the confidence that dogma could be justified by reason and ended when the progress of thought showed this confidence to be untenable.

The first philosophical problem to attract attention was the conflict between the realists and the nominalists about the nature of universals. This was suggested by statements made by Boethius and by the fourth-century Neo-Platonist Porphyry. The more extreme forms of realism, following Plato, affirmed that

---

[4] Henry Osborn Taylor: *The Medieval Mind*, II, 91, 93.

general classes and categories—universals, in other words— really existed outside the minds of the human beings who conceived them and were, in fact, more real than the individual objects they were used to describe. This belief in the reality of abstractions was derived from the Platonic assumption that if something could be thought about, it must actually exist. For the nominalists, on the other hand, universals were merely words, and only individual things were real.

This controversy began before the end of the eleventh century; the first important nominalist was Roscelin of Compiegne, born about 1050, and the first strong defender of realism was William of Champeaux, born in 1070. For these men the problem was largely a matter of logical analysis, its underlying social implications being unrealized, and their views were supported and opposed mainly in terms of their applicability to Christian dogma. Such doctrines as the Trinity and transubstantiation, for example, could not easily be reconciled with nominalism. The intensity of the conflict suggested, however, that more practical issues were at stake, though these did not become explicit until much later. The movement of medieval thought from realism to nominalism reflected the more general movement of Western society toward individualistic and rationalistic attitudes. Realism gave support to the belief in the reality of the Church and other organic bodies and in the authority they claimed over their individual members; it also implied that the classes into which feudal society was divided were more real than their individual members. The gradual development of nominalism in the later Middle Ages reflected both the decline in ecclesiastical authority and the rise of economic and social individualism; and by breaking down the whole medieval conception of the universe as a hierarchical order, that development prepared the way for a completely new cosmology in which the basic reality was not God but matter in motion.

The first decisive step in the process of separating reason and faith was taken by Abelard, who began teaching early in the twelfth century while still in his twenties and became a lecturer in the Paris cathedral school in 1115. One may believe his protestations of orthodoxy. He was no doubt speaking with complete sincerity when he declared: "I do not wish to be a philosopher if I must resist St. Paul; I do not wish to be Aristotle if I must separate myself from Christ."[5] In interpreting non-Christian writings, he claimed the right to give them Christian meanings which their authors would have disclaimed, on the assumption that any truths they contained must be in harmony with Christian doctrine.[6] Yet it is impossible not to recognize that there were innovations in Abelard's approach to philosophy. Earlier theologians had begun with the truth of Christian dogma, known by direct experience, and had sought to find rational interpretations of it. But for Abelard there were two truths: that revealed to the Church and that discovered by reason. He assumed that they were in harmony with each other, and the main purpose of his philosophy was to demonstrate this harmony. But there can be no doubt that this separation of reason and faith, in spite of Abelard's confidence that they could be reunited, represented a potential threat to Christian belief. In recognizing the dangers of trust in the independent power of reason, St. Bernard and Abelard's other clerical opponents were showing more foresight than Abelard himself.

Abelard's contributions to philosophy were not of major importance in themselves. Their significance lay in the spirit that pervaded them. In all his writings one can detect a tendency to shift authority from divine revelation, as known to the believing Christian, to the reason of the individual, though this tendency was, of course, not carried very far and was important only because it marked the beginning of new attitudes which were developed by later thinkers. He insisted that only through the exercise of reason could one ascertain the truths of faith, demonstrating this, in *Sic et Non,* by a series of quotations from the

---

[5] Letter 17.
[6] Brehier: op. cit., p. 158.

Bible and the early Fathers apparently supporting opposite sides of religious questions (it should be added that Abelard was not the first to compile such a list, and that he borrowed much of it from Yves de Chartres). In his attitude to the nominalism-realism dispute he was clearly on the side of nominalism, though he regarded himself as seeking a middle ground according to which universals had no independent existence but inhered in individual objects and could be grasped by the mind as concepts. And in his ethical doctrines he insisted that sin consisted essentially of sinful intentions, shifting the whole emphasis from the objective act to the motivations of the actor.

All these deviations from what had previously passed as orthodox doctrine might have been accepted as tenable by Abelard's fellow philosophers, and did, of course, foreshadow the future development of Western thought. Unfortunately Abelard was the type of person who must always create enemies for himself. Fond of admiration and applause, which he earned not so much by his strictly intellectual abilities as by the eloquence of his lectures and the glamour of his personality, he was always the center of attention, and those who refused to idolize him were inevitably antagonized by him. His early career was a series of triumphs which made him the idol of the students of Paris but which were won by means of intellectual battles with competing philosophers whose intellectual deficiencies Abelard brutally exposed. His last twenty-five years, beginning in 1117 with his tragic love affair with Héloise, consisted mostly of misfortunes, which culminated in his condemnation for heresy by a Church council at Sens, in which St. Bernard was the leading figure, and in his death in the monastery of Cluny two years later, in 1142.

He survives in the memory of posterity chiefly because of his association with Héloise. The letters which they allegedly exchanged after many years of separation seem not to have been known before the thirteenth century and are of doubtful authenticity. Yet they show so much psychological insight, and are so true to what we know from other sources about the characters of the putative authors, that it is perhaps easier to accept them as genuine than to attribute them to some literary genius otherwise unknown to history. Abelard is revealed as a man of genuine piety counseling his former mistress to turn to God, but still, with his desire for applause, as a partially flawed personality. Héloise, as Professor Gilson has remarked, shows herself not only a woman but a Frenchwoman, regarding love for a man as the center of her existence and performing everything demanded of her (including immuring herself in a convent), asking only to be loved in return. Another letter, certainly authentic, gives its readers a higher opinion of the Middle Ages and of humanity in general. Nothing could surpass in tenderness and tact the letter in which Peter the Venerable, Abbot of Cluny, informed Héloise of the death of Abelard and assured her that they would be united in eternity. This remarkable letter deserves quotation at some length.

It was granted us to enjoy the presence of him—who was yours —Master Peter Abaelard, a man always to be spoken of with honour as a true servant of Christ and a philosopher. The divine dispensation placed him in Cluny for his last years, and through him enriched our monastery with treasure richer than gold. No brief writing could do justice to his holy, humble, and devoted life among us. I have not seen his equal in humility of garb and manner. When in the crowd of our brethren I forced him to take a first place, in meanness of clothing he appeared as the last of all. Often I marvelled, as the monks walked past me, to see a man so great and famous thus despise and abase himself. He was abstemious in food and drink, refusing and condemning everything beyond the bare necessities. He was assiduous in study, frequent in prayer, always silent unless compelled to answer the question of some brother or expound sacred themes before us. He partook of the sacrament as often as possible. Truly his mind, his tongue, his act, taught and exemplified religion, philosophy, and learning. So he dwelt with us, a man simple and righteous, fearing God, turning from evil, consecrating to God the latter days of his life. At last, because of his bodily infirmities, I sent him to a quiet and salubrious retreat on the banks of the Saone. There he bent over his books, as long as his strength lasted, always praying, reading, writing, or dictating. In these sacred exercises, not sleeping but watching, he was found by the heavenly Visitor; who summoned him to the eternal wedding-feast not as a foolish but as a wise virgin, bearing his lamp filled with oil—the consciousness of a holy life. When he came to pay humanity's last debt, his illness was brief. With holy devotion he made confession of the Catholic Faith, then of his sins. The brothers who were with him can testify how devoutly he received the viaticum of that last journey, and with what fervent faith he commended his body and soul to his Redeemer. Thus this master, Peter, completed his days. He who was known throughout the world by the fame of his teaching, entered the school of Him who said, "Learn of me, for I am meek and lowly of heart"; and continuing meek and lowly he passed to Him, as we may believe.

Venerable and dearest sister in the Lord, the man who was once joined to thee in the flesh, and then by the stronger chain of divine love, him in thy stead, or as another thee, the Lord holds in His bosom; and at the day of His coming, His grace will restore him to thee.[7]

The remainder of the twelfth century produced no more philosophers of the first rank and marked no advance beyond the positions assumed by Anselm and Abelard. Possibly Abelard's condemnation checked further speculation. Instead of propounding new ideas, men of learning produced surveys and summaries of accepted doctrines. Honorius of Autun compiled a widely read *Summa* of theology, while Peter Lombard composed *Sentences,* which became a kind of textbook of accepted beliefs. This philosophical truce was ended about the end of the century as a result of a new influx of Arabic influences and of hitherto unknown Greek writings, especially a number by Aristotle. Christian theologians were then impelled to recognize the need for a new major effort in the rationalization of belief, the result being the great synthetic systems of the thirteenth century.

---

[7] Quoted in Taylor: op. cit., II, 52.

9

Medieval Literature

The Latin language, which during the Carolingian period had been used only for the imitation of the classics, came to life again during the early Middle Ages. It remained for several centuries the preferred medium of self-expression for the educated part of the population. The language continued to change and was no longer frozen by the prestige of the classics and the imitation of classical models. In fact, technical innovations which spread to all branches of medieval literature were made first by the writers of medieval Latin, not (as might have been expected) by poets writing in one of the vernaculars. Some of the Latin poems of the twelfth and thirteenth centuries, written in a style wholly different from that of the classics, remain among the finest masterpieces of Latin literature. It was not until the humanist movement of the early Renaissance, with its reverence for classical Latin and its repudiation of the linguistic innovations of the Middle Ages, that Latin became again a dead language, this time remaining so.

The most significant line of development in early medieval poetry was the gradual growth of new verse techniques based on rhyme and accent in place of the classical counting of long and short syllables. It is a curious fact, difficult to account for, that this change in verse techniques parallels and typifies the whole transition from classical to Western culture. Apparently the new Western sensibility could find poetic self-expression only in the new forms. Although the beginnings of the new poetry are already to be found in the fourth century, or even earlier, they did not become fully established until six or seven hundred years later.

Rhyme and accent were used in a very rudimentary form in some early Christian hymns, and it is probable that they were derived from the marching songs of Roman soldiers and other forms of popular verse from earlier periods. Thus the new techniques originated among the lower classes, not among the educated groups, and derived much of their quality from the fact that they were intended to be sung rather than recited. All early medieval poetry was, in fact, accompanied by music, which was regarded as equal in importance to the words. But throughout the whole Dark Age the new kind of poetry developed very slowly, apparently with little recognition of its importance. Dark Age poets who took themselves seriously, like those at Charlemagne's court, invariably reverted to quantitative verse, in addition to borrowing elaborate figures of speech and conventional allusions to pagan gods. As we have seen, the first complete and deliberate employment of rhyme is to be found in verses written by an Irish monk in the seventh century. In this field, as in others, the earliest expressions of the new forms of creativity are to be found in the British Isles, where the classical heritage was less dominant and less inhibiting than on the continent.

Learned poets, such as those associated with the school of Chartres, continued to imitate the classics through the Middle Ages; but from the eleventh century on the new kinds of Latin poetry were being written with an astonishing freshness and vigor both by hymn-writers and by the anonymous authors of student songs. Victorine monks, especially Adam, produced notable religious poetry, but the greatest of medieval hymns were products of the Franciscan tradition in Italy in the thirteenth century. Thomas of Celano wrote the Dies Irae, in which rhyme and accent are used with incomparable effect like a series of hammer blows to express the horrors of the day of judgment, while the tender rendition of the sorrows of the Virgin Mary, the Stabat

Mater, was the work of the eccentric Jacopone da Todi, who was driven almost crazy by the death of his wife, abandoned a promising legal career to roam the Umbrian roads crying out his sins and sorrows, and eventually joined the Franciscans, though he was often on the verge of heresy in his denunciations of the sins of the regular clergy.

A very different aspect of medieval life was represented by the student songs, often known as Goliardic from a mythical Rabelaisian figure known as Golias who was supposed to have composed them. Several manuscript collections have survived, and some of them seem to have been in circulation as early as the tenth century. These are products of a kind of psychic underground which celebrated natural desires and pleasures as vigorously as the official theology condemned them. Written and sung by university students, most of whom probably ended their lives as pillars of the clerical hierarchy, they exemplified the duality that characterized all aspects of early medieval culture. The glorification of a frankly sexual love and of drinking and gambling coexisted with the doctrines of an ascetic religion.

In the long run, however, the growth of literature in the vernaculars was more important than the survival of Latin. Both hymns and student songs were minor literary forms, whereas the vernacular literature of the early Middle Ages, particularly that written in northern France, presented a comprehensive view of life which can fairly be described as of major scope and depth.

A literary genre may originate among an intellectual elite and be designed for edification and instruction; or it may be intended to provide entertainment for the uneducated. Both kinds, at first sharply divided from each other, were to be found in the early Middle Ages; and as has happened at some other periods (with the drama of Elizabethan England, for example) the literature of entertainment proved to have more vitality, more social and cultural significance, and more potentialities for development. Often inartistic and crudely sensational, it inculcated a profoundly realistic morality, though this had little or no relationship with the official ethical code supposedly preached by the Church; and it gradually acquired refinement and sophistication and an awareness of individual emotions, thus paralleling and promoting the general advance of civilization. It both reflected social conditions and served as a means for that gradual rediscovery of the individual which was the central theme of medieval cultural development.

Even during the darkest period of the Dark Ages there were professional entertainers. The Germanic peoples had their scops, or bards, who celebrated the achievements of the tribal warriors and enjoyed a relatively high social status. The Roman world had its *mimir* or *scenici* (actors), who could recite poetry, play musical instruments, and dance, juggle, or perform acrobatic feats according to the tastes of their audience. Aided by wars and disorders, the Church succeeded finally in closing the theaters (in Italy they seem to have survived until the sixth century), which were always, and not without reason, regarded as strongholds of sexual depravity, but it could not eliminate the *mimus,* who continued to subsist as a migratory entertainer through the Dark Ages, thus transmitting a tradition of professional skill from ancient to medieval and modern civilization.

In the course of time the *mimus* and the scop became merged with each other, and the result was the *joculator,* or jongleur, whom we first see clearly in the eleventh century. Like the *mimus,* the jongleur had to be adept in half a dozen different skills which would hold popular audiences, and like the *mimus* he was viewed with deep suspicion by the Church, which often persuaded secular governments to legislate against him; but he inherited from the scop the special function of singing, and sometimes of composing, epic lays about the glory of war. His most famous appearance in history occurred in 1066 at the battle of Hastings. "In the very van of William's army at Senlac," remarks Professor Chambers, "strutted the minstrel Taillefer, and went to his death exercising the double arts of his hybrid profession, juggling with his sword and chanting an heroic lay of Roncesvalles." [1] Taillefer, however, who was permitted by Duke

---

[1] E. K. Chambers: *The Medieval Stage* (London, 1903).

William to strike the first blow against the Saracens, was apparently more highly regarded by his clientele than were most jongleurs. A passage in the thirteenth-century Provençal romance *Flamenca* illustrates with humorous exaggeration the normal status of the profession. An aristocratic wedding feast is described as attracting more than fifteen hundred jongleurs. At the conclusion of the feast, after the guests had washed their hands and been supplied with wine and cushions, all the jongleurs stood up together and performed their various acts, juggling, tumbling, singing, reciting, and playing instruments in frenzied and humiliating competition.

In this humble occupation are to be found the main sources of Western poetry and Western music. As in ancient Greece, the first literary form to emerge was the epic poem, or *chanson de geste*. This was wholly feudal in its values and point of view, though the subject matter generally consisted of episodes from the Carolingian period. The struggle with the Mohammedans on the Spanish frontier was the favorite theme, though a number of *chansons* deal with the wars of barons against each other or against the emperor. The *chansons* must have been composed and chanted primarily for the entertainment of feudal barons, but an itinerant jongleur who had failed to find a welcome in a castle hall could no doubt earn a night's lodging by performing for a peasant audience.

There has been considerable controversy about the origins of the *chansons*. They first began to be studied during the Romantic movement by critics who believed in the virtues of anonymous folk art and were therefore inclined to stress their derivation from the old Germanic tribal lays. This view was challenged early in the twentieth century by Joseph Bedier, who argued that jongleurs were employed by monasteries along the most famous pilgrimage routes, especially the route to the grave of St. James of Compostella in northern Spain, to entertain travelers and publicize the shrines. This theory is supported by some of the detailed geographical information contained in the poems, but it is noticeable that most of them display more accurate knowledge of northern than of southern France, thus indicating northern provenance. Bedier's insistence that nothing in the *chansons* antedates the twelfth century is surely excessive. The poems as we have them must have been preceded by earlier versions transmitting memories of the Carolingian dynasty.

Most of them are composed in iambic pentameters, grouped in *laisses* of varying length in which all the lines end with the same vowel sound. In some later examples this reliance on assonance gives place to rhyme. More recent critics have emphasized the evidences of deliberate artistry and the presence of classical reminiscences, especially of borrowings from the *Aeneid*. The humble jongleur, it appears, despite the degrading necessity to combine poetry with juggling and acrobatics, was sometimes a man of learning and a self-conscious creator.

Many passages in the *chansons* are crudely sensational, displaying little more realism or refinement than a modern comic strip. Jongleur arithmetic, like much jongleur geography, is wholly reckless, and a single Christian warrior, as he likes to proclaim himself in the boasting monologue ("gab") with which he builds up his self-confidence before a battle, is usually a match for several thousand Saracens. The descriptions of single combats quickly become monotonous for modern readers, who, unlike the original audience, have not enjoyed the personal experiences needed to appreciate the finer points of medieval combat. The details are frequently gory, with much emphasis on the flow of blood and on limbs hacked off and entrails hanging. Altogether typical is the occasion in one of the *chansons* when a warrior is described as tearing out the entrails of a dead opponent and flinging them in another enemy's face. Religious sentiment rarely becomes more subtle than the simple assertion of the *Chanson de Roland* that "the pagans are wrong and the Christians are right" (line 1015). There is little respect for the clergy unless, like Archbishop Turpin, they are also valiant warriors, and the abrupt reminder in the *Chanson de Roland* that Archbishop Turpin has fought the pagans not only in battle but also by "very beautiful sermons" (line 2243) strikes a wholly incongruous note. The belief in the Christian God means simply that he will usually protect those who fight his battles and will reward them with paradise, while the Saracen deities (Mahomet, Apollo, and Tervagan, according to the *Chanson de Roland*) do nothing effective to help their worshippers. There is, of course, the usual trust in relics. Women play a minor role, the men being much more interested in fighting than in love. Sexual propositions mostly come from females, especially from Saracen princesses, who supply the only element of romance. Although marriage is treated with respect, husbands are considered within their rights when they give their wives bloody noses or otherwise maltreat them.

Yet in spite of all the brutality, the whole spirit of the *chansons* is profoundly moral, though the morality is definitely feudal and not Christian. The ideal warrior is valiant (*preux*), generous, truthful, and above all loyal to his lord and to all his feudal obligations. That he behaves like a good vassal is the highest praise. Corresponding qualities are expected of the king, who must recognize the rights of the barons and be guided by their counsel. Thus the *chansons* describe an ideal feudal society and inculcate the values needed to sustain it. It is, however, significant that the powers of the king are definitely limited and that he is often portrayed as a somewhat weak-willed and unreliable character. The baronial audiences of the *chansons* were often in rebellion against the monarchy and preferred not to hear it praised. Even Charlemagne, who is presented as an awe-inspiring white-bearded hero two hundred years old, is easily deceived, while his son Louis, who figures in many of the *chansons,* inspires no respect whatever.

The strongest moral emphasis, however, is placed not on feudal values but on a deeper and more universal quality. The heroes of the *chansons* most often come to grief because of their lack of *mesure* (moderation and proportion). Arrogant, impulsive, and excitable, they fail in self-control. This recalls the ancient Greek doctrine that *hybris* would always evoke a corresponding nemesis, though the punishment of *hybris* was the work of the gods, who easily became jealous of human beings, while the awareness of the dangers of *démesure* was more rationalistic and had little connection with any religious belief. But in either case the advance of society from barbarism to civilization required that the ruling class should learn the habit of self-control. The inculcation of this simple and very necessary lesson was the chief social function performed by the *chansons*.

The earliest surviving example of the genre, the *Chanson de Roland,* is by universal consent also the greatest, especially the first 2,400 of its 4,000 lines. A simple tale of valiant warriors brought to destruction partly by treachery and partly by their leader's lack of *mesure,* it is much more primitive than the *Iliad* in both language and characterization, but it evokes the same tragic sense of life. It was based on a historical memory which must have been handed down by earlier generations of jongleurs; we know from Einhard that when Charlemagne returned from his Spanish campaign, his rear guard, led by Roland, was cut to pieces, though this was done not by Saracens but by Christian Basque mountaineers. In the *Chanson* Roland is appointed to command the rear guard through the machinations of his enemy, Count Ganelon, who has plotted with the king of the Saracens to bring about his destruction. Roland is then attacked in the pass of Roncevaux by a vast Saracen army; but when his friend Oliver entreats him to blow the horn that will bring Charlemagne to the rescue, he is too proud and too concerned about maintaining his reputation for valor to admit the need for help. This is the display of *démesure* that causes the catastrophe. In the ensuing battle the Christians display prodigies of valor, slaughtering immense numbers of Saracens, but all of them are finally killed. Roland, the last survivor, finally recognizes his error and blows the horn, but splits his temples in the effort. In the later and somewhat anticlimatic sections of the *Chanson,* Charlemagne returns and takes vengeance on the Saracens, kills their king in single combat, forcibly baptizes all the survivors (except the queen, who is given the privilege of a voluntary conversion), and puts to death Ganelon and thirty of his relatives (in accordance with primeval custom it is assumed that treachery and guilt go by families). The poem ends with the aged emperor summoned by the Archangel Gabriel to march against enemies of Christianity who are making trouble in another quarter of his empire. "His eyes shed tears, he pulls his white beard." Thus the battle against the pagans is unending.

The best surviving manuscript of the *Chanson* bears the name Turoldus, though it is uncertain whether this refers to its author or merely to its transcriber. Whoever composed it knew how to build up tragic tension in a starkly simple narrative of events. A few brief reminders of the Pyrenean local echo through the poem: "high are the mountains, and the valleys shady, the rocks brown, the defiles sinister" (814–15); "high are the mountains and shady and great, the valleys deep, the waters violent" (1830–1). Otherwise the *Chanson* never wanders from its central theme, which is presented with no psychological subtleties; and although the subject is the struggle between the two religions and the Mohammedans are able to win victories only because of Christian errors, the whole spirit of the poem is tribalistic and pre-Christian. The French are vassals of the true God and must extend his territories through force of arms; and the cause of Christianity is identified with that of "sweet France" (the reiterated and moving application of the word *douce* to the homeland of the Christian warriors seems to be a reminiscence of the *Aeneid* and late Latin epics). Much of the poetic effectiveness of the *Chanson* is derived, moreover, from a sense of fate which is primitive rather than Christian and makes another parallel with the Homeric view of life. Charlemagne suspects the treachery of Ganelon and weeps because of his forebodings of the death of Roland, but he is unable (for reasons that are never explained) to change the arrangements for the rear guard. This feeling of an inescapable tragic destiny belongs to the deepest level of the poem.

The tone of austere dignity and elevation which distinguished the story of Roland is not achieved in the other *chansons*. The favorite hero of the wars with the Saracens is William of Orange,[2]

---

[2] There is no connection with the Dutch independence leader of the sixteenth century.

the historical original of whom was apparently a cousin of Charlemagne who was appointed Count of Toulouse. He was also known as William of the Crooked Nose, which was changed in later *chansons* (through a confusion of the words *courbe* and *court*) to William of the Short Nose, giving rise to a story that the end of his nose had been sliced off in battle. Though an impeccable nobleman, patriot, and Christian warrior, William was a character with a broad popular appeal, having an immense appetite for food, a passion for fine horses, and a vigorous, though rather elementary, sense of humor. His wife Guibourg, who had originally been married to a Saracen but had been captured and converted by William, was the ideal feudal lady, feeding and massaging her husband when he came home exhausted from battle, encouraging him in defeat, and ably managing the affairs of his immense household.

The *Chanson de Guillaume* is generally regarded as the best of a cycle of some twenty-five *chansons* dealing with the exploits of William and other members of his family. The first section contains many reminiscences of the *Chanson de Roland,* though it never attains the same tragic intensity. One hundred thousand Saracens invade the region of the Gironde by sea, and William's nephew Vivien goes with other French warriors to repel them. Since the French number only ten thousand, some of them wish to postpone battle and send to William for reinforcements; but Vivien, like Roland, insists that "this would be a shame for the Christians, pride and joy for the pagans." In a battle fought on a desolate seashore all the Frenchmen are slaughtered; the courage, sufferings, and final death agony of Vivien are described in great detail, with a number of echoes of the story of the crucifixion. The *Chanson de Guillaume* then drops to a cruder and less heroic level. William whose home is apparently at Barcelona (the geography is utterly confused), hears the news and leads an army of thirty thousand against the Saracens, who have been delayed by contrary winds and are still encamped on the same seashore; but in four days of fighting all the Frenchmen are killed except William himself. He escapes and returns to Barcelona in a state of discouragement, but begins to feel better after Guibourg has set before him a shoulder of boar, a roast peacock, two large cakes, and a large loaf. He finishes them off and also drinks seven liters of wine without looking up from the table or offering anything to Guibourg, upon which she remarks with affection that "whoever eats and drinks so well cannot fly like a coward from the battle or disgrace his lineage" (line 127). Guibourg has also found thirty thousand new recruits by spreading a story that the Saracens have been defeated and men are needed to help in collecting the booty. William leads out this new army, and once again all of them are killed except William and another of his nephews, a boy named Guiot. But God then intervenes with a miracle, and William and Guiot put to flight all the Saracens, win the battle, and avenge the death of Vivien. In another section, apparently of later date, William finds Vivien still alive and is able to give him Holy Communion before he expires, thus assuring his entry into paradise. He then seeks help against another invasion from the ignoble King Louis and fails to get it, but is aided by a mysterious giant who has been a slave in the king's kitchen. This turns out to be Guibourg's long-lost brother, who has been kidnapped and brought to France in childhood and who is now duly baptized and provided with a Christian wife and with seven castles and the fiefs attached to them.

Another group of *chansons* deal with baronial warfare, giving remarkably realistic pictures of the feudal anarchy. An outstanding example is *Raoul de Cambrai,* a somber and tragic masterpiece which illuminates the whole history of the Middle Ages. Its hero, a French Achilles, is a model feudal warrior in his valor, his prowess in battle, and his generosity to his dependents; but when he is wronged, his anger is wholly uncontrollable. King Louis has deprived him of his inheritance, the lordship of Cambrai, and has then promised to give him the lordship of Vermandois. But this is claimed by the sons of the previous count, Herbert, who can be dispossessed only by force. (The subject matter of this *chanson* belongs to the period when the transmission of feudal fiefs by heredity had not yet fully replaced royal appointment, while the close relationship between nephews and maternal uncles must be a reminiscence of a much earlier phase of social development when inheritance was still matrilineal.) Instigated by his uncle, the implacable Guerri the Red, Raoul leads an army into Vermandois, and the horrors of feudal warfare are graphically described. In particular, Raoul burns the town of Origny, including a convent where a hundred nuns perish in the flames. He shows his *démesure* by this utter ruthlessness and also by his desire to eat meat in Lent and by blasphemously proclaiming, while engaged in combat, that "neither God nor man nor all the saints" (line 151) can save his enemy from death. A prolonged battle follows, in which Raoul's army is reduced from ten thousand men to one hundred and forty and that of the sons of Herbert from eleven thousand to three hundred, and finally Raoul himself is killed. His victorious opponent, Bernier, the most sympathetically portrayed character, has been caught in a conflict of feudal loyalties, since he has served Raoul as his squire and been knighted by him but is the illegitimate son of one of the sons of Herbert and one of the nuns of Origny. Loving Raoul, he has done his best to dissuade him from his acts of *démesure* and has changed sides only after a violent quarrel. The death of Raoul does not end the poem, since five years later his young nephew Gautier is of age to resume the feud, instigated thereto by Raoul's mother and uncle. Refusing all suggestions of mutual forgiveness, he engages Bernier in single combat, and the two warriors begin to hew each other to pieces. They are stopped from killing each other by officials of the king, who bring them to the palace to be healed of their wounds but lodge them in the same bedchamber, where they continue to hurl threats and abuse at each other. An abbot finally persuades Gautier to give up his plans of vengeance, and then abruptly everything is changed by the discovery that the king, whose injustice toward Raoul was the initial cause of the whole tragedy, is proposing to disinherit both Gautier and the family of Herbert. The leaders of the two factions immediately become close allies, bluntly denounce the king for his misdeeds, rally their followers, plunder and burn the city of Paris, and return to their homes to prepare for war. On this typically feudal note the original poem ends, the later sections being late and feeble additions. Nothing could give a clearer picture both of the values and mutual loyalties of the ideal feudal order and of the violent and intense emotionalism which prevented the ideal from ever becoming an effective reality.

By what means could the barbaric ruling class described in the *chansons* be induced to learn self-control, gentle manners, and respect for spiritual and cultural values? What psychic force was strong enough to persuade these men of violence to acquire the attitudes and habits of civilization? Twelfth-century France found an answer to this question in the idealization of sexual love.

One might have expected religious belief to serve as the main instrument of ethical progress, as had happened in the development of other civilizations. The advance of Greek society beyond the barbaric conditions described in the Homeric poems, for example, had been promoted by the worship of the Olympian gods, especially of Apollo, as interpreted by the priests of Delphi. But early medieval Europe had inherited a religious system which could not easily be applied to actual social conditions. Persons who took Christian values seriously were generally impelled to abandon worldly society and seek redemption in monastic retirement. Meanwhile the feudal nobleman could hope to satisfy his Maker by the performance of such ritualistic requirements as attendance at Mass, pilgrimages to the tombs of saints, and generosity to the clergy. Through the circumstances of its early history, medieval Christianity had largely failed to develop moral standards that were relevant to the daily lives of the ordinary laymen. What was needed was both a higher code of conduct and some positive motivation for adopting it. But as a result of the ascetic and otherworldly emphasis of Catholic Christianity, effective moral development occurred outside the official religions system, and to a large extent in actual opposition to it.

The concept of love as an agency of civilization was invented in southern France by the troubadours. The earliest whose work has, in part, survived was William IX, Duke of Aquitaine and Count of Poitou from 1087 to 1127, though it would appear from his poems that he was conforming to conventions already well established. The movement lasted into the thirteenth century, and the names of some four hundred and fifty troubadour poets have survived. The advent of the troubadours was an event of vast literary and cultural importance both because they were the originators of the whole Western tradition of lyric poetry in the vernaculars and because they propagated new emotional attitudes and values which were to remain favorite themes of European literature through the later Middle Ages and the Renaissance and to have a lasting and profound effect on the whole European view of life. By exploring individual emotion and developing a vocabulary and literary forms and techniques for giving it expression, they made an essential contribution to the process of self-discovery which constituted medieval man's most important cultural task. Their services in the early development of Western music were of almost equal importance, though handicapped by the lack of an adequate system of notation.

The troubadour movement was a product of the Midi. Governed by great feudal nobles and their vassals, the most powerful of whom were the Duke of Aquitaine and the Count of Toulouse, the people of the region had little sense of allegiance to the King of France. They were separated from the northern French by linguistic differences, speaking various dialects that were closer to the original Latin. The dialect adopted by the troubadours has become known as Provençal, though it was actually derived mainly from the usages of the Limousin, which became standard for the literature of the whole region, presumably because this was the original home of the new poetry. The whole Midi had preserved more memories of Roman civilization than northern France and had been less deeply affected by the Germanic conquest. Although society was organized on feudal principles, it was less barbaric than that of the north and more open to new intellectual influences. Class lines were drawn less rigidly, so that the nobleman and the bourgeois could associate with each other almost as equals, and there was relatively little religious intolerance. Large Jewish communities had been established in a number of southern cities ever since Roman times, and were rarely disturbed by their Christian neighbors; there was even some willingness to promote cultural and commercial interchange with the Mohammedans of Spain and northern Africa. Christian beliefs seem, in fact, to have been taken less seriously in the Midi than in any other area in the domain of the western Church, for which reason this became the main breeding-ground not only of nonreligious poetry but also of religious heresies.

There has been a prolonged, and still unsettled, controversy about the literary sources of the new poetry. Love poetry had been written in Arabic since before Mohammed, and had subsequently acquired a mystical tendency through contact with Neo-Platonism. The troubadours seem to have borrowed some of their verse forms and imagery from the Arabic poets of Spain. But the distinctive features of the new poetry—the exaltation of women and the treatment of love as an ennobling power—were alien to the Mohammedan tradition and do not seem to have Arabic parallels. The essential originality of the troubadour convention becomes equally clear when it is contrasted with its other obvious source, the poetry of Ovid. Ovid's *Art of Love* was studied by the poets of twelfth-century France with a solemnity that its author would have found utterly bewildering, and its tongue-in-cheek advice about the techniques of winning and holding a lover (which concluded with some highly practical suggestions to women about matching the positions they assumed in sexual intercourse to the shape of their bodies) was treated as having almost scriptural authority. But when Ovid urged the male to beg humbly for his mistress's favors, and if necessary to shed a few tears, he was merely showing him how to play the most effective gambits in the game of seduction. When the troubadours repeated these recommendations, they were entirely serious. Love had acquired a meaning which it had never had in any earlier culture and which it has partially retained in Western society down to the present day. For the classical poets it had generally been depicted as a consuming and destructive passion, as exemplified in the lives of Helen, Medea, and Dido. The troubadours were the first to regard it as an instrument of moral growth.

A more plausible explanation for the origins of the new doctrine of love is sociological. Troubadour poetry may have acquired much of its specific quality from the conditions of feudal life. It was mostly composed in feudal castles; and though some of the poets were, like William of Aquitaine, themselves great noblemen, most of them belonged to the minor gentry or the bourgeoisie, and while they enjoyed more social esteem than the jongleurs of the north, they were equally dependent on patronage for their livelihood. The wives of feudal noblemen were usually married at an early age for social and economic reasons to husbands who neglected them, and troubadour poetry may have owed much of its popularity to the discovery that these women were interested in love and responsive to flattery. All its dominant conventions—the assumption of feminine superiority (which was usually defined in feudal terms, the poet considering himself as his lady's vassal) and of the ennobling powers of love, the insistence that love and marriage were incompatible, the reprobation of the jealous husband, the emphasis on secrecy, the suggestion that while sexual consummation was the proper end of love, it was almost beyond the lover's hopes—can be interpreted as reflections of the relationship between the great feudal lady and the troubadour of lower rank.

But while the new doctrine of love may have had its roots in the feudalism of the Midi, it should not be supposed that it can be wholly explained in sociological terms. What may have originated partly as a kind of game and partly as a device for securing patronage had consequences that were profoundly serious and far-reaching. Having been stimulated by the social milieu to an idealization of women and of sexual desire that had no precedent in earlier cultural attitudes, the troubadours went on to explore new emotional possibilities. Despite the lover's tears and sighs, it was love that gave meaning and value to his existence and served as a motive for self-improvement. Love was "the gay science" and the only true source of joy. "He is truly dead who does not feel in his heart the sweet savor of love," affirmed Bernart de Ventadour. "What is life worth without love? What is it but ennui for the others? May God never hate me to the point that I love for a day or month after having fallen into the ranks of those ennuyed ones, deprived of all desire of love." [3] Declared Peire Rogier: "I have so well fixed my heart on the joy [of love] that I cannot prevent myself from singing; for from my infancy this joy has nourished me, and without it I would be nothing; and I see well that all that is not love makes men base and vile." [4]

There was no ambiguity about the ultimate wishes of the troubadour lyricist; he wanted to sleep with his lady. Some troubadour poetry was frankly and even coarsely sensual—some of the poems of William of Aquitaine, for example. A favorite genre was the *aubade,* which presented two lovers awakened at dawn by a friendly watchman and complaining that the night had been too short. But in a majority of the poems the lover was primarily concerned with the joys and torments of unsatisfied desire and scarcely dared to hope for consummation. A typical troubadour attitude was expressed by Bernart de Ventadour: "When I see her, my eyes, my face, my pallor bear witness of it. Fear makes me tremble like a leaf in the wind, and I have no more reason than a child. That is how I am dominated by love. Ah, for a man thus conquered, a woman should have pity. Noble lady, I ask you nothing except to accept me as a servitor. I will serve you as a good lord no matter what recompense obtain." [5]

The analysis of the lover's emotions and of the rights and duties of a love relationship was often pursued to extremes which

---

[3] Quoted in Alfred Jeanroy: *La Poésie Lyrique des Troubadours,* I.
[4] Quoted in Jeanroy: op. cit.
[5] Quoted in Jeanroy: op. cit.

must seem tiresome and ridiculous to most modern minds. A kind of playful scholasticism of love was developed, which retained an extraordinary fascination for sophisticated persons until the end of the Renaissance, as passages in the comedies of Shakespeare bear witness. It has even been suggested, in fact, that the troubadours actually preferred the state of unsatisfaction, that they were not really interested in normal love at all, and that their poetry was the expression of a morbid repudiation of the whole physical world.[6] One may agree that they often seemed more interested in the emotion than in the object and that they deliberately exaggerated the obstacles and impediments in order to increase the intensity of their desire. There was an element of masochism about the whole attitude, which occasionally developed into a longing for death.

The troubadours knew, however, that when sexual desire is wholly uninhibited, it remains merely a physiological appetite. It acquires spiritual meaning and becomes associated with a true respect for the loved personality only in proportion as it is kept under control. The troubadour situation, unreal and somewhat ridiculous as it may appear to the modern mind, may be regarded as a necessary means for transforming sex from a mere animal coupling into a sentiment loaded with spiritual and moral values. The artificiality of much of the poetry written by the troubadours and by their imitators in other languages, therefore, should not blind us to its importance in the development of civilization. In the *chansons de geste,* which faithfully reflected feudal society before the twelfth century, nobody ever stopped to analyze an emotion because nobody was capable of the necessary effort of inhibition. In the troubadour lyrics, for the first time since the advent of the barbarians, the most powerful of human appetites was subjected to rules and controls, used as material for introspective examination, and treated as a means for ethical improve-

---

[6] See Denis de Rougemont: *Love in the Western World,* translated by Montgomery Belgion (New York, 1940).

ment. For in order to please his lady, the lover would display *mesure* and gentle manners, be loyal, generous, and courageous, and avoid anything brutal or discourteous. He would, in fact, as was repeatedly emphasized, behave like a true lord and not like a *vilain*.

Troubadour poetry was obviously hostile to Christian teaching. It is true that some of the troubadours ended their lives in the bosom of the Church, becoming monks and even bishops. The most moving of the surviving poems of William of Aquitaine, apparently written near the end of his life when he was about to go on pilgrimage to Compostella, affirms his desire to repudiate the pomp and pleasures of the world and seek salvation.[7] But throughout his earlier life, according to a contemporary chronicler, William had been the enemy "of all modesty and all sanctity,"[8] being several times excommunicated because of his scandalous life, and similar statements could probably have been made of most of his successors. A poetry that idealized sexual desire and glorified adultery was wholly unacceptable to the Church. Some of the troubadours, moreover, who borrowed the imagery of religious devotion to describe the sufferings and rewards of love, could fairly be accused of blasphemy. The whole movement was possible only because the Church throughout the Midi had little control over the lay population. Yet in the long run the new doctrine of love, purged of its excesses, may be regarded as serving the moral values of Christianity, though not perhaps the Christianity of the Catholic Church. In later centu-

----

[7] "I have been a friend of prowess and of joy; but now I must separate myself from both in order to depart to him with whom all sinners find peace. I have been greatly jovial and gay; but Our Lord no longer wishes that it be thus; now I can no longer support the burden, so close I am to the end. I have left all that used to charm me, the chivalrous and pompous life; since it pleases God, I resign myself and I ask him to hold me among his own. I ask all my friends that after my death they come, all of them, and honor me greatly; for I have known joy and gaiety, both far and near and in my home. But today I renounce joy and gaiety; I quit the vair and the gray, and the precious furs."

[8] Quoted in Jeanroy: op. cit.

ries the kind of ideal love taught by the troubadours gradually become disentangled from the adulterous associations that it had acquired from the troubadour situation and became the foundation of Western marriage.

The troubadour movement served the values of civilization in more subtle ways. It was a step forward in Western man's discovery of himself, providing him with a vocabulary for certain forms of self-expression and self-exploration. As Professor Jeanroy has remarked, "the poet takes himself as the subject of his songs; proudly camped in the face of the public, he does the honors of his own heart with a complaisance which will not be found again to the same degree until the romantic movement." [9] This capacity for honest observation was, of course, limited, and the modern reader is likely to be more aware of the conventionalized elements in troubadour poetry than of its originality. Medieval man, the poet as well as the theologian, remained generally incapable of looking at an object and describing what he saw. There are many references to nature in the troubadour poems—to the season of spring, which was the most appropriate time for love, and to the songs of birds, especially larks and nightingales; but they all give the impression of being culled from books. The actual landscapes of southern France—the sunlit gardens of Provence, the misty chestnut groves of the Limousin, the vigorous vegetation of the plains of Langeudoc, the snowy peaks of the Pyrenees —are conspicuously absent. Nor did the troubadours individualize the ladies whom they loved; their descriptions of feminine beauty are so conventionalized that they all seem to be writing about the same person. Every lady has a skin white as snow and red as a rose, blond hair, white teeth, and a slender well-proportioned figure. Once the tradition had been established, in fact, poetic composition became mainly a matter of following rules, and there was less room for genuine personal confession. One cannot assume that all troubadour poems were necessarily auto-

---

[9] Jeanroy: op. cit., II, 62.

biographical; the biographies which record the love affairs by which they were supposedly inspired, and which became attached to the poems during the thirteenth century, are mostly fictitious, and should properly be regarded as forerunners of the *Decameron*. It is interesting that one of the greatest of the poets, Arnaut Daniel, was placed by Dante in the region of purgatory reserved for the purification of homosexuals. Modern appreciation of the movement is further impeded by the fact that a troubadour poem was intended to be sung, and the tune was an integral part of the composition. Writing in rhymes and accents and inventing verse forms of great subtlety and complexity, the troubadours were the main founders of the whole Western poetic tradition, but they have survived because of their historical importance rather than because of the intrinsic value of their achievement.

The element of convention is probably less manifest, and modern appreciation may therefore be easier, in the poems of hate rather than in those of love. Besides love lyrics the troubadours also wrote *sirventes,* which might deal with any current moral or political question but which tended to be predominantly satirical, often with a strong autobiographical element. A *sirvente* was originally a poem written by a *sirven,* or retainer, of a nobleman to advance his interests. Many give a vivid portrayal of the feudal disorder, the most lively being those of Bertran de Born.

It is probable that by the early years of the thirteenth century the troubadour movement had exhausted its potentialities, though poetry in the Midi might have assumed new forms. But what actually ended the movement was the Albigensian Crusade.[1] For nearly thirty years southern France was overrun by warriors from the north, fighting nominally to destroy the Albigensian heresy but actually to impose the rule of the monarchy and to secure booty for themselves. From this bloody and destructive enterprise the civilization of the Midi never recovered.

----

[1] See pp. 240–2.

The last major figure in the troubadour movement, Peire Carde-
nal, recorded his sentiments in a series of twenty bitter *sirventes*
denouncing the greed and arrogance of the Catholic clergy and
of the so-called crusaders from the north.

Meanwhile the troubadour conventions and verse techniques
had spread to virtually every other Western country. Their diffusion into northern France began before the middle of the twelfth
century, and is generally associated with the marriage of William
of Aquitaine's granddaughter Eleanor. This egotistical, strong-
willed, and pleasure-loving lady was married in 1137 to the
King of France, Louis VII, by whom she had two daughters.
These subsequently became the wives of two of the greatest of the
northern noblemen, the Counts of Blois and Champagne. Meanwhile Eleanor had grown bored with King Louis, whom she
described as a monk rather than a king; after obtaining an annulment of her marriage, she became the wife of Henry Plantagenet,
Count of Anjou, who inherited the throne of England in 1154
and displayed until his death in 1189 all the demonic drive and
the political skill that had generally distinguished the Angevins
since their emergence in the ninth century. By her second marriage Eleanor had four sons, Henry the "Young King" (who died
prematurely in 1180), Richard Coeur de Lion, Geoffrey of
Brittany, and John Sans Terre, the second and fourth of whom
subsequently became kings of England. An indulgent mother and
an intolerable wife, Eleanor encouraged her sons to rebel against
their father; she was held by him in well-deserved captivity for
the last sixteen years of his life, although she retained enough
vigor to emerge after his death and govern England as regent in
turn, for each of her two surviving sons. There is no good reason
for supposing that either Eleanor or any of her children had any
deep appreciation of aesthetic values, but they regarded the kind
of poetry written by the troubadours as an embellishment to
feudal life. Eleanor herself introduced the new style into the
English and French courts and was the subject of love poetry
written by Bernart de Ventadour. Her daughter Marie of Champagne became a leading patroness of literature; her son Henry

was closely associated with Bertran de Born, who mourned his death in a well-known elegy; and Richard Coeur de Lion (whose personal inclinations seem to have been homosexual) even wrote a few poems himself.

The love poets of northern France (the trouvères) copied the troubadours in style and subject matter, but were generally less mystical in their view of love and less inclined to place women on unapproachable pedestals. From France the new attitudes spread to Germany, where the early thirteenth century was the great age of literary *Minnedienst* (love service). The *Minnesänger* mostly preferred to celebrate marriage rather than adultery, though the best-known and most charming of German love poems, the *Unter den Linden* of Walther von der Vogelweide, is frankly and delightfully sensuous. Meanwhile the more mystical aspects of the troubadour convention were developed in Italy, eventually flowering into the *dolce stil nuovo* of Dante and his friends, in which the love of a beautiful woman became a means for achieving spirituality.

In northern France the main literary importance of the new view of love was in helping to produce the romance, which gradually replaced the *chanson de geste* as the favorite literary form. Written largely for feminine, or at least for mixed, audiences, the romance gave expression to the new ideals of chivalry. Its central figure, the knight errant, was the perfect feudal hero, devoted to feats of arms and the pursuit of glory, but using his strength to punish oppressors and protect the weak, and habituated by the practice of courtly love to self-control and refinement. Unlike the *chanson de geste*, the romance was wholly devoid of any element of social realism; its values were individualistic, each knight pursuing glory for himself alone, and its subject matter was a dream world with no relationship to actuality. With the rise of the monarchy and its bourgeois allies, feudal society of the late twelfth century was already losing much of its original *raison d'être* and showing symptoms of decadence, and the romances displayed a strong tendency toward escapism. Yet the chivalrous ideals which they inculcated proved to have an extraordinary vitality and have continued to have some influence on European society down to modern times.

Many romances were written on classical themes; ancient Greek and Roman legends, especially that of the Trojan War, were retold in terms of medieval chivalry, as were also stories about the wars of Charlemagne. But the favorite subject was the Arthurian legend. Its immediate source was the *Historia Regum Britanniae* of the Welsh chronicler Geoffrey of Monmouth, which was completed about 1147. This was translated into French, with some additions, by the Norman poet Wace in 1155. Geoffrey was indebted to Welsh traditions, which may have been recorded by a shadowy Welsh or Breton poet called Breri or Bleheris. Other stories of Celtic provenance, particularly those of Tristram and Iseult and of the Holy Grail, had apparently been preserved in Brittany and quickly became attached to the Arthurian legend, though we do not know how they reached the French poets. The extent of the Celtic influence has remained a misty and controversial subject, but it is reasonably certain that the French poets responsible for the development of the legend took their material from Celtic sources, though they reworked it in terms applicable to twelfth-century feudalism and chivalry. The main attraction of the legend was the conception of a group of knights engaged in seeking adventures, righting wrongs, and paying court to beautiful women. It was characteristic of feudal conditions that King Arthur himself quickly became a shadowy and somewhat ineffectual figurehead, unable even to retain the fidelity of his queen, while the spotlight shifted to the various knights in his entourage.

Probably the only romances that retain much appeal for modern readers are those dealing with Tristram and Iseult, who had no real connection with King Arthur's court. This story of guilty and doomed lovers retained its original Celtic flavor; its theme was not the courtly and ennobling love of the troubadours but the destructiveness of a compulsive passion. The whole legend—the first fateful meeting of the lovers in Ireland, their separation at the Cornish court, their flight into the forest and the hardships of their life alone with each other, their final deaths—is drenched with the tragic and primeval sorrow that had always been a characteristic element in the literature of the Celtic fringe.

Most of the other Arthurian romances are lacking both in intensity of feeling and in awareness of any kind of reality. Displaying none of the recognition of the material bases of feudal society that had distinguished such *chansons de geste* as *Raoul of Cambrai,* they reflected the spirit of leisure-class feudal society after it had become decadent. Knights ride out in search of adventure; for no particular reason they engage in single combat with other knights, who often turn out to be friends or relatives; they wander through vast forests, rescue beautiful women held captive by giants or Saracens, are made welcome in strange cities, meet an occasional Christian hermit (the organized Church is conspicuously absent), and see various supernatural marvels. In due course they return to King Arthur's court and recite their experiences. These tales are dreamlike in their lack of logical sequence, their fantasy quality, and their total disregard of realistic geography and chronology, but they are devoid of the hidden emotional significance that gives intensity to a genuine dream. The modern reader, not interested in the detailed accounts of knightly combats, quickly begins to ask for some recognition of the material necessities of the life of chivalry. What do these knights and ladies eat, where do they sleep, where are the estates that support them and the peasants who labor for them? Such questions remain unanswered.

Perhaps the main interest of the romances is derived from the relics of Celtic mythology embedded in them, although these are retained solely for their picturesque and melodramatic flavor, without any awareness of their original meaning. Some romances contain, for example, accounts of enchanted countries, where knights and ladies are held as captives, which were apparently derived from Celtic myths of the world of the dead. The whole Grail legend, with its Fisher King suffering from an incurable wound through which his land has become waste, the young knight of the same family who was to redeem the land by asking the right question, and the symbolism of the lance and the bowl, was plainly derived partly from a primitive fertility cult and partly from a puberty ritual. In medieval romance it was given a Christian coloration by the assertion that the bowl (originally a female sex symbol) contained the blood of Jesus and had been brought to Glastonbury by Joseph of Arimathea after the crucifixion and had subsequently disappeared. Knights were supposed to go in search of the Grail, which became a symbol of divine grace, and could find it only if they had lived pure lives. Yet the Fisher King, his incurable wound, and the desolation of his kingdom still remained in the story, like fragments of a pagan temple built into a Christian church, in spite of their total loss of significance.

From these strictures, however, one group of romances must be excluded: the verse tales of Chrétien de Troyes, which were probably written between 1150 and 1175. These comprise *Érec and Énide, Cligès, The Story of the Cart* (also known as *Lancelot*), *Yvain*, and an unfinished *Perceval*. They conform to the general pattern of the Arthurian romance; in fact, Chrétien has sometimes been supposed to have invented the whole genre; but they display a sophisticated lightness of touch and a capacity for psychological analysis unequaled by any other French medieval author. Chrétien cannot be ranked as one of the world's great writers—his verse is pedestrian and his scope is much too limited—but he is a figure of vast importance in literary history, since he can fairly be considered as the founder of the Western novel.

Chrétien knew all about the troubadour concept of courtly love, but *The Story of the Cart* is the only tale in which he fully accepted it, and this, as he explains at the beginning, was written at the request of Queen Eleanor's daughter Marie of Champagne, who apparently dictated the plot. Lancelot sets out to rescue Queen Guinevere from captivity in an enchanted country, proves his fidelity by undergoing all kinds of sufferings and humiliations on her behalf (including transportation in a cart normally used for taking criminals to execution—hence the title), and is finally permitted to spend a night with her. If one can judge by the number of illustrations of the story in medieval art, this was much the most popular of the tales. But in his other writings Chrétien definitely prefers married love to adultery as a subject for poetry and is explicitly critical of troubadour doctrine. The plot of *Cligès* is modeled after that of Tristram and Iseult, the lover and his mistress being the nephew and the wife of the Byzantine emperor; but morality is preserved, after a fashion, by the invention of a drug which prevents the emperor from actually embracing his wife while giving him the illusion of doing so. *Érec and Énide* and *Yvain* both deal with married couples, and both of them present a conflict between love and honor; instead of being a stimulus to knightly deeds, love is an impediment to it. The problem is not worked out on any very profound level, but there is an underlying seriousness in Chrétien's writing, in spite of his apparent flippancy. He was fascinated by the image of a knight going out on some kind of quest (presumably for salvation, though the goal is never very clear), reaching his objective through the exercise of knightly virtue, and thereby redeeming the victims of enchantment. These themes are most fully developed in the unfinished *Perceval,* which deals with the Grail legend. Chrétien's quests are presented with much more vividness and intensity than those in other Arthurian romances, and they have religious overtones, but specific references to Christian doctrines and institutions are remarkably scanty.

Chrétien's stories have retained their power to entertain. The narrative flows quickly and smoothly, with a delightful variety of characters and episodes. Marvels and miracles are described with an engaging insouciance. Despite the leisure-class audience for which he is writing, he is aware of the economic basis of feudal life and occasionally stresses the humanity of servants, craftsmen, peasants, and other members of the submerged class of *vilains*. In *Yvain* the victims of enchantment whom the hero must rescue are women condemned to exploitation in a kind of silk factory. Above all, Chrétien is interested in human emotions, especially the emotion of love. The soliloquies in which his leading characters describe their feelings often strike the modern reader as somewhat labored and artificial; the modern novelist has more effective ways of describing emotional states. But this was the beginning of a new tradition, and the understanding of human psychology had not yet acquired much depth or subtlety. From Chrétien there runs a clear line of descent to the masters of the modern French novel. In spirit, in fact, he is already closer to Marcel Proust than to the *Chanson de Roland,* which had probably been composed only a half-century before he began to write.

IO

Architecture and Art

The most satisfying aesthetic achievements of the Middle Ages were the great cathedrals.[1] Architecture was the dominant art form of the twelfth and thirteenth centuries; and while there was a vast production of other visual arts—sculpture, mosaic, mural painting, and stained glass—these remained subsidiary to the buildings in which they were placed and had no independent development. One of the most significant features of the cathedrals was the comprehensiveness with which they incorporated so many different aspects of medieval society. While the total effect was an assertion of the truth of Christian beliefs, the

---

[1] An architectural style is an expression of the view of life of the society which produces it. Recognition of this fact leads to implications not always realized in aesthetic theory. An exact imitation of a Gothic cathedral built in the twentieth century does not have the same aesthetic impact as an original medieval building, yet the difference is not to be found in the material structure; it can be found only in what the spectator brings to the act of appreciation, including the necessary historical information. All art is communication (it is still to be judged as communication even when what is being communicated is too difficult for more than a small number of sophisticated persons to grasp). An original medieval structure is meaningful in proportion to the spectator's capacity to appreciate what it communicates. But the state of appreciation which the builders hoped to induce occurs in the mind of the spectator, and hence includes the relevant historical and aesthetic knowledge. A modern imitation of such a building, while it has the material needed to produce an aesthetic response, has little of significance to communicate.

216

detailed carvings and colored windows reflected all the vigor and variety of daily life. Prior to Dante (who was the beginning of the Renaissance), imaginative literature never succeeded in synthesizing the various discordant elements in medieval culture. But in the cathedrals they could be set side by side without overt conflict, and remain subordinate to structures which affirmed the supremacy of the divine order.

Originating in a fusion of barbaric and Mediterranean traditions, medieval architecture and art flourished chiefly in areas where neither of these traditions was strong enough to overwhelm the other. While forms and building techniques were chiefly of Mediterranean provenance, the spirit of medieval art continued to reflect the influence of the Celtic and Germanic heritage, with its preference for a kind of dynamic abstractionism. The more characteristic styles of medieval art never established any deep roots in the Mediterranean countries. Up to the later thirteenth century, Byzantine influences remained dominant in Italy and to a lesser degree in southern France and Spain; and these areas took little active part in artistic development. Germany also contributed little during the early stages, its art running parallel with its political attitudes, which were dominated by the myth of the Roman Empire. During the early Middle Ages, German art tended either to copy Carolingian models or to fall under Byzantine influence, which was reinforced when the Emperor Otto II married the Byzantine princess Theophano in 972. Theophano brought with her numerous manuscripts and other *objets d'art,* which for a long time set the aesthetic standards of the German imperial court and of any nobles and ecclesiastics interested in art patronage. Meanwhile, even more than in literature and philosophy, northern France was the area of highest artistic creativity.

Through the Dark Ages, church buildings continued to be copies of Roman models, and while there was some innovation, there was no decisive break with the classical tradition. The ground plan of the typical Christian church had been derived from the Roman basilica, a public meeting hall for judicial or other official purposes. This could easily be adapted to forms of public worship which, unlike worship of the pagan gods, mostly took place indoors. The original basilica was rectangular, with rows of pillars marking off aisles and a nave. Soon after the adoption of the basilica form by the Church, the far end began to be rounded into an apse holding the altar, while the addition of transepts gave the building the form of a cross. At a later period the central space between the transepts was often set apart as a choir. Roofs were generally of timber. Less frequent were churches of central rather than cruciform plan: round, square, octagonal, or formed like a Greek cross with all arms of the same length. Numerous basilica-form churches, many of them quite large, were built in France under the Merovingians. The church of St. Martin of Tours, for example, erected late in the sixth century, was 160 feet long and 60 feet wide, and had 120 marble columns and 52 windows. Since none of the larger and more important buildings have survived, we cannot form any judgment of their aesthetic quality; but it is plain that Merovingian architecture was wholly of Mediterranean origin, with no incorporation of Germanic elements. The same can be said of most Carolingian architecture, which—like the Carolingian revival of learning—went back to classical models.

In the eleventh century the increase of wealth, along with the slow growth of law and order, made large-scale church-building possible, especially by the monasteries. The result was the emergence of a distinctive style generally known as Romanesque. This was not yet a wholly original expression of the Western spirit. Full originality came only with Gothic halfway through the twelfth century. Romanesque was a transitional style, largely derived from Mediterranean and Eastern sources, though unlike its Dark Age predecessors it contained much that was new and distinctive and was not a mere imitation of earlier buildings. The earliest examples of Romanesque were mostly in southern Europe, in Lombardy and in Catalonia. Italy remained largely faithful to Romanesque forms throughout the whole of the Middle Ages, until its return to classical models in the early Renaissance. But probably the finest examples of Romanesque were in northern France, where it exhibited constant innovations leading by slow degrees to the final consummation of medieval building in Gothic.

The most obvious qualities of Romanesque were its appearance of massive strength, its unity and harmony, and its emphasis on horizontal rather than vertical lines. It may be regarded as the visual equivalent of a religion which was seeking to impose form and order on a largely anarchical society and which had not yet begun to encourage philosophical speculation or to be translated into terms of individual emotional experience. The observer was not lifted above himself into new states of consciousness, but he was given a massive sense of order and security. In Romanesque are to be found the force and confidence with which the Church affirmed its faith in Catholic doctrine. But the richness and variety of human life were excluded from it, nor was there any note of mystical exaltation. Human emotions were to be controlled and dominated rather than assimilated. In the words of Pierre Lavedan, it "differed from the preceding style because it imposed on its intellectual disorder a strong dominating idea—an abstract logic, which later gave way to the spontaneous naturalism of Gothic. . . . The combination of masses in Romanesque buildings always gives an impression of balance rather than uplift; horizontality dominated verticality." [2]

Romanesque churches generally retained the basilica form, and the most significant innovation was that the roofs were beginning to be made of stone instead of timber, and were therefore vaulted and were strong enough to be surmounted by stone towers. (The treatment of the roof was the most significant individual factor in the whole evolution of medieval building.) Barrel vaults, with round arches, were the most frequent form, though a few Romanesque churches carried domes. In some churches the nave was built higher than the two side aisles, thus

---

[2] Pierre Lavedan: *French Architecture,* pp. 69, 89.

making possible a clerestory above the roofs of the aisles to provide lighting for the nave. Other examples of increasing architectural complexity were the inclusion of an ambulatory linking the two aisles and the gradual proliferation of chapels in place of the single apse.

The same emphasis on the need for a transcendental order pervaded the sculptures which, with increasing density, were incorporated into the buildings, especially beside the doors and in the tympanum above the main entrance. Romanesque sculpture presented figures of Christ and the apostles and of his Old Testament predecessors, but these were not fully realistic. With their slender and elongated bodies, their large rectangular heads, their clinging draperies and off-balance postures, they gave expression, with the full consciousness and intention of the artist, to doctrines that still emphasized the transcendental. As has been noted earlier, Christ was most often portrayed with concentration on the divine and not the human aspects of his double nature, frequently appearing in the role of judge at the end of the world. The figures of Christ in the scenes of the last judgment at Véze- lay, Moissac, and elsewhere show him as the stern lord and ruler of the world, not yet as the suffering savior. This was an art which expressed the need for spiritual powers capable of domi- nating the chaos of the material world and of human society. In spite of its concentration of the human figure, sculpture still showed abstractionist tendencies. Yet in spite of its lack of real- ism and its tendency to keep to two dimensions, northern Roman- esque art conveyed much more sense of movement than did that of Mediterranean countries, as was shown particularly in the swirling draperies in which its human figures were often swathed. Similar qualities were displayed in the numerous wall paintings in Romanesque churches; outstanding examples are the impres- sionistic and extraordinarily dynamic figures in the church at Tavant, between Tours and Poitiers.

Romanesque began to give place to Gothic about the middle of the twelfth century. And while Romanesque had developed chiefly in the monastery churches, Gothic evolved mainly in the urban cathedrals for lay worship, reflecting both the increase of available money and the growing confidence in the possibility of an orderly world in which religious dogmas could be translated into emotional terms instead of being blindly obeyed. Gothic was not wholly urban, however, since the new style in its simplest forms was adopted by many of the Cistercian abbeys.

There is no easy way to define Gothic. Three architectural novelties are usually associated with it: ribbed vaulting, which enabled the entire weight of the structure to be carried on a kind of skeleton of ogives, thus making it possible for most of the wall space to be used for windows; pointed arches, which gave additional strength to the vaulting; and flying buttresses, which bore much of the weight of the roof and towers and thus made additional height possible. But all these features were to be found in buildings that were not yet Gothic. Both ribbed vaulting and the pointed arch had, in fact, been invented in the Near East and applied in a number of different buildings before they were adopted by the architects of northern France. Gothic can be identified only by the general impression, not by any specific technical details. Its essential qualities cannot be exactly defined, but may be described as luminosity and an illusion of movement upward. These two qualities may be regarded as the material equivalents of the essential character of medieval religious belief.

Designed for public usage and appreciation and therefore dependent on public support, financially and otherwise, architecture has always been the most socially significant of the arts; and whenever a distinctive style becomes widely established, it must be regarded as the reflection of the general view of life of the society which has produced it. Building materials are, of course, conditioning factors in architectural evolution: Athens could not have built the Parthenon exactly as it was without the marble quarries of Mount Pentelicon, nor could northern France have built the cathedrals if it had not been rich in different varieties of limestone. Similarly, the growth of a style is due, in part, to the invention of new techniques: if medieval French craftsmanship had been less adept, Gothic would not have been so fully expressive of the medieval spirit. But the main factor in architectural development is always the view of life of the society responsible for it. Materials and techniques are limiting factors, but they are not causal. What architects and their patrons wish to convey, not of course because of any conscious intention of reflecting social forces but simply because their tastes and preferences are socially determined, is always the fundamental reason for the growth of a style. Once the intention has become established, the solution of the technical problems involved is of secondary importance, although it may require several generations for appropriate building methods to be devised and the implicit tendencies of the style to be fully realized.

Who was responsible for the development of medieval architectural styles? The actual designing and building were, of course, the work of professional craftsmen, and such documents as the notebook of Villard de Honnecourt show their interest in observing and recording new technical and aesthetic devices. But it is obvious that the cathedrals could not have been built in new styles without both clerical and general public approval. Romanesque evolved mainly in the monastery churches; and although the assertion that the monks themselves did the building has been shown to be mythical except in a very few instances, they must have given general support to the new style. But the cathedrals were built in cities and intended for public use. The individuals primarily responsible were the bishops; their most necessary task was to raise large sums of money, often in competition with each other. In some instances, as at Laon, the bishops were in conflict with leading groups among the townspeople; but normally cathedral-building had the enthusiastic support of the laity. Yet the conscious motivations which produced these aesthetic masterpieces were often crudely materialistic. The whole Gothic movement was made possible only by the rapid growth of urban prosperity and by the belief of wealthy citizens that the investment of their capital in these spiritual enterprises would bring in higher returns than spending it on direct economic expansion. If they had been asked to define their motives, most of them would probably have declared that they hoped to win the approval in their worldly affairs of Jesus and the saints, and more especially of the Virgin, in whose honor many of the cathedrals were built.

Even cruder and more materialistic considerations were often involved. Cathedrals were often built to house miracle-working relics, and relics were valuable not only because they cured diseases but also because they were good for business. The cathedral of Chartres, for example, contained the sacred tunic of the Virgin Mary, worn during the birth of Christ. When the cathedral burned down in 1194 (this was already the sixth building on the same site, most of the earlier ones having also burned), the townspeople, after recovering from their resentment at the failure of the Virgin to protect her shrine and having been duly encouraged by the discovery that the famous tunic was still intact, resolved to build a seventh cathedral mainly because it would attract merchants and other travelers to the annual fair. Yet the new cathedral which resulted from these utilitarian considerations was one of the most beautiful creations of western Christendom. Beauty does not come into being by accident, and what is important about the rebuilding of Chartres is not the expressed motivation but the unexpressed aesthetic sense of the authorities responsible for it and their belief that this sense would be appreciated by the Virgin.

Who invented Gothic? The new style seems to have first appeared in the abbey church of St. Denis, more particularly in the rebuilding of the nave about the year 1140, and at about the same time in new cathedrals at Chartres and Sens. And there is considerable support for the proposition that insofar as the style was devised by anybody in particular, the credit should be given to the Abbot of St. Denis, Suger. Born into a peasant family, entering the abbey at an early age, becoming involved in political affairs, and rising to the post of chief adviser to King Louis VI and virtually prime minister of France, Suger seems a most unlikely person to be an aesthetic innovator. Undoubtedly much of the credit for the new style should go to the master masons whom he employed; but the main lines of the original conception appear to have been worked out by Suger himself (according to Suger's own autobiographical letters and other writings). It is significant that he was on close terms of personal friendship with the two other architectural innovators, the bishops of Chartres and Sens.

In some degree the new style appears to have had political implications. St. Denis was the chief abbey of France, the burial place of its patron saint, and the home of the oriflamme, the standard used in battle by the kings of France. When the nave was dedicated, Suger invited all the prominent men of the kingdom, including the king himself, and the occasion was used to emphasize a kind of parallelism between the heavenly and the French hierarchies, thus elevating the monarch into a kind of symbol of Christ and thereby increasing his prestige by conveying a mystical sense of his royal role. It is significant that Gothic became especially associated with the royal domain, at this time restricted to the Île de France, and that as the domain expanded, the new style accompanied it.

But the main purpose of Gothic was to represent religious doctrine, in accord with the medieval belief that all material things were only symbols of transcendental truths. This symbolization was performed by the actual structure of the Gothic building, which was therefore exposed to view, not largely covered up, as in Romanesque. This may be regarded as visible geometry; and it is significant that according to Plato's *Timaeus,* the one Platonic dialogue known to the early Middle Ages, geometry was what God had made the world of. The arches and the vaulting, which carried the eyes of the observer upward, conveyed a feeling of soaring; while by a kind of optical illusion the buttresses seemed not so much to be supporting the structure as to be tethering it to the earth and preventing it from flying into the empyrean.

In addition to this illusion of movement, the other main feature of Gothic was its luminosity. One of the main purposes of this method of building was to make possible a maximum employment of the wall space for stained-glass windows; and as the light of the sky was refracted through these brilliantly colored windows it acquired an active quality, and the material of the building seemed real only insofar as it was touched by the light. Suger, it has been said, was "infatuated with Light." In describing St. Denis he declared that "the entire sanctuary is thus pervaded by a wonderful and continuous light entering through the most sacred windows. . . . The work which nobly shines makes our minds shine so that they may go through true lights to the true light, where Christ is the true door." This emphasis on light reflected the medieval belief that it particularly symbolized divinity. Light, in fact, was so closely associated with God that it seemed to have become more than symbolic. For medieval mystics light virtually *was* God. This identification began in the writings of Dionysus, and was expounded by various theologians, particularly by Hugh of St. Victor, who was a friend of Suger. A similar intoxication with light can be found in later mystics like St. Bonaventura, and even in scholars with more scientific interests, such as Robert Grosseteste; and it pervades the *Paradiso* of Dante. Thus when the worshipper in a Gothic abbey or cathedral observed the brilliantly colored windows, and saw the apparently dynamic quality of the light and how it brought to life objects within the building and constantly moved with the movements of the sun and the changing cloud patterns in the sky, he felt that he was indeed watching the direct manifestation of divine power. It was especially appropriate that this conception should have been developed first in an abbey dedicated to Dionysus, and (in view of his identification with the patron saint of France) that the abbey should symbolize not only the all-pervasive power of God but also the God-created authority of the kings of France.[3]

As cathedrals grew bigger and craftsmanship more skillful, an immense variety of human figures and natural objects was presented within the Gothic structure, thus symbolizing the diffusion of religious truths throughout the natural world. Sculpture,

---

[3] For Suger, see Erwin Panofsky: *Meaning in the Visual Arts*, pp. 128–33.

however, was clearly subordinated to architecture, and consisted mainly of human figures which were attached to the walls and doorways and could not be seen in the round. Man's existence was meaningful only through belonging to the divine order. But the trend was toward greater realism and humanization. Typical Gothic figures were shaped like human beings, no longer being elongated as in Romanesque; and the faces had more expression and less solemnity. Occasionally, as in representations of the blessed on judgment day, they were shown with smiles. Christ, moreover, was no longer the stern judge of the world; nor had he yet become the suffering victim preferred in the later Middle Ages. Most frequently in Gothic he was a king, while the Virgin was presented as a beautiful and stately queen.

In presenting nature as an expression of the ideal the Gothic period corresponds in artistic development to the fifth century B.C. in Greece. Yet the differences in the sculpture of the two periods are conspicuous and important. For the Greeks, divinity could be presented as wholly immanent in human forms; the gods were essentially idealized men and women, limited in power and representing beauty and euphoria rather than any exalted ethics. Greek sculpture thus presented independent human figures, not necessarily attached to temples. These were largely nude or semi-nude, and have a sense of organic energy emanating from vital centers within the body. But for the Gothic sculptor, man was an instrument of transcendental divine powers, and hence was presented as subordinate to buildings which symbolized religious beliefs. The bodies were draped, and the draperies were portrayed with no special concern for the bodies beneath them, the figures deriving their power not from within themselves but from the architectural ensemble. In these respects Gothic sculpture may perhaps be regarded as less expressive than that of Greece. But the most significant difference was in the quality of the spiritual emotion. The Greek figures were products of a relatively simple age which had not yet fully grappled with the realities of sin and suffering, and its deities represented an ideal happiness, not yet accepting the full responsibilities of man's tragic destiny.

The euphoria of the Greek gods quickly degenerated after the fifth century into mindlessness and irresponsibility. The medieval artist, on the other hand, inherited a more complex tradition in which evil could not be brushed aside but must somehow be integrated into any total conception of the universe. Gothic sculpture, inferior to that of classical Greece in purely aesthetic qualities, was loaded with a more complex awareness of human experience. The smile that occasionally appeared on the faces of its human figures was more constrained and less spontaneous, bought at a heavier cost, and less easy to maintain.

Meanwhile, in the less conspicuous parts of the cathedrals, other impulses were receiving sculptural expression. Craftsmen were portraying scenes from daily life, realistically rendered leaves and flowers, real and imaginary animals, and grotesquely diabolical faces and figures. Thus, by a kind of relaxation of official discipline, a psychic underworld, somewhat in contrast with the severity of orthodox beliefs, was becoming visible. Theoretically, all the art of the cathedrals was supposed to convey religious truths for the benefit of illiterates; but much of it could have had little spiritual meaning for the average worshipper. The stories and characters that it represented were not easily identified and were often misinterpreted, and some of them were purely playful. Thus every mode of being, both natural and supernatural, was capable of being synthesized into the cathedral structure. But while the Gothic cathedral contained the whole of nature, it was itself the expression of a drive to move beyond and above the natural order. The dynamic abstractionism to which natural objects were subordinated should perhaps be regarded not as Christian but as northern. In its deeper implications, in fact, Gothic can almost be interpreted as negating the Christian values which it was supposedly expressing.

Classical architecture, most impressively represented in the Parthenon, had conveyed a faith that ideals were to be found in nature. Buildings had remained close to the earth and had blended with the environment, the external view being much more important than the interior, while the glowing and rounded columns had seemed almost organic and alive. The classical style had gradually given place in the Roman period to an architecture that repudiated nature, almost ignoring external appearance and concentrating on the shaping of an inner space through which the individual worshipper could feel a sense of absorption into a metaphysical reality. Beginning with some of the buildings of late paganism, this had achieved its supreme expression in the Hagia Sophia in Constantinople. Gothic, on the other hand, sought both to incorporate nature and at the same time to transcend it. In spite of its impulse toward a movement upward, it remained (unlike late classical and Byzantine structures) an integral part of the environment, the sense of soaring being conveyed as strongly in an external view as in the interior. The detailed decoration, moreover, was increasingly naturalistic, even the grotesque and the obscene being capable of incorporation into the Gothic whole. This was the expression of a culture that was beginning to synthesize the doctrinal affirmations it had inherited from the past with the exuberant delight in natural things that marked the progress of secular society forward from barbarism. What Gothic especially conveyed, however, was not the sense of peace and serenity which has been the most usual characteristic of religious art but the feeling of movement. The worshipper did not merely achieve a sense of participation in some form of comprehensive reality, whether natural or supernatural. This was a style that pointed to action as well as to meditation, expressing a belief that man achieved salvation neither by submitting to nature nor by repudiating it but by overcoming it. And in spite of the assimilation of all natural elements, the ultimate reality to which the dynamism led was not organic but abstract. Whereas classical architecture, with its rounded pillars and smooth lines, had idealized organic shapes, Gothic was an architecture in which almost everything ended in a point and nothing was rounded, not even the columns supporting the roof which had gradually replaced the rounded pillars of the classical past. Thus the statuary and pictures were absorbed into a totality which was both dynamic and basically non-naturalistic, in much the same way that animal shapes and human heads had been absorbed into abstract designs in the illuminated manuscripts of the Dark Ages in the British Isles and Carolingian France.

Was there an element in the Gothic achievement that went deeper than Christian beliefs? It expressed man's confidence in his capacity to soar, though the destination was heaven. What is implied, in fact, was not only a striving for salvation but also man's sense of his own limitless capabilities. No architectural style before the twentieth century has done that more powerfully. In subordinating both nature and man himself to an abstract creation it contained an element that was fundamentally inhuman. While it foreshadowed the achievements of Western man in making himself master of the world, it also suggested the *hybris* that may eventually bring him to self-destruction.

This was the style that blossomed in the Île de France and constituted medieval man's most impressive achievement. Its great period lasted for something like a century. Between 1180 and 1270 no less than 80 cathedrals and 2,500 abbey churches were built in France alone. By aesthetic standards Chartres, one of the earliest Gothic structures, and Notre Dame, of the early thirteenth century, were never surpassed; but in the drive for more height and more luminosity there was for a long time a steady progression. Buildings became taller, window space more expansive, and decoration more complicated. A kind of climax was reached with Beauvais, begun in 1247. This had a vault with a height of 160 feet, as contrasted with the 95 feet of Suger's abbey of St. Denis and the 98 feet of the highest Romanesque building, the abbey church of Cluny. But at Beauvais the builders overreached themselves; it proved to be impossible to maintain such a high structure with such limited supports, and after the vault had fallen in 1284, no further attempts were made to complete the nave, the cathedral remaining only as a choir and towers. Meanwhile Gothic had spread in full vitality but with some local divergences through England and through western Germany, and less effectively into Spain and some towns of northern Italy.

A parallel development can be traced in the illustrations of illuminated manuscripts, the only visual art form which remained independent of cathedral architecture. After the initial fusion of classical representationalism with northern two-dimensional abstractionism in the British Isles and Carolingian France, the methods of the illustrators evolved with a momentum of their own, without further external influence. Human figures gradually acquired a plastic three-dimensional solidity and became capable of movement, instead of being used to express transcendental forces. In the manuscripts, as in the sculpture of the cathedrals, Gothic man was presented realistically. Meanwhile the decorations of initial letters became increasingly elaborate, and (as in some of the sculpture) a playful psychic underworld found expression in this humble medium, just as a Bohemian delight in wine and women was manifested in the Latin songs of the wandering scholars. The manuscript decorations gradually began to include dragons and other fanciful wild animals, human beings in various grotesque forms, and even naked women.

Architectural degeneration began to show itself in the fourteenth century. The parts were becoming more important than the whole, the builders losing the sense of organic unity which they had displayed during the great period; and expressiveness began to outrun what was expressed. Later Gothic was marked by an increasing elaboration of decoration. In sculpture there was a new emphasis on suffering, Christ now being portrayed largely as the crucified one, with a realistic rendering of pain. The world, it now appeared, was chiefly a place of suffering, not ennobled by a sense of higher purposes. More definitely degenerate was a kind of sentimentality, often displayed in portrayals of the Virgin, who became more often a French peasant girl and occasionally a woman with overt sexual appeal.

Gothic did not wholly lose its vitality for a long period. The late fifteenth century saw one of the greatest masterpieces of Gothic painting, the Pietà of Villeneuve, in which Christ was presented as suffering but with a forceful dignity and restraint. And the same period saw a kind of revival of the best features of

Gothic, free from the later elaborations, in the provinces of Touraine and Champagne. Gothic lasted into the sixteenth century, and it did not wholly disappear until it was ousted by the new Renaissance styles which had developed in Italy and were now spreading north of the Alps.

.   .   .

Another art form, choral music, was so closely associated with church architecture, and developed so clearly along parallel lines, that it calls for mention in the same chapter. The Christian liturgy from the beginning consisted largely of the singing of Biblical sentences, the tunes being apparently derived from Jewish and other Near Eastern sources. Any use of instruments was for a long time forbidden because of their association with pagan rituals. There was much antiphonal singing in Christian services, the precentor singing the words of psalms or of gospel passages and the congregations replying with long-drawn-out alleluias. This constitutes the only kind of Dark Age music of which we have much knowledge. The progress of all kinds of music was for a long time impeded by the lack of any adequate system of notation. Popular songs without Christian content presumably existed, and—as with the hymns composed in the fourth century by St. Ambrose—they may have exerted some influence on the development of religious music, but we have no record of them.

Until late in the Dark Ages the Christian liturgy did not yet have any fully set form, and different congregations were able to make innovations. These were more frequent in northern Europe than in the Mediterranean countries. As with the visual arts, new developments seem to have originated in the British Isles and subsequently to have been adopted into northern France and the Rhineland during the Carolingian period. Unity was imposed in the time of Charlemagne, the so-called Gregorian chant becoming standard for the whole western European culture area. And although Gregorian chant was attributed to the Roman Church, and Pope Gregory the Great was considered its main author, it actually owed much to northern and British provenance and was not wholly welcomed by the papacy. The Carolingian period also saw some progress in the development of an adequate system of notation, though the most important advances came in the eleventh century with the work of Guido of Arezzo.[4]

The general adoption of Gregorian chant gave Western civilization a form of music marked by "evenness, steadiness and symmetry." As Dom David Knowles has said, it "is wide in its range of emotional expression, majestic, spiritual, and austere beyond all other forms of the art, exquisitely spontaneous and pure in its melody, and extremely subtle and sophisticated in its technical perfection."[5] This phase in musical development closely paralleled the Romanesque phase in architecture. Like the Norman abbeys and cathedrals of the eleventh century, music exhibited a dignity and an inner force reflecting a determination to impose law and order upon the anarchy of the phenomenal world.

Musical progress came about initially through the expansion of the liturgy and the incorporation of new elements. Extra words, known as sequences, began to be interpolated in the singing of the alleluias—an innovation which appears to have been first publicized by a tenth-century monk named Notker belonging to the monastery of St. Gall in Switzerland. In the tenth and eleventh centuries, it has been said, "Gregorian art showed a tendency to large and elaborate constructions exhibiting endless melismata of embellishment."[6] Music, moreover, began to be instrumental as well as vocal, religious antagonisms to instruments being gradually forgotten, though the human voice continued to dominate music until the late Renaissance.

The most important musical innovation was choral polyphony, which may be regarded as equivalent to the architectural

---

[4] See Denis Stevens and Alec Robertson: *Pelican History of Music,* I, 246.
[5] Quoted in Stevens and Robertson: op. cit., I, 159.
[6] Paul H. Lang: *Music in Western Civilization,* p. 78.

growth of Romanesque into Gothic. While it appears to have originated in Britain, a full recognition of its importance came only with its adoption into the French cathedrals late in the twelfth century. Notre Dame became the chief center of the new music, and its first acknowledged master, whose name was Leonin, was attached to this cathedral late in the twelfth century.

One of the special achievements of the Gothic style was the capacity to create a transcendent unity out of disparate elements. It presented a synthesis of a wide variety of human and animal shapes, these sculptural items being unified by the general design. Thus the whole of creation was presented in symbolic form in a single cathedral, with special emphasis on what man needed to know in order to secure his own salvation. Choral polyphony exhibited the same quality in sound. It was no longer considered necessary for every singer to be singing the same melody and the same words at the same time. Several different passages were sung at the same time and were presented as parts of a broader union, built up by individual contributions. The final result was a balance of forces. The individual listener "must make his choice, select a part and follow it, and then become a part of the polyphonic web." [7] There is a close parallelism between this unification of sounds and the balancing of ogives in the roofs of Gothic cathedrals, both being intended to convey a sense of actual multiplicity controlled and unified by divine power.

Later developments in music were predominantly secular; the innovations in the liturgy were extended to nonreligious music. There had been a considerable development of musical entertainment during the early Middle Ages. The troubadours had been composers of music as well as of lyric poetry (until the Renaissance it was taken for granted that poems were to be sung, or at least recited, not merely read). The fusion of religious and popular music was displayed mainly in the motet, which was a polyphonic performance, composed for several different voices, but

---

[7] Lang: op. cit., p. 137.

generally secular in subject matter and no longer associated with the cathedrals. Other forms of music continued to be written, but through the later Middle Ages the widespread interest in music (the capacity to sing and perform on an instrument was an essential part of a gentleman's education) was expressed chiefly in the composition of motets. There was an intense interest in music among educated persons and a considerable development of musical theory. During the fourteenth and fifteenth centuries, France, Italy, and the Netherlands all contributed to musical growth and produced important individual composers.

Meanwhile the democratic element always present in the liturgy, though for a long time kept under clerical control, had led to the growth of popular religious drama. Instead of merely singing alleluias, along with the additional words authorized by the clergy, members of religious congregations began to assume different roles and sing the appropriate words. This led them to act out episodes in Biblical stories and lives of saints, the liturgy thus giving birth to the mystery and miracle plays. The medieval drama remained an essentially democratic art, enabling ordinary men and women to participate actively in what was regarded as a form of religious worship. It continued to be popular until the Renaissance introduced some knowledge of the classical drama, especially that of Seneca, thus leading to a fusion of different traditions which, at least in Spain and England, produced a theater of first-rate creative performance.

I I

The Later Middle Ages

During the twelfth century the creative energies of the new civilization had found expression with remarkably little awareness of cultural conflict. The West was, of course, by no means peaceful; there were wars between Pope and emperor, between kings and their vassals, and between the rising cities and their feudal superiors; but for a long time these did not lead to any questioning of first principles. Yet the two great institutional and value systems of medieval society—feudalism and the Church—represented fundamentally different views of life. And while religious thinkers were translating the dogmas of an ascetic and otherworldly Christianity into terms comprehensible to the medieval mind and accessible to human emotion, secular poets were recommending warriors to display a wholly worldly moderation and were glorifying an adulterous courtly love. Much of the cultural activity of the twelfth century was, in fact, non-Christian, if not overtly anti-Christian.

Yet for a period a synthesis of all the major cultural trends seemed to be possible, despite the intellectual contradictions between them. The great Gothic cathedrals succeeded in combining Christian belief with delight in natural objects. Of similar significance was the appearance of individuals who embodied both feudal and Catholic values with a grace and apparent harmony which acute cultural conflicts would have made impossible. A man like Louis IX, the only French king who attained, and was worthy of, the honor of sanctification, summed up the finest aspects of the medieval spirit.

King of France from 1226 to 1270, Louis respected the law, refused to engage in wars of conquest for territories to which he was not entitled, and displayed in ruling his kingdom both a scrupulous sense of justice and firmness of a kind too often lacking in saintly kings. This firmness could extend even to the hierarchy of the Church when he believed that its members were claiming more than their due. Combining justice with a discriminating charity (he contributed vast sums in alms for the unfortunate), he showed himself both masterful as a king and at the same time humble as a Christian. His friend and biographer, Jean de Joinville, liked to remember him sitting against a tree in the wood of Vincennes after Mass, surrounded by his councilors and listening to any of his subjects who wished to make requests or complain of unjust treatment. France prospered under his rule and enjoyed more peace, both internally and externally, than at any other period of the Middle Ages. St. Louis was even able to put an end to the private wars which had been the curse of feudalism.

Yet St. Louis shared most of the superstitions of the time. He believed in the efficacy of relics and paid to the emperor at Constantinople immense sums for Jesus' crown of thorns and a piece of the true cross. The Sainte Chapelle in Paris, with its glorious array of blue windows, perhaps the ultimate Gothic achievement in luminosity, was built to house these precious objects. When he was in danger of shipwreck while crossing the Mediterranean, he lay on the deck wearing only a shirt, with his arms spread crosswise, praying to the sacred host in front of him. He had no tolerance for enemies of Christianity and warned unlearned persons to have no dealings with Jews lest they be led astray. "And so I say unto you," Joinville represents him as saying, "that no man, unless he be a very good clerk, should argue with them; but the layman, when he heareth the Christian law reviled, should not defend it but by his sword, wherewith he

236

should pierce the vitals of the reviler as far as it will go." [1] In accordance with these beliefs Louis was an ardent crusader, and was absent from his kingdom for no less than six years, first leading his army against the Mohammedan forces in Egypt, where he was defeated and captured, so that his subjects had to raise an immense sum to ransom him, and then spending four years directing the affairs of what survived of the Christian Kingdom of Jerusalem. His mode of life in his later years was highly ascetic. He wore a hair shirt, had himself regularly scourged with iron chains, and heard two Masses daily. All this made him a suitable candidate for sainthood, and (according to Joinville) his corpse, buried at Marseilles, worked "very fair miracles."

Louis was fortunate in having a biographer who could convey the flavor of his personality; but all the records of his time portray him not only as a saint but also as a human being endowed with the kind of charm that is possible only for those who have achieved an inner integrity. The Italian chronicler Salimbene, who saw him at the outset of his Crusade, remembered him as "spare and slender, having the face of an angel, and a countenance full of grace." [2] And if one adds that he was somewhat dominated by his mother, the famous Blanche of Castile, who served as the very efficient ruler of France before Louis was of age, and that little love was lost between Blanche and her daughter-in-law, this reminder of human problems makes the qualities of the royal saint even more vivid.

The ideals that had animated St. Louis, however, were rapidly ceasing to be practically effective. The later Middle Ages saw one of those basic transformations of values and allegiances that mark the end of a historical epoch. In the course of the thirteenth century the Roman Church lost much of the popular support on

---

[1] Jean de Joinville: *History of Saint Louis,* translated by Joan Evans (Oxford, 1938), I, 10; II, 122.

[2] Quoted in G. G. Coulton: *From St. Francis to Dante* (London, 1907), p. 140.

which its influence depended. There was a growing resentment against its claims to power and financial support and against the corruption of the clergy. Meanwhile, the feudal order, which had always been an order in theory rather than in reality, was giving place to new forms of political authority. In France, Spain, and England the main residuary legatee of both the Church and the feudal order was the national state headed by a strong monarchy, which was now becoming the main source of order and focus of popular loyalties. While the rise of the state meant a loss of the sense of the unity of western Christendom, it brought about a great increase in administrative efficiency and in the enforcement of law and order.

Clerical claims to supremacy over secular authorities, which had first been strongly asserted by Gregory VII in the eleventh century, seem to have reached a kind of climax with Innocent III, who was Pope from 1198 until 1216. He asserted a responsibility to rebuke all forms of sin (including sins committed by kings) and proudly affirmed that God had "entrusted to Peter not only the universal church but the government of the whole world." [3] Innocent was a statesman of the highest skill and determination, and he was also fortunate in that (apart from King Philip II of France) he had no formidable opponents. For a few years his claims were accepted—verbally, at least—by most of western Europe.

The political claims of the papacy were accompanied by an attempt to impose intellectual and cultural orthodoxy, if necessary by force. During the twelfth century the creative powers of the new Western civilization had been exercised with remarkable freedom and variety. The thirteenth century, on the other hand, was an age of attempted synthesis and consolidation; and this brought to an end the great period of medieval creativity. The Church now sought to absorb whatever could be reconciled with its dogmas—this was the age of the great scholastic system-build-

---

[3] Henry Osborn Taylor: *The Medieval Mind,* II, 303.

ers who attempted to organize the whole range of thought—but tendencies which could not be harmonized with orthodox doctrine met with growing intolerance. Threatened both by popular movements of protest against its wealth and corruption and by the influx of new ideas from Arabic sources, the Church resorted, for the first time in Western history, to organized repression and persecution of heresy. This unprecedented use of force proved ultimately to be self-defeating, leading to skepticism and rebellion and to the general cultural disintegration of the later Middle Ages.

In actuality, western Europe had never been monolithic in its religious beliefs. That medieval society was ever wholly loyal to the Catholic Church is a myth fostered by Catholic propagandists. Heretical movements were always numerous and widespread, especially among the poorer of the bourgeoisie, but we cannot judge them fairly because all that we know of them comes from orthodox sources. During the twelfth century a number of sectarian movements denounced the wealth and privileges of the clergy and demanded a return to the poverty and simplicity of gospel Christianity, thus illustrating the dangers to the Church of unrestricted Bible-reading. The most popular of these movements was that of the Poor Men of Lyon, or Waldensians, founded about 1170 by the merchant Peter Waldo. They were condemned by the Church as heretical in 1184, but continued to increase. In order to check such movements the Pope ordered in 1229 that the Bible be read only in Latin and that the Psalter should be the only section of it permitted to laymen. But anticlerical sects continued to increase, especially in the towns of northern Italy.

Other sectarian movements, equally hostile to the clergy, revived the millennial fantasies that had been a disturbing element in Christian teaching from the beginning. False prophets arose, probably self-deluded, but making messianic claims and promising a rapid advent of the age of the Holy Spirit when all men would obey the spirit within them, which had been promised by a long line of Jewish and Christian mystics ever since the Old

239

Testament prophets. In 1110, for example, a prophet called Tanchelm appeared in Flanders, denouncing the clergy and promising the millennium. Until he was killed in 1115 he won mass support among the poorer classes in the Flemish cities.

The most formidable of the heresies, and the chief reason for the Church's resort to persecution, was the Albigensian, or Catharist, movement, which spread through most of southern France during the twelfth century. According to Catholic sources —and no others are available—this was a revival of the Manichaean heresy of the third and fourth centuries. Surviving in Armenia, it had spread to Bulgaria and other Balkan countries in the later Dark Ages and had apparently been brought to the West through commercial contacts. Preaching a dualism of good and evil which seems to have been suggested by the Zoroastrian religion of Iran, the Albigensians declared that the world had been created by the spirit of evil and that salvation could come only from freeing oneself from everything that was tainted by materiality, and more particularly from sexual desire. They denounced the wealth and arrogance of the established clergy, and this won them wide support from many who by no means shared their ascetic ideals, including many of the troubadours.

The Albigensians were accused by the Church of gross immoralities, apparently on the assumption that they denied marriage rather than sex. Actually the leaders of the movement—the *perfecti* who were pledged to live fully ascetic lives—displayed an impressive saintliness and were willing to suffer torture and execution rather than deny their faith. By the end of the twelfth century they seem to have won the respect of most of the population of the Midi, including both nobles and commoners, and had built up an elaborate organization, with headquarters in a castle at Montsegur, an almost inaccessible mountain in the eastern Pyrenees. Throughout the Midi, and also in parts of northern Italy, they were a serious threat to Christianity.

The Church had not previously resorted to the persecution of heretical groups. As early as 385 several Spaniards who had espoused the "Priscillianist" heresy (also a form of Manichaeanism) had been executed by the secular authorities; but this action had met with strong disapproval from clerical leaders and had not established a precedent. In the course of the twelfth century a number of heretics had been put to death, but these killings were the result of popular hysteria or the anxiety of secular governments to maintain order and uniformity rather than of clerical policy. In 1204, Pope Innocent launched a missionary campaign to end Albigensianism in southern France; but peaceful methods of persuasion proved ineffective, and after a papal legate was murdered and the murderer went unpunished, the Pope resorted to sterner measures. In 1209 he called upon Christian warriors to organize a Crusade against the heretics, promising that they could keep for themselves any lands they conquered from Albigensian nobles. This resort to force was accompanied by the use of inquisitorial methods to discover heretics, and persons found guilty were turned over to the secular authorities for execution. The Inquisition, at first left under the control of the local bishops, was made directly responsible to the papacy in 1231.

The Albigensian Crusade was one of the most horrible episodes in medieval history, surpassing even the crusaders' conquest of Palestine in brutality and destructiveness. During more than a quarter of a century Catholic nobility from northern France engaged in a series of campaigns for the conquest of the Midi, destroying the tolerant and easygoing civilization in which the troubadours had flourished. The famous statement attributed to the papal legate when the crusaders massacred all the inhabitants of the city of Béziers—"Kill them all, for God will know his own"—is probably fictitious, but it certainly reflects the attitudes of the crusaders. Religion soon ceased to be the main motivation for the war, which became primarily a struggle to extend over southern France the rule of the monarchy and the northern nobility; and many good Catholics soon found themselves fighting on the same side as the Albigensians for political reasons.[4]

---

[4] Like King Pedro II of Aragon, who was killed in battle in 1213. A good Catholic, Pedro had been one of the first kings to assume the responsibility of preventing heresy in his kingdom. His defeat and death in battle apparently

Albigensianism, however, was finally destroyed, the last episode of the war being the capture in the year 1245 of the fortress of Montsegur and the slaughter of the Albigensian *perfecti* who had taken refuge there.

Having claimed political as well as spiritual authority, and having sanctioned the use of force in defense of the Catholic faith, the papacy had embarked on a course of action which proved eventually to be suicidal. During the middle decades of the thirteenth century it became involved in a long conflict with the Emperor Frederick II and his successors, which kept all of Italy in constant turmoil and led to increasingly urgent demands for money from the Catholic laity all over western Europe.

The fourth emperor of the Hohenstaufen dynasty, Frederick inherited through his mother the Norman kingdom of Naples and Sicily. Born and brought up in Italy, he spent little time in Germany, concentrating most of his energies on the government of his southern Italian kingdom and identifying himself with the traditions of the Mediterranean civilizations, Roman, Byzantine, and Arabic. Mostly self-educated, he spoke seven languages, encouraged the development of Italian poetry, wrote a book on falconry that had genuine scientific value, made scientific experiments, liked to travel accompanied by a whole menagerie of unusual animals as well as a corps of male and female entertainers who were alleged to compose a kind of bisexual harem, and was, in general, the exemplar of a rationalism that was wholly alien to medieval ways of thinking. While Louis IX embodied the best aspects of medievalism, Frederick, known to his contemporaries as the Wonder of the World, represented the future. His most important achievement was to build a new kind of bureaucratic state in his kingdom of Naples and Sicily, guided as far as possible by rational principles of government. He regulated eco-

---

resulted partly from his having spent the previous night enthusiastically enjoying the women provided for his entertainment by his southern French hosts. When the time for action came, he had barely enough energy left to climb onto his horse.

nomic activity, promoted learning, and provided efficient methods of enforcing justice, but did not tolerate individual freedom. Although he was himself somewhat of a freethinker—how much so remains controversial—and although he was on friendly terms with Arabs and Jews and employed them in his government, he did not permit Christian heresies, regarding them as a cause of disorder. Like the Italian despots of the Renaissance, he treated the state as a kind of work of art created by an absolute ruler, showing no concern for individual rights or concepts of legitimacy.[5]

With two authorities in Italy, both of them claiming supreme power though animated by wholly different ideas, conflict was inevitable, and the later years of Frederick's reign were filled with bloody, prolonged wars between Pope and emperor. These civil wars spread to most of the north Italian cities and led to the divisions between the Guelph and Ghibelline factions which were the main curse of Italy for the next two centuries—Guelph was the name of a German princely family friendly to the papacy, and Ghibelline was an alternative name for the Hohenstaufen. Frederick died in 1250, but the papacy continued the struggle with younger members of his family for another decade until all of them had been destroyed. The papal victory was achieved largely because of the assistance of the French, who had temporarily acquired a dominating position in the affairs of Italy. A victory won on such terms was, however, worse than defeat. The claims to universal rule which had been affirmed by Innocent III had degenerated into demands for wealth and power. Such at

---

[5] Little of enduring importance can be attributed to the last of the Hohenstaufen emperors; but he was the kind of individual who continues throughout later history to have a personal appeal. Along with other Hohenstaufen rulers, he occupies a coffin in the cathedral of Palermo. (The words are chosen carefully—the coffins are above ground, and are not located in any kind of tomb.) On June 13, 1967, somebody placed flowers beside his coffin. According to the guide employed by the cathedral authorities, the flowers belonged to a German resident of Palermo who wished to remind the Sicilians of the greatness of men of German origin.

least was the conviction of many of the lay population who continued to support Christian beliefs but could no longer see the existing Church or its hierarchy as embodying them. For devout individuals a visit to Rome was a particularly disillusioning experience, for clerical greed and self-seeking were nowhere more conspicuous than in the capital of Christendom.

The fall of the Hohenstaufen brought to an end the attempt of the Holy Roman emperors to combine Italy and Germany under one government. Later emperors were mostly concerned only with German affairs, though they signally failed to establish any effective central government; and the whole imperial myth, which Western civilization had inherited from its Roman predecessor, ceased to have any practical effect or importance, though it was still accepted by intellectuals (such as Dante). But the papacy now confronted more formidable opponents in the growing national states, the main causes of conflict being financial. While Rome was making increased demands for money from churches in all western countries, the western monarchies were insisting that the clergy should contribute more heavily to the expenses of the secular governments. The inevitable conflict came during the pontificate of Boniface VIII (1296–1303), who had asserted papal supremacy over all secular authorities even more uncompromisingly than Innocent III. Disagreements with the French King Philip IV evoked in 1303 the bull *Unam Sanctam,* in which Boniface affirmed that subjection to the Pope was altogether necessary for salvation for all human beings. French authorities, aided by Italian antipapalists, retaliated by seizing Boniface and physically maltreating him—a shock which caused his death within a few days. The French subsequently put pressure on the College of Cardinals to bring about the election of a French prelate who established himself not at Rome but at Avignon. During this "Babylonian Captivity" the papacy largely represented French interests, and in consequence retained little respect from other European peoples. Worse was to follow, for an attempt to restore the papacy to Rome led in 1378 to the "Great Schism" with rival pontiffs at Rome and at Avignon.

1. *These three reproductions of parts of the Lindisfarne Gospels were made in northern Britain late in the eighth century. They illustrate the beginning of the fusion of northern abstractionism and the representationalism of the Mediterranean artistic tradition. Two of the reproductions are almost wholly abstract and are strongly influenced by Irish art of the so-called Dark Ages. This picture of St. Matthew attempts to present a realistic portrait but fails completely to convey any sense of three dimensions.*

2. *a. This church of St. Peter, built at Toscanella, Italy, during the twelfth century, illustrates the Romanesque style of architecture.*

b. Mathilda's Abbey Church at Caen. A forceful example of Norman Romanesque in the later years of the twelfth century.

3. *The doorway of the Abbey of Moutiers-St.-Jean, in Burgundy, built in the thirteenth century. Typical of Gothic during its best period. Particularly notable is the human quality of the two figures, who are shown as independent of the building.*

4. *The cathedral of St.-Pierre at Beauvais. Built during the middle decades of the thirteenth century, this was the culmination of the Gothic style. Its builders overreached themselves, and after the choir collapsed in 1284, no attempt was made to rebuild it.*

5. *In the early Middle Ages, Christ had been represented as the triumphant judge and king. During the period of the medieval decadence, emphasis was shifted to the human and suffering Christ. This* Pietà *was made in Touraine about the year 1500.*

6. *Flemish art of the fifteenth century was crowded with figures, most of them of middle-class origin, richly colored, and expressing satisfaction with life as it was. These pictures are the work of an anonymous painter generally known as the Master of the St. Barbara Legend. They portray King David giving a letter to Uriah, and the Queen of Sheba bringing gifts to King Solomon.*

ITALIAN ART BEFORE GIOTTO

7. *a.* OPPOSITE, TOP: *Mosaics in the church of Santa Maria in Trastevere, Rome. Portraying Jesus, the Virgin Mary, and various saints; made in 1145.*

b. BOTTOM: *The Virgin and various angels and saints; painted in Florence in the thirteenth century by Cimabue. Both pictures lack movement and action, and try to express spiritual realities by means of rows of human figures.*

8. *The resurrection of Lazarus by Giotto, painted in the chapel of the Scrovegni in the cathedral, Padua, in about the year 1305. Giotto revolutionized Italian art by depicting human beings realistically, but the realism was restricted to the figures in the foreground.*

9. OPPOSITE: *Stefano da Zevio's* Virgin in the Rosegarden *and Gentile da Fabriano's* Journey of the Magi, *both painted early in the fifteenth century, illustrate the dreamlike quality and secular magnificence of the "International Gothic" of the later Middle Ages.*

10. Peter and the Tribute Money, *painted by Masaccio shortly before his premature death in 1428. After Giotto, for a hundred years, Italian art had made little further progress toward realistic representation. Then the rules of perspective were discovered, making it possible for artists to paint convincingly three-dimensional pictures. The first to do so was Masaccio.*

11. *The Pazzi Chapel, Florence, designed in the 1440's by Brunelleschi and exemplifying the originality of post-Gothic Italian architecture. The campanile in the background, attached to the church of Santa Croce, retains a Gothic quality.*

12. a. This portrayal of the condottiere Gattamelata was made by Donatello in the 1440's. The first figure of a man on horseback since Roman times, it illustrates the delight in human vitality which characterized Renaissance man in general and Donatello in particular.

b. The Tempietto (cloister of San Pietro in Montorio, Rome) built in 1503 by Bramante. A round building surmounted by a dome, it expresses the spirit of the Renaissance in spite of its failure to meet the functional requirements of Christian worship.

13. *a. Ghirlandaio's last supper, painted in the 1470's, was strictly representationist.*

b. Leonardo's, nearly a generation later, exemplified the faith in the creative insight of the artist, which was leading to the abandonment of realism.

c. For Tintoretto, working in the 1570's, religious truth came through mystical insights, and the conflict about realism had become meaningless.

THREE VERSIONS OF THE LAST SUPPER

14. *This portrayal of St. Peter's miraculous draft of fishes, painted by Raphael shortly before his premature death in 1520, shows how the art of the high Renaissance was departing from realism. The placing of the figures in this picture is realistically impossible, though this will not be noticed by the spectator without careful examination.*

15. *Portrait of Lucrezia Panciatichi, painted early in the sixteenth century by the mannerist Angiolo Bronzino. Mannerism reflected the uncertainties of Italian art after the great age. Its sense of insecurity is strikingly reflected in the facial impression and body posture of this portrait.*

16. *The sixteenth-century château of Chenonceaux, in the Loire Valley. The lower floors are Renaissance in spirit, but Gothic reminiscences domi-nate the roof.*

Normality was not restored until 1417, when the Council of Constance succeeded in winning general recognition for a single pontiff, Martin V, with headquarters at Rome.

Thus the inability of medieval man to make a workable separation between spiritual and political authorities, the consequent involvement of the Church in secular affairs, and the growing resentment against the corruption of the clergy led to the downfall of the institution which implemented and symbolized the belief in the unity of Christendom. The papacy never fully regained its position of leadership; for more than a century after the Great Schism it was largely involved in Italian politics, attempting to safeguard itself by winning full control of the papal state, while its attitudes were deeply affected by the secularism of the Renaissance. During the Schism there had been much advocacy of a transfer of authority from the papacy to a general council; but although the leaders of this so-called Conciliar Movement made significant contributions to political theory, they were unable to make them practically effective. Insofar as religion survived as a positive and constructive force, it mostly took the form of a mysticism which was markedly individualistic and had little use for institutional forms.

Meanwhile the other great institutional and value system of the early Middle Ages was also disintegrating. The decay of feudalism and the rise of monarchy were most complete and most significant in France, where they came about by a slow evolutionary process. At the beginning of the Middle Ages the French king was merely the apex of the feudal pyramid and was dependent on the great feudal magnates for armed forces and most of the other appurtenances of sovereignty. Only in his own feudal domain, which originally consisted of a small province surrounding the city of Paris, did he exercise effective authority. The extension of royal power was brought about by the elimination of the great magnates and the expansion of the king's domain. This was largely accomplished during the reign of Philip II (1180–1223). Later kings somewhat reversed the process by granting duchies to their younger sons, but without full feudal powers. Thus

France was again partially disunified in the later Middle Ages, and was not definitively reunited until the end of the fifteenth century, when Brittany, the last of the great feudal fiefs, was added to the royal domain.

Accompanying this geographical expansion was the construction of effective machinery of government, free from feudal restrictions. The kings gradually assumed authority to maintain an army under their own direct control, to collect in taxes whatever money was needed for the expenses of government, and to supervise the administration of justice. Royal officials, mostly of middle-class origin and university-trained, composed a new bureaucracy, whose powers were deeply resented by the old noble families. In the new order literacy and loyalty to the crown counted for more than noble birth and prowess in battle. As was declared by Guillaume de Nogaret, an official under King Philip IV (1285–1314), "They are not nobles, but they are chevaliers of the king; the king has taken them for his men; from that their honor, from that their dignity. They are in infinite number in the kingdom." [6] The rise of the monarchy was generally supported by all those groups who—for economic or other reasons—wanted to put an end to the endemic violence of feudal society, and particularly by the bourgeoisie. In the course of the thirteenth century the monarchy became strong enough to end private warfare among nobles, and thereafter the right to wage war was a royal monopoly.

Meanwhile economic changes were causing a gradual erosion of the system of mutual obligations of which feudalism consisted. With the steady increase of trade and the use of money, the customary services owed by the peasants to their lords could often be commuted into money payments. The traditional lord-and-serf relationship changed into one of landlord and tenant, which normally benefited both parties. This meant that the peasants became legally free and were no longer attached to the soil,

---

[6] Quoted in Wallace K. Ferguson: *Europe in Transition,* p. 176.

while the lords generally found it more convenient to have money rather than labor at their disposal. But because the payments due from the peasants were not normally subject to change and because the increase of money in circulation resulted in a slow but fairly steady inflation, the change worked in the long run to the detriment of the nobility. In the later Middle Ages, in fact, the minor nobility was losing much of its former authority and independence, for a number of different reasons. Coats of armor, for example, were becoming more elaborate and more expensive, and were often beyond the resources of the lesser nobles.

Thus a new kind of society was coming into existence, a society in which ambitious individuals without hereditary advantages could acquire wealth and prestige and in which socio-economic relationships involved money payments rather than personal services and pledges of allegiance. Yet for a long time there was little conscious awareness of this social transformation. The belief in feudal values endured long after they had largely ceased to be practically effective in the organization of society. Throughout the later Middle Ages, and in some degree down to relatively recent times, it was still widely assumed that noble birth carried with it certain special virtues and that the qualities of the warrior lord were superior to those of the merchant or the royal official. The cult of chivalry was strongest in the fourteenth and fifteenth centuries, long after it had ceased to be meaningful as a social force. Feudal ideals, represented by the image of a knight in armor uninterested in materialistic gains and prepared to risk his life in noble causes, have, in fact, retained their glamour down to the twentieth century, and have had appreciable effects on social attitudes, despite the sharp discrepancy between conceptions and realities.

The growth of royal power brought with it a transfer of loyalties, without which it could not have become effective. In the earlier stages of the rise of the monarchy, kings had continued to regard themselves in feudal terms, claiming simply the rights and powers to which feudalism entitled them. This had remained true as late as the reign of Louis IX. But it gradually became apparent that, in reality, the king was accumulating powers that went far beyond feudal concepts. These new powers brought him into direct relationship with French people of all classes and ranks, so that the monarchy could no longer be regarded simply as the apex of the feudal pyramid. Thereafter the primary loyalty of every Frenchman was given to the state, and to the king as its representative, and not to his immediate superior in the feudal hierarchy.

This change became explicit in the reign of Philip IV (1285–1314). The growth of centralized government and the transfer of administrative, judicial, and fiscal powers from the feudal lords to the crown made a new theory of government essential. Philip's advisers—nobody is sure how far the initiative was taken by members of the royal bureaucracy and how much the king himself contributed to it—turned from feudal to classical principles. In this shift they were strongly influenced by the study of Roman law in the universities. The king was to be regarded as the successor of the Roman emperor, endowed with the same absolute powers and responsible only to God. This claim was facilitated by the decline of the so-called Holy Roman Empire of the German kings into little more than a legal fiction, and by the conflict between the French king and the papacy. But in making imperial claims for their master the French lawyers and bureaucrats were, of course, unable to adopt the main traditional justification for such claims. The emperor had been regarded as the God-appointed ruler of the whole human race, and hence as the preserver of peace and the symbol of unity. It is true that one of Philip's spokesmen, Pierre Dubois, argued that the empire should be transferred from the German to the French king, but no attempt was made to implement this proposition. In practice, western Europe was split into several different states, each with its own government claiming absolute powers.

What was important was the fact of royal supremacy rather than the theory by which it was justified. And as this supremacy meant a transfer of individual loyalties and allegiances, it was necessarily a slow and protracted process. Philip IV was almost an absolute monarch, but during the fourteenth and fifteenth centuries royal powers were temporarily weakened by several ineffectual rulers, some of whom were too strongly influenced by the ideals of feudal chivalry. And although the growth of the national state meant more peace and order, more administrative efficiency, and a more rational approach to political problems, the emotional attitudes and the arguments by which it was supported remained medieval and pre-scientific. The Western mind was still obsessed with the ideal of unity, though this ideal had been transferred from Christendom as a whole to the national state, and it was still accustomed to support its political beliefs with cosmological arguments which would appear to the modern mind to be mere analogies, but which were then regarded as fundamental truths. There was no basic change in the quality of political thinking until the seventeenth and eighteenth centuries, when the defense of unity and kingship by cosmic analogies gave place to the equally necessary, but equally irrational, doctrine of natural rights.

France became the standard example of royal absolutism. The political evolution of Spain was complicated by the long war with the Mohammedans and by the division of the Christians into several different kingdoms. She achieved political unity under the rule of Ferdinand and Isabella in the fifteenth century, but both politically and culturally there continued to be sharp divisions among the Spanish provinces. The dominance of Castile, which stood for unification, was resisted by other sections of the country. In the third of the national states, England, a similar growth of a royal power capable of enforcing unity culminated in the sixteenth century in the rule of the Tudor dynasty. But English political development was more complex than that of France and Spain, though there was little awareness of this fact or of its importance. In England the powers of the monarchy were legally limited by Parliament, and the individual citizen was regarded as having rights which government could not violate. In spite of what looked like Tudor absolutism, England became a pioneer in the creation of new political institutions leading toward government by the people.

12

Late Medieval Thought

Meanwhile the movement of Christian thought was running parallel to that of Christian politics. Scholastic philosophy attempted to organize the whole of human thought and ended with the recognition that this was impossible and that scholastic principles could be maintained only by force or authority, not by rational argument. Confronted by the growing strength of non-Christian ways of thinking, theologians attempted to organize the whole of the Christian view of life into a comprehensive system which would fuse faith and reason and provide answers to all possible questions. The twelfth century had been an age of new beginnings in theology, in which doors had been opened for new forms of thinking. The great system-builders of the thirteenth century, despite their relatively liberal and optimistic conceptions of human nature, were attempting to close doors. Having carried the effort to rationalize theology to its farthest-possible limits, they were followed in the fourteenth century by thinkers who affirmed that faith and reason were ultimately irreconcilable and by the consequent collapse of the whole scholastic enterprise.

The most important new threat to Christian doctrine was the growing influence of Aristotle, who reached the West through Arabic intermediaries and accompanied by Arabic interpretations, especially those of the twelfth-century Spanish philosopher Ibn Rochd, generally known to the West as Averroës. A vast number of translations into Latin were made of Arabic works of science and philosophy and of Greek works from Arabic versions. This activity took place chiefly in Spain and was sponsored by tolerant clergymen, especially by Archbishop Raymond of Toledo. The most active of the translators was Gerard of Cremona, who arrived in Toledo about the year 1165 and is said to have translated no less than seventy-one Arabic works. The result was that Western scholars became acquainted with almost the whole corpus of the works of Aristotle, along with Arabic commentaries which tended to give them a Neo-Platonic coloration.

Thus the West was now being introduced to a system of thought which affirmed that philosophy was independent of theology and might arrive at truths contrary to those of religion. According to Averroës there were two kinds of truth, each of them valid in its own sphere. And according to Aristotelian philosophy God was not the Person of Christian theology who had made the universe and continued to govern it and to be concerned with human salvation and damnation. The universe existed eternally, and God was an impersonal principle of perfection engaged in the contemplation of his own being and imparting movement to the universe by his mere existence. Nor did man have an individual soul capable of surviving the death of the body; his soul would be absorbed into the divine being, and would not retain any separate identity. Early in the thirteenth century, teachers of philosophy in western Europe were beginning to explore these Aristotelian conceptions, and were therefore accused of Averroism. We hear especially of David of Dinant and Amaury of Bène, both of whom taught at the University of Paris, and at a later period of Siger of Brabant, who rather puzzlingly was placed by Dante in paradise. All these men were natives of the Netherlands, which was coming to rival northern Italy as a center of bourgeois wealth and intellectual independence.

Because Aristotelianism led to these non-Christian doctrines, the Church was initially hostile to it, and for a generation or more even prohibited it from being taught. During the second

half of the thirteenth century, on the other hand, scholastic philosophers began to incorporate Aristotelian doctrines into Christianity, making a distinction between truths accessible to the
human reason and truths that could be known only through
revelation. The two forms of truth were not in contradiction with
each other, but were known through different channels. This
change of attitude was of immense importance, though in the
long run it proved to be an ineffective method of defending
Christianity from rationalistic criticisms.

Prior to the advent of Aristotelianism, Christian thought had
mostly adhered to the lines laid down by St. Augustine, whose
philosophy had retained a strong element of the Platonism he had
absorbed before his conversion. For Augustine, as for all thinkers
in the Platonic tradition, knowledge was not derived from sensuous observation and experience. The senses were misleading
and could not lead to truth. Truth came from the direct contemplation of the divine ideas, which were innate in the human soul
and known by intuition. For Christian philosophers they were
more or less identical with God himself. Thus Christian thinkers,
enlightened by divine grace, had a direct mystical knowledge of
spiritual realities. These realities were known by divine revelation
and were taught to nonbelievers by the Church. Because heretics
and nonbelievers were required to accept Christian doctrine on
the authority of the Church, this attitude often appeared to be
hostile to freedom of thought and to the growth of rationalism, as
in Bernard's condemnation of Abelard. But it must not be forgotten that faith in the dogmas of the Church was corroborated by
the spiritual experience of believers. This could not be conveyed
in words, but it gave to Christians a sense of certainty derived
not from logic but from the feeling of immediate apprehension
of spiritual realities. The essence of Christianity was the sense of
submission to the will of God, of identification with Jesus, and of
the forgiveness of sins, all of which were interpreted as made
possible by divine grace. In spite of the degeneration of popular
Christianity during the Dark and Middle Ages into a system of
magic-working little higher than the forms of paganism which it

had superseded, the experience of grace continued to be known by saints and philosophers. It was the premise of all Christian thinking; and it should be remembered that all systems of thought, scientific as well as religious, are based on premises which transcend rational proof, although they may be corroborated by appeals to reason and to experience.

In the thirteenth century, however, Christian philosophers found themselves confronted by a dilemma. The Platonic and Augustinian tradition could be maintained either by appeal to the authority of the Church or by appeal to the spiritual experience of individuals. But the reliance on authority would necessarily block all intellectual progress, and was made increasingly untenable by the growth of rationalistic and critical attitudes derived from the encounter with Arabic thought. The appeal to direct personal experience, on the other hand, might open the way to radically new ways of thinking which would undermine the whole structure of organized Christianity, as had been shown in the growth of popular heresies; and the Church, as an authoritarian institution, was not bold enough to expose itself to this kind of danger. In order to escape from this dilemma, Christian thinkers began to repudiate the whole Platonic and Augustinian distrust of reason and to present Christian doctrine as a rational structure defensible by means of logical argument. Truth was no longer based either on authority or on inner intuition, but was approached by deduction from sensuous experience and observation. In the later years of the thirteenth century, therefore, though with many misgivings and reversals of direction, the Church moved away from Platonism and turned toward the rival Aristotelian tradition, which was largely derived from the Arabs and purported to present most of the structure of belief in rational terms.

Thirteenth-century philosophy was almost monopolized by the two orders of friars; and whereas the Dominicans adopted Aristotelianism, the Franciscans mostly remained faithful to the Augustinian tradition. The leading Franciscan scholastics were Alexander of Hales, who died in 1245, and his greater pupil,

Bonaventura (1221–74). Bonaventura's biography of St. Francis retains little of the uniquely personal flavor which was well preserved in the less formal memoirs of less learned Franciscans; but he was apparently a gentle and overly conscientious individual, and his premature death was attributed to overwork. In addition to teaching and writing philosophy, he served for seventeen years as minister-general of the Franciscan order. Bonaventura was faithful to his master in his reliance on mystical experience, and in his philosophy reason remains definitely subordinate to faith. "The clarity of philosophic knowledge is great according to the opinion of worldly people," he declared, "but it is little in comparison with the clarity of Christian knowledge." [1] Philosophy thus derived its preconceptions from faith, and its function was to elucidate them. To the questions that were beginning to perplex rationalistic thinkers—whether the universe was eternal or created in time, in what manner did the soul survive after death, how far was human knowledge reliable—Bonaventura gave firmly Christian answers, even when they appeared to conflict with reason. Certain basic truths, such as the existence of a personal God, were prior to knowledge and necessary for it, and hence could not be made subject to argument. They were known to the human soul by direct intuition.

The first Christian philosopher to accept Aristotelianism was Albert of Cologne (1201–80), a scholar of the true German vintage whose voluminous writings covered virtually the whole range of human thought. His most original contributions were in the sciences, especially in botany, but he is important in the history of philosophy chiefly because he was the teacher of Thomas Aquinas (1225–74), who—despite his relatively short life—was the greatest of the scholastic system-builders. Thomas was Italian-born, coming from a noble family with royal connections in the kingdom of Naples, but like almost all the scholastics he both studied and taught at the University of Paris. In his

---

[1] Quoted in Emile Brehier: *The Philosophy of the Middle Ages,* p. 280.

immense synthetic structure the attempt of medieval thinkers to produce a harmony of faith and reason reaches its climax.

Late in life Thomas had mystical experiences which apparently changed his philosophic attitudes. "Such things have been revealed to me" he told a friend, "that what I have written seems but straw." [2] Lest it be assumed from the general tenor of his writings that he was a wholly prosaic thinker, it should be recorded that he was the author of some of the greatest of medieval hymns, particularly of the famous *Pangue lingua*. But the main bent of his philosophy was toward minimizing the role of mystical experience in validating Christian beliefs and toward strengthening reliance on rational argument. His most important innovation was to substitute an Aristotelian epistemology for the traditional reliance on Plato. The knowledge of realities was not innate, as the Platonists had declared, but was deduced from sensuous apprehension. The human soul "is not naturally gifted with the knowledge of truth, as the angels are, but has to gather knowledge from individual things by way of the senses." "God can be seen in his Essence by man only if separated from this mortal life." [3] There was nothing in the human intellect that was not first in the senses, and all general concepts were deduced from sensuous experience. Thomas admitted that certain Christian dogmas could not be proved by rational arguments, though they were not to be regarded as contrary to reason; but they had to be accepted on faith, as derived from revelation. This applied, for example, to the belief in the Holy Trinity and to the doctrine that the world had been created in time and was not eternal. But wherever possible Thomas relied on sensuous experience and rational deduction from it rather than on Christian faith and the authority of the Church. In so doing he taught a view of man which was both lower and higher than Christian theology had

---

[2] Quoted in Philip Wicksteed: *Dante and Aquinas* (London, 1913), p. 93.

[3] Thomas Aquinas: *Summa Theologica,* translated by the Fathers of the English Dominican Province (1927–35), 3-76-5, 1-1-12-11.

traditionally maintained. By denying that the soul was "naturally gifted with the knowledge of truth," he hoped to make Christian doctrine invulnerable against any attack based on claims to mystical experience. At the same time by showing that Christian doctrine could be defended by means of rational argument, he hoped to refute the Averroists and other philosophical opponents of orthodoxy.

The Thomistic synthesis, presented in the vast *Summa Theologica,* with its 631 topics for discussion and its 10,000 objections and replies, is at first sight one of the most impressive intellectual structures ever built by a human mind. It resembles a Gothic cathedral in its comprehension and apparent unification of virtually every aspect of human experience; and it is Gothic also, in a more subtle way, in a kind of passion for elaboration for its own sake. There is an audacity in Thomas's display of logical virtuosity that recalls the audacity with which medieval builders sought to combine the greatest possible height with the widest possible spread of window space. Contemplating this immense network of argumentation, the human mind is—at first sight—stunned into admiration and acceptance. But as soon as one ventures to analyze the principles on which it is based, one finds that the union of Aristotelian and Christian thought is not so complete as one might have supposed, and that one of the purposes of Thomas's logical virtuosity is to conceal certain dangerous fissures in the argument. The Thomistic synthesis is, in fact, a product primarily of intellectual ingenuity, not of the emotional drive that gives vitality to philosophical argument or of the observation of previously unrecognized facts which leads to new hypotheses. And for this reason one finds in it little that a human being can live by or that can stimulate him to further discoveries. One can admire the smoothness and skill with which Thomas sets out to organize the whole range of human thought; but the greatest philosophical systems, like those of Plato and Augustine, have been great not because of logical ingenuity, in which they have often been deficient, but because of the emotional pressure which impelled their creation.

Thomas began by attempting to prove the existence of God. This proof depended on conceptions which for Thomas, as for Aristotle and almost all other classical and medieval thinkers, were self-evident and therefore in no need of demonstration. The world was regarded as finite, from which it followed that an infinite series was impossible; there must therefore be a first cause and a being who was absolutely and not relatively good. According to Aristotelian views of physics, moreover, there could be no motion without a mover. Objects remained static unless they were pushed. There must therefore be some ultimate cause of the movements of the material world, and this cause would only be spiritual. God moved all things, both by originally imparting motion to them and by finally drawing them back to himself by the attraction of his divine perfection.

Thus according to the traditional cosmology it was impossible not to believe in some kind of divine being. But the Thomistic proofs of the existence of God ceased to command assent as soon as men began to suggest that the universe was not finite but infinite and that movement did not require a mover. Such suggestions were beginning to cause speculation among philosophers within a half-century after Thomas's death.

From the Aristotelian proofs of God's existence, moreover, it was no easy jump to the Christian view of God. A philosophic hypothesis rather than a direct object of human knowledge, the supreme being of Aristotle had been inactive and uninterested in human affairs. Accepting the Aristotelian deity, Thomas declared that "God's intellect is his substance," that he knew all things because his essence contained everything, and that his knowledge was the cause of everything.[4] From this chilly and impalpable entity how could one arrive at the highly emotional Person, capable of both compassion and indignation, whom Christianity had inherited from Judaism and who was presented in the Christian Bible? The Aristotelian deity seemed scarcely capable of an

---

[4] Thomas Aquinas: op. cit., 1-1-14-4; 1-14-5-13.

act of free will. He was so intellectualized that he seemed bound by standards of justice and goodness which he had not himself created.

Thomas was unable to support belief in the Christian God either by an appeal to direct experience or by rational argument. God might occasionally give a mystical knowledge of himself to a human being, but this was an act of divine grace. The human intellect was not formed to know God directly; as though seeing him in a mirror, it could only deduce his existence from the contemplation of his creation. Even mysticism, moreover, was—according to Thomas—an intellectual experience. By divine grace the human mind might attain to the knowledge of God and might even see the whole creation as God saw it; but this was very different from the sense of emotional union with the divine being which was the standard mystical experience. Despite his efforts to rationalize as much of Christian belief as possible, Thomas had to recognize that the whole of the specifically Christian conception of God was derived from revelation and dependent on faith; it could not be deduced from philosophical concepts. The Aristotelian supreme being and the Christian creator of the universe had, in reality, no relationship to each other, despite Thomas's efforts to evade this uncomfortable conclusion.

The Christianization of Aristotle's view of man led to even greater difficulties. For Aristotle every object consisted of a union of form and matter; though the dichotomy was logical rather than real, as neither form nor matter could be regarded as capable of existing independently of the other. This view appears to have originated in Aristotle's biological studies, though he extended it—not very usefully or convincingly—to the physical sciences. It was the form that imparted life, energy, and a sense of purpose to living creatures. A being achieved perfection to the extent that its form was fully actualized in matter. In man the form was therefore to be identified with the vital principle that Christians called the soul. But the form was also common to the whole species; it was what brought man into being and enabled him to be recognized as such by others (the Aristotelian dichot-

258

omy of form and matter belonged both to biology and to epistemology). Individualization was due to matter, the form having
no separate identity until it became actualized. Thus according to
Aristotelian principles the continuance of individual existence
after form and matter had become separated by death was apparently impossible. Thomas provided an answer to this problem,
but his solution was merely a verbal formula incapable of practical utility or validation. Form, he declared, individualized itself
by becoming united with matter; thus every human soul was a
distinct individual, though it could not exist apart from matter
(this was in accord with the doctrine of the corporeal resurrection, which was very different from the Platonic belief in the
immortality of the soul, though Christians rarely seem to have
accepted all the implications of such a doctrine). Thus Aristotle
and Christianity were reconciled on paper, though the reconciliation had no practical meaning or result.

Of more practical importance were the ethical discrepancies
between Aristotle and the Christian gospel. Thomas's view of
human nature was largely Aristotelian, particularly in his insistence—so different from the gospel emphasis on loving God and
one's neighbor—that "the ultimate beatitude of man consists in
the use of his highest function, which is that of the intellect."
Thus the practice of contemplation is superior to the charity
taught by Jesus and Paul. In accordance with Aristotelian conceptions, Thomas's view of human nature is mostly optimistic,
with relatively little emphasis on original sin. He repeatedly affirms that "everything seeks after its own perfection." "Everything has this aptitude towards its natural form, that when it
possesses it not, it tends towards it; and when it possesses it, it is
at rest therein." Nobody desires evil, which is essentially a negation; and if men are guilty of evil, it is because of a disorder in
their desires rather than from positive depravity. "Never would
evil be sought after, not even as an accident, unless the good that
accompanies the evil were more desired than the good of which
the evil is the privation." [5] This optimism extends to Thomas's

---

[5] Thomas Aquinas: op. cit., 1-1-12-1; 1-1-6-1; 1-1-19-1; 1-1-19-9.

political views, which may be described as generally liberal. Sovereignty belongs to the people, though it should normally be delegated to a single ruler. But the king should govern in accord with law, and may be removed if he is guilty of violating it. The positive laws of the state derive their authority from conformity with the God-created law of nature and reason. "Human law has the nature of law in so far as it accords with right reason; and in this it is clear that it is derived from the eternal law. But to the extent that it departs from reason, it is called unjust law, and thus it has not the nature of law, but rather of violence." [6] Unlike more sin-conscious Christian theorists, Thomas did not make any sharp distinction between the ideal society envisaged by natural law and what was practically possible. For many Christian thinkers such institutions as private property were contrary to natural law but necessitated by man's sinful state. Thomas, on the other hand, declared that they were additions to natural law devised by human reason and were not to be regarded merely as the consequences of sin.

All these aspects of Thomas's thinking are distinguished by a pagan sobriety and good sense and an elevated view of human nature. With good reason he has been described as the first Whig. It is therefore with a sense of shock that one finds him expounding the orthodox Catholic doctrines of election and damnation, without any mitigation of their severity. Only those individuals who have been chosen by God will achieve salvation. "Why he chooses some for glory, and rejects others, has no reason except the Divine Will." The number of the damned will be immensely larger than those of the saved. And "in order that the happiness of the saints may be more delightful to them and that they may render more copious thanks to God for it, they are allowed to see perfectly the sufferings of the damned." [7]

Thus in Thomas's writings about man one finds two different

[6] Ewart Lewis: *Medieval Political Ideas*, I, 52.
[7] Thomas Aquinas: op. cit., 1-1-23-5; 1-1-23-7; 3-94-1.

conceptions side by side, with little attempt to reconcile them. On the one hand is the classical and humanist ideal of a natural perfection; on the other hand the Christian ideal of renunciation of the world and the flesh and of union with God. A similar dichotomy was to be found in Aristotle, who had propounded two different ideals, that of the great-souled man of action and that of the contemplative life; but the Aristotelian division had been much less sharp because of the lack of the sense of sin and of the need for grace. With Thomas the duality becomes manifest in the assertion that man needs grace for two different reasons.[8] Corrupted by original sin, he cannot be cured of his imperfections and achieve a natural goodness without the assistance of grace. But above and beyond the ideal of natural goodness, which had been achieved in the Garden of Eden before the fall, is the hope of a supernatural good for which a second influx of grace is necessary. Thus the mystical union with God is presented not as man's natural fulfillment, but as an added consummation beyond what Adam was capable of before the fall.

Thomism did not immediately win official approval. Thomas's adoption of Aristotelianism was too thoroughgoing for immediate acceptance. As a Dominican, moreover, he incurred the hostility of the rival Franciscan order. In 1277, three years after his death, the Bishop of Paris, Étienne Tempier, issued a decree condemning as heretical 319 propositions derived from Aristotle and Averroës, three of which were specifically ascribed to Thomas. Encouraged by this official sponsorship, Franciscan and Augustinian philosophers launched a series of assaults on the Thomistic position, and only after half a century of controversy did Thomas's advocates clear his name of charges of heresy. He was finally canonized in 1323, and thereafter he was generally regarded as an authoritative spokesman of Christian doctrine.

The great figures in the history of human thought are those who make new observations or give expression to new forms of

---

[8] Thomas Aquinas: op. cit., 2-1-109-2.

emotional experience and are not primarily concerned with logical consistency. Thinkers of this kind, who are truly creative, exercise a continuously fructifying influence on later generations. But Thomas's main endeavor was to provide explanations of phenomena which would be intellectually self-consistent and would give the illusion rather than the reality of understanding. Like his master Aristotle, he worked out a series of formulas which were based on logic rather than on observation and which had no practical validation and could not lead to new discoveries. These formulas were used to give an appearance of harmony between Aristotelianism and Christianity, but because they were verbal rather than real, they had no vital efficacy. By his excessive emphasis on the intellect as the highest quality in both God and man, moreover, Thomas can fairly be accused of surrendering the vital core of the Christian view of life. For Jesus and Paul the essence of Christianity was love (*agape*), and this had always been known by the mystics, even if it was too often forgotten by the power-hungry ecclesiastical hierarchy of the Roman Church. Thus the main effect of Thomism was to serve as a barrier to further theological advance. When the Church gave its official sanction to the Thomistic system, it was attempting to freeze Christian beliefs and showing its fear of new ideas and further philosophical progress. Thomas was, in fact, the last first-rate figure who can be called a Catholic thinker. After him there were Catholics who thought, but their thinking was, in greater or lesser degree, divorced from their theological beliefs.

Just as the attempt of the thirteenth-century papacy to make itself the one supreme authority led to a general loss of faith in its pretensions, so Thomas's attempt to unify all Christian thought was followed by a disintegration of the whole scholastic enterprise. The movement of thought after Thomas can, in part, be interpreted in narrowly philosophical terms. Disturbed by the inner weaknesses of the Thomistic system and by its inconsistencies with Christian experience, later philosophers reacted against its rationalistic assumptions and tried to work out ways of thinking more in accord with experience. In general, they tended to separate the realm of faith from that of reason and to enlarge those areas of Christian doctrine which were regarded as derived from revelation rather than from rational demonstration. They attributed prime importance to the will rather than to the intellect; and they insisted that individuals alone were real and that universals were mental conveniences. These tendencies brought the scholastic movement to a rapid conclusion. Scholasticism had meant—essentially—the attempt to harmonize faith and reason, and it ended when this attempt was abandoned in the belief that harmony was impossible.

By an unusual paradox—this is possibly the only example in the whole history of thought of official censorship producing good results—the condemnation of Aristotelianism in 1277 had an invigorating effect on intellectual development. Philosophers were stimulated to believe that an omnipotent God was not necessarily compelled to work in conformity with Aristotelian physics and metaphysics. Possibly God had made the universe in accord with other and more mysterious principles, which further investigation might uncover. The attack on Thomism helped to promote a critical examination of Aristotle's laws of motion, as well as of his metaphysical dichotomies, and this, in turn, led eventually to the world-view of modern science. But although modern physics can be traced back to the early fourteenth century, it was not until the seventeenth century that its full importance became manifest.

These new philosophical tendencies, however, were not solely the result of the progression of thought; they also reflected the general spirit of the age. Western development in the late Middle Ages was marked by a loss of faith in the affirmations that had formerly maintained unity and by the growth of an individualism which often frankly repudiated all allegiance to ideal motivations. Men were losing the sense of an ideal order embodied in social forms and institutions and giving them meaning and justification. This was an age of political and cultural fragmentation, and this fact was reflected in, and also influenced by, the movement of philosophy.

A Franciscan of British origin, Duns Scotus, may perhaps be regarded as the last of the great scholastics. Deserving his title of Doctor Subtilis, Duns was the most complex of medieval thinkers. He was much too difficult a thinker to acquire any wide influence. In fact, later generations were inclined to dismiss his writings as unintelligible, as a result of which the name "Duns" (or dunce) acquired the derogatory connotations it has always retained. But his philosophy was a true reflection of the disintegration of the medieval world-view.

The main tendency of Duns's work was to expose the inadequacy of the philosophical devices with which Thomas had unified his universe. One was left with a universe of disjunct entities in which all relationships were unintelligible and there was no way by which the human mind could acquire any certain knowledge. To an increasing extent, in fact, philosophy was now generally regarded as dealing, at best, with probabilities. Certainty, it was affirmed, could be reached only by faith.

Emphasizing freedom in both God and men, Duns set the will above the intellect. God had created the universe by an act of will, not of intelligence; and man approached God primarily through love rather than through understanding. Duns also set out to clarify the confusions inherent in the Thomistic conception of man as a union of form and matter, though he succeeded only in adding to its complexity. Recognizing the dangers to Christian belief of the Thomistic identification of the soul with the Aristotelian form, he declared that the soul was itself a compound of form and matter; a spiritual entity comprised matter just as much as a corporeal entity. And in order to evade the anti-Christian implications of the doctrine that attributed individuation to matter, Duns postulated a separate principle by which each individual achieved identity, which he called *haecceitas* ("this-ness"). And because every *haecceitas* was a separate entity and not to be considered as part of a larger system, the universe of Duns Scotus was, in the last resort, without intelligible order and unity. It was held together by forces which could not be grasped or defined by the human mind.

264

Duns's philosophy seems largely a catalogue of negations, and what it especially negated was the rationalism of St. Thomas. But it cleared the ground for new and more creative views of life. Elevating the will above the intellect, it made possible a reassertion of the values of mystical experience. Undermining the verbal formulas which Thomas had borrowed from Aristotle, it demonstrated the need for some wholly new approach to the understanding of the cosmos. And though it had little direct influence on intellectual development, either in Duns's lifetime or afterward, it was a true reflection of the late medieval sensibility.

13

The Medieval Decadence

Except in Italy, and to a lesser extent in Flanders and England, the fourteenth and fifteenth centuries were devoid of cultural creations of major importance. Although the values and institutions that had inspired the medieval efflorescence had largely ceased to be socially effective, they continued to determine thinking among the upper classes and to command verbal assent. Western society was undergoing fundamental economic and political changes, but there was not yet any general awareness of the importance of the new forces. Feudal ways of thinking were still predominant in spite of their lack of practical relevance. Perhaps the dominant aspect of Western culture during this period was the attempt to evade the realities which were undermining the traditional social structure.

There was an uneasy awareness of the decay of accepted values, but no new value system had been formulated. In consequence, men were no longer guided by any clear affirmations about the meaning and purpose of human life, and much of their way of living was characterized by a lack of order and balance and by gross inconsistencies. Both open sensuality and the fear of death and damnation were apparently more acute than in earlier periods, and professions of chivalric honor were often combined with practices of extreme barbarity. As Johan Huizinga has remarked, the life of the later Middle Ages "bore the mixed smell of blood and of roses. The men of that time always oscillate

266

between the fear of hell and the most naive joy, between cruelty and tenderness, between harsh asceticism and insane attachment to the delights of this world, between hatred and goodness." [1]

Much of the cultural activity of the period, including particularly its art and literature, was frankly escapist. Realities could not be integrated into any generally accepted view of life, and men were therefore unable to adopt any positive attitude toward them. This was particularly true of one major catastrophe which originated outside the processes of social development and hence must be considered as accidental. The bubonic plague, generally known as the Black Death, reached western Europe as a result of commercial contacts with the East, and in its first and most destructive outbreak during the years 1348–50 it killed, according to the best available evidence, no less than one third of the total population. Several later outbreaks, though less deadly, prevented anxiety from subsiding. The fourteenth century was also marked by agricultural decline, resulting in some years in widespread famines. Apparently the population expansion of the early Middle Ages had brought into cultivation all the usable land, and much of the soil was now losing its fertility. Thus medieval man had objective reasons for an increased fear of death—a death for which religious belief offered no plausible justification and which could not easily be reconciled with prevalent views of human life. The inevitable sense of panic resulted both in increased sensuality and in religious hysteria. But although the Black Death had traumatic effects, it must not be considered as the primary cause of the medieval decadence. How a society reacts to catastrophe is determined by its internal tendencies; and if it has enough healthy vitality, the effects are limited.

Almost equally incomprehensible to the ruling classes was a series of peasant and working-class rebellions. The feudal class structure no longer appeared to the lower classes to be just and

---

[1] Johan Huizinga: *The Waning of the Middle Ages* (Anchor Books), p. 27.

rational. Its mythical and ideological supports were crumbling, and the rule of the nobility was losing that conviction of legitimacy without which there can be no effective social order. To this challenge from below, the aristocracy could respond only with violence: a violence which was an expression of fear and which was not modified by any chivalric values. Chivalry applied only to conflicts within the knightly class.[2]

There were three major peasant outbreaks—in Flanders in 1323, in France in 1357 (the "Jacquerie"), and in England in 1381—along with a number of relatively minor movements in Germany and elsewhere. In each of them the peasants displayed murderous fury against their upper-class oppressors but were eventually crushed and massacred by the authorities with even greater bloodshed. Yet it cannot be said that the peasants were actually more exploited than their more submissive ancestors of the early feudal period. The revolts were provoked by specific grievances—the continued imposition of various feudal dues by the lords, and heavy taxation, mostly for war purposes, by governments—but in general the changes in western European society in the late medieval period were working to the advantage of the peasant class. They profited by the commutation into money payments of the services traditionally due to their lords, and—after 1348—by the decrease in the numbers of the laboring class caused by the Black Death. The rebellions were an example of the general rule that such struggles are likely to be initiated by classes who are rising in the social and economic scale and who are encouraged to fight against oppression because they are moved by hope rather than by despair.

In Flanders and England the revolts were more than mere

---

[2] The Scottish nobles were almost constantly at war with their English counterparts. Yet when there was a peasant rising in England, the Scots offered to give help in suppressing it—a gesture which the English nobles appreciated, though they did not accept it. See Jean Froissart: *Chronicles of England, France, Spain, and the Adjoining Countries,* translated by T. Johnes (New York, 1901), I, 228.

blind outbreaks of class resentment. They were accompanied by the preaching of positive radical and democratic ideals, largely inspired by Biblical sources and propagated by itinerant preachers who continued the tradition of the Spiritual Franciscans. The English preacher John Ball, according to Froissart's *Chronicles,* used to declare that "matters cannot go well in England until all things shall be in common; when there shall be neither villeins nor lords; when the lords shall be no more masters than ourselves . . . Are we not all descended from the same parents, Adam and Eve? And what can they show, or what reason can they give, why they should be more masters than ourselves?" [3] Thus the main ideological support of the class hierarchy—the assumption that nobles were born noble, and that villeins were villainous—was now being challenged.

In one province of western Europe radicalism developed not only among the peasantry, but also in the cities. The clothing and other industries of Flanders had made it by the thirteenth century the richest section of Europe with the possible exception of northern Italy. Politically, it was by law a part of France, but the immediate authority was the local count, and the French kings never succeeded in permanently adding it to their domain. Radicalism developed among the weavers and other urban workers as well as among the peasants, and through much of the fourteenth century Flanders was the scene of stormy and extremely complex civil wars, ending with the definitive restoration of upper-class authority in 1382. Subsequently it came under the firm rule of the dukes of Burgundy, and its industrial prosperity diminished as a result of competition with the growing cloth industry of England. But through the whole later Middle Ages, Flanders was a center of radical ideas both in religion and in politics; the subversive effects in other countries were apparently substantial, though hard to trace.

Having survived the plague and crushed the peasants, the

---

[3] Quoted in Wallace K. Ferguson: *Europe in Transition, 1300–1520,* p. 270.

aristocracy continued to keep reality at arm's length. Characteristic of all aspects of late medieval upper-class life was an adhesion to outmoded forms without regard for considerations of utility. Manners were elaborately ritualized, with excessive concern for questions of rank and status, despite the inordinate waste of time that resulted from such concerns. All strong emotions, whether of joy or sorrow, received public manifestation by means of prescribed ceremonies, as though the naked feeling had become too dangerous and destructive for direct expression. Much of the character of upper-class society was expressed in its clothing, which had never been more elaborate or less utilitarian. "No epoch," Huizinga declares, "ever witnessed such extravagance of fashion as that extending from 1350 to 1480."[4] Male costume, as displayed in the paintings of artists catering to the upper class (such as those of the Limburg brothers), was especially bizarre, featuring pointed shoes whose excessive length made locomotion difficult, cylindrical or pointed bonnets, and hoods draped above the head in the form and color of a cock's comb.

Public ceremonials were a frequent feature of the life of the age, reflecting its contradictory oscillations between sensuality and religious fear. The festivities with which a city gave welcome to a visiting prince were likely to include an array of naked women enacting the choice of Paris or some similar classical legend; yet on other occasions men were reminded of the realities of death and damnation by flagellants marching in line with bare backs, each of them being publicly beaten by the man behind him. Such extreme assertions of human sinfulness were disliked by the Church, which regarded the flagellants as potential heretics likely to ignore clerical authority, but they reflected something deeply felt by the men of this epoch. One of the favorite subjects of popular art was a line of skeletons engaged in the "dance of death." Despite the growth of rationalism, in fact, the religious fears and superstitions of this epoch were in some ways stronger

---

[4] Huizinga: op. cit., p. 249.

and more primitive than in the high Middle Ages, when all such emotions were given expression through the forms prescribed by clerical authority. It was in the fifteenth century that the danger of witchcraft began for the first time to arouse serious and sustained alarm among both the clergy and the masses of the population. In 1461 the city of Arras passed through a period of hysterical panic in which a number of its citizens were condemned as witches and put to death. This was the first of many such outbreaks occurring in all Western countries and lasting through the sixteenth and seventeenth centuries. The Middle Ages had, in this regard, maintained more rational attitudes.

Meanwhile the aristocratic class continued to claim social and political superiority and to pursue its customary activities as though society were still wholly feudal and its claims to leadership were still accepted by the mass of the people. Warfare was still regarded as the most noble of all activities, provided that it was conducted in accord with the rules and practices of chivalry. The chivalric ideal retained such prestige, in fact, that kings and princes professed to be guided by it in pursuing warlike policies, brushing aside all realistic considerations of economics and affecting to seek an immortal glory that could be earned only by showing prowess in personal combat. Crusading was still regarded as the highest form of warfare, and kings and princes were constantly taking oaths to regain Christian ownership of the Holy Land, though somehow they never managed to fulfill these promises. These chivalrous professions were made by a number of English and French kings, but were especially popular with the dukes of Burgundy. The original duke, a younger son of the French king, acquired the duchy in 1364, and for more than a century he and his successors tried to build it into a separate principality, controlling the territories between France and Germany and also absorbing the Netherlands. The project came to an abrupt and catastrophic ending with the defeat and death in battle of Duke Charles the Bold in 1477, but for many years the dukes maintained the richest and most splendid court in Europe. The wealth with which the court was maintained came from the cities of the Netherlands, which the dukes had inherited by means of a series of fortunate marriages. But there was no general recognition of this fact, and the dukes and their chroniclers preferred to give the credit for the rise of the duchy to the heroism and devotion of the Burgundian knighthood. The dukes continued to pay at least lip service to chivalric ideals, which—according to the Burgundian chronicler Molinet—had originated with no less an individual than the Archangel Michael in his primeval conflict with Lucifer.

With many of the princes of the later Middle Ages, chivalry was merely a device for justifying upper-class rule, but it had its more serious aspects. Chivalric ideals seem to have been partially responsible for provoking one of the most senseless episodes of the period, the so-called Hundred Years War between France and England. Actually there were two wars, the first fought from 1337 to 1380 and the second from 1415 until 1453. Each of them began with English victories, leading to English annexations of parts of France; and in each of them the French ultimately regained what they had lost. The wars were fought almost wholly on French soil, apart from occasional raids into northern England by the Scots, who allied themselves with the French. During the periods of English dominance, English armies engaged in plundering expeditions over large areas of France, meeting with remarkably little French resistance.

Nominally provoked by the claim of King Edward III of England to be (through his French mother) the legal heir to the throne of France, the war had some rational political and economic causes. The two countries were in conflict over the control of the French province of Guienne, while the status of Flanders, nominally French but in practice self-governing and closely linked by economic ties to England, was another source of dissension. But the prolongation of the struggle and of the consequent devastation of much of France was in large measure owing to the desire of kings and noblemen on both sides to win immortal glory by pursuing the only occupation to which they were trained and habituated. Since the crusading era had ended and private war had been abolished by the monarchies, the chivalric ideal could now find expression only in conflicts between the new national states. And while the English kings invaded France with small but disciplined armies consisting not only of knights in armor but also of plebeian archers armed with a new and most effective weapon, the longbow, the French nobility insisted on fighting by the traditional methods which had prevailed since Carolingian times, regarding the charge of knights in armor as the only tactic appropriate to chivalric ideals and refusing to allow their individualistic greed for glory to be impeded by any notions of mass discipline.

The most famous historian of the first phase of the war was the Flemish-born Jean Froissart, who wrote in French but spent part of his life in England and wrote largely from an English point of view. His chronicle is filled with the beauty and glamour of warfare. He liked to portray its visual aspects—the spectacle of knights riding out to battle with banners flying and the sunlight glittering on their armor. When he described the actions of his characters, the desire to display prowess by feats of arms was generally as much as was needed by way of motivation. But Froissart's values were all askew, as is likely to happen in an age that has lost any clear conception of the meaning of human life. Despite his glorification of chivalry, he was well aware that one of the main objectives of the knights was to capture noble prisoners who could then be held for ransom. Killing them instead of capturing them was uneconomic as well as inglorious. Sordidly materialistic considerations were in fact deeply entwined with the whole chivalric code, and the notion that knights fought only for glory was maintained as a kind of legal fiction. On the other hand, persons of lower rank—and all persons below the knightly level, wealthy bourgeoisie as well as peasants, were lumped together without distinction—could be slaughtered freely. Only when the carnage passed all reasonable limits, as in the massacre of all the inhabitants of Limoges by the orders of King Edward's son, the famous Black Prince, did Froissart feel that any moral condemnation was called for. Except in such extreme instances, chivalry was essentially a game with little connection with political and economic realities, and to exhibit the qualities of knighthood was more important than to achieve victories. After the Black Prince had captured King John of France in the battle of Poitiers, he consoled his royal prisoner by telling him that "in my opinion you have cause to be glad that the success of this battle did not turn out as you desired; for you have this day acquired such high renown for prowess that you have surpassed all the best knights on your side." [5]

The most extraordinary illustration of the perversity of the chivalric ideal was the behavior in battle of the French nobility, as exhibited in three large-scale engagements—those of Crécy (1346), Poitiers (1356), and Agincourt (1415). On each of these occasions the French regarded the charge of armed knights either on horseback or on foot as the central feature, disregarding both the increase in the weight of coats of mail, which made charging increasingly difficult, and the emergence of the plebeian longbow into a weapon which could slaughter horses and even pierce armor. The French, apparently, regarded their outmoded battle tactics as a source of honor and even of pleasure, and this was more important to them than life and victory. It is, in fact, difficult to explain their conduct in battle unless we suppose that they enjoyed the prospect not merely of fighting but of being killed. At Crécy the French engaged in a series of disorderly and unplanned charges against the English lines and were easily slaughtered by the opposing bowmen. At Poitiers the French elected to fight on foot, regarding horses as too vulnerable; but the results of the battle were the same. During the second phase of the war, in which it was the turn of the English to be defeated, the French adopted more realistic methods of warfare, devised by a leader of relatively low social status and professional standards of generalship: Bertrand Du Guesclin. Yet when the war was renewed in 1415 by King Henry V, the nobility was again in

---

[5] Raymond L. Kilgour: *The Decline of Chivalry,* V, 463.

control of the French army. Even more startlingly than at Crécy and Poitiers, they exhibited the propensity of human beings under the influence of outmoded codes of conduct to display a lemminglike urge toward self-destruction. Armor had grown even heavier, so that any knight who lost his footing needed assistance in getting up. Despite his handicap, and also despite heavy rains which had left ankle-deep mud in front of the English line, the French again elected to fight on foot. Those French knights who survived the showers of English arrows staggered into the enemy lines almost too exhausted to lift their arms and were easily destroyed by plebeian English infantry equipped with knives and hammers. Some four thousand Frenchmen were killed at Agincourt, by contrast with less than one hundred English.

These spectacular English victories had no lasting results; they demonstrated the senselessness of chivalric ideals, but they by no means brought them to an end. But the war had some positive significance, at least for France, in giving a religious aura to the new forces of nationalism. This last phase of the war, during which the English were for the second time deprived of their conquests of French territory, was distinguished by the appearance of Joan of Arc, the peasant girl from Domremy. At the age of seventeen she persuaded the French dauphin to give her military command and actually turned the tide of warfare by leading the French to victory at Orléans. No character in Western history seems more improbable, yet the records of her trial for witchcraft after she had fallen into the hands of the English make it plain that the traditional story of her achievements must be accepted as authentic. Her main significance in history is in exhibiting and symbolizing the growth of French nationalistic loyalties. Her claim that she had been ordered to expel the English invaders by angelic and saintly voices marked a new development in the rise of nationalism to priority among the different forms of loyalty. For the next five hundred years patriotism was to remain the strongest of political sentiments with most Frenchmen and with most of the citizens of other Western countries.

The escapism of the chivalric ideal found expression also in the arts. Much of the literature of the period was wholly unrealistic, giving expression to emotions by means of recondite symbolisms and occasionally recommending a direct sensuality which showed no respect for the moral doctrines of Christianity. Art tended to emphasize the sensuous magnificence of upper class life. The *Romance of the Rose,* written in the thirteenth century, remained immensely popular despite bitter condemnations by churchmen who would have liked to have seen it banned, and it may be regarded as the most typical literary expression of the medieval decadence.

The *Romance of the Rose* has not retained much appeal for modern readers, its allegorical method of expressing emotion having become wholly outmoded; and its exploration of all the intricacies of courtly love has come to appear merely tiresome. But for the more enthusiastic of its medieval readers it had almost Biblical authority. This was particularly true of some 4,000 lines of the first part, which was written by Guillaume de Lorris about the year 1240. The subject is the progress of a love affair, love being represented as a garden, while the hoped-for consummation is equated with the picking of a rose. What makes the book almost incomprehensible for most modern readers is that all the emotions which hasten or impede love's consummation are personified and described as though they were human figures. Thus pride, shame, envy, sloth, and so forth appear as separate characters. By this means the author succeeds in presenting a detailed psychological analysis of the growth of love, in spite of the dreamlike quality of his work; and his descriptions of the garden have a freshness and vividness which can still appeal to readers who are unaccustomed to his method of describing human emotions.

Guillaume de Lorris apparently died before completing his work, and for some forty years the lover was left with his desire still unconsummated. Then a sequel of 22,000 lines was added by a writer variously known as Jean Clopinel and as Jean de Meung. This illustrates another aspect of the late medieval view of life: a frank glorification of sensuality, unchecked either by religious doctrine or by the code of courtly love. The author rambles over the whole field of human knowledge with encyclopedic scope and little concern for relevance; but his general attitudes are emphatically expressed and startingly unorthodox. Bitterly and contemptuously hostile to the clergy and wholly unromantic in his views of women, he transfers to sex the values and attitudes of mystical experience. Nature created men and women in order that they might give each other sexual pleasure and thus replenish the earth; and it is sheer perversity that leads human beings to violate nature's laws by practicing chastity. Jean looks back regretfully to a golden age in the past when there were no laws or institutions, "all shared earth's gift in common lot" (line 8858), and copulation was not restricted by any notions of monogamy. After long diatribes against chastity, Jean eventually returns to the lover waiting in the rose garden; the god of love captures the tower where Danger, Shame, and Fear have been guarding the rose; and Welcome admits the lover to the inner sanctuary and encourages him to pluck the flower.

The *Romance of the Rose* was the only late medieval French writing of major importance, and for the following two hundred years French poets mostly continued to produce second-rate restatements of the tradition of courtly love, varied only (as in some of the works of Eustache Deschamps and François Villon) with gloomy meditations on the imminence and universality of death. These had a directness and an intensity of feeling that was lacking in the poetry of love. The refrain of Villon, *Où sont les neiges d'antan,* and his reminder of what death does to the human body expressed realities which were deeply felt by late medieval society and from which it was no longer protected by any strong hope of religious salvation.

The art of painting displayed similar tendencies. The deep religious reverence of early medieval art had almost disappeared. Artists now worked mostly for lay patrons of the upper class, who enjoyed portrayals of a fairy-tale world of brilliant colors and idealized noblemen superior to all the unpleasant exigencies of actual living. On the other hand, artists also cultivated a meticulous realism in the rendering of detail, with a lack of creative organization which betrayed the age's general loss of faith and which paralleled the growth of nominalism in philosophy.

The former of these tendencies was exemplified in the so-called International Gothic, which may be regarded as beginning with the work of Jean Pucelle in the 1320's and was displayed chiefly in the illumination of manuscripts. By this time Italian painting was being revolutionized by masters like Giotto in Florence and Duccio in Siena with a new concern for the rendering of three-dimensional space and of plastic bodies. The French and Flemish practitioners of the International Style were influenced by the Italians in their techniques, but they had none of the sober, solid, bourgeois view of life which characterized the work of Giotto. Their aristocratic patrons wanted an escapist art with rich colors and idealized figures and landscape backgrounds. The International Style reached its peak early in the fifteenth century with the work of the Limbourg brothers, whose masterpiece was the illuminated *Book of Hours* produced for a French prince, the Duke of Berry. Twelve magnificently colored pictures illustrate the twelve months of the year, most of them having as background an idealized feudal castle or palace. In the foreground peasants portrayed with a Giottoesque solidity perform appropriate tasks, or ladies and gentlemen, magnificently attired and retaining the unsubstantiality and elongated elegance of earlier Gothic figures, entertain themselves. Despite the reality of the peasant laborers, the whole of these compositions has an idyllic atmosphere far removed from the harsh realities of actual living.

Meanwhile religious art was still being produced in large quantities, but the spirit of reverence displayed during the period of High Gothic was giving place to virtuosity of craftsmanship and to a sensuous realism which sometimes approached blasphemy. Only occasionally, as in the late fifteenth-century pietà of Villeneuve, did artists give direct and powerful expression to religious feeling. In architecture this was the age of the Flamboyant, which may be described as Gothic that had gone to seed. It was characterized by a proliferation of details obscuring the main lines of the structure. The loss of religious idealization can be traced especially in portrayals of the Virgin. A queen in the great Gothic period, she became a very human young woman in the north portal of Notre Dame of Paris, carved about 1255. In the Vierge Dorée of Amiens, a decade or so later, she was beginning to display sexual allure, and this was carried further in the fourteenth-century Virgin of the choir of Notre Dame, with her fastidious features, thin lips, and plucked eyebrows. This tendency reached its climax in the fifteenth-century painting of Jehan Fouquet, who modeled Mary after the king's mistress Agnes Sorel and portrayed her with one naked breast and an air of passive sensuality.

14

New Views of Man
and the Universe

The culture of late medievalism, however, was not all so pretentiously unreal. The fourteenth and fifteenth centuries were marked not merely by the survival of feudal values that had lost their relevance to social conditions, but also by the beginnings of new views of life that were destined to dominate European culture for several centuries.

The main underlying intellectual change was the growing acceptance of individualism as a positive good. The philosophers of the thirteenth century had created systems intended to limit and hold in check the claim of the individual to form his own views of the world. But when the scholastic synthesis ceased to command assent, there was no longer any effective intellectual barrier to individual exploration. In the fourteenth and fifteenth centuries, to an increasing extent, individual thinkers began to flout collective authority. They claimed direct access to the Holy Spirit through mystical contemplation—an attitude which was to lead eventually to the Protestant Reformation; they adopted an extreme nominalism in their views of science, thereby laying the groundwork for the new world of Copernicus and Galileo; and they developed new art forms which concentrated on the realistic rendering of individual figures.

14 · New Views of Man and the Universe

Closely associated with the new individualism was the new concept of the infinity of space, which contrasted sharply with the limited spherical universe that previous cosmologies had accepted as self-evident. This began to take shape in the writings of certain late medieval philosophers, though it did not win general understanding and acceptance for several centuries. But a new feeling about space was developing in the late Middle Ages, although most of its implications were not yet apparent. It is shown in art both in Italy and in northern Europe, and was especially manifested in the formulation of rules of perspective intended to present a realistic view of space as continuous, three-dimensional, and infinite. The new concept of space marks perhaps the sharpest difference between the medieval and the modern mind, the more so because a finite and an infinite space are equally beyond the scope of the human mind, and the choice between them therefore depends on sociological preferences, not on scientific proof. Paradoxically, the modern view is possibly the more confining because it places man clearly within a spatial universe which is described in wholly materialistic terms and is not imbued with any spiritual values; and although man can attempt to explore the universe with his mind, he knows that he is inescapably tethered to a particular place within it. In spite of its Ptolemaic assumptions, the medieval mind, on the other hand, believed that the ultimate realities were outside place and time and that man could commune with them through mystical experience and after the death of the body.

Once the attempt to unify reason and faith had been abandoned and it was recognized that divine omnipotence was not limited by Aristotelian standards of rationality, new affirmations became possible. Creative thinkers and artists moved in various new directions which had little or no connection with each other. Reality itself began to appear as paradoxical and ultimately incomprehensible, and there was no longer the sense of security derived from the assumption that Christian theology, as taught and defended by the organized Church, had the answers to all necessary questions. But while the new ways of thinking were less reassuring and more anxiety-producing, they opened the way for new discoveries. Thinkers began to speculate more boldly and penetrate into deeper mysteries than during the great age of Catholic faith. And while the Franciscans turned outward and began to develop an approach to nature which led eventually to the world-view of modern science, some of the Dominicans, abandoning their earlier Aristotelianism, turned inward and arrived at mystical experiences that were almost beyond the scope of Christian theology as it had previously been understood. Both these movements emphasized the evidence of experience and did not accept the limitations of scholastic rationalism. That the whole mystical movement represented a break with traditional ecclesiasticism was indicated by its use of the vernacular languages rather than Latin. Its roots were in middle-class lay society, and the main motivation of its leading figures was to cure the anxieties of those individuals who could no longer find spiritual support in traditional Catholic institutions.

The greatest of the Dominican mystics was the southern German philosopher Johannes Eckhart, better known by the title Meister (1260–1327). This extraordinary individual, while fully accepting the dogmas of the orthodox faith, at least in his own belief, interpreted them in new ways and moved beyond them into realms of spiritual experience which no previous Christian mystic had ventured to explore. Penetrating through Christian dogmas to that ultimate sense of spiritual union with God from which Christianity derived its vitality, and which it shared with other religions that filtered it through different theological and ethical systems, he went beyond orthodoxy rather than going against it. Yet his affirmations were so bold and so novel that clerical disapproval was to be expected, and twenty-eight propositions ascribed to him were actually condemned as heretical in 1329, two years after his death.

For Eckhart, as for all true mystics, religion began with the negation of self-will, detachment from all worldly preoccupations, and total surrender to the divine being. "To be full of things is to be empty of God, while to be empty of things is to be full of God." "When a free mind is really disinterested, God is compelled to come into it." This union with God would express itself in a life of active benevolence. "What we have gathered in contemplation we give out in love." Unlike most mystics, Eckhart taught that the way of Martha was superior to the way of Mary, and giving a cup of water to a thirsty man was more important than a mystical ecstasy. But in defining the essence of the religious life Eckhart went further than any earlier Christian mystic in affirming the unity of man and God. In conformity with the teaching of Christian theology, mystics had declared that man, though like God, could never lose his individuality and become swallowed up in God, even though this insistence on separation, which had its source in the theology of Judaism, may perhaps have been contrary to what they experienced. But for Eckhart the ultimate core of the self was divine. "There is a principle in the soul untouched by time and flesh, flowing from Spirit, remaining in the Spirit, itself altogether spiritual. In this principle is God, ever verdant, flowering in all the joy and glory of his actual self." In the mystical union the human soul was swallowed up in divinity. "The soul imbibing God turns into God as the drop becomes the ocean." "The 'I' is reduced there to utter naught, and nothing is left there but God." This was the supreme human experience, and by it the soul passed outside of space and time and became one with eternity; and just as man had a higher and a lower self, so one must distinguish between the God who acted in, and upon, the world and the ultimate Godhead who transcended all spatial and temporal processes and remained forever unmoving and almost beyond all concepts of personality.

From this affirmation of a supreme reality which could not be described in words, Eckhart went on to define most of the doctrines of Christianity as metaphors for ineffable truths, though he did not deny that they were also literally true. The incarnation meant the constant rebirth of the divine spirit in the human soul, and this was more important than the historic birth of Christ from the Virgin Mary. The kingdom of heaven referred neither to the expectation of a new world-order in Time nor to the salvation of the elect after death, but to the union with the eternal Godhead, beyond space and time, which was possible for the human soul here and now. "A man beholds God in this life in the same perfection, and is blessed in exactly the same way, as in the after life." [1]

In essentials, Eckhart's view of life was identical with that of the great mystics of other religions. As Rudolf Otto has shown, it can be closely matched with the doctrines of the ninth-century Indian philosopher Sankara; and as the parallels resulted not from any mutual influence, but from similarity of experience, they may be regarded as evidence for the authenticity of that experience. In mysticism all the great religions meet, and institutional and doctrinal differences become unimportant. Eckhart came closer to the central core of spiritual experience, and was less inhibited by specifically Christian dogmas, than any previous Christian mystic.

Nevertheless, there are certain distinctive flavors about Eckhart's thinking, not so much in its basic affirmations as in the manner of expression and the emotional overtones; and these may be ascribed partly to his Christian upbringing and partly to Germanic traditions and the Germanic environment. The whole spirit of Eckhart's mysticism has a dynamic quality which can fairly be described as Gothic in its stress and striving and its effort to reach the higher realm without losing contact with the realm of ordinary human living. It is dynamic especially in its emphasis on Christian practice, so different from the quietism of contemplation generally preferred in the Asian religions. Unlike many of his Christian predecessors, Eckhart did not lose contact with material realities; he had no use for visions or magical powers of healing and guidance, nor did he advocate any extremes of asceticism. Many of his recorded sermons deal warmly and sensibly with the daily problems of Christian living.

Even more characteristic of Eckhart's dynamism is the em-

---

[1] Quotations from Eckhart in R. B. Blakeney: *Meister Eckhart* (New York, 1941), pp. 84, 85; and Rudolf Otto: *Mysticism, East and West,* translated by B. Bracey and R. Payne, pp. 22, 180, 207, 211.

phasis on vitality and creativity in his conception of God. His Godhead is constantly in action; he is life and creation *in excelsis,* and is thus very different from the chilly aloneness of the God of Plotinus. The most highly flavored of Eckhart's sayings are those in which he endeavors to convey some conception of this Gothic being. "I am that I am . . . It indicates also such a boiling up and pouring out of itself in itself, scalding and melting and bubbling itself within itself, light penetrating life, itself whole penetrating the whole self. On this account John 1 says: 'In Him there was life.' For life is as it were a gushing up, a thing welling up in itself, pouring any part of itself into any other part, before it runs forth and bubbles over without." [2]

Eckhart spent part of his active life as a preacher at Strasbourg, and it was partly because of his influence that mysticism became a vital force in various parts of the Rhineland for the remainder of the Middle Ages. During the fourteenth century there was a loosely organized group of mystics who called themselves the Friends of God. They were not overtly hostile to the organized Church, and managed to avoid accusations of heresy; but they were deeply aware of the corruption of most of the clergy, and they remained somewhat aloof from institutional religion. The two best-known of the Friends were Johannes Tauler and Henry Suso, both of them Dominicans and direct disciples of Eckhart; but most of the group preferred to remain laymen. Among them was a Strasbourg banker, Rulman Merswin, who founded a retreat, known as the House of the Green Isle, on the Ill River, where devout persons could live in retirement, and who was also the author of a considerable body of mystical writings. But the outstanding pietistical work produced by the movement was the *Theologica Germanica,* the author of which has remained unknown.

From the Rhine Valley mysticism spread to the Netherlands, where the leading figures were Jan Ruysbroek, who retired to a hermitage in the forest of Soignes near Brussels, and Gerard

---

[2] Otto: op. cit., p. 171.

Groote of Deventer, who founded the Brethren of the Common Life. Groote was probably the principal author of the religious meditations known as the *Imitation of Christ,* which were put together and published in the fifteenth century by Thomas à Kempis and generally bear his name. From the Netherlands mysticism was carried to England, where the fourteenth century saw such mystical writers as Richard Rolle of Hampole, Juliana of Norwich, and the anonymous author of *The Cloud of Unknowing.*

This individualistic approach to religion, devaluing institutional Christianity and emphasizing the personal experience of God and works of charity, helped to bring about the Protestant Reformation (Luther was deeply influenced by the *Theologica Germanica*). More directly it led to the various mystical sects which emerged after the Reformation in the Rhineland and the Netherlands and had a considerable influence on religious development in England and the United States.

The disintegration of scholasticism made possible the development of new ways of thinking not only about inner religious experience but also about the external world. The premises underlying the scientific view of reality were partially formulated early in the fourteenth century, though it was not until the seventeenth century that their importance became fully manifest.

Science had already had a long history in the Western world, though its growth had been impeded by religious dogmas and superstitions. Western civilization from the beginning, in fact, had shown itself more favorable to scientific progress than had its classical predecessor. How far this was due to its religious belief is not easy to determine. One might have expected that Christianity, with its emphasis on the divine creation of the world, would have promoted the study of God's handiwork. The early thirteenth-century encyclopedist Vincent of Beauvais declared that to behold "the magnitude and beauty and permanence of his creation" should inspire men with reverence.[3] But this attitude

[3] Quoted in A. C. Crombie: *Medieval and Early Modern Science,* I, 174.

286

did not promote a scientific study of the creation, at least not before the later Franciscan movement. Most Christians continued to regard nature as simply a storehouse of analogies for theological beliefs, not as a source of new knowledge. Meanwhile men continued to rely on various magical devices for the control of natural evils. How could there be any substantial medical progress when a saint's relic was considered a universal panacea, often no doubt with successful results when the ailment was psychosomatic?

What apparently made Western civilization more scientifically inclined than the civilization of Greece and Rome was its greater interest in technological progress. Starting as early as the eighth and ninth centuries, Western development was promoted by a number of technical innovations: iron plows, some understanding of crop rotation, new devices for drainage, mills driven by wind or water, looms and spinning wheels, new ways of using iron and other metals, new methods of making glassware. These inventions did not, of course, interest philosophers and other men of learning, but they reflected something of vital importance in the spirit of the new civilization. The classical civilization had made no appreciable scientific advances after the third century B.C., largely because of the belief that any kind of manual labor was degrading and should be left to slaves, and also because of the assumption, established by Plato and only partially denied by Aristotle, that knowledge was attained by the contemplation of divine ideas, not by practical experiment. Thus classical philosophy, motivated by reactionary political attitudes, had been led to an impasse from which it never succeeded in escaping. But the West did not rely on slave labor and had plenty of incentive for seeking labor-saving devices; nor was its ruling class eager to affirm that contemplation was superior to labor. Especially important in the early growth of Western technology were the monasteries, whose inmates had impelling reasons to promote labor-saving inventions.

Technology had little direct relationship with science; but it encouraged an understanding of the value of experiment and a belief that through the understanding of nature man could learn to control it. Western science from the beginning was concerned not only with knowledge, but also with power, and without this practical motivation its development would have been much more limited. A similar emphasis on power was displayed by Arabic scientists, from whom the West acquired a mass of detailed information about specific sciences, though this was not accompanied by the kind of general theory needed for major advances.

Scholasticism had started with general principles which were regarded as largely self-evident and of divine origin, and had attempted to reach specific phenomena by deductive reasoning. Science proceeded in the opposite direction, beginning with phenomena and trying to induce general principles which could then be tested by experiment. Some understanding of the need for direct observation of nature, free from theological prepossessions, was displayed in the early Middle Age. As early as 1130, Adelard of Bath, after a prolonged visit to Arabic countries, wrote a dialogue, called *Quaestiones Naturales,* in which he urged the direct study of nature. Nature, he declared, "is not confused and without system, and so far as human knowledge has progressed it should be given a hearing. Only when it fails utterly should there be recourse to God. . . . Those who are now called authorities reached that position first by the exercise of reason." [4] By the thirteenth century, a few individuals were beginning both to understand the importance of experiment and to foresee what science could do to increase man's power over nature. Probably the ablest of them was Robert Grosseteste (1175–1253), an Oxford scholar who ended his life as Bishop of Lincoln. Grosseteste took virtually all knowledge as his field, but his major contributions to science were in the study of optics, to which he was attracted by mystical as well as by practical motivations. The medieval scientist, like the medieval architect,

---

[4] Crombie: op. cit., I, 26.

regarded light as so peculiarly symbolic of divine grace as to be virtually identical with it; and Grosseteste sought to find in light the first cause of matter and motion. But despite these mystical considerations he understood the nature and importance of experiment, which is beautifully described in some of his writings.

Grosseteste was also a pioneer in understanding the importance of mathematics. The Hindu numerals, adopted by Arab scholars in the ninth century and hence misnamed "Arabic," had been introduced into Europe in the year 1202 by Leonardo Fibonacci, a Pisan merchant who had traveled in Arab countries. Now for the first time the West had a system of enumeration which made calculation easy and which included a symbol for zero. Some knowledge of algebra and trigonometry quickly followed, and exact measurement began to be applied in various fields—in weights and measures, for example, and in the measurement of time; mechanical clocks were first used late in the thirteenth century. This led to the recognition, first fully expressed by Grosseteste, that all physical science must be based on mathematics.

The most famous of Grosseteste's pupils was Roger Bacon (1214–92), whose scientific knowledge became legendary and who was perhaps more important as a symbol of the new scientific spirit than for his concrete achievements. A man of immense and varied learning, but with a character marred by egotism and cantankerousness, which prevented him from receiving full recognition from his contemporaries, he made relatively few new discoveries, but is remembered for his understanding of scientific method—he was the first person to speak of "experimental science"—and as prophet of scientific technology. His chief surviving works are the *Opus Maius* and the *Opus Minus,* finished in 1267 and addressed to the Pope (who apparently never read them). These are statements of how science could best be promoted and how much it could increase man's power over nature, though scientific observations are confusedly mingled with religious fantasies and with denunciations of the moral degeneracy of his contemporaries. Posterity has preferred to remember Bacon's predictions of airplanes, automobiles, steamships, and other marvels, though these were not accompanied by an understanding of how they could be constructed. As Emile Brehier has remarked, there was a strong element of Jules Verne in Bacon. He should perhaps be classified as the founder of science fiction.

Thus before the end of the thirteenth century advanced thinkers had arrived at an understanding of the fundamentals of scientific method. There had also been an accumulation of knowledge about most of the specific sciences, much of it acquired from the Arabs, though considerable additions had been made by Christians. These advances had been welcomed by enlightened churchmen, and there had been relatively little conflict between science and theology. But of more fundamental importance in the development of Western thought was the formulation of a new general world-view in accord with scientific attitudes. This started early in the fourteenth century, though it did not win general acceptance among men of learning until the seventeenth century. It was in direct conflict with certain religious beliefs, and its sources were philosophical and sociological rather than directly scientific.

The new ways of thinking denied the "realism" (in the medieval sense of the word) that had dominated early medieval philosophy and had still been partially maintained by St. Thomas. Regarding universals as mere mental conveniences, not as actually existing, fourteenth-century thinkers insisted that only concrete particulars had reality. The new philosophy thus reflected the growing individualism of late medieval society and the breakdown of the belief that corporate institutions were more real than the men and women who belonged to them. The exponents of this late medieval "nominalism" generally gave support to individualistic tendencies whenever these came into open conflict with the spokesmen of the old order. Thus they were on the side of radicalism in politics as well as in philosophy, besides being in accord with the development of the natural sciences.

An accompanying tendency was to regard the universe as infinite, not as the closed system, with the earth at its center and heaven composing the circumference, which the medieval mind had inherited from the Greeks. This change in point of view was not itself scientific, but it led indirectly to important scientific advances: to the abandonment of the Aristotelian conception of motion as requiring a mover, to the recognition that the same laws of mechanics applied to the whole universe (in contrast with the traditional belief that stars and planets moved by principles different from those governing sublunar bodies), and eventually to the heliocentric theory of the solar system. The new view was obviously of immense psychological importance, and was directly contrary to traditional religious doctrines and to certain passages in the Bible. If the universe was infinite, then the earth was no longer the center of it, and this could not easily be reconciled with the whole Christian conception of salvation. How could men continue to believe that Christ was the Son of God if the earth was merely one of an infinite number of similar bodies in an infinite universe? The sources of the new view can only have been sociological, and are to be found in a general change of sensibility in Western society, though it was not generally accepted for several centuries. Western man was beginning to feel himself hemmed in by the traditional clerical and political authorities and was acquiring greater confidence in his own powers of exploration. The new views were a protest against the claustrophobic quality of the medieval universe. They were an expression of the same impulses that, on the practical level, led in the fifteenth century to the early voyages of discovery.

The most important precursor of the new view of the universe was an English Franciscan, William of Occam (1300–48), who is remembered chiefly as a thoroughgoing nominalist. Making a radical separation between theology and philosophy, the sphere of faith and the sphere of reason, he claimed freedom to pursue intellectual inquiries without feeling any obligation to reach conclusions that would harmonize with religious belief. Universals, he asserted, did not, and could not, really exist. They were merely signs invented by the human mind to refer to qualities that were common to groups of individual objects. "No universal

really exists outside the human mind in individual substances." [5]
"Every positive thing outside of the soul is by that very fact
singular." [6] This dismissal of universals was supported by the
principle known to later generations as Occam's razor, according
to which it was unnecessary to postulate several causes for any
phenomenon if one was adequate. This was stated by Occam as
"a plurality must not be asserted without necessity." [7]

Jettisoning most of the intellectual baggage that medieval
philosophy had inherited from Plato and Aristotle and clearing
the ground in order to make possible a new beginning, Occam
repudiated the complex Aristotelian conception of quadrupal
causation; one could know only that certain phenomena were
generally followed by certain other phenomena. He denied the
doctrine that any action at a distance was impossible, thus implying that movement might be explained as caused by distant
attractions and repulsions and need not be attributed to forces
directly in contact with moving objects. He rejected the belief
that celestial matter differed from earthly matter in being incor-
ruptible, and thus implied that the same laws of mechanics applied to the earth and to the heavens. And he came close to
asserting that the universe was, or at least might be, infinite
instead of finite, and that motion, once started, would continue
by its own impetus until checked or diverted by some opposing
force, and therefore did not require the constant intervention of a
first mover.

The practical implications of William of Occam's nominalism became apparent when he supported the claims of the
emperor in a controversy with the Pope, writing a number of pam-
phlets in which he argued that the emperor was directly responsible to God, not to the Pope as God's intermediary. Principles of
right and justice were transmitted by God to individual human

---

[5] Quoted in Maurice de Wulf: *History of Medieval Philosophy*, p. 183.

[6] Etienne Gilson: *History of Christian Philosophy in the Middle Ages*, p.
490.

[7] Crombie: op. cit., I, 231.

beings, not to the corporate entity known as the Church or to the Pope as its representative. The nominalist philosophy implied a denial of the existence of such corporate entities. The Pope spoke simply as an individual, in spite of the authority with which he was endowed, and had no legitimate power over secular rulers in political matters. Church and state should be separated from each other, and the Church should be concerned solely with man's supernatural salvation, which belonged to the sphere of faith, not of reason. Thus nominalism pointed toward a liberal conception of individual rights and partially toward democracy. These implications were developed further by a number of other nominalist thinkers, particularly by Marsiglio of Padua (1270–1342), whose *Defensor Pacis* attacked papal authority and presented a theory of popular sovereignty, and by several members of the Conciliar Movement of the early fifteenth century, which tried unsuccessfully to reform the Church by transferring authority from the Pope to a general council.

That this kind of philosophy was in accord with the spirit of the age was shown by the appearance during the fourteenth century of a number of other philosophers (some of them Dominicans or Cistercians, though the majority continued to be Franciscans) who adopted Occamist nominalism and in some instances went further toward the emerging scientific world-view than William himself. A long series of teachers at the University of Paris made a radical separation of philosophy from theology, insisted that all we knew of causation was the experience of uniform succession, denied the existence of universals, and adopted new theories of motion.

As early as 1320, François de Marchia appears to have denied that motion required the continuous activity of a mover, and thus to have foreshadowed Galileo's principle of inertia. More explicitly, Jean Buridan, rector of the University of Paris in 1327 and again in 1349, attributed movement to an internal impulse which continued of its own momentum once it had been acquired. Thus the eternal movement of the heavenly spheres could be explained as having been caused by a primeval impulse the effects of which were conserved indefinitely. There was no need to postulate the constant intervention of a celestial power. From these revolutionary views of physics it was easy to pass to the suggestion that the earth was in motion and not the static center of the universe. This suggestion was actually made, though presented as a possibility only, by Jean Buridan and by a somewhat younger scholar, Nicolas d'Oresme. Proof of these suggestions came, of course, at a much later period. The scientific world-view began with hypotheses, not with observations and calculations, and these hypotheses were reflections of the spirit of the age.

The mystical individualism of the new modes of sensibility were directly reflected in art—especially, of course, in Italy, where the Renaissance was well established, but also in the Netherlands. The new beginnings in Flemish painting can be dated about the year 1420 and reflected a new scientific world-view as well as the new mysticism. The Flemings had some contacts with Italian art, and to some extent the influences were mutual; but basically Flemish art was indigenous to Flanders. In addition to its parallelisms with philosophic thought, it was significant in its emphasis on realistic representation of human beings and its reflection of middle-class points of view. Its initial leaders were the van Eyck brothers, Hubert and Jan, and the movement retained much of its vitality throughout the fifteenth century. Flanders was at this period still the richest area in northern Europe, owing chiefly to its cloth industries; and though it had suffered acutely from class conflicts, it had now achieved temporary peace and stability through the firm control exercised by the dukes of Burgundy. Its wealth and its urban development prepared it to support a new kind of painting. Most of the sponsors of the new art were bourgeois merchants who preferred portraits and other secular subjects. The van Eycks gave them an art which differed from realistic representation only in its more brilliant coloring.

More important issues were involved, of which most contemporary sponsors and critics probably remained unaware. Like the

Italians of the same period, the Flemish masters were struggling to express a new sense of space as continuous and three-dimensional. Their work paralleled that of the Italians, though there was less emphasis than in Italy on the calculations of perspectives. Art was now committed (for some five hundred years) to the presentation of the concrete material world, not of the inner world of subjective emotion and religious belief. Unlike the Italians, however, the van Eycks and their pupils presented reality as a mass of details with little attempt at organization or synthesis. Their pictures portrayed figures with a masterly sense of realism and included richly crowded backgrounds, everything being brilliantly colored. But the sense of order and unity which characterized the greatest art, and especially that of the Renaissance in Italy, was missing. Flemish pictures are, in fact, generally cluttered with too many figures, all of which are admirably portrayed, but which convey a sense of overcrowding. Consider, for example, Jan van Eyck's *Madonna of Chancellor Rodin,* which shows the Chancellor sitting opposite the Virgin and her child, while in the background between them the spectator sees snowy mountains, a wandering river, and a whole city, with innumerable buildings and inhabitants. It is an astonishing *tour de force,* but it does not display the creative organizing power of the greatest art. As with the nominalist philosophers, reality is represented as a mass of individual details, and there are no positive affirmations. Michelangelo a century later stated criticisms about Flemish art in which there is much truth, though they were perhaps expressed with too much severity. He complained that it sought simply to render natural objects with minute and meticulous accuracy, and that it lacked the order and unity imparted by the truly creative artist.

The fact that most of the work of the van Eycks was always secular in tone and usually in subject matter did not mean that religion was wholly excluded, though there was little religious feeling in such works as the van Eycks' famous altarpiece *The Adoration of the Lamb.* But the mysticism which had developed in the Netherlands alongside the secularism of bourgeois life inspired much of the work of Roger van der Weyden, who was contemporary with the van Eycks. A gifted master of the later fifteenth century, Hugo van der Goes, portrayed religious experience with an intense emotionalism that drove him to monastic seclusion and eventually to madness. The religion of the painters was as individualistic as that of the mystics.

The later fourteenth and the fifteenth centuries were less productive in philosophical speculation, possibly because of the turmoil caused by the Hundred Years War between France and England; but one bold thinker summed up the more important philosophical tendencies of the time, both its mysticism and its new conceptions of the universe. This was Nicholas of Cusa (1400–64), a German-born cleric who originally supported the Conciliar Movement and was an active reform leader but subsequently accepted papal supremacy and was rewarded with a cardinalate. In the intervals of a busy life he wrote a highly original work of speculation known as *De Docta Ignorantia* ("Concerning Learned Ignorance"). This book accepted all the new conceptions stated by, or implicit in, the new philosophy: the infinity of the universe, the movement of the earth, the importance of mathematics as the most certain of the sciences, the application of the same rules of motion to the earth and the heavens. But Nicholas's main concern was to transcend science and end with a mystical union with God. Human knowledge was at best relative and self-contradictory. But in God, who was both the center and circumference of the infinite universe, all contradictions were resolved and all opposites met each other. Thus medieval philosophy ended, as it had begun, with God, but the mathematical deity of Nicholas presided over a very different kind of universe from the closed and finite system of the early Christian philosophers.

From the point of view of the ordinary individual without scientific training, the most revolutionary of the new concepts was the shift of the earth from the center of the universe to the status of a minor planet revolving around the sun. This new astronomy, foreshadowed by fourteenth-century scholars, was first formulated in detail by Copernicus, a Polish scholar who—apart from some early education in Italy—spent his life in East Prussia. His work was published in 1543, many years after its author had first formulated his new view of the universe. And it is significant that this intellectual revolution, possibly the most important change in point of view in all human history, was initially caused not by new observations or new mathematical solutions of astronomic problems but by a change in sensibility. Man's picture of the universe now demanded heliocentricity. Copernicus's theory, as originally worked out in mathematical terms, was "neither more accurate nor significantly simpler than its Ptolemaic predecessors." [8] But as Copernicus himself recognized, the real appeal of sun-centered astronomy was aesthetic rather than pragmatic. Scholars were now willing to accept the new astronomy because it harmonized with their new feelings, not because it was mathematically more convincing. The mathematical proofs of the Copernican system were of secondary importance and were not fully worked out until the seventeenth century.[9]

The change from a finite to an infinite space is perhaps the sharpest difference between the medieval and the modern view of the universe. Is it possible that a similar transformation of space conceptions may mark a similar difference between the modern cosmology and whatever is destined to succeed it? The modern mind has envisaged space as containing what can be seen and touched. Every object occupies a particular point in space; otherwise it does not exist. But this conception does not apply to sound, which has no particular location and can be heard at any

---

[8] Thomas S. Kuhn: *The Copernican Revolution,* p. 171.

[9] The element of claustrophobia in the change from a Ptolemaic to a Copernican universe is clearly shown in the writings of Giordano Bruno (1548–1600). "The Nolan," he declared, meaning himself, "has given freedom to the human spirit and made its knowledge free. It was suffocating in the close air of a narrow prison-house whence, but only through chinks, it gazed at the far-off stars. Its wings were clipped, so that it was unable to cleave the veiling clouds and reach the reality beyond." Quoted in William Boulting: *Giordano Bruno* (London, 1914), p. 125.

point within the appropriate radius. In terms of a visual spatial universe, sound is inexplicable. Is it possible that the human race may at some point substitute a sound universe for our present visual conceptions? One cannot say. And that earlier change was inexplicable, although it had some connection with the growth of individualism both in thought and in social action.

PART III

THE RENAISSANCE

15

The Renaissance in Italy

While the culture of medieval France was succumbing to decadence and disintegration, a new movement of creativity was developing in Italy. The Italian Renaissance, which carried individualism and rationalism far beyond the limits reached in France, was well under way by the middle of the fourteenth century and retained its vitality until the middle of the sixteenth. It contributed little to science or technology and produced no philosophy of lasting significance; but it was responsible for achievements of immense importance in the visual arts. In these media it gave expression to a new confidence in human potentialities and a new sense of the reality of the world of space and time which marked an even sharper break with the sensibility of medieval man than that made by late medieval nominalism.

How far Italian civilization had a continuous history from Roman times is difficult to estimate. Throughout the whole of the Dark Ages, city life, with its arts and crafts and its schools of grammar and rhetoric, seems never to have disappeared wholly. Rome had remained the home of the papacy, though its population had dropped from above one million to—at the lowest point —perhaps twenty thousand, most of whom lived in misery and squalor, not interested in the crumbling ruins of ancient glories by which they were surrounded. Through most of the Middle Ages, Rome was dominated by a few noble families whose incessant factional conflicts frequently determined papal elections.

Perhaps a dozen other cities had had a similarly continuous existence from Roman times. But more important than these physical survivals was the transmission of memories. Educated Italians never wholly forgot that their ancestors had once been the rulers of the Mediterranean world and the chief protectors of its order and civilization. Despite their political submission to the Germanic conquerors from the north, they continued to regard themselves as members of a superior people and to hope for the re-establishment of Italian supremacy, or at least for the unity and independence of Italy.

Neither the Ostrogothic and Lombard kingdoms nor the Holy Roman Empire of Charlemagne and the German emperors had any deep or lasting effects on Italian culture, and Italy played only a minor role in the institutional and cultural developments of medieval civilization. The Italians remained largely unreceptive to social and aesthetic trends that were derived from the Germanic heritage. Neither feudal institutions nor Gothic art styles ever established any deep roots in Italian society.

During the early Middle Ages, Italy had contributed to the growth of Western culture not as an innovator but as an intermediary. She had served as a meetingplace of the three civilizations into which the Mediterranean world had been divided. Although northern Italy formed part of the Latin Catholic culture area and was included, nominally at least, in the Holy Roman Empire, close connections with Byzantium continued. A number of Dark Age Popes were of Greek descent, and the definitive separation of the Greek and Latin churches did not come about until the eleventh century. Parts of southern Italy remained Greek for a long time, as they had been before the rise of Rome. The Byzantine Empire retained political control over parts of Italy until the year 1071, when its last foothold, the town of Bari in Apulia, was captured by the Normans of the kingdom of Sicily. Meanwhile, commercial connections were of increasing importance. In the early Middle Ages, several Italian cities developed trade connections with the eastern Mediterranean area, and Venice, in particular, became a main medium for the transmission of Byzantine and Levantine influences to western Europe. Romanesque architecture flourished, but Italian art and some church buildings remained Byzantine in style until the beginning of new Renaissance art forms in the thirteenth and fourteenth centuries.

Arab influences were less obvious, though perhaps of almost equal importance. They were transmitted mainly through Sicily, which was controlled by the Arabs in the later Dark Ages and conquered by the Normans only in the latter decades of the eleventh century. A vigorous, ruthless, and realistic people, the Normans rapidly forgot their initial religious intolerance. Their kingdom, which comprised the southern parts of the Italian peninsula as well as Sicily, continued to be partly Arab in the ethnic origin and religious belief of its inhabitants and became a center for the transmission of Mohammedan learning and technology. The Norman kings of Naples and Sicily, followed in the thirteenth century by the Emperor Frederick II, borrowed political ideas and institutions from the Eastern autocracies and built up an absolutist and bureaucratic state.

The Renaissance developed mostly in northern Italy, and early in the Middle Ages this had become an area of self-governing city-states. In theory they were under the rule of the emperors, but after 1176, when a league of rebellious northern cities defeated Frederick Barbarossa in the battle of Legnano, most of them were for all practical purposes independent. Thus a society developed comparable to that of ancient Greece or of the still earlier Sumer in Mesopotamia. The city-state has always been the most stimulating, and also the most turbulent, of political institutions, chiefly because governmental affairs can easily become the concern of every citizen instead of being directed by some remote and consequently mysterious authority. The city-state had always been the central institution of the classical civilization—even the Roman Empire had been considered a league of cities during its great period—and the reappearance of the city as a political and moral unit in medieval Italy owed something to earlier memories and traditions.

Rural Italy was mostly divided into big estates, the owners of which were regarded as members of the nobility; but feudal institutions were never widely established and quickly disappeared. Most of the noble families of northern Italy preferred to live in the cities and to participate in city politics, though they often continued to display a feudal arrogance and propensity toward violence, building themselves fortified towers on city streets and becoming involved in prolonged family feuds with each other. According to the twelfth-century German chronicler Otto of Freising, "Almost the whole country pertains to the cities, each of which forces the inhabitants of its territory to submit to its sway, and there is hardly a man of rank or importance who does not recognize the city's authority. They surpass all other cities of the world in riches and power." [1]

Political independence was accompanied by economic growth. By the thirteenth century, northern Italy had become the richest part of Europe and was moving into the capitalistic phase of economic development. Its supremacy was due originally to its control of trade between western Europe and the East. Numerous luxury articles of small bulk were imported from Constantinople and the Levant, some of them coming originally from areas in more remote parts of Asia. Merchants were at first itinerant, traveling with their wares to markets in northern France, the Netherlands, and England. As trade expanded, mercantile operations became more extensive and more complicated. Control was exercised by large business houses in the Italian cities whose leading members no longer traveled but stayed at home; and elaborate devices for keeping accounts and recording profits and losses were developed. As the fifteenth-century humanist Leon Battista Alberti declared, "It befits a merchant always to have ink-stained hands." [2] The use of bills of exchange made unnecessary the transportation of money. By the thirteenth century, several northern Italian business firms had branches and connec-

---

[1] Quoted in Wallace K. Ferguson: *Europe in Transition, 1300–1520*, p. 32.
[2] Ferguson: op. cit., p. 103.

tions in the leading western European cities and were gradually assuming the functions of banking houses capable of making loans to kings and noblemen. Meanwhile, rivalries between seaport cities for control of the trade with the Orient were becoming more intense; Venice, Genoa, and Pisa were the leading contestants.

Commercial expansion was followed by a growth of industry, particularly of textiles, which were especially important in Florence. Most industry was carried on by small independent craftsmen who themselves retailed the goods they made. But some industries gradually came under capitalist control, wealthy merchants acquiring ownership, while the workers were reduced to the status of wage-earning proletarians. This was notably true of the Florentine woolen industry, which according to the fourteenth-century historian Giovanni Villani gave employment to about one third of the city's working population.[3]

This growth of economic complexity had important political repercussions. In the early Middle Ages, when the cities first achieved self-government, authority belonged mostly to patrician merchants and to the nobility. But as trade and industry expanded, there were demands for political rights on the part of new groups—merchants who had more recently risen to wealth, industrial entrepreneurs, wage-earning proletarians. Through the thirteenth and fourteenth centuries there were incessant and murderous struggles for political power and economic advantages both between classes within the same city and between different cities. The political situation was further confused by the claims of the papacy to temporal power, the conflicts between the papacy and the Holy Roman emperors, and the intervention in Italian affairs of the French monarchy, initially on the pretext of supporting the papacy. Class struggles in the Italian cities were complicated and intensified by these broader conflicts for power and privilege.

---

[3] Ferguson: op. cit., p. 111.

The final outcome resembled what had happened in the Greek cities before the rise of democracy in Athens. Most of the Italian cities came, sooner or later, under the rule of despots. There were some attempts to establish democracy, most notably in Florence during the middle decades of the fourteenth century. But the Florentine richer classes regained control in 1382, and in 1434 the city came under the rule of the Medici, who were willing to dispense with the appearances of power as long as they could enjoy the realities. Venice remained a republic and maintained a stability which was the envy of other states, though it was rigidly controlled by rich mercantile families, with no element of democracy. Two smaller cities, Siena and Lucca, also remained republican. Every other city-state had surrendered its freedom before the end of the fourteenth century.

The despots achieved power by various means, sometimes by popular choice and sometimes by force; and some of them sought to legalize their rule by purchasing a title (such as vicar, duke, or marquis) from the emperor. They usually tried to make their rule hereditary, generally with success except when their heirs displayed marked incompetence. Except when they flagrantly misused their powers for selfish purposes, they undoubtedly had the support of the majority of their subjects, who found that dictatorial rule, however corrupt, was preferable to incessant civil war. Yet the rule of the despots was never fully legitimized, and this lack of accepted legal authority was of immense importance for the whole development of the Renaissance. Legal supremacy still belonged to the emperor, and during the early phases of the Renaissance, idealists disturbed by the lack of political order and unity, such as Dante and Petrarch, continued to hope for an effective restoration of full imperial authority. When the futility of these hopes for the revival of the Roman Empire became apparent, the Italians had to recognize their dependence for the maintenance of any kind of peace and order on governments frankly based on force and fraud. This was a society that offered plenty of opportunities to individual adventurers who were guided by their own creative or destructive impulses rather than by any generally accepted principles of morality and justice. It promoted a maximum of individual initiative and political experimentation, and stimulated that confidence in human powers which was the dominating theme of Renaissance art and literature.

Most of the despots aspired to expand the area under their rule and pursued policies of expansion over the countryside and over smaller cities in the vicinity. This resulted in numerous outbreaks of interstate warfare, but the fighting was now done mostly by mercenary troops, led by *condottieri*. These professional soldiers were hired by the despots whenever they went to war, while the civilian population preferred to spend their time more profitably. Some *condottieri* were unscrupulous adventurers who aspired to become despots themselves, while others were honorable men who had chosen warfare as their profession and respected the contracts under which they had been hired. For obvious reasons warfare between opposing *condottieri* was usually not very bloody. As long as the Italian cities were not threatened with conquest by foreign powers, this can be regarded as a highly civilized way of settling interstate conflicts.

By the middle of the fifteenth century, Milan, Florence, and Venice had emerged as the three leading states in the north. Many of their smaller rivals had been absorbed and deprived of independence; but some other northern cities, such as Mantua, Ferrara, and Urbino, continued to be governed by their own local despotic dynasties. Venice had definitely surpassed her rivals for commercial control of the eastern Mediterranean, and Genoa and Pisa had sunk into relative insignificance. Meanwhile, central Italy was nominally under the rule of the papacy; but the removal of papal headquarters from Rome to Avignon had led to a kind of interregnum during which most of the cities in the papal state came under the control of local despots. For a century after the restoration of the papacy to Rome in 1417, the Popes had to devote themselves primarily to regaining their temporal power over the papal state, their religious functions being of secondary importance. In the south, the kingdom of Naples and Sicily was still in being, but it was for a long time in dispute between French and Spanish dynastic claimants. After the death of Frederick II in 1250, it ceased to be a center of intellectual activity, and its contributions to the Renaissance were unimportant.

Interstate warfare, previously almost incessant, was temporarily ended in 1454, when the three leading states of northern Italy came together in the Peace of Lodi. This was followed by a defensive league, covering almost the whole country, which was designed to maintain peace and to provide for defense against possible foreign invasions. The next forty years were free from major wars. Outbreaks of violence continued occasionally to disturb the life of the cities. Lorenzo de' Medici, for example, narrowly escaped assassination in 1474 in a conspiracy promoted by the Pope, and his younger brother was actually killed while attending Mass in the cathedral of Florence. Some other cities, notably Perugia, continued to be torn apart by bloody family feuds. But political passions were less obsessive than in the past, and this was the most peaceful epoch that Italy had enjoyed since the fall of Rome.

The special quality that distinguished Renaissance society from that of the Middle Ages was an emphasis on the reality of the material world in space and time. Medieval man, while showing in his behavior that space and time were realities, professed to believe that their main importance was to symbolize higher spiritual forces which could not be expressed directly. But for Renaissance man what was visible and tangible really existed, and it was unnecessary to look for anything beyond. This led to the recognition that man was an individual with an independent existence, capable of formulating his own conceptions of truth and of morality. In his philosophical and religious formulations, Renaissance man continued to be influenced by medieval thinking. But in the visual arts the new views of reality led to an artistic revolution.

In the fourteenth century, Italian painters, no longer seeking to convey transcendental truths by means of visual symbols, set out to reproduce natural forms, on the assumption that art should be judged by the success with which it copied nature. This was probably the most radical and the most abrupt change of sensibility in all aesthetic history.[4] And because the artists of the Renaissance portrayed human beings who seemed capable of independent movement and action, having a life of their own apart from the framework of the picture or—in sculpture—the structure of the building, they promoted an individualistic view of life. As art developed through the fourteenth and fifteenth centuries, it became more richly and lavishly colorful in its appeal to the senses, presenting a world that was filled with natural beauties and invitations. In its art, if not in its professed beliefs, Renaissance Italy affirmed that this world was more real than any hypothetical afterlife; and if mankind still needed spurs for the pursuit of high achievement, they were to be found not in the promise of celestial salvation, but in the quest for worldly glory.

The Renaissance was, in part, a continuation of humanizing tendencies that had begun in medieval France. The debt of Italy to France was especially evident in early Italian literature, which began in imitation of the troubadours. The individualism of the Renaissance had, moreover, been foreshadowed in the nominalism of late medieval philosophy. More broadly, the Renaissance can be regarded as the logical sequel of the French efflorescence in the movement of Western civilization toward individualism and rationalism. But to the Italians themselves it appeared not as a logical development beyond medievalism, but as a revolt against it. With considerable truth they regarded themselves as repudiating northern and Germanic influences and rediscovering native qualities which could be traced back to the ancient Roman civilization. Attitudes emerged that had always been latent in the

---

[4] Almost equally radical, but much less abrupt, was the revolution of the late nineteenth and early twentieth century which ended the dominance of representationism that had begun with Giotto and reasserted the preference for symbols and abstractions. But whereas medieval art had given expression to religious beliefs, modern art was mostly irreligious and affirmed the power of modern man to create his own truths, both intellectual and emotional.

sensibility of Mediterranean peoples and were presumably to be attributed partly to environmental influences and partly to cultural traditions. The Mediterranean peoples, unlike those of the north, had always been inclined to regard reality as sensuous, objective, visible, and tangible, and had always been aware of man as existing in the natural world and seeking natural goals and consummations. Ancient Greece had discovered man, free from the distortions of transcendental religious beliefs, and this Greek humanism had been partially preserved, though with strong Oriental nonhumanist associations, by Byzantium. Similarly, the Italians of the Renaissance were rediscovering human nature, and in so doing were recapturing their own traditional bent, free from the influences of northern and Oriental mysticism.

Rejecting the Germanic elements in medieval culture, the Italians regarded themselves as reaffirming the Greco-Roman tradition. In its narrower connotations the Renaissance meant a rebirth of classical culture. This, indeed, was the origin of the name "Renaissance," which was first used in the sixteenth century by the art historian Vasari. Medieval France had begun the process of assimilating and revivifying the an and classical heritage, translating it from empty dogmas lived experience, but it had not worked back beyond the belief a attitudes of the age of Constantine. It had known much of the earlier classical literature—medieval scholars had a wider acquaintance with the classics than has often been recognized—but it had been unable to understand and digest it. The Italians, on the other hand, carried the process of rediscovery as far as the age of city-state republicanism, and believed themselves to be engaged in a complete reconstruction of the classical culture. But in supposing that they were primarily endeavoring to copy the ancients, the Italians of the Renaissance were not fully recognizing their own capacity for innovation. The imitation of classical values and art forms was only one aspect of the Italian achievement, and it had less importance than Italian scholars and patrons of learning supposed. Renaissance artists and intellectuals made use of their

Latin heritage for support in their rebellion against aspects of medieval culture which they felt as alien or restrictive; but much of the achievement of the Renaissance was profoundly original and reflective of a new post-medieval sensibility.

The man of the Renaissance was not in all ways more enlightened than the late medieval man whom he superseded. Emphasizing human glory and the pleasures of the senses and regarding human life primarily in aesthetic terms, he had little interest in philosophical speculation or in scientific discovery. Leonardo da Vinci's scientific investigations were exceptional, and it is significant that Leonardo never made them public. The scientific world-view toward which late medieval nominalism was moving did not win general acceptance from educated men until the seventeenth century. Throughout the Renaissance, antiscientific and superstitious beliefs persisted to a surprising degree; and some of them, being supported by the authority of the ancients (such as the belief in astrology), became even stronger than during the Middle Ages.

Renaissance culture, moreover, to a greater extent than that of the Middle Ages, reflected the attitudes of the upper classes. The support for the new literature and learning, and in a lesser degree for the new art, was provided by the despots and by rich merchants. There was nothing democratic about the Renaissance. Popular tastes, indeed, lagged behind those of the upper classes, being slow to accept the new standards in art and literature. And while many of the despots displayed a surprising degree of artistic sophistication, they had a tendency to prefer an art which did not grapple too profoundly with the realities of human life, communicating chiefly enjoyment of a richly colored fantasy world. Much Renaissance painting and almost all of its literature, especially during the fifteenth century when the rule of the despots was most firmly established, lacked essential seriousness.

One of the important achievements of the Renaissance was to develop new norms of upper-class behavior. Ideals of education were revolutionized by scholars and schoolmasters in order to suit the needs of a wealthy and leisured aristocracy which, unlike the medieval nobility, was interested in many other activities besides warfare. The new standards of culture retained much of their influence down to the twentieth century, the gentleman, fortified with an education based primarily on the classics, having replaced the chivalric warrior as the ideal type. But it was always plain that this was an upper-class ideal, and one of the functions of a classical education was simply to differentiate the member of the ruling class from the man of the people who had no access to this singularly useless branch of learning.

These new norms were predominatingly secular—the gentleman respected religious belief but did not cultivate it too enthusiastically—and provided no remedy for the political problems resulting from unchecked individualism. Renaissance man, repudiating medieval ideals of social order, had originally supposed that both political and aesthetic standards were to be found partly in the study of nature and partly in the imitation of the ancients. But it gradually became apparent that he was underestimating his own creative powers. Faith in these powers became the main unifying principle of Renaissance Italy, but with very different results in the arts and in social life. In the arts, the masters of the late fifteenth and early sixteenth centuries, no longer regarding themselves as simply copying natural forms, claimed to be creative in the same way that nature was creative and to have a godlike power to produce things wholly new. This mystical view of the artist's function was corroborated by the actual experience of artistic creation as the product of compulsive inspirations welling up from the depths of the human personality. The most conspicuous feature of the work of Leonardo, Raphael, and Michelangelo was its sense of an underlying aesthetic order and harmony; but this sense was derived from the artist's own creative power and was not to be found in nature. In politics, on the other hand, order was impossible unless it was believed to be derived from objective and transcendental standards. While Renaissance individualism led, in the arts, to the culmination of human creativity in Michelangelo, in practical life it ended in an amoralism whose most outspoken representative was Machiavelli.

Meanwhile the Renaissance spread to northern and western Europe, but outside Italy it appeared as a largely alien movement, not as a revival of earlier traditions. Spain, France, and England assimilated whatever elements of the Renaissance could be reconciled with their own cultural heritages, but much of its view of man evoked fear and antagonism. Two radically different views of life were now competing with each other, and the exploration of the conflict between them and the search for some underlying harmony became the main themes of sixteenth-century arts and letters.

16

Dante, Petrarch, and Giotto

The best point at which to begin the study of the Renaissance is the work of Dante, who—like other great poets, such as Homer and Shakespeare—was backward-looking in his explicit view of life, but forward-looking in its deeper implications. His conscious purpose was to state the established conceptions of man's nature and destiny, and his work constituted a synthesis of the whole cultural and spiritual heritage of Western man, extraordinary both in its comprehensiveness and in its grasp of what was central and essential. Yet the *Divine Comedy* contained discordant elements which were not fully reconciled with each other and which foreshadowed the breakdown in later generations of medieval ways of thinking and the emergence of new views of man.

In the age of Dante, cultural leadership passed from France to Italy; and while the whole achievement of medieval France was available to the Italians, they were severely selective in what they adopted from it. Much of French literature had developed out of a feudal society and had been strongly marked by feudal attitudes; but the urban and capitalistic society of northern Italy preferred to stress different values. And though the French had been by no means ignorant of the classical background of Western literature and thought, they had not accepted it as an intrinsic and indispensable element in their cultural heritage. In Italy, however, there was a deep sense of a continuing tradition from Roman sources. Italian culture was both Christian and Roman, each element being of vital importance and supposedly endowed with divine authority.

The most immediate French influence was troubadour poetry. Early in the thirteenth century, poets at the court of Frederick II began to compose love poetry in the vernacular. This was
the first use of Italian for literary purposes, the vernacular being
much slower in replacing Latin than in other Western countries.
Later in the century, troubadour conventions spread from Naples
to Tuscany. But the northern Italian poets, beginning with Guido
Guinicelli of Bologna and continuing with Guido Cavalcanti and
with his younger friend Dante, used the troubadour techniques to
express a fundamentally different attitude to life. The reverence
for femininity that had flourished at the feudal courts of southern
France could not be transferred to the more rationalistic society
of the Italian cities. The troubadours had represented love as an
ennobling and civilizing emotion, but its goal had been sexual
consummation; and as the troubadours considered nothing
higher than sexual love (even though it was sometimes regarded
as superior if it fell short of carnal fulfillment), the troubadour
attitude had remained essentially anarchical. But the Italians
broadened the concept of love to include the desire for all worthy
things, even including philosophical learning, and transformed
the loved woman into a symbol of all virtue and knowledge. Love
thus ceased to be anarchical and became the motive power which
led the individual to the understanding and acceptance of his role
in an orderly universe. This was best exemplified in the poems
written by Dante in honor of Beatrice and published as *La Vita
Nuova*. The poets responsible were described by Dante as writing
in a *dolce stil nuovo*, a sweet new style, though Dante seems to
have been referring to the directness and spontaneity with which
they wrote rather than to their philosophical orientation. "I am
one," he declared, in defining the style, "who, when love breathes
in me, take note and in that manner which he dictates go on to set
it forth." [1] Love, in this new and comprehensive sense (though

---

[1] Dante: *Purgatorio*, xxiv, 52. This and subsequent quotations from the
Divine Comedy are from the prose translation by Philip Wicksteed and
H. Oelsner in the Temple Classics.

for Dante it remained definitely *eros* and not *agape*), was the main motive power in the universe, the link between God and man, and the source of order.

Born into a society in which warfare, both civil and inter-state, had long been chronic, and himself compelled to spend his later years in exile from his native city of Florence, Dante was obsessed by the need for order; and what was perhaps most medieval in his thinking was his conviction that a moral and political order was inherent in the structure of the universe, disorder being the result of man's disobedience to the divine will. But Dante differed from most other medieval thinkers in stressing the duality of the Western tradition, the sources of order being Roman as well as Christian. This was due, in part, to his deep conviction that the papacy should confine itself to spiritual leadership and should not assume political functions, which were the proper responsibility of the empire. His whole work was pervaded with a deep hostility to the policies pursued by the thirteenth-century Popes, which he regarded as ruinous both for the Church and for Italy.

Dante's prose treatise *De Monarchia,* written in the hope that the current emperor, Henry VII, would reassert imperial authority and restore order in Italy, was an extreme statement of the medieval belief in unity. Mankind was an organic whole, and freedom and justice required that its oneness be embodied in the will of a single ruler whose personal interests would be identified with the good of all. Such a ruler would "desire all men to be made good," "one will dominating and ruling all the rest to oneness." This had been achieved under the Roman Empire, which had become the ruler of the world by divine support. "The world was never quiet on every side except under Divus Augustus, the monarch, when there was a perfect monarchy," and Christ had chosen this period for his birth and had been—politically—a subject of the emperor. Dante went on to deduce that the empire was directly responsible to God and was not subordinate to the papacy. Man had two objectives, blessedness in this life and blessedness in the next, and hence needed two authorities: "the supreme pontiff, to lead the human race, in accordance with things revealed, to eternal life; and the emperor, to direct the human race to temporal felicity in accordance with the teachings of philosophy." [2]

In the *Divine Comedy,* Dante's purpose was to describe the divine order which pervaded the universe and to show how it was exemplified in the lives of individuals. His conception of the cosmos was essentially medieval, but there were significant changes of emphasis. His view of life was more humanistic, positive, and optimistic than that of most medieval theologians; and in his awareness of (and admiration for) the human individual, seen not as a specimen of a group or class but presented with all his personal force and idiosyncrasies, he gave expression to the qualities developed in the new urban society of northern Italy. For Dante, as for all profound spokesmen of the Western tradition, freedom and order were ultimately in harmony. By realizing his true nature and becoming more fully himself, man learned to love God and become a part of the divine order. The whole *Comedy* was primarily a study of the different kinds of love, both the true love which unites man to God and the destructive love which leads man astray. When directed toward its proper objective, love is the source of order, and what is experienced by the poet in his journey through the next life is the process of moral growth by which man learns the dangers of wrongly directed love and acquires the true love which brings harmony with the divine will and the sense of freedom and peace. Love, in fact, is the main motivation of God as well as of man. The last line of the *Comedy* speaks of "the love that moves the sun and the other stars," while even hell is the creation of love as well as of power and wisdom.

Thus the innate desire for good is the motive power of all human striving. "Like to the lark who soareth in the air, first singing and then silent, content with the last sweetness that doth

---

[2] Dante: *De Monarchia,* i, 12, 15, 16; iii, 16.

sate her, so seemeth to me the image of the imprint of the eternal pleasure, by longing for whom each thing becometh what it is": so Dante summarized the human situation in the *Paradiso* (xx, 73). Man had gone astray by loving wrongly, but he could achieve regeneration by learning to love rightly, and in the process of salvation the intellectual understanding of the good (though made possible by grace and a right will) preceded love for it. One could not love the good unless one first had knowledge of it (*Paradiso*, xiv, 40; xxviii, 109; xxix, 139). But once the individual had come to know what was worthy of love, he no longer required the guidance of any external authority and could safely follow his own desires. After he had passed through purgatory Dante was informed by Virgil that he was now free to do what he pleased and had become his own Pope and emperor. "Free, upright and whole is thy will, and 'twere a fault not to act according to its prompting. Wherefore I do now crown and mitre thee over thyself" (xxvii, 140). Throughout the *Divine Comedy* there is little emphasis on the doctrine of original sin and little recognition of diabolical temptation. The devil, in fact, is represented as motionless, wedged into the center of the earth like a worm in an apple, and freezing everything in his vicinity by the beating of his wings, while God is the ultimate source of all movement.

In the *Divine Comedy*, as in the *De Monarchia*, Dante accepted classicism as a source of truth almost on the same level as Christianity, and apparently saw no areas of conflict between them. The whole poem is, in fact, permeated with the classical heritage, which—for Dante—was still living. The ancient Roman deities had been so thoroughly allegorized that Dante could speak of them, and of various episodes in classical mythology, with no trace of condemnation or disbelief. The *Paradiso* actually begins with a prayer to Apollo for inspiration. An even more striking example occurs in the seventh book of the *Inferno*. The pagan goddess Fortune, favorite deity of the classical decadence, appears as an agent of God in distributing prosperity and catastrophe, God apparently retaining no direct control over such movements. In Canto XIII of the *Paradiso,* St. Thomas Aquinas offers an Aristotelian explanation for the imperfection of most human beings in terms of form and matter and the failure of matter to be fully molded by form, thus implicitly denying the Christian belief that everything had been created by God and that imperfection was the result of sin. The denial of salvation to virtuous pagans is a Christian dogma which Dante obviously found disturbing; and while he placed most of the pagan heroes and sages in the *Inferno* (though they did not suffer any positive torments), he did succeed in putting into heaven two pagan rulers (the Emperor Trajan and the legendary Trojan Ripheus) and in affirming that on judgment day many who had not known Christ would be closer to him than many professing Christians.

Confidence in an ultimate harmony of freedom and order, as expressed in the *Divine Comedy,* is the spiritual foundation of the whole Western tradition and an essential prerequisite of any movement of high creativity. It was this confidence that made the Renaissance possible, though with much more emphasis on freedom and a weaker insistence on order than had been displayed in the Middle Ages. But if one studies the detailed presentation of human beings in the *Comedy* rather than its formal intellectual framework, one becomes aware of certain discrepancies which led ultimately to the breakdown of the synthesis Dante had attempted to affirm, and which foreshadowed not only the growth of the Renaissance but also its final disintegration. According to Christian doctrine man became most fully himself in proportion as he learned to shun perverse or disproportioned love and to center his desires upon God. But in the *Divine Comedy* it is the souls in the *Inferno* who most vividly represent the potentialities of the human individual.

We should not, of course, suppose that Dante intended his description of the next world to be taken as literally true. He used Christian notions of the afterlife in order to present an interpretation of human nature in this world, the *Comedy* being a vision of man's failures and potentialities. Sin is its own punishment, and the souls in the *Inferno* are there not only because of the wrath of

God and his desire to manifest his justice, but—more significantly—because they have chosen sin and, even when aware of
their damnation, are incapable of feeling regretful or repentant.
In the murky air of hell with its gloomy landscapes and its long
and varied sequence of torments, there are many examples of
human malevolence and bestiality, but the strongest impression
that Dante conveys, perhaps in spite of his own conscious intentions, is that man can confront the certainty of eternal punishment and yet remain defiantly himself. The souls of the damned
are not broken by their fate, and in many instances do not lose
their nobility or cease to be lovable. Thus the heretic Farinata
raises himself from his fiery tomb "as if he entertained great scorn
of hell"; Jason retains his regal aspect and seems to shed no tear
for pain; and the thief Vanni Fucci shouts defiance of God. And
because the damned are without hope for the future, they are
almost all concerned with worldly glory, asking Dante to recall
them to the memory of living men. For some of them Dante
retains love and admiration, especially for his friend and teacher
Brunetto Latini, damned because of homosexuality, who appears
"like one of those who run for the green cloth at Verona through
the open field; and of them seemed he who gains, not he who
loses" (x, 36; xviii, 83; xv, 122–5).

The characters in the *Inferno* are all sharply individualized,
being described with that vividness and extraordinary concision
in which Dante excelled all other poets. And this quality is much
more fully displayed in the *Inferno* than in the two later sections
of the *Comedy*. For in his insistence on being himself in defiance
of all authority, and in his concern for worldly glory rather than
for salvation, the man of the *Inferno* is the man of the Renaissance.

In the *Purgatorio,* which presents man striving to achieve
right love, there is a decline in intensity, and the dramatic sense
of conflict which pervades the *Inferno* gives place to the dreamlike visionary quality of medieval painting. The characters retain
their individuality, and some of them still display the self-asser-
tiveness that had characterized them on earth. The poet Sordello,

for example, seems "haughty and disdainful" (vi, 62). But the main emphasis is on the struggle of these potentially blessed characters to rid themselves of self-will and submit to the divine order. They are no longer concerned with earthly glory, and memories of earthly life are much fainter than in the *Inferno.* The charm of the *Purgatorio* is pictorial rather than dramatic. As in the Thomist philosophy, the process of salvation is presented in two stages. At the top of the mountain of purgatory there is the earthly paradise, which men may enter after they have achieved terrestrial perfection, and this is presided over by a mysterious figure named Matilda (whom Dante seems to have invented), and is described as filled with sensuous beauties, somewhat like a Botticelli painting. But man also needs grace to achieve supernatural perfection, to be enjoyed in heaven, and this is spiritual rather than material, and can no longer be symbolized as a garden.

In heaven man is swallowed up in the celestial choir and wholly loses his individuality. The keynote of the *Paradiso*—and indeed of the whole poem—is expressed in the third canto in the words of Piccarda: "His will is our peace" (iii, 85). God is presented primarily in terms of light, a conception which was almost universal in medieval art and which was regarded as more than merely metaphorical, and the souls of the blessed are similarly seen as points of light kindled by the light of God. As literature the *Paradiso* is an extraordinary *tour de force,* since it succeeds in conveying the sense of space and light with little concrete imagery. But the souls of the blessed engage in too much theological explanation for the benefit of their terrestrial visitor, and the atmosphere is too rarefied for most readers to follow him easily.

As soon as Dante enters heaven, he mistakes the souls whom he encounters for mere reflected images, and beyond the second circle, in the sphere of Mercury where he encounters Justinian, he no longer makes any reference to the physical features of any of the souls. The higher he climbs, the more completely the souls lose all separate identity. In the sphere of Jupiter, for example, which is the sixth of the nine circles and is dedicated to justice, more than a thousand good kings are gathered together in the form of an eagle; and while each speaks separately in the first person, they are so closely united with each other that only one sound can be heard. "So do we feel one glow from many coals as from those many loves there issues forth one only sound out of that image" (xix, 19). Goodness means unity and harmony, whereas evil produces conflict. This sense of unity reaches its climax with God himself, who appears not as a person but—in accord with mystical experience—as simply oneness. "Oh grace abounding," declares Dante after his vision of divinity, "wherein I presumed to fix my look on the eternal light so long that I consumed my sight thereon! Within its depths I saw ingathered, bound by love in one volume, the scattered leaves of all the universe; substance and accidents and their relations as though together fused, after such fashion that what I tell of is one simple flame" (xxxiii, 82–9). Dante does not appear to be writing as one who had himself enjoyed the mystical union with God, but his portrayal of God as above and beyond personality and to be experienced primarily as a universal oneness is true for all authentic mysticism.

Medieval in his formal thinking, but a man of the Renaissance in much of his sensibility, Dante marks one of the great divides in the cultural development of Western man. He may be said, in fact, to have taken the best from both worlds. The *Divine Comedy* is, among other things, a triumph of architectonics, combining the sharpest sense of individuality with the maintenance of a general pattern of unity. After Dante, and in part because of him, there is a decisive change in the intellectual atmosphere of Italy, despite occasional throwbacks to medievalism and the retention of many of the impedimenta of medieval thought. But the sense of unity disappeared, and was not recaptured (though in a very different form) until the High Renaissance of Leonardo, Raphael, and Michelangelo. Giotto, Dante's contemporary, marked even more sharply a similar divide in the development of painting.

16 · Dante, Petrarch, and Giotto

In the work of Dante one is always aware of tension between the growing spirit of individualism and the traditional religious values. But with the next major figure in Italian literature, Petrarch (1304–74), who was born a generation later than Dante, medieval and Renaissance attitudes are presented side by side with a curious lack of any sense of conflict. Despite a professed adherence to the whole of Christian theology, a Renaissance emphasis on human individualism and a Renaissance desire for worldly glory seem to count more heavily than the ascetic values of medievalism. Petrarch was, in fact, the first person since the end of classical civilization to win fame by purely intellectual and aesthetic achievements. His strongest bent was toward personal exploration in a spirit not of moral self-condemnation but simply of intellectual curiosity, for which reason he may be regarded as the first modern man, although he found stimulation and encouragement in the *Confessions* of St. Augustine, which remained his favorite book. In spite of his orthodox beliefs, he was closer to Montaigne than to St. Bernard; and in some most important qualities he set the standards for the whole of the Renaissance.

Born at Arezzo in northern Italy, his parents being Florentine exiles, Petrarch spent much of his early life at the papal court at Avignon and fifteen miles away at his country cottage at Vaucluse, on the river Sorgne. Here he became widely famous as the author of the sonnets addressed to Laura. In later life Petrarch abandoned the Italian vernacular, pouring out a series of letters and essays in Ciceronian Latin and writing a Latin epic poem, entitled *Africa,* in imitation of Virgil. More lastingly important was his work in the discovery and diffusion of classical Latin writings, which made him the principal founder of the humanist movement. These activities made him the most widely known and sought-after man of his time. He traveled widely, sometimes on diplomatic missions, was welcomed by kings and city governments, and spent much of his later life in Milan and Venice.

Petrarch won his most enduring reputation for the aesthetic qualities displayed in his early love sonnets. Unlike Dante's Beatrice, Laura remained a real person and was not transmuted into a symbol of transcendental values. In actuality, it appears, she was a woman of Avignon who acquired a husband and twelve children, and who was known to Petrarch for twenty-one years before her death from the plague in 1348. But Petrarch's relations with her seem to have been purely poetic, and his love did not prevent him from keeping a mistress by whom he fathered two illegitimate children. The sonnets which he wrote in praise of Laura started a fashion which continued to flourish for hundreds of years, most memorably perhaps in Elizabethan England. Yet Petrarch himself wished afterward to repudiate them, describing them as "trivial verses, filled with the false and offensive praise of women." [3] After the age of forty he boasted that he had remained celibate, though this seems to have been due primarily to his conviction that one could not live the life of a sage if one were distracted by the pursuit of women rather than to any Christian revulsion against fleshly desire.

Some of Petrarch's later prose writings can best be described as essays—a literary genre which one cannot find in the Middle Ages; and in them, as also in his correspondence (written in Latin), one finds a strong autobiographical interest and a curious tolerance of inconsistent values. This is well exemplified in his *De Vita Solitaria*. "I believe," he declares, "that no noble spirit will ever find repose save in God, in whom is our end, or in himself and his private thoughts, or in some intellect united by a close sympathy with his own." Elsewhere he speaks of serving God, developing our minds, or leaving our remembrance to posterity as equally valid goals. Thus the values of Christianity and those of pagan philosophy are placed on the same plane as equally worthy of respect. Throughout his praise of solitude he refers both to Christian hermits (sixty of them) and to pagan philoso-

---

[3] Quoted in a selection of Petrarch's letters, *Petrarch, the First Modern Scholar and Man of Letters*, translated by James Harvey Robinson (New York, 1898), p. 79.

phers as examples of a wise asceticism, but the motivation is not salvation but personal happiness. "Let each man decide according to his own preference," he declares. There is no suggestion of human sinfulness, of duties owed to God, or of the danger of eternal damnation. Petrarch, moreover, sounds more medieval than he actually was because of the medieval quality of his vocabulary. Men had not yet developed a suitable language for the expression of the new spirit. It is with some sense of shock that one encounters occasional statements that sound fully medieval: denunciations of Christian kings for failing to crusade against the Turks, for example, and attacks on women recalling those of the more misogynistic medieval saints. It was characteristic of Petrarch that he should have climbed Mount Ventoux (close to his home at Vaucluse) simply to admire the view—medieval man had displayed no interest whatever in the aesthetic aspects of nature—but that when he reached the top he should have found his sentiments most closely expressed in a passage from St. Augustine depreciating all worldly things. Typical of his new concern with the self was his complaint of "varying moods, which were rarely happy and usually despondent." A medieval theologian would have pronounced him guilty of *accidia*.[4]

In cultural history, Petrarch figures as perhaps the principal founder of the movement for the revival of the classics, generally known as humanism. Classical literature had, of course, been studied during the Middle Ages, but it had been interpreted as subordinate to, and in harmony with, Christian theology. With humanism it was used to support an attitude of revolt against medieval views of God and man. In its early phases the growth of humanism was closely connected not only with the change of ethical and philosophical values, but also with the assertion of an Italian national consciousness. Italian scholars cultivated a sense of political and cultural continuity. Italy had once given peace

---

[4] Petrarch: *De Vita Solitaria,* translated by Jacob Zeitlin, 1-1-1, 91-10-3, 1-4-1.

and justice to the entire world (this myth of Roman universality was affirmed by Petrarch almost as vigorously as by Dante); the empire had been overthrown by the northern barbarians; now the time had come to restore both the empire of the Romans and their more enlightened culture and art forms. This view of history was strengthened by the hope of ending the incessant civil wars in Italy. For Petrarch, as for Dante, national unity meant the restoration of the empire. He hailed the coming of the Emperor Charles IV to Italy in 1354 almost as fervently as Dante had welcomed Henry VII, and with equal futility. But one episode in his life indicated the possibility of another solution: when in 1347 a young Roman, Cola de Rienzo, attempted to revive the Roman republic, Petrarch hailed him with enthusiasm as the restorer of ancient liberties. Unfortunately Rienzo was able to hold power for only a few months. Most of the humanists continued both to maintain the myth of the empire and to glorify one-man government, as represented by the despots upon whom they were largely dependent for their livelihood. Julius Caesar, the first emperor, remained a hero, and Cicero was blamed for trying to preserve the republic instead of devoting himself wholly to philosophy. Thus the revivification of the classical tradition was—for the time being—not carried back to the republican phases of the classical heritage.

Petrarch's enthusiasm for the revival of the classics led him to a reinterpretation of history which may be regarded as the invention of the concept of the Renaissance. Before Petrarch there had been no sense of discontinuity in history; for Dante, for example, the Roman Empire still existed, though it was now ruled by Germans rather than by Italians. For Petrarch, on the other hand, the end of the empire in its original form marked a sharp break in historical development and the beginning of a long period of barbarization. He distinguished between *historiae antiquae* and *historiae novae,* the latter being a time of "darkness" (*tenebrae*) in spite of the triumph of Christianity. Thus a long dark age had intervened between the ancient civilization and its revival in Petrarch's own time. Petrarch, however, thought of this

326

largely in political rather than cultural terms. The great days when Rome had ruled the world had ended with the triumph of Germanic barbarism, but Petrarch hoped for their re-establishment. His zeal for the revival of classical Latin, in place of the corrupt Latin of the Middle Ages, was closely associated with his Italian nationalism. Petrarch's conception of history was also significant in recognizing the reality of time and the location of man within it in much the same fashion as the painters were now placing man within a realistic three-dimensional space.

The other major Italian writer of the fourteenth century, Petrarch's young Florentine friend Giovanni Boccaccio (1313–75), provided a similar example of a Renaissance sensibility only partially emancipated from medieval beliefs, though his religious misgivings became important only in his later life. As a young man he was concerned almost exclusively with the world of the senses—at least in his writings—and was apparently totally devoid of moral scruples. Spending some years at Naples, which was already notable for its frivolous atmosphere, he fell in love with a young lady of the court, Fiammetta by name; and his earlier writings were dedicated to her, presenting a love that was frankly physical, without the idealizing effects that Dante had found in his love for Beatrice and—to a lesser degree—Petrarch in his love for Laura. This glorification of physical desire pervaded the *Decameron,* which Boccaccio completed in 1353 at the age of forty. The stories in his book, allegedly told to each other by seven young women and three young men who had taken refuge from the Black Death of 1348 in a villa outside Florence, are mostly concerned with extramarital sexual adventures and mishaps, described without a trace of moral condemnation. That friars and other clerics are frequently shown engaging in such adventures might be regarded as a sign of hostility to the Church, but is actually presented as though the inability of the clergy to respect their vows of celibacy was an accepted and understandable fact. Most of the stories were not new, but were collected from folk tales, French *fabliaux,* and other manifestations of the psychic underground of medieval society; but in

Boccaccio's retelling of them they enter the mainstream of Western literature.

The world of the *Decameron* is, of course, not realistic, but highly artificial: the young and ardent attain their ends, while the old and the hypocritical come to grief. But the desire celebrated by Boccaccio is precisely that which had been treated as the especial source of wickedness by the medieval Church. In order that the Renaissance glorification of human nature could be accepted, it was necessary to affirm the normality of physical desire. In the fourteenth century such audacity was hard to maintain, and Boccaccio came in later life to regret the *Decameron*. He even thought of entering a monastery, though Petrarch persuaded him to devote himself instead to classical studies. His later life was spent as a scholar and teacher, and he was the first Italian humanist to become familiar with Greek.

Meanwhile a revolution was occurring in the visual arts. This was a direct reflection of the change in sensibility and was not a deduction from new ideas and beliefs, so that the break with the past was much sharper and more immediate than in literature. The principal innovator was Giotto, Dante's friend and contemporary, who was universally accepted by later Italian painters and art historians as the founder of modern art. As the sculptor Ghiberti declared in his *Commentaries,* written a century after Giotto's death, he "introduced a new art. . . . Wonderful works were executed, especially in the City of Florence and in many other places. Many of his disciples were as gifted as the ancient Greeks. Giotto saw in art what others had not attained. He brought the natural art and refinement with it, not departing from the proportions." [5] The art historian Vasari, writing in the sixteenth century, said that with Giotto "art rose from humble beginnings to the summit of perfection." [6]

Giving expression to the belief that the material world was an

---

[5] Quoted in Elizabeth Holt: *A Documentary History of Art,* I, 153.
[6] Quoted in F. H. Gombrich: *Art and Illusion* (New York, 1951), p. 61.

ultimate reality, not merely a storehouse of symbols for transcendental truths, the new art can be regarded both as marking a new phase in the secularization of the Western sensibility and as a reassertion of attitudes that at a much earlier period had seemed characteristic of Italy.

Before Giotto, Italian art had remained Byzantine. Solemn Virgins and Pantocrators, portrayed against gold backgrounds suggesting the light in which divine power became manifest, invited the spectator to turn away from the world of the flesh and the devil. Superb examples of Byzantine art were to be seen in Sicilian churches, especially those of Palermo and of Monreale, and in the island church of Torcello among the lagoons that girdled the city of Venice, while mosaics from earlier periods were preserved at Ravenna and in some of the churches in Rome. But most of the Italian art before Giotto was of inferior quality, the work of artisans with little aesthetic sense. In architecture there was one outstanding building in the Byzantine style, the cathedral of St. Mark in Venice. But with the change of sensibility the whole art of Byzantium suddenly began to seem crude and meaningless.

Giotto was immediately preceded by a somewhat shadowy figure, Cimabue, who retained Byzantine techniques but tried to convey more human emotions. More important was the work of several sculptors of the Pisano family, especially of Nicolo and his son Giovanni, whose bas-reliefs conveyed a feeling of plasticity, rather than the purely linear sense characteristic of earlier sculpture, and displayed a new sense of movement and of emotional intensity. But Giotto was the main innovator, marking a revolutionary change of sensibility which has few, if any, parallels in art history. It is significant that his art was almost immediately accepted as in tune with the new temper of north Italian bourgeois society. Giotto had a long and successful career, never lacking patrons and remaining astonishingly productive.

Giotto's greatness was universally attributed to the fact that he copied nature and presented figures that gave the illusion of living reality. Boccaccio declared that there was "nothing that

Giotto could not have portrayed in such a manner as to deceive the sense of sight." [7] Later Florentine painters were to go much further in deceiving the eyes of spectators, and by their standards Giotto seems still half-medieval. The background of his pictures is often omitted altogether, or else it consists of buildings that are wholly unrealistic and lacking in any sense of perspective. Boccaccio's praise is an indication of how much the spectator brings to the appreciation of a work of art and reads into it. It is only by contrast with his Byzantine and medieval French predecessors that Giotto appears to be copying nature. But his main achievement was to convey a sense of physical reality in his figures, if not in their environment. Giotto's men and women appear to have mass and volume; they arouse the tactile imagination and seem capable of being touched and felt. And as soon as he had demonstrated the possibilities of realistic presentation, this suddenly appeared as the standard by which all art should be judged, and the fact that earlier painters had pursued other objectives was forgotten.

Giotto's subject matter remained religious, but his primary concern was with human beings, even though they might be saints or apostles. His men and women are reassuringly corporeal, with none of the transcendental aloofness of the Byzantines. The solid fleshiness of his figures is one of the more obvious hallmarks of Giotto's style. These are genuine human beings, not queenly Virgins and omnipotent and awe-inspiring Pantocrators. And the center of interest in a Giotto picture, the main subject around which the lines are organized, is almost always a human experience. The figures are shown in conversation, or acting upon each other, not in silent and motionless confrontation of the spectator. Man and not God is the central theme; and even if the man is Francis of Assisi or some other saint, he is still capable of the normal human emotions of love, fear, wonder, and dismay. In Giotto's art, André Malraux has declared, "man has regained

---

[7] Quoted in Gombrich: op. cit., p. 61.

the old self-mastery of the Roman but without his pride. Giotto was perhaps the first Western artist whose faith gave every Christian his due of majesty." This conception of "the honor of being a man" was to "traverse all later Italian art like the muffled persistent sound of a subterranean river." [8] A study of Giotto reinforces the more humanistic elements in Dante, especially if one remembers that Dante knew and admired him, and that Dante's conception of art, as explained in the *Purgatorio,* was wholly representational.

The naturalness of Giotto's figures was his most obvious innovation, but his work had deeper implications. Implicit in it was a radically new conception of the whole meaning and purpose of art. As art was thereafter regarded as a copy of nature, no longer as a symbolization of spiritual truths, a picture ceased to be considered as an object in its own right and was regarded as a kind of window presenting a view of part of the material world. With this two-dimensional medium artists tried to convey a three-dimensional space. The attempt to convey the illusion of three dimensions owed something to the revived study of classical sculpture and bas-reliefs. Both Byzantine and late medieval art, moreover, in spite of their lack of interest in the material world, had usually presented a kind of stage space, so that their pictures portrayed a little depth, though of a very limited kind. But the new painting rendered space as infinite and continuous, and this was not derived from either Byzantine or French traditions. The new sense of space paralleled the development of philosophical thought in the later Middle Ages, though its expression in art preceded full philosophical formulation. It was an aspect of the new consciousness of Western man and was finding expression also in late medieval philosophy. Painters of later generations carried the new sense of space much further than Giotto had, and by exploring its implications they eventually moved beyond the

---

[8] André Malraux: *Les Voix du Silence,* translated by Stuart Gilbert (New York, 1953), p. 266.

assumption that the purpose of all art was to copy nature, the material world being regarded as the basic reality.

While Florence was evolving a new form of art, a kind of Byzantine afterglow was illuminating the rival city of Siena, which never fully emerged from the Middle Ages. The Sienese displayed some of the new sense of the infinity of space, though they presented it as an ambient medium rather than through the mass and volume of their figures. These were mostly copied not from life, but from the Byzantines, although they also showed some French Gothic influence. There is no easy explanation for the differences between the art of the two cities, but in some degree they persisted through the whole Renaissance. Florentine art remained more massive, geometrical, and intellectual, concentrating on design and on the portrayal of human figures, while the art of Siena was more linear, mercurial, lyrical, and mystical and tended to emphasize color.

Duccio (1278–1319), a little older than Giotto, was the main founder of the Sienese school. A brilliant colorist, he created a kind of fairy-tale world in which Christian figures were presented for their pictorial charm rather than with any sense of religious awe or any intensity of emotional experience. Duccio was a delightful storyteller, sometimes described as the last great painter of the Middle Ages, and he had every artistic virtue except the sense of life. His virtues were transmitted to his most gifted pupil, Simone Martini (1285–1344), who spent his later life at the papal court at Avignon. For sheer beauty of line and color Martini was unsurpassable, but his work offered an escape from reality rather than an enhancement of it. His famous *Annunciation,* with its delicately shrinking and reluctant Virgin, portrayed against a gold background, with thin cheeks, an elongated nose, and parchment complexion, like a youthful princess in an Oriental fairy tale rather than the Mother of Christian belief, conveyed the flavor of a rich but decadent sophistication, with no relationship to the more vigorous and progressive forces in the Italian society of the time. Martini's affiliations were with late medievalism rather than with the pullulating life of the

Italian cities; and he was an important influence in the growth of International Gothic.

Siena continued to be an important art center through the fourteenth century, and some of its painters pioneered in new directions. For example, the Lorenzetti brothers, Pietro and Ambrogio, attempted to produce illusionist landscapes and town panoramas, though they lacked the knowledge of perspective needed for convincing representation. Both in Siena and in Florence, however, the middle decades of the century saw a temporary reaction back to a fully medieval sensibility and medieval artistic styles. The 1340's were a time of serious economic difficulties in both cities, with repeated bad harvests and numerous mercantile bankruptcies. In 1348, moreover, came the first attack of the Black Death, followed by milder repetitions in 1363 and 1374. These reminders of the uncertainties of human life evoked an acute sense of human sinfulness and a revival of the more ascetic types of religion. It was also significant that in both cities this was a period of democratic ascendancy, and the masses were less disposed than the rich merchants to appreciate a realistic and humanistic art. An episode in Sienese history illustrates the change in popular sentiment. An old Roman statue, apparently portraying a naked Venus, had been found in 1335 and had been considered appropriate for public display. In 1357, on the other hand, economic distress and defeat in a war with the Florentines caused the Sienese to conclude that their tolerance of pagan sensuality must have been offensive to God. The statue was consequently broken into small pieces, and these were secretly buried in Florentine territory.

The artistic results were to be seen at Florence in pictures like the Strozzi Chapel altarpiece (c. 1354) of Andrea Orcagna and the Virgin of Nardo. Departing from the warm humanity of Giotto, painters once again presented Christ and his mother as figures of transcendent majesty. Christ was more frequently shown as the stern judge of mankind and less often as its suffering savior. There was less movement and less individuality than in the work of Giotto, more use of brilliant red, blue, and gold backgrounds, and more emphasis on the reverence due the Church and its priests. Similar trends were seen in Siena, but perhaps the most characteristic work of this period was the terrifying *Triumph of Death* in the Campo Santo at Pisa, which was probably the work of Francesco Traini.

17

The Quattrocento

In its narrower and more literal meaning the Renaissance was the rebirth of classical culture, and this aspect of the movement was in the ascendant during the last half of the fourteenth century and the first half of the fifteenth, being especially represented by the scholars who called themselves humanists. There had been earlier so-called Renaissances, at least according to modern historical nomenclature, such as that fostered by Charlemagne and that of the cathedral schools, more especially of Chartres, in the twelfth century. But these had consisted mainly of revivals of the study of Latin literature, with no attempt to return in spirit to the ancient civilization. Culture had remained basically Christian and northern despite the borrowing of certain elements from the classics. As Erwin Panofsky has remarked, the culture of antiquity had to be decomposed before any aspects of it could be assimilated into the new northern cultures. The Italian Renaissance, on the other hand, attempted a real revival of the past, seeking to assimilate classical attitudes in their totality.[1]

The original impetus for the Renaissance had been largely political, at least according to Petrarch's interpretation of it. Italian intellectuals hoped to restore the Roman tradition because they wished to put an end to domestic strife and foreign interven-

---

[1] Erwin Panofsky: *Renaissance and Renascences in Western Art,* p. 100.

tion. But there were more significant social and moral reasons for the continuance of the humanist movement.

The northern Italian cities had developed a new kind of society which needed new values and views of life. Medieval society had glorified the warrior nobleman and the monk; but the dominant groups in the Italy of the Renaissance had no particular respect for chivalric prowess; and though they continued to profess belief in Christianity, they were by no means inclined to repudiate the world and the flesh. This was true of the wealthy mercantile and banking families, and more especially of the despots and their courtiers and officials. New standards of morals and manners had to be formulated, both to provide the new ruling classes with appropriate codes of behavior and interpretations of human experience and to justify and legitimize their privileged position in society. To a large extent these new standards could be derived from the classical past, particularly from the writers of the later Roman republic and the early empire. In the philosophical writings of Cicero, Seneca, and others, the humanists could find a high ethical idealism which—unlike the Christianity of the Middle Ages—did not advocate withdrawal from the world and which stressed the development of all aspects of the human personality rather than exclusive concentration on spiritual or intellectual achievement.

The humanists were primarily educators. This, in fact, was the original meaning of the word. It was derived from the Latin *humanitas,* and according to the second-century writer Aulus Gellius, this word had "about the force of the Greek *paideia,* that is, what we call education and training in the liberal arts." [2] The most lasting and important achievement of the humanist movement was to transform education by making classical studies its main subject and by aiming at the production of well-rounded human beings accustomed to life in leisured upper-class society and to physical activity as well as to mental and moral discipline.

------

[2] Quoted in Wallace K. Ferguson: *Europe in Transition, 1300–1520,* p. 291.

The Italian universities mostly remained strongholds of medieval methods of education until a later period, but the humanists founded schools which were often supported by, and closely associated with, the courts of northern Italian despots. Especially notable among the schoolmasters of the Renaissance were Guarino da Verona at Ferrara and Vittorino da Feltre at Mantua. The new educational ideals inculcated norms of behavior that were much broader and nobler than those of medieval chivalry; but they remained definitely aristocratic in their purpose and appeal. The Renaissance was not a popular movement, and one of the aims of the classical education was to give the upper classes a training in subjects that were not available for the masses and that could be presented as sources of esoteric wisdom.

Meanwhile, humanist scholars were also engaged in recapturing as much as possible of the Roman past. They searched monastery libraries in Italy and elsewhere for forgotten manuscripts, developed critical methods of establishing accurate texts, made collections of classical sculptures and other remains, and themselves wrote essays and learned studies in Ciceronian Latin. While the main emphasis was on Roman antiquities, the study of Greek, which had been generally unknown during the Middle Ages, began in 1397 when a Byzantine scholar, Manuel Chrysoloras, was invited to teach at the University of Florence. Also important in spreading Greek studies was a joint council of Greek and Roman clerics held in Italy in 1438 to discuss religious reunion and joint action against the threat of Turkish expansion. The council failed in its primary objective, but it led to new contacts between Italian and Byzantine scholars. In the later fifteenth century, Platonic studies had an important influence on Italian culture, replacing the Aristotelian emphasis of later medieval philosophy.

This growth of classical scholarship led to critical analyses of the authenticity of various documents important in Christian history, thus promoting a general spirit of religious rationalism. Lorenzo Valla, for example, engaged in textual criticism of the New Testament, and proved that various Christian writings—

those attributed to Dionysius the Areopagite, for example—
dated from much later periods than had formerly been assumed.

Officially the humanists and their disciples remained Christian, though the religion which they professed was actually closer to paganism in its rationalistic emphasis and its ethical tendencies. But as long as they made no open attack on the traditional beliefs, they were in no danger of being disciplined or silenced by the Church. The papacy of the fifteenth century was largely absorbed in conflicts between the Italian states, and its attitude toward doctrinal controversies was more tolerant than at any other period. The humanists were therefore able to introduce a rationalist spirit into religious doctrines, to preach an ethic which attached more importance to glory in this world than to salvation in the next, and to defend the enjoyment of sensuous pleasures. Perhaps the most important of all the new attitudes was the shift of emphasis from the life of contemplation to one of intense social activity. Renaissance men could see little to be valued in monastic seclusion and advocated an active life both for glory and for the achievement of moral and social ideals. The performance of civic duty was now exalted above contemplation; and although this revaluation of morality was in imitation of the classics, it was represented as being in accord with true Christian doctrine. This ethical revolution owed much to Petrarch, though in other moods he could exalt the contemplative life as fervently as any of the hermits of the *Thebaid,* but without the same concentration on the winning of eternal salvation. The new morality seems to have been first fully affirmed in the writings of Coluccio Salutati (1331–1406), a humanist scholar who served for many years as Chancellor of Florence. Still thinking largely in Christian terms, Salutati turned from Thomism to Augustinianism and exalted the will above the intellect and active love above contemplation, but continued to affirm that love was the gift of divine grace. Another humanist who was also a public official, Leonardo Bruni, carried further this new ethical emphasis; and, deriving his view of man mainly from Aristotle rather than from the theologians, he declared that devotion to

338

civic duty was in accord with the nature of man, no divine grace being needed to produce it.

As most of the humanists were free-lance intellectuals who had to live by their wits, they attached themselves to despots and to rich men who were eager to win prestige by patronizing the new learning. Under such conditions it was difficult for them to maintain high standards of political and personal morality; and the man of letters who sold his intellectual skills to the highest bidder became a not unfamiliar figure in Renaissance Italy. The intellectuals' lack of financial independence was an unfortunate aspect of the Renaissance because it made it difficult for them to recognize the values of political liberty. The Rome which they sought to re-establish was the Rome of the early empire, not of the republic.

There was, however, one Italian city-state—Florence—where humanism became associated with political liberty and republican government. This occurred near the end of the fourteenth century and had most important effects on the whole later development of the Renaissance.

The reasons for the cultural pre-eminence of this city throughout most of the Renaissance, from the time of Dante and Giotto to that of the young Michelangelo, are not easy to discover, but undoubtedly an important factor was the persistence of a faith in individual liberty which gave self-confidence and a spirit of independence to its citizens. In Florence the republican and communal attitudes that had developed in many of the northern Italian cities during the early Middle Ages still retained some vitality. Despite a stormy political history and prolonged conflicts—bloody but politically invigorating—between oligarchy and democracy, the Florentines remained reluctant to submit to despotic government. In actuality, the city was not governed democratically; and the glorification of republican virtue may be regarded as more a myth than a reality. After 1382, political power belonged to the oligarchy, and the poorer citizens were disfranchised; nor was there much liberalism in Florence's rule over a number of subject cities in Tuscany. But a myth that is generally accepted has creative power. In spite of the rule of the upper classes, there appears to have been a widely diffused sense of civic loyalty and civic pride and a conviction that Florence was superior to other cities in the personal freedom and the opportunities enjoyed even by the poorest of its citizens.

At about the end of the fourteenth century the Florentines found themselves threatened by Milanese imperialism. The despot of Milan, Giangaleazzo Visconti, had made himself master of most of northern Italy and apparently aspired to unify the whole country, so that the Florentines became involved in a desperate struggle for independence. The immediate threat ended with the death of Giangeleazzo in 1402, though it was renewed by other despots several times during the next half-century. In this crisis the Florentines saw themselves as championing freedom against tyranny. This civic idealism was fully shared by the leading humanist scholars of Florence. The situation led to a far-reaching revision of the whole classical heritage, which in Florence was henceforth identified with republicanism rather than with Caesarism.

The ancient world, it was now affirmed by the Florentines, had been capable of great achievements only as long as it was free. Despite the reluctance of the Florentines to disagree with Dante, Brutus, who had tried to save the Roman republic, was now regarded as a hero, while Caesar was portrayed as the main author of the Roman decadence. In order to give Florence a proper role in this rewriting of ancient history, the legend that it had been founded by Caesar was repudiated. It was now supposed to owe its origin partly to the Etruscans, who were represented as the enemies of Roman imperialism, and partly to a group of Roman settlers in the age of the Republic. These views won general acceptance among Florentine scholars and political leaders, and were given classic expression in some of Bruni's orations, which were consciously modeled after Pericles's Funeral Speech, and in his *History of the Florentine People*. Florentine humanists thereafter argued that the ideal scholar, instead of devoting himself solely to intellectual pursuits, should live as an active member of society, marrying, raising a family, and taking an active part in political affairs.

Florentine intellectuals continued to profess faith in man's right to liberty, despite their inability to make their faith practically effective. In the 1430's the city came under the rule of the Medici, who for most practical purposes could be regarded as despots, though they controlled the city by influence and indirection rather than by any open exercise of power. Their policies, moreover, tended to favor the mass of the population rather than the wealthy classes; and they showed too much moderation and good sense to provoke much open opposition. The combined rules of Cosimo and his grandson and successor, Lorenzo, covered half a century (1434–92). Subsequent attempts to re-establish republican government proved to be ineffective, and the Medici were finally restored, this time with the official titles of despotism as well as the realities. In a speech composed in 1428 Bruni declared: "Equal liberty exists for all . . . the hope of winning public honors and ascending is the same for all, provided they possess industry and natural gifts and lead a serious-minded and respected way of life; for our commonwealth requires *virtus* and *probitas* in its citizens. Whoever has these qualifications is thought to be of sufficiently noble birth to participate in the government of the republic . . . This, then, is true liberty, this equality in a commonwealth; not to have to fear violence or wrong-doing from anybody, and to enjoy equality among citizens before the law and in the participation in public offices. But now it is marvelous to see how powerful this access to public offices, once it is offered to a free people, proves to be in awakening the talents of the citizens . . . Since such hope and opportunity are held out in our commonwealth, we need not be surprised that talent and industry distinguish themselves in the highest degree." [3] The last attempt to maintain the republic collapsed in 1530. Yet Florentine art and intellectual life were permeated

---

[3] Quoted in Hans Baron: *The Crisis of the Early Italian Renaissance,* I, 21.

with a deep faith in man which owed much of its vitality to the belief in the ideals of republicanism, despite the recognition that these were no longer viable. This was true of Michelangelo and —despite his authorship of the famous *vade mecum* for would-be despots, *The Prince*—of Machiavelli.

With the assimilation by Florence of the city-state phase of classical civilization, the revivification of the ancient heritage was substantially complete. Ever since the early Middle Ages the Western mind had been working backward in the process of translating the heritage from empty dogma to relived experience, and this had been particularly the function of the Italians. Thus the movement of Italian thought and culture closely paralleled that of the classical civilization but moved in a reverse direction. Otto III, the tenth-century emperor who had dreamed of reviving the Roman *imperium* in close alliance with the Pope, may be regarded as corresponding to Constantine, Francis of Assisi to Jesus Christ, the Emperor Frederick II to Augustus, and Dante to Virgil. This was followed by the efflorescence of a city-state and predominantly bourgeois and secular society resembling that of the classical world before it had been unified by Rome. Its culmination, in a kind of revived Periclean age, came in the late fifteenth and early sixteenth centuries, Michelangelo marking the peak of its artistic creativity as Phidias had marked that of fifth-century Greece. These correspondences were not merely coincidental. The Italian mind was actually assimilating the classical heritage, working back from its religious to its more secular phases; and at each period it became capable of absorbing only the corresponding aspects of the classical development.

In other cities, contemplation continued to be praised because civic duty was ruled out by political despotism. Later Renaissance thinking on these subjects continued to accept, at least nominally, a Catholic framework, though the glorification of nature and of an active life produced results that were far from orthodox. A real devotion to the pleasures of the senses and to the quest for worldly glory was only partially disguised by affirmations of orthodoxy. Thus Lorenzo Valla in his *De Voluptate* wrote a dialogue in which orthodoxy was nominally reaffirmed, though the strongest effect was the glorification of the senses. Similarly, Cardinal Sadoleto wrote a dialogue, *De Philosophia*, assuming as his own role the defense of religious contemplation, but putting into the mouth of his friend Inghirami (a cleric and papal official, preacher, Vatican librarian, and secretary to the college of cardinals) an exaltation of worldly glory, wisdom being defined as "a kind of civil and popular philosophy inciting men to actions splendid and glorious in the sight of the multitude and making them great, powerful, noble and, in short, the first of all men." [4] This hope for glory in this world was the real doctrine of the Renaissance. Similarly, Pietro Pomponazzi denied the immortality of the soul on philosophical grounds, being an Aristotelian rather than a Platonist, but saved his orthodoxy by insisting that he still believed in it as an article of faith, however impossible it might be rationally. One can find in almost all Renaissance thinkers a tendency to appeal to nature as normative and to deduce from it a justification of pleasure as intrinsically good. Yet there was no direct denial of Christianity, and not merely from prudential motives. All the philosophy of the Renaissance represented an attempt to keep worldly and otherworldly values in a harmony which was necessarily uneasy and unexamined. This was true also at a later period of the Christian Humanism of northern countries, as exemplified in Erasmus and in such English poets as Edmund Spenser. Both Christianity and the glorification of nature had such force that it was believed that both could be affirmed despite gross inconsistencies.

Meanwhile the arts continued to develop, though somewhat handicapped by the continuing emphasis in Renaissance thinking on the perfection of the ancients and the barbarity of medievalism.[5] The surviving classical buildings and sculptures, which had

---

[4] Quoted in Eugene F. Rice: *The Renaissance Idea of Wisdom*, p. 74.

[5] The Renaissance view of the Middle Ages as a period of darkness was generally accepted until the eighteenth century. The subsequent idealization of medieval culture originated in the Romantic movement, and was due, in part,

attracted little aesthetic attention for a thousand years, began to find appreciation during the fourteenth century. In a letter written about the year 1380, for example, a disciple of Petrarch named Giovanni Dondi describes his ecstatic excitement at viewing the ancient art still surviving in Rome and insists on its vast superiority over all modern works of art. It was probably fortunate that not enough of ancient art survived to make exact imitation possible. Little was known of classical painting; and from what survived of sculpture and architecture the moderns acquired chiefly a knowledge of new techniques which could be applied to the expression of a different view of life. The extent to which Renaissance artists actually copied the classics was frequently exaggerated by critics of the period. Despite some borrowing from the classics the main purposes of art continued to be the copying of nature, the glorification of man, and the placing of both nature and man in the infinite three-dimensional space which was now demanded by the new sensibility of Western civilization.

---

to the reaction against the somewhat effete and formalistic classicism that had followed the Renaissance and in part to the Romantic quest for anything exotic or sensational. The so-called Gothic architecture (a word that was originally applied to the cathedrals to indicate that they were barbaric) was regarded in the eighteenth century as supremely ugly. By a total transformation of aesthetic values it was seen in the nineteenth century as supremely beautiful. The recapture of the values of medieval art led to a general appreciation of all aspects of medieval culture, which considerably exaggerated their importance. Admirers of the Middle Ages regarded them as asserting a belief in order and unity and hence as offering an escape from the chaotic multiplicity which they felt to be the main characteristic of modern society. The most influential spokesmen of this medievalism, at least in the English-speaking world, have been Henry Adams and T. S. Eliot. These men made the fatal mistake of judging medieval society by what it said about itself. It certainly believed in order and unity, but this was a reaction against the chaotic state of actual society and had no basis in actual ways of living. The more chaotic medieval society became, the more it resorted to escapist unrealities in its theoretic ideals. The favorite medieval occupation was sacking a city. And where were medieval ideals when the crusaders were massacring the entire population of Jerusalem? Any close analysis of any part of medieval society always reveals that the general anarchy was even worse than we had supposed.

344

These motivations led early in the fifteenth century to new developments in the visual arts which carried them far beyond the affirmations originally made by Giotto. Giotto and his disciples had endowed human figures with a sense of corporeal reality, but they had not known how to make the backgrounds visually plausible or to convey a feeling of distance, and their works had therefore failed to present a fully three-dimensional space. These problems were solved early in the fifteenth century by the invention of mathematical rules of perspective. This was apparently the work of Filippo Brunelleschi, known chiefly as an architect. Perspective was first applied convincingly in painting by Tommaso Guidi, called Masaccio, and its rules were worked out in more detail by Leone Battista Alberti, a man of very varied talents known chiefly as an architect, and by the painter Piero della Francesca. Antonio Manetti, in his biography of Brunelleschi, written late in the fifteenth century, defined perspective as "part of that science which aims at setting down well and rationally the differences of size that one sees in far and near objects, such as buildings, plains, mountains, and landscapes of all kinds and which assigns to figures and other things the right size that corresponds to the distance at which they are shown." [6] This invention had intoxicating effects on many of the painters who applied it, causing them to regard painting as primarily a science concerned with the revelation of the ultimate realities of the material world, the artist as a kind of higher mathematician whose work was based on geometry. The confusion of roles was strengthened by the fact that most Renaissance artists were, in fact, expected to know how to construct buildings, erect bridges, and engage in military engineering. The knowledge of nature displayed by the men who painted it was identified with the power to manipulate it for practical ends.

Florence continued to be the main creator and carrier of the Renaissance, and three men of genius dominated its art during

---

[6] Quoted in Elizabeth Holt: *A Documentary History of Art,* I, 170.

the early fifteenth century: the architect Brunelleschi, the sculptor Donatello, and the painter Masaccio. These three great innovators marked out the lines that art was to follow until the end of the Renaissance. Along with two other sculptors, Lorenzo Ghiberti, the maker of the famous bronze reliefs on the doors of the Baptistery, and Luca della Robbia, chiefly remembered for his work in terra-cotta, they were fully appreciated by their contemporaries, who recognized that they were witnessing major new achievements in the visual arts. As Alberti declared of these five creators, they had "talent for every noble thing not to be ranked below any who was ancient and famous in these arts." [7]

In his own day Brunelleschi was the most widely influential of the group, perhaps because he had an amiability not often displayed by great creators, then or now. Vasari declared that "he lived as a good Christian and left to the world the savor of his goodness . . . From the time of the ancient Greeks and Romans until now there has been no man more rare or more excellent." Beginning as a goldsmith and sculptor, he was defeated by Ghiberti in a competition for the making of the Baptistery doors, and subsequently turned to architecture after a prolonged visit to Rome during which he made a careful study of ancient building methods, particularly those employed in the Pantheon. He was generally regarded as having restored architecture to its correct classical lines, as practiced by the Romans and lost, even in Italy, during the centuries of Gothic aberration. Brunelleschi, however, took from the ancients only what he needed, primarily building methods rather than basic designs, and used them to convey a new sensitivity which was as sharply different from medieval architectural traditions as that which Giotto had expressed in painting. Horizontal rather than vertical lines, domes and cupolas instead of towers and spires, flat ceilings or rounded arches and barrel vaults rather than pointed arches and ogives, rows of round pillars with classical flowered capitals rather than Gothic

---

[7] Quoted in Holt: op. cit., I, 206.

columns—above all a masterly sense of unity and harmony, all the details being organized into simple easily comprehended designs based on carefully measured mathematical proportions— these appealed to the sensibility of Renaissance Italy, rather than the sense of mystery, of celestial powers beyond human comprehension, and of upward aspiration that had been conveyed by the vast complexity of the great cathedrals. A cathedral had been the work of generations, each of which had added something of its own without regard for any central plan. It had grown with a kind of organic life of its own, the efforts of craftsmen being guided by a common acceptance of stylistic requirements rather than by comprehensive blueprints worked out by any conscious intelligence. But a Renaissance building (with a few notable exceptions, such as St. Peter's in Rome and the cathedral of Florence) was clearly the work of a single mind shaping materials in accord with arithmetical harmonies.

Perhaps the most significant aspect of Renaissance architecture was its preference for church buildings that were circular or formed like a Greek cross with all the four arms of equal length. The long nave of the Gothic churches had been designed to draw the worshipper toward the high altar, conveying a sense of his subordination to divine powers. But a Renaissance church was planned to be viewed from a single central focal point. Standing in the center, the spectator was able to enjoy the beauty around him; man, and not God, had become the measure of all things. The first design for a round church was drafted by Brunelleschi for Santa Maria degli Angeli in Florence in the year 1434, but this building was never completed. Thenceforth most Renaissance architects preferred this kind of design in spite of its obvious unsuitability to the needs of Christian worship. There are beautiful examples in Leonardo's notebooks. Even the new basilica of St. Peter's in Rome, as planned by Bramante in 1506, was based on the Greek cross, abandoning the long nave which had been the traditional form for a thousand years. This deep-rooted Renaissance preference is one of the most striking examples in architectural history of the determining influence of an epoch's sensibility and view of life, functional requirements being considered of secondary importance or actually sacrificed.

Once the break with the Gothic tradition and the emergence of a new style had become manifest, Italy's long distaste for northern art forms was expressed with a new vigor and confidence. Brunelleschi's contemporary Filarete, author of a treatise on architecture, regarded the superiority of round over pointed arches as scarcely in need of justification: "The reason round arches are more beautiful than pointed ones is plain; everything that impedes the vision either more or less is not as beautiful as the line that the vision follows, and thus the eye has nothing to hinder it. And this is the round arch, as you see. . . . Cursed be the man who invented this wretched Gothic architecture. Only a barbarous people could have brought it to Italy." [8] This view of Gothic remained standard throughout the Renaissance. Vasari, for example, writing in the sixteenth century, spoke of "those grotesque and ugly features" which were to be found in medieval art, and spoke of Gothic as "this curse of building . . . which has polluted the world." "May God preserve all lands," he declared, "from the intrusion of such thoughts and such a style of craftsmanship."

The new style was to dominate architecture throughout the Renaissance and beyond, but Brunelleschi's personal note was a grace and airiness and delicacy not easily reproduced by his later imitators. His most famous creation, the vast dome of the cathedral of Florence, is not typical of his style. Soaring 113 feet above its supporting walls, it was an engineering *tour de force,* built from 1420 to 1434 (the shell of the building, designed by Arnolfo de Cambio, had been set up more than a century earlier), a massive object that lacks the grace of Brunelleschi's less pretentious works. Perhaps the most characteristic of his buildings is the Pazzi Chapel. Airy columned arcades surround an elegant rectangular chamber surmounted by a small cupola.

---

[8] Quoted in Holt: op. cit., I, 87, 249.

Within the chapel, neither projection nor play of shadows break the geometrical regularity of the spacing of the formal moldings around the white walls. The rectangular portal with its fluted columns and flowered capitals and lunette reliefs formed the style of innumerable Renaissance doors. Man was definitely in control of matter, and was shaping it into a unity supposedly copied from the unity of natural beings but actually created by man himself.

Meanwhile Brunelleschi's friend Donato, universally known by the affectionate diminutive Donatello, was displaying in sculpture an assured mastery which won him fame and highly paid commissions all over northern Italy during a period of nearly sixty years. In keeping with the new sense of the independence of man, sculpture was now emancipated from its medieval subordination to architecture; and although Donatello carved a number of reliefs for church altars and façades, many of them portraying crowd scenes conveying an extraordinary sense of movement, his most characteristic works were fully rounded and movable statues of individuals. The hallmark of his work was a frank delight in human strength and beauty and in all varieties of character that mankind was capable of producing. A number of his subjects were religious; and he could produce a tender crucifixion and an ascetic, sin-conscious Magdalen and John the Baptist, but there was little suggestion that these were intended to inspire special devotion. They were realistic studies of human psychology, on the same level as Donatello's secular portraits. Perhaps his most typical works were the nude and boyish David triumphing over the head of Goliath, the figure of St. George with its calm and self-confident virility, and the portrait of the Venetian general Gattamelata ("Honey Cat") with its superb rendering of physical strength and pride and practical intelligence, the first equestrian statue since Roman times. No art could have been more humanistic. There was little of the weight of thought and the melancholy which Michelangelo later was to put into the human face and figure. Donatello saw life in terms of its infinite possibilities for human achievement, not as tragic.

By contrast with the other leaders of this generation of gen-

349

ius, Masaccio has remained an obscure figure of whom almost nothing is known except that he died, while still a young man, during a visit to Rome. Yet he was the first painter to take a decisive step forward in the movement toward realistic representation that had been initiated by Giotto. Masaccio made an effective use of the principles of perspective. Giotto had portrayed human figures convincingly, but he had scarcely advanced beyond a stage space, the backgrounds of his pictures mostly remaining obscure or unrealistic. But with Masaccio art became suddenly fully three-dimensional. His characters are located in the visual world, the hills and buildings in the background of his pictures being delineated with as full a realism as the characters themselves. His men and women, moreover, convey a sense of tactile reality and of an extraordinary energy and corporeal vitality which—for the modern spectator—make a much sharper break with the whole Byzantine and Gothic inheritance than Giotto had achieved. This was a full expression of the new Renaissance view of man; and later artists could elaborate and diversify it, but they could not go further in the movement toward naturalism. Every important later Florentine artist studied the methods of Masaccio, who may be described as a painter's painter, in the recognition that (as Leonardo declared) he "showed by perfect works that those who are led by any guide except Nature, the supreme mistress, are consumed in sterile toil." [9] Yet his total production was meager and has been badly preserved. The work which exercised such a potent influence over three generations of artists consists primarily of a few frescoes illustrating the life of St. Peter in the Brancacci Chapel in the church of Santa Maria del Carmine in Florence.

With these new developments in the arts, the whole conception of a Renaissance was broadened and clarified, and a view of cultural history took shape which owed much to Petrarch, but

---

[9] Quoted in Rachel Annand Taylor: *Leonardo the Florentine* (New York, 1928), p. 60.

was first fully expressed by the sculptor Ghiberti in his *Commentaries,* written early in the fifteenth century. According to Ghiberti the art of the ancient world had been inspired by pagan beliefs and had consequently been destroyed by the Christian Church. "Idolatry was persecuted in such a way that all the statues and pictures of such nobility, antiquity, and perfection were destroyed and broken to pieces. And with the statues and pictures, the theoretical writings, the commentaries, the drawing, and the rules of teaching such eminent and noble arts were destroyed. In order to abolish every ancient custom of idolatry it was decreed that all the temples should be white. At this time the most severe penalty was ordered for anyone who made any statue or picture." The decline of culture had then been hastened by the barbarian invasions, and art had been wholly dead for six hundred years. Then the Greeks (i.e., the Byzantines) had tried to restore the art of painting, but "feebly . . . and with great crudity . . . for the people of that age were as rough and crude as the ancients were skilful." [1] Finally Giotto had appeared, followed by other great men, and art had entered upon a new epoch, largely based on a return to the sound principles of the classics. This interpretation of art history remained standard throughout the Renaissance and, indeed, until the revival of appreciation for medieval art and architecture during the Romantic movement of the late eighteenth and early nineteenth centuries. It illustrates the total inability of the new Renaissance man to comprehend and sympathize with the objectives of the Christian art either of Byzantium or of the medieval West.

In writing about the arts the new movement was represented as a return not only to nature, but also to the classics, the former being most prominent in painting and the latter in architecture, while sculpture represented both tendencies. It was not easy to reconcile these two conceptions, but gradually a new interpretation developed which was expressed especially by Leone Battista

---

[1] Quoted in Holt: op. cit., I, 153.

Alberti. The essence of classical art, it was suggested, was its use of the correct aesthetic proportions, and these proportions were supposed to be exemplified in the human body and therefore to be regarded as natural. Thus in all three of the visual arts adherence to the right proportions was in accord both with nature and the classics. But this concept of what was natural was far removed from the direct copying of natural appearances and the realistic representationalism which had been the avowed aims of Giotto and Masaccio. It pointed the way to the belief in man's power of independent creativity which was first fully affirmed in the so-called High Renaissance of the period of Leonardo and Michelangelo. Alberti was so strongly convinced of this power that he almost equated the artist with God. "Whatever was done by man with genius and with a certain grace," it was said, "he held to be almost divine." [2]

The most extreme statement of the divinity of art was made by the art historian Giorgio Vasari a century later. "The origin of these arts was nature herself—the first image or model, the most beautiful fabric of the world—and the master was that divine light infused into us by special grace, which has made us not only superior to all other animals, but has exalted us, if it be permitted so to speak, to the similitude of God himself." [3]

The middle decades of the quattrocento saw no other innovations of major importance—it was not until near the end of the century that Leonardo initiated a new trend—but there has never been a period of Western history when art expressed more sheer enjoyment of the possibilities of line and color or more confi-

---

[2] Quoted in J. B. Ross and M. M. McLaughlin, eds.: *The Renaissance Reader* (New York, 1958), p. 492.

[3] Quoted in Holt: op. cit., I, 140. There is a psychological connection between individualistic attitudes and the sense of vista in three-dimensional views of space. This is demonstrated in the psychological tests worked out by Hermann Rorschach. A strong feeling for vistas leads to the realization that all observations are relative to the position of the observer, and hence that truth is subjective and nothing is absolute. This was the basis of Renaissance individualism.

dence in human powers. The hallmark of the painting of this period was its delighted exploration of life in this world. While Christian belief and legend continued to provide most of the subject matter, the tone became progressively more secular. Christ and the saints were located within a three-dimensional space, and were portrayed as human figures, not as cult-images.[4]

The artist was still considered a craftsman working to fulfill the wishes of those who employed him and was expected to display competence in half a dozen different occupations—most artists of this period had their initial training in the workshops of goldsmiths. The conception of the artist as an original genius giving expression to his own insights and formulating his own standards was expressed in the middle years of the fifteenth century by critics like Alberti and in the next generation—with an even more justifiable arrogance—by Leonardo, but it was never generally accepted by the artist's patrons. The tastes of employers continued, therefore, to have a determining influence on the tone and subjects of art. Artists had to satisfy the preferences of rich merchants and of despots; and while most of their

---

[4] Some of the more unbelievable aspects of Christian dogma become unhappily conspicuous when they acquire visual representation in painting. A notable example is the doctrine of the Trinity, as portrayed by (among other artists) Masaccio, Dürer, and El Greco. How can the relationship between God the Father and his son Jesus be made intelligible? Most painters have concentrated on one or the other and have not attempted to define the relationship. Thus Michelangelo, for example, presents in the Sistine Chapel God the Father creating man; this is an almost convincing portrayal of the Christian deity, and certainly surpasses any other rendering of him. Jesus has no part in it, but is reserved for the stellar role in Michelangelo's portrayal of the last judgment more than thirty years later, from which God the Father is excluded. When God the Father and his son appear in the same picture, it is difficult for the painter to differentiate between them in any meaningful way. In practice, God is usually shown as somewhat larger, more fully bearded, and wearing antique clothing (his headdress resembles the tiara worn by the Pope on formal occasions). It is evident that it was Jesus and not God who was the victim on Calvary. At this point orthodox Christian doctrine becomes so meaningless that it is difficult not to be a little blasphemous. What kind of father did God become when he allowed his son to be crucified?

patrons accepted the basic premise of all Renaissance art—its belief that aesthetic standards were derived from nature—they had a tendency to ask for an art that would provide them with pure enjoyment and would not presume to explore new aspects of reality.

Florence retained its leadership and its prestige as a school of the arts, and most of its artists retained a high sense of aesthetic responsibility, though an escapist tendency showed itself under the Medici. The invention of perspective had intoxicating effects, and it soon became customary for painters to present their figures in front of immense panoramas fading gradually into blue distances, the valley of the Arno being the favorite example. But the central subject of all Florentine art continued to be the human figure, though the new emphasis on the background was a constant reminder that man was an inhabitant of the material world. And although no Florentine painter who flourished during the half-century between Masaccio and Leonardo can be compared with these two major figures, there were perhaps a dozen who made contributions of their own. The central line of Florentine art was the increasing mastery of techniques appropriate to the new view of man, and a number of artists approached this task in a rationalistic and scientific spirit, regarding the rules of perspective not as conveniences, but as revelations of ultimate reality. This was true especially of Uccello and—in spite of the naïve religiosity expressed in his paintings—of Fra Angelico. Other artists are remembered because they made some special innovation in subject matter or technique which was then adopted by their pupils and successors. Thus, for example, Veneziano developed special skills in depicting figures in movement, Verrocchio explored the representation of twilight, Pollaiuolo pioneered in the portrayal of nudes, and Ghirlandaio presented scenes from the life of Christ and the saints which were largely realistic renderings of middle-class life in Florence. These and other painters, though themselves of secondary importance, prepared the way for the summation of the Renaissance view of man in the great masters of the early sixteenth century. And in spite of a fondness for scenes of violence and bloodshed (for reasons unexplained the artists of this period loved to portray the beheading of Holofernes by Judith, and of John the Baptist at the request of Salome) the period was characterized by a growing confidence in man which was far removed from any doctrine of original sin and was exemplified in vivid portrayals of pleasures and adventures.

Meanwhile a number of other northern Italian cities had become artistic centers; and some of them developed special styles of their own, presumably because some individual master impressed his influence so strongly that his successors continued to work along the same lines. Siena, following Duccio, continued to display a lyrical quality in paintings that were exquisitely colored and organized but lacking in vital force. The Umbrian hill town of Perugia produced a series of masters, beginning with Pinturicchio and continuing with Perugino and his pupil Raphael, who pioneered in the effective organization of figures in a three-dimensional space. Their somewhat sentimental and ethereal figures showed no recognition that the political life of Perugia probably surpassed that of every other Italian city in assassinations, acts of treachery, and wholesale massacres. Ferrara, governed by the relatively enlightened Este dynasty, produced in Cosimo Tura and his pupil Cossa painters who loved hard and rocky landscapes peopled by figures even more grotesquely stony and austere than their surroundings. Sharply in contrast, Venetian artists were beginning to find expression for the riches and luxury and the wholly secular concerns of the great commercial city. Giorgione and the brothers Bellini, Giovanni and Gentile, while almost equal to the Florentines in the design of their figures, added a love for rich harmonious colors which became the special characteristic of the Venetian school.

Escapist tendencies were stronger in northern Italy than in Florence. Most of the cities were firmly under the rule of despots, with none of the republican traditions which—in spite of the Medici—were strongly preserved at Florence, and most of the despots wanted an art that would be highly decorative, without realistic tendencies. In its earlier phases, the art of the north was strongly influenced by the International Gothic that had been cultivated by the French nobility during the feudal decadence. Its products were richly colored, fanciful and exotic, and often crowded with brilliantly attired aristocratic figures who might be shown going on a journey through romantic landscapes. This was the art of men like Gentile da Fabriano, Umbrian-born but working mostly in the north, who loved to portray fair knights and lovely ladies riding past masses of flowers under golden skies with faces aglow with happiness. The work of such men, incomparably delightful when considered as decoration but lacking in the feeling of weight and mass which could convey a sense of reality, may be regarded as the sunset of the age of chivalry. Later in the fifteenth century, similar tendencies found expression in the work of the Florentine Benozzo Gozzoli, especially in his *Journey of the Magi*. This presents resplendent princely figures, most of them young and gay and utterly unlike the magi of Christian tradition, riding through fantastic mountain country with no thought for anything but their own enjoyment and magnificence of attire. Several of the figures represented young men of the Medici family, and the whole composition illustrated the kind of escapism which even Florence produced under Medici influence.

Two masters, neither of them Florentine, did their most important work during the middle decades of the quattrocento, presenting new versions of the strength and dignity of man. These were Mantegna, who derived his name from his native city, and Piero della Francesca. Presenting an artistic version of humanism, Mantegna identified himself completely with the world of ancient Rome, copying figures from Roman columns and presenting them in front of backgrounds dominated by Roman temples. Mantegna's Rome, which had actually little to do with reality, sheds new light on the humanist movement. His highly idealized men and women, displaying an astonishing sense of calm mastery and self-assurance, represented the ancient world not as it was, but as Renaissance Italy liked to imagine it. Rome, as Mantegna romantically affirmed it, had

356

created a civilization which glorified human strength and beauty, with no need for Christian humility or for other-worldly salvation. A similar glorification of man pervaded the work of Piero della Francesca, who was born in an Umbrian village but did much of his work in the Tuscan city of Arezzo. Approaching art in a highly intellectual spirit, he studied and wrote about perspective as though it were a branch of science. His pictures, all nominally on religious subjects (best known is his series on the history of the true cross), are pervaded with a sense of man's trust in his own inner strength and completeness. Motionless and self-controlled, the men and women of his pictures confront each other without communicating, and one has a sense that the smallest change would destroy the unity of the whole picture. They are, like the *haeccitates* of Duns Scotus or Leibnitz's monads, self-contained and in need of nothing which they cannot of themselves supply out of their own resources.

The work of such men pointed forward to the affirmation of man's creative powers that characterized the High Renaissance. Artists could no longer regard themselves as simply copying nature, ignoring the subjective organizing principles which gave their work its unity and coherence. And without such an affirmation art would be likely to slip back to a sentimental medievalism. This tendency was exemplified in the work of the most prominent late fifteenth-century Florentine painter, Sandro (Alessandro) Botticelli. A master of linear design whose work had an immense charm and delicacy, Botticelli turned his back on the main tendencies of Florentine art up to his time. He was not interested in conveying a sense of weight and mass that would give his figures reality. He built his pictures out of flowing lines, which gave an appearance of movement to figures that had no weight. Many of them were presented as floating in space, their feet doing no more than touching the ground. His men lack masculine strength and his women are devoid of sexuality. They inhabit a fairy-tale world, both gay and melancholic but never real. His Virgin and his Venus have the same face, being modeled—according to legend—after a lady loved by one of the younger Medici; but as neither of them belongs to the material world, one can accept this resemblance without any sense of blasphemy. Botticelli had learned technical lessons from his Florentine predecessors, but his work was close in spirit and tone to the International Gothic.

While the aesthetic taste of the despots and their courts was a disturbing factor in the development of the visual arts, in poetry it was a dominating influence. Since the time of Giotto, painting had been regarded as a search for ultimate realities, and this tradition of seriousness had been too firmly established wholly to give place to the desire for sophisticated entertainment. But in Italian literature there was no continuing tradition. After Dante and Petrarch came a long hiatus caused by the acceptance of the humanist insistence that all serious work had to be written in Latin.

For more than a hundred years after the *Decameron* no important work of literature was written in Italian. The movement for the revival of classical Latin was in the ascendant, and Dante's convincing defense of the vernacular in his *De Vulgari Eloquentia* was apparently forgotten. Yet posterity has not cared to remember any of the imitations of Cicero and Virgil produced by the humanists, except for nonliterary reasons, just as Petrarch's lasting literary fame is based on his early Italian sonnets and not on his Latin epic, *Africa*. Genuine masterpieces cannot be produced in a dead language, and the Latin of the humanists had ceased to be spoken more than a thousand years earlier. Other forms of Latin had remained partially alive throughout the Middle Ages, but the humanists had nothing but contempt for the language of the scholastics and of the medieval hymns and Goliardic songs. By breaking with the living tradition and insisting on returning to the classical forms, the humanists—by a curious paradox—were actually responsible for finally killing the language they so admired, though the growth of the vernaculars had already made it moribund.

When poetry again began to be written in the vernacular in the late fifteenth century, it was lively, amusing, and technically extremely skillful, but not serious. The more ambitious examples took their subject matter from the French *chansons de geste* and the romances, which had become familiar to the Italian people in popular versions rendered by anonymous street singers and were now delicately spoofed for the pleasure of the aristocracy. This comic retelling of the exploits of Charlemagne and his peers and other medieval heroes began in the entourage of Lorenzo de' Medici with the comic epic entitled *Il Morgante Maggiore,* the author of which was Luigi Pulci. But the main center of poetry during this period was the court of Ferrara, which had been governed by the Este family since the early Middle Ages and was more sympathetic to chivalric values than were other Italian cities. Two long poems dealing with material supplied by the *chansons* were its chief literary products: the *Orlando Innamorato* of Matteo Maria Boiardo and the *Orlando Furioso* of Lodovico Ariosto. Orlando is the Italian form of Roland, and the stark, single-minded warrior of Roncesvalles is transformed into a romantic and chivalrous knight-errant in love with the princess Angelica, daughter of the King of Cathay. Of the two authors, Ariosto has been generally regarded as the more skillful and the less serious. He creates a world resembling that portrayed by Fabriano: a world filled with rich colors, handsome knights and beautiful ladies, improbable adventures, a fairy-tale atmosphere, and nothing of reality. Theoretically, this is placed in the eighth century, and the French are doing battle with the Saracens; but this background is barely mentioned. Knights and ladies wander away in quest of each other and cover hundreds of miles of land and sea in a single afternoon; motivations are obscure, though they generally have to do with love; men are sometimes carried on the backs of sea monsters to strange countries or by hippogriffs to the moon; and while men may lose their wits, the mood of the poem never becomes tragic. Mostly the moral atmosphere has the purity that generally characterized the tales of chivalry, but occasionally the recital is varied with a bawdy story. Ariosto's fertility in inventing episodes is inexhaustible; and whenever anything is in danger of becoming monotonous there is a sudden change of character and scene. And though this is wholly a fantasy world, the author can still show his virtuosity in the subtle and delicate analysis of human emotions. Ariosto has never become popular in northern countries (though Spenser borrowed heavily from him in writing *The Faerie Queene*); but he expresses something permanent in the Mediterranean temperament.

The most enlightened of the courts was that of the Montefeltro dynasty, who reigned as dukes of Urbino. Federigo da Montefeltro, duke from 1465 until his death in 1482, was a professional *condottiere* who spent the money he earned by fighting other people's wars partly in building a library and partly for the benefit of his subjects. He was succeeded by his son Guidobaldo, whose interest in learning and the arts was shared by his wife Elisabetta, who belonged to the Gonzaga family, rulers of Mantua. It was the court life of Guidobaldo and Elisabetta that was celebrated in *The Courtier* of Baldassare Castiglione, a native of Mantua who served various different princes, but spent the happiest years of his life (from 1504 until 1508) at Urbino. *The Courtier* is a series of dialogues, allegedly taking place in the year 1507 during four evenings and participated in by some thirty interlocutors. Its theme is the ideal nobleman, and its sensitivity to moral and aesthetic values makes this book an enduring memorial of some of the finer aspects of the Renaissance. Castiglione's portrayal of court life is thoroughly realistic. He recognizes that the nobleman must seek honor and reputation and that there is no value in noble deeds unless other people hear about them. It will add to the nobleman's reputation if he displays the quality of *sprezzatura,* which means that he should give the appearance of performing difficult feats easily and spontaneously, without visible effort. And his aim should always be the winning of glory in warfare, not economic gain. Thus Castiglione's morality is definitely worldly, with no suggestion of the ascetiscism of the Middle Ages, though the dialogues end with a long speech in praise of Platonic love delivered by a future cardinal named Pietro Bembo, and it is affirmed that the proper aim of love is marriage. But Castiglione succeeds in convincing his readers that Guidobaldo and Elisabetta were actually as devoted to culture and virtue as they were reputed to be, and the whole book has a charm derived from the life of the court of Urbino which cannot be paralleled in Renaissance writing.

18

High Renaissance

A new phase in the history of Renaissance art began with the advent of Leonardo da Vinci, whose first major painting, *The Virgin of the Rocks,* was painted early in the 1480's, With Leonardo came a new emphasis on man's power of independent creativity. The function of the artist was not merely to copy natural appearances, but to select and organize them in accordance with his own subjective conceptions of beauty and significance. This new view of the meaning of art inaugurated the so-called High Renaissance, which lasted through the early decades of the sixteenth century, its major figures, in addition to Leonardo, being Raphael and Michelangelo.

For Giotto and for Masaccio and their admirers, nature meant chiefly the outward appearance of things, and painting had been judged by representational standards, its value supposedly depending on the degree with which it rendered the illusion of material realities. But obviously any great painter does more than merely copy appearances, and the early Renaissance critics who professed to judge art in these terms were not fully aware of their own values. The greatness of representational art depends not on its closeness to appearances, but on how those appearances are organized by the artists. What human creativity adds to nature is the essential element. As Renaissance artists and critics became aware of this, they continued to affirm that nature was the artist's model, but what was meant by nature underwent a subtle change.

This change of attitude is reflected in Alberti's treatise on architecture, which was completed in 1452. According to Alberti, the function of the artist was not merely to copy natural appearances, but to produce beauty, and this required creative activity. He defined beauty as "a harmony of all the parts, in whatsoever subject it appears, fitted together with such proportions and connections, that nothing could be added, diminished or altered, but for the worse." [1] Elsewhere in the same treatise he spoke of beauty as arising from congruity. "The business and office of congruity is to put together members differing from each other in their natures, in such a manner that they may conspire to form a beautiful whole." [2] This law of congruity was to be found in every production of nature, so that in adhering to it the artist was now conceived of as imitating not merely the works of nature, but nature itself, and nature was regarded as a creative power directed and inspired by God. Art was no longer judged solely by illusionist standards, though these were still expected to be followed, but was considered as also a revelation of higher truths.

As art developed, there was a growing emphasis on the subjective elements in artistic creation. This tendency was already implicit in the adoption of rules of perspective. The originators of these rules believed that they were scientific laws, yet in actuality they should be considered in large measure as practical conveniences necessitated by the fact that artists were trying to transcribe a three-dimensional world in a two-dimensional medium. Human beings, with their two eyes, do not see the world from a single point. Perspective made the process of human vision neater and more orderly than it actually was. Implicit in it, moreover, was an individualistic conception of truth, which was now regarded as varying according to the observer's point of view. Reality was nature as man perceived it, and each angle of vision

---

[1] Elizabeth Holt: *A Documentary History of Art,* I, 230.
[2] Holt: op. cit., I, 236–7.

had its own validity. The ultimate outcome of this artistic evolution was reached with the great figures of the High Renaissance. Godlike perceptiveness and creative power were attributed to the individual artist, who was now regarded as an inspired man of genius superior to all rules and conventions. The act of seeing had become more important than the objects that were seen.

The greater artists of this period continued to insist that they were following nature, and they did, in fact, continue on the whole to conform to representational standards, although they also claimed a new freedom to depart from them in order to serve higher artistic purposes. But in speaking of nature they were giving expression to their sense of the creative process as one of discovery rather than of invention, its achievements conveying the sense of inevitability which is one of the hallmarks of great art. This deep, nonrational confidence that what man is affirming is discovered rather than invented is characteristic of all ages of high achievement. The bases of order and truth and beauty are felt as given, not as fictions, and man sees himself as communicating things that come from a higher transcendental source. Modern man may prefer to regard this source as wholly internal, feeling that the artist is giving release to deep forces within his own psyche; but the feeling of inspiration given by great artistic creations remains, however it may be interpreted. When Renaissance painters lost this sense of inevitability and began to regard art as an expression of subjective fictions, as happened with the "mannerism" of the middle decades of the sixteenth century, the great period of Renaissance painting came to an end.

The belief in man's creative powers was asserted in philosophy by Marsilio Ficino and his fellow Platonists. The Renaissance was not a very productive period in abstract thought, either in quantity or in quality; and Ficino is of interest because he expressed the spirit of this time rather than for the intrinsic importance of his thought. The study of Platonism—actually of the Neo-Platonism of Plotinus rather than of the original doctrines of Plato himself—was introduced into Italy by Byzantine scholars attending the Council of 1438. In 1462, Ficino was endowed by

Cosimo de' Medici, receiving a villa and a library; and he gathered around him a group of Platonic enthusiasts who engaged in informal studies and discussions and became known as the Platonic Academy. In addition to translating works by Plato and Plotinus, Ficino wrote original works, especially his *De Religione Christiana* and *Theologia Platonica,* both of them published in 1474. These attempts to fuse Christianity and Platonism may be regarded as foreshadowing the aesthetic theories of Leonardo and Michelangelo.

Asserting the divinity of the human soul, which he considered as actually a part of God and a sharer in God's creative powers, Ficino probably affirmed a higher conception of humanity than any other philosopher in history. Man's supreme faculty, he declared was his imagination rather than his capacity for logical thought, and this enabled him to share in God's creativity and to identify himself with all the other beings in the universe, whether above him or below. "The images of the divine entities whence it sprang," Ficino said of the human soul, "it carries within itself as the reasons and models of the lower things that it recreates as it were of its own. It is the center of all and possesses the forces of all. It can turn to and penetrate this without leaving that, for it is the true connection of things. Thus it can be called rightly the center of nature, the middle point of the universe, and the chain that links the world together." [3] "The effort of the soul is directed toward this end: that the soul in its own way will become the whole universe." [4] Man could not only enter into all other beings by the power of his imagination; he could also exercise powers of independent creativity which made him actually the rival of God. "Since man has observed the order of the heavens, when they move, whither they proceed and with what measures, and what they produce, who could deny that man

---

[3] Quoted in Giorgio de Santillana, ed.: *Age of Adventure* (Boston, 1957), p. 57.

[4] Quoted in Ernst Cassirer et al.: *The Renaissance Philosophy of Man,* p. 200.

possesses as it were almost the same genius as the Author of the heavens? And who could deny that man could somehow also make the heavens, could he only obtain the instruments and the heavenly material, since even now he makes them, though of a different material, but still with a very similar order?" [5] The human soul, in fact, "in the arts and in governments is the rival of God." [6]

Similarly ecstatic affirmations of the greatness of man were made by Ficino's young disciple Pico della Mirandola, who died at the age of thirty-one after making an immense reputation both for learning and for personal charm. In his *Oration on the Dignity of Man,* he represents God as saying to man: "The nature of all other beings is limited and constrained within the bounds of law prescribed by us. Thou, constrained by no limits, in accordance with thine own free will, in whose hand we have placed thee, shall ordain for thyself the limits of thy nature. We have set thee at the world's center that thou mayest from thence more easily observe whatever is in the world. We have made thee neither of heaven nor of earth, neither mortal nor immortal, so that with freedom of choice and with honor, as though the maker and moulder of thyself, thou mayest fashion thyself in whatever shape thou shalt prefer." [7]

When the artists of the High Renaissance affirmed that they were following nature, they felt that they were capturing a deeper reality which could be described as nature only by a kind of metaphor. Leonardo declared that "the mind of the painter must transmute itself into the very mind of nature and be the interpreter between it and art." [8] Painting, in fact, was "the grandchild of nature, for all visible things are produced by nature and these her children have given birth to painting. Hence we may justly

---

[5] Quoted in Giorgio de Santillana: op. cit., p. 15.
[6] Quoted in Anders Nygren: *Agape and Eros,* p. 657.
[7] Quoted in Cassirer: op. cit., pp. 224–5.
[8] Quoted in Sidney J. Freedberg: *Painters of the High Renaissance in Rome and Florence,* p. 9.

call it the grandchild of nature and related to God." [9] Michelangelo went even further in his emphasis on the creative power of the artists, actually equating it with the knowledge of God. "Fine painting," he affirmed, "is nothing other than a copy of the perfections of God, and a remembrance of his painting, and lastly a music and melody which only the mind is capable of hearing, with great difficulty." The artist, in fact, "is capable of inventing what has never been found before." [1]

With the advent of the High Renaissance, each major artist was more fully individualized, all his works bearing the unmistakable imprint of his own special view of reality, and there was an inevitable shift of the spectator's interest from the actual work to the personality behind it. The value of art came to depend primarily on the depth of insight displayed by its maker, and this was an innate gift which might be improved by study but could not be acquired by study alone. The great artist was a man of individual genius, and this was displayed in everything that he created, even in sketches and other unfinished works. Michelangelo was being goodhumoredly contemptuous of his rival Raphael when he suggested that he did not get his art from nature but from long study. Thus the artists of the High Renaissance were making claims for themselves that put them on a par with the saints and prophets. This was in sharp contrast with the medieval artist's role of hired craftsman working in accord with established techniques to satisfy the demands of the patrons who employed him. No artist could have been more fully aware of his own high merits than Leonardo or Michelangelo. And both of them had a strong propensity to leave their works unfinished, as though they were primarily interested in the original conceptions and resented the labor needed to transcribe them fully.

What one feels most strongly in the works of the High Ren-

---

[9] Quoted in Nesca Robb: *Neoplatonism of the Italian Renaissance* (New York, 1935), p. 225.

[1] Quoted in Robert J. Clements: *Michelangelo's Theory of Art*, pp. 18, 20.

aissance is the creative energy with which the artist organizes his
subject matter and imposes order and unity upon it. Alberti's
definition of beauty as a harmony of all the materials, resulting
through congruity in a unified whole, was now realized much
more forcefully and fully than in the works of any earlier artists.
No art could have reflected more fully the belief in man's native
power to master the world of appearances. Classic art has been
defined by Roger Fry as art "which to provoke emotion depends
on its own formal organization" and does not "count on the
association of ideas which it sets up in the mind of the spectator."
This use of the word "classic" formulates one of the essential
differences between the art of the quattrocento and that of the
period inaugurated by Leonardo. The range of material capable
of incorporation into a work of art was, moreover, very much
extended. Leonardo's ambition was to render not only the physical appearance of human beings, but also their inner emotions. A
figure, he said, "is not praiseworthy if there does not appear in it
the action that expresses the feeling of its spirit." The painter
should portray "man and the intention of his soul"; [2] and the
latter was, of course, much more difficult because it could only be
suggested and could not be directly stated. This conception of the
function of art was held even more strongly by Michelangelo,
who was primarily a creator of human figures and who succeeded
in conveying the whole gamut of human emotions.

The innovating genius of Leonardo can be fully appreciated
if one compares his *Last Supper* (begun in 1495) with a painting of the same subject which was made by Ghirlandaio about
the year 1480. Ghirlandaio was in many ways typical of the
quattrocento. Most of his pictures, despite their religious subject
matter, actually consisted of scenes taken from the Florentine life
of his own day. Everything in his pictures conformed with realistic standards of representation; yet although he made use of rules
of perspective, he still preferred to line up his figures so that they

---

[2] Quoted in Freeberg: op. cit., p. 10.

faced the spectator with a two-dimensional effect. His *Last Supper* presented Jesus and his disciples arrayed along one side of a table, Judas alone being placed (according to long-established tradition) in isolation on the other side. Each of the figures displayed a different emotional reaction. Through the windows above them the spectator was given a view of various exotic trees and flying birds. The picture, however, was wholly lacking in any sense of unity or organizing energy. It remained a mass of details, each of which had to be studied in isolation from the rest, and the eye of the spectator was given no guidance or direction.

Leonardo's portrayal, on the other hand, presented itself, from the very first glance, as a unity; and however carefully one studied the details, one never lost awareness of the total effect. The disciples were organized into four different groups, with Christ alone in the center; but each group and each individual was integrated into the whole and derived significance from contributing to it. And although the line of the table imposed a horizontal and somewhat two-dimensional feeling, this was offset by a whole series of vertical lines and by the sense of perspective established by the two side walls in the background. The unity of the picture, moreover, was astonishingly dynamic. In detail the picture was full of movement and emotion. Each of the disciples, aroused by Christ's statement that one of them would betray him, was portrayed in vigorous movement expressive of the most violent reaction; and Christ alone remained calm and motionless. Thus the picture presented an organic synthesis of human feeling and activity, organized around its central theme, which was the greatness of Christ and his relationship to his disciples. Everything in the picture contributed to this total effect, and there were no such irrelevant details as the trees and the flying birds in the background of the Ghirlandaio version. So naturalistically convincing was the portrayal that only the most alert of spectators was likely to notice that, in actuality, it was quite unrealistic. In order to obtain a heightened effect, Leonardo was bold enough to depict a physical impossibility. The table was far too small to accommodate all the disciples, but the picture was organized so skillfully that the lack of space has usually gone unnoticed.

Illegitimate son of a Florentine lawyer, Leonardo made his initial reputation in Florence. But at the age of thirty he went to Milan, where he spent seventeen years in the service of the despot Ludovico Sforza. After Sforza's fall in 1499, he returned to Florence, but he apparently preferred to work for a patron; and after a brief period in the employment of Cesare Borgia, he spent his last years in the pay of the King of France. Leonardo's contemporaries recognized that he had inaugurated a new epoch in the development of painting, both in his insistence on the formal unity of a picture and in his unsurpassed capacity for expressing movement and emotion and producing effects of light and shadow. And they mostly accepted him at his own valuation as a creative genius. The half-dozen major works on which his artistic reputation depends are indeed a unique and unsurpassed achievement. But the man seems greater than what he produced, and there is an enigmatic quality about him which makes him both mysterious and inexhaustibly interesting.

He was always concerned with the solution of problems, and his fascination with the powers of the human intellect could lead him to embark with apparent enthusiasm on trivial or destructive occupations. During his stay at the court of Ludovico Sforza he was willing not only to work on *The Last Supper* and other works of art but also to give his talents to the devising of court festivities and entertainments; and he seems to have had no moral scruples about serving Cesare Borgia as a military engineer. By such activities he made himself useful to his patrons and earned his livelihood. But he seems always to have maintained his aloofness, never revealing himself fully—an attitude that was probably partly the result of his homosexuality (this probably never became overt; his whole attitude toward sexuality seems to have been one of revulsion). Meanwhile he was confiding a large part of his mental activities and speculations to his notebooks, which were kept strictly secret. The contents in fact never became fully known until the late nineteenth century. The modern world thinks of him largely as a scientist; and he certainly showed an astonishing capacity to foresee later scientific discoveries and technical inventions. But as most of his work remained unknown until three and a half centuries after his death, he had little influence on his contemporaries and cannot be regarded as an important figure in scientific history. His science was closely associated with his art; in both spheres he was interested in the solution of problems and regarded such solutions as discoveries of divine and natural law.

Yet it was always art that he felt to be his real profession, and he undertook it with such a sense of dedication that he was apparently too conscientious to work with any facility. According to Vasari, he "felt that his hand would be unable to realize the perfect creations of his imagination, as his mind formed such difficult, subtle, and marvellous conceptions that his hands, skillful as they were, could never have expressed them." [3] Vasari declares that on his deathbed he spoke of his lack of productivity in art as though it were a sin. And more than that of any other Renaissance painter, his art was removed from the world of actuality. Strange landscapes filled with unusual rock formations and flowing waters; and the enigmatic, slightly smiling, and highly spiritualized faces which he gave to all his women, to Mona Lisa and to Leda no less than to the Virgin—from what compelling psychic sources and what visions of the spiritual world these were derived remains mysterious. No figure of the Renaissance seems to have gone further into the psychic world or to be more wholly beyond our comprehension.

Leonardo should perhaps be regarded as a forerunner of the High Renaissance rather than a full participant in it. It did not become clearly apparent that art had entered a new phase until 1508, when two great masters, Raphael and Michelangelo, began work in the Vatican under the direction of Pope Julius II. Filled with worldly ambition and demonic energy, although al-

---

[3] Giorgio Vasari: *Lives of the Artists* (Everyman's Library), II, 157.

ready sixty years of age when he assumed the papacy in 1503, Julius aspired both to establish effective papal sovereignty over a large area of central Italy and to make Rome into a center of the new art and learning. Henceforth Rome did, in fact, displace Florence as the main center of the Renaissance. Julius seems originally to have had no special preferences in art—he invited all the most highly reputed painters to Rome, regardless of style —but once Raphael and Michelangelo had started work, he had taste enough to recognize their pre-eminence and give them the necessary support. Without his patronage the High Renaissance would have assumed different forms and might not have been so clearly differentiated from earlier periods.

Born in Urbino and studying art first under Perugino at Perugia and afterward under various masters at Florence, Raphael was only twenty-five when he started work in the Vatican, and he spent most of the remainder of his short life in Rome. His contemporaries were dazzled and amazed by his artistic skill and facility and by the unfailing courtesy and generosity which distinguished him so markedly from his great rival, Michelangelo. No great artist has been so loved or has been so unfailingly rewarded with worldly prosperity and popularity. Both in his skill and in his subject matter he may be regarded as the culminating figure of the whole Renaissance. The immense murals in the Pope's rooms in the Vatican, along with innumerable lesser works, including no less than fifty different Madonnas, made him the most productive of all artists before the great Venetians, though much of the detail in his later pictures was filled in by students and assistants. He was not in the first rank, perhaps, in imbuing his figures with the sense of movement and plastic solidity or in conveying emotion; but he was unerring in his capacity for giving his pictures a unified form. No other painter was his equal in space composition. What he chiefly expressed, moreover, was a sense of harmony which may be regarded as one of the aims of the Renaissance—harmony especially between the pagan and the Christian elements in Western culture. In Raphael's art Zeus and Jehovah seem to be fused with no feeling of conflict or incon-

371

gruity. A similar harmony of elements usually regarded as discordant seems to have characterized his life. He loved many women, and according to Vasari his premature death was partly caused by an especially wild night of debauchery, resulting in a fever which his doctor tried to cure by bleeding. Yet this did not prevent Vasari from declaring that "those who copy his virtuous life will be rewarded in heaven." [4] In his life, as in his art, pagan morals could be combined with the Christian hope of redemption.

Yet precisely because the work of Raphael was the consummation of the whole Italian Renaissance, it lacks the note of individuality and the sense of tension which are necessary for continued high appeal. Everything came to him too easily. The men of the Renaissance had hoped for the fusion of pagan and classical traditions, but this fusion could not actually be achieved except in relatively superficial terms. A thousand years of the Christian sense of sin and the Christian sanctification of human suffering could not be obliterated; and the most interesting Renaissance works of art are those that convey not an easy harmony but a continued conflict. Raphael could portray happiness and human glory; but there is little suffering in his pictures, and little of that sense of mystery, like an intimation of another world which we can feel but can never see, which is conveyed so strongly by Leonardo. Raphael's murals summarized the positive achievements of the Renaissance, but in so doing they emphasized its limitations. And while one is awed and delighted by Raphael's skill in marshaling such a multitude of human figures with such a consummate sense of order and unity, one feels that a single unfinished figure by Michelangelo conveys a deeper and more powerful sense of the meaning of human life than the whole vast sweep of the Vatican murals. Only in some of Raphael's later easel paintings does he reveal a growing sense of complexity which suggests that he was capable of greater things than any he actually produced.

---

[4] Vasari: op. cit., II, 249.

Nobody could have been less like Raphael than his great rival Michelangelo, the last great artist of the Florentine school and the crowning figure of the whole Renaissance. Lonely, morose, and cantankerous; uninterested in all other human beings except the members of his family and a few personal friends; contemptuous of all the comforts and graces of social life; fully aware of his own greatness and ready to make the highest claims for it—Michelangelo was the prototype of the isolated and self-directing man of genius. He had to the full the Italian quality of *terribilità,* which means to be possessed by the most intense and demonic emotional drives. If one were to judge from his surviving letters, he was motivated chiefly by the desire for money, not for himself but in the hope of winning aristocratic status for his brothers and nephews (who constantly disappointed him); yet he fully recognized his own importance. He treated Pope Julius and his other patrons as his social equals; and to complaints that his figures in the Medici Chapel were not sufficiently lifelike, he replied that in a thousand years nobody would care what the Medici princes had looked like. Born and trained in Florence and spending his mature life partly in Florence and partly in Rome, he died, active to the end, at the age of eighty-nine. Yet he completed relatively few works, much of his life being spent on projects that remained unfinished or abortive, though when he had a clear road ahead of him, as in the painting of the Sistine Chapel, nobody could work with more speed and intensity. His patrons are much to blame for failing to make the best use of his talents. But everything that he touched, even the slabs of marble that he laid aside half-finished, showed the unmistakable imprint of his personality. And everything conveyed the tragic sense of human life, both its greatness and its misery, which was Michelangelo's hallmark, and by which he transcended the art and ideals of his time. Though pressure from his patrons made him a painter and an architect, he would have preferred to remain exclusively a sculptor of the human figure. No other great artist has had subject matter so narrowly delimited. Yet in the bodily and facial expressions of human figures he could somehow give a

sense of conveying on the most profound level the whole meaning
and significance of human life.

It is indeed paradoxical that the greatest figure of the Renaissance should have been so different from his forerunners and
contemporaries. He had none of their joy in material appearances, their delight in rendering the life of their time in pictures
with bright colors, crowded with a variety of human figures.
Himself a believing and pious Christian, almost Protestant in his
sense of direct dependence on God, he was untypical of his age
except in his artistic skill and his veneration for the art of classical antiquity. Retaining the values of sculpture even when he was
engaged in painting (as in the Sistine Chapel), he had little
interest in color and none in the realistic representation of the life
around him. Of many painters of the Florentine school he must
have felt as he did about the Flemings: that they had no concern
for significant form.[5]

Michelangelo was not devoted to beauty for its own sake,
although no figures could have been more beautiful than some of
his Madonnas, such as the *Pietà* at St. Peter's in Rome or the
Madonna at Bruges. Art, for Michelangelo, had higher functions
than a mere pleasure in attractive forms and colors and in the
realistic rendering of daily life. It was a revelation of the nature
of God. Michelangelo expressed this conception in Neo-Platonic
terms, at least in the poems written in his old age for his friend
Vittoria Colonna. "My eyes longing for beautiful things," he told
her, "together with my soul longing for salvation have no other
power to ascend to heaven than the contemplation of beautiful
things." "Nor does God, in his grace," he affirmed in another

---

[5] "They paint in Flanders expressly to deceive the outer vision, either things
which delight you or about which you may speak no ill, such as saints or
prophets. Their painting is of patches, masonries, plants in the fields, shadows
of trees, rivers and bridges, all of which they call landscapes, with many figures
here and many there. And all this, although it may appear good to some eyes,
is done truly without reason or art, without symmetry or proportion, without
attention to selection or rejection, and finally, without any substance or muscle."
Quoted in Clements: op. cit., p. 207.

poem, "show himself to me in any other aspect more clearly than in a beautiful human veil." [6] But it was impossible for a man of Michelangelo's complex sensitivity to rest secure in Plotinus's affirmation of salvation as a flight of the alone to the alone. The Christian sense of sin and the Christian love for the rest of mankind could not be dismissed so easily. What gives the work of Michelangelo such intensity is the conflict between his simple, pious Christianity and the pagan exuberance of the Renaissance, and this actually makes him the truest interpreter of his time, in spite of his uniqueness—an interpreter on deeper levels than were reached by any of his contemporaries. Coming to maturity at the height of the Renaissance, he foreshadowed the disillusionment with worldly glory and the revival of Christian piety which, during his later years, brought the whole movement to an end. As C. R. Morey has declared, "Michelangelo's powerful inhibited figures reflect the disparity between Christian emotion and the antique ideal, free human will and the will of God; the rational forms of classic sculpture were not made for the ecstasy of a Christian mystic; they writhe in the possession of an unfamiliar spirit and betray, by brutal distortion, incongruous proportions and discordant composition, the force of the collision of medieval Christianity and the Renaissance." [7]

This sense of disharmony became stronger as Michelangelo grew older. Even in his youth he never conveyed the feeling of spontaneous delight in the richness of earthly life of which earlier Florentine art had been so full. But his early works, such as his statue of David, expressed a pleasure in human strength and vitality, combined with a sense of the seriousness of human obligations and ideals. This seriousness was carried further in the ceiling of the Sistine Chapel (completed in 1512), with its rendering of the Old Testament elements in the Christian tradition. It was imbued with a religious awe and reverence, but the

---

[6] Quoted in Clements: op. cit., pp. 9, 111.

[7] Charles Rufus Morey: *Mediaeval Art,* p. 62.

world remained essentially intelligible and just. Michelangelo was perhaps the only painter in all Christian history capable of making a worthy figure of God; and though his God was a being who inspired awe, he appeared as essentially reasonable and benevolent. This trust in the ultimate rationality of God and his creation was implied in the whole structure of the design, the innumerable different figures portrayed on the ceiling composing a unified whole. Man, especially as represented by Adam before the fall, was a creature of singular beauty and intelligence, capable of understanding the works of his creator.

In Michelangelo's later works, however, life became increasingly gloomy, harsh, and incomprehensible. Nothing could convey a sense of sadness and of longing for death and for the sleep that foreshadows it more plaintively than the Medici tombs (started in 1525). The brooding and melancholy faces of the two Medici princes and the four reclining figures supposedly representing different times of day and night all seem somnolent and drugged, facing realities only with the greatest reluctance. Michelangelo himself summarized the mood of his work in a four-line poem. "Dear is my sleep, but more to be mere stone, so long as ruin and dishonor reign. To see naught, to feel naught, is my great gain. Then wake me not, speak in an undertone." [8]

In the works of his old age the world was not only tragic but also incomprehensible, and this led to changes of artistic technique, which meant a break with the whole early development of Renaissance art and foreshadowed the coming of a new and more conflicted era. In some of his architectural designs, such as those for the Medici Chapel, there were elements of irrationality and disharmony which broke with the classical tradition that had been established by Brunelleschi; but the main work of his old age was *The Last Judgment* on the wall of the Sistine Chapel, completed in 1541, when he was sixty-six. In this picture adher-

---

[8] Translated by John Addington Symonds, and quoted in his *Life of Michelangelo* (London, 1893), p. 324.

ence to the rules of perspective and the other principles by which painters had sought to imitate nature was abandoned. Nor were there any remnants of the attractive human forms and the bright colors and landscapes which even the most religious-minded of Florentine artists rarely failed to include. This somber mass of naked human forms, shown in every possible variety of posture and movement, responding to the stern command of a Christ who does not bear the slightest resemblance to the bearded, pitying, and suffering figure of the gospels, can inspire every spectator only with awe and horror. Mary alone, sitting at Christ's right hand, shows some human warmth of feeling and pity at the frightening events that are taking place.

19

Mannerism and

Machiavelli

In the painting of the High Renaissance freedom and order seemed to be in harmony. Only an intensely individualistic society could have produced Leonardo and Michelangelo; but their work had passed beyond individualism, affirming an ideal order not dependent on any external authority but derived from the depths of the human spirit. Although individual human beings were no longer presented as separate and independent entities, as in much of the work of the Quattrocento, they still retained a life and character of their own. They were subordinated to the general design, but the design was immanent in the individuals, and not arbitrarily imposed on them.

On the political and social level there was nothing equivalent to the artistic sense of order. Italian society had lost the feeling of moral and religious unity and to an increasing extent was dominated by an egotistical and self-seeking individualism, wholly devoid of moral scruples. The growth of anarchy led eventually to a reaction back to earlier forms of order and brought the Renaissance to an end.

The process was hastened by foreign interference. Both France and Spain, having recently achieved unification by strong monarchies, were ready for imperialist expansion. Aggressive

378

energies that had formerly been occupied with internal conflicts could now be directed outward. It was the misfortune of Italy that she offered so many tempting prizes to foreign conquerors. Despising these interlopers, whom they liked to identify with the barbarians who had destroyed the Roman Empire a thousand years earlier, the Italians were unable to expel them. The lack of national unity, the egoism of the despots, and the reliance on hired *condottieri* for military services had ruinous effects. Italy could have been saved from foreign rule only if it had been united into a national state. But the Italians had no spiritual or emotional attitude, which could provide a mystique for patriotic loyalties, no moral reserves which could be evoked to cope with this kind of emergency. Instead of joining forces against the foreigners, most of the rulers of the Italian states tried to make use of them to further their own ambitions in interstate conflicts. For generations most of them had been accustomed to rely on intelligence and intrigue in pursuing private interests, and they had lost the capacity to deal with brute force.

In 1494 the King of France, Charles VIII, led an army into Italy, primarily in order to assert a hereditary claim to the kingdom of Naples. The threat of French control of Italy alarmed the Spaniards and led to a long period of intermittent conflict between the two powers. Charles VIII, young and foolish, was quickly driven back across the Alps, and died shortly after. But his immediate successors, Louis XII and Francis I, continued to be attracted by Italian adventures; and though Naples quickly became a Spanish possession, Milan remained a bone of contention. Meanwhile another cause of disturbance was the political ambition of the papacy, which sought to control most of central Italy. Cesare Borgia, acting for his father Pope Alexander VI (1492–1503), made himself notorious, even among the Italians, by the methods he employed in this objective, but the death of his father put an end to his career. The objective was largely accomplished by Julius II (1503–13), Michelangelo's patron, who was more at home on a battlefield than in a church and despite his advanced age (he was born in 1443) had a driving energy and an ambition equal, though in a different sphere, to Michelangelo's.

The wars continued until 1559, with intervals of an unstable peace, and ended in the total victory of Spain, which dominated Italy for several generations. One episode has a special significance in the history of the Renaissance. In 1527 a Spanish army, strengthened by a large corps of German mercenaries, descended upon Rome, where the Pope (Clement VII, of the Medici family) had invited attack by allying himself with the French. The resultant sack of Rome, followed by several months of occupation by soldiers who were totally out of control, put an end to the cultural predominance that had belonged to Rome for a generation and gave a shock to all educated Italians. There had been little respect for traditional morality in the Italy of the Renaissance, but there had been a faith in man's capacity to civilize himself, and this was wholly negated by the barbaric savagery displayed in the wholesale looting, raping, and murdering in the most revered city in Christendom. As Erasmus declared, "This was not the end of a city but the end of a world."

Meanwhile events happening elsewhere were diminishing the importance of Italy in the Western world. The voyages of discovery meant a shift of economic power from the Mediterranean countries to those bordering on the Atlantic and undermined the long-established control of the trade between western Europe and the Orient which had been so profitable to Venice and other Italian cities. Even more significant in bringing Italy's cultural predominance to an end was the Protestant Reformation, beginning with Luther's denunciation of the papacy in 1517. National churches, largely controlled by the secular authorities, took the place of Catholic internationalism in northern Europe; and church lands were confiscated and distributed among lay owners. Thus the wealth and power that had accrued to the papacy, and indirectly to Italy in general, were vastly reduced. Any further growth of Protestantism was prevented by the drastic purification of clerical practices in the Counter (or Catholic) Reformation, but as this meant not only a reformed clergy but also a revival of clerical authority and the imposition, at least in principle, of strict moral standards upon the laity, it brought the Renaissance to an end.

Under the circumstances any other outcome was impossible. Moral standards and political loyalties were so thoroughly eroded that Italian society could save itself from total disintegration only by submitting to political and moral authoritarianism. But one political commentator hoped for a different solution, in accord with Renaissance rationalism and individualism. This was the Florentine Niccolò Machiavelli. Devoted to the union of Italy as the only way of expelling the foreign barbarians, Machiavelli asked how a new state could be created in a society which no longer accepted any form of authority as legitimate. This was the central subject of all his writings. His method, as he himself pointed out, was similar to that of the painters. Like them, he turned for guidance partly to antiquity and partly to nature.

The rule of the Medici in Florence had temporarily ended in 1494, Lorenzo's son and successor, Piero, having proved himself incompetent; and the republic had been restored. Machiavelli served the republican government in several official positions, and always preferred it as superior to despotism. With the return of the Medici in 1512 (brought about by a Spanish army), he went into exile, though he subsequently made overtures to the new Florentine government, in the hope that it could be persuaded to adopt policies favorable to Italy. But the Medici made no response, and Machiavelli spent his last years, until his death in 1527, writing books in rural retirement. In his *History of Florence,* he analyzed the process of political decay which made republican government impractical, attributing the main blame for Italy's political problems to the papacy, which was incapable of establishing national unity and unwilling to allow it to be accomplished by any of the secular states. In *The Prince* he discussed the methods to be adopted in creating a new state. And in the most important of his works, the *Discourses on the First Ten Books of Livy,* he dealt in broader terms with the problems of creating a new state, taking his examples not from contempo-

rary despotisms but from the early history of the Roman republic.

Machiavelli was the first commentator to write about politics
in wholly rationalistic terms, as the science of power, and to
consider religious belief as simply a device for promoting the
necessary political loyalties and ethical standards. Yet his views
of human society were much too simple to be genuinely realistic
and were largely based not on observation, but on *a priori* reasoning derived from a few simple premises. The central problem
with which he was concerned—how to create and sustain a new
state in a society which lacked any concept of legitimacy—was,
in fact, insoluble, so that all Machiavelli's reasoning ended in
futility. His chief importance in history is to be found not in any
constructive formulation of conclusions but in his symbolizing a
view of life which horrified most of his contemporaries, even in
Italy.

By nature, Machiavelli believed, man was wholly evil. His
desires were insatiable and could be controlled only by strict
social discipline. "Nature has created men so that they desire
everything but are unable to attain it." [1] Political history therefore consisted largely of conflicts for power, mostly provoked
by the desire of the upper classes to rule and the disincli-
nation of the popular classes to obey.[2] Machiavelli made no
detailed analysis of economic factors or of class characteristics,
and did not explain how moral judgments could fairly be applied
to a world in which self-seeking was universal, or from what
principles they could be derived. But it is plain that he regarded
virtue, by which he meant chiefly patriotic loyalty and valor in
warfare, as always a social product brought about by wise legislation, the welfare of the state being the ultimate standard of value.
Religion was a necessary means for the promotion of virtue, and
no government could achieve security without it. "Everything

---

[1] Niccolò Machiavelli: *Discourses,* translated by C. E. Detmold (New York,
1940), 37.

[2] Machiavelli: *History of Florence,* 3–1.

that tends to favor religion (even though it were believed to be false) should be received and availed of to strengthen it." "As the observance of divine institutions is the cause of the greatness of republics, so the disregard of them produces their ruin; for where the fear of God is wanting, then the country will come to ruin unless it be sustained by the fear of the prince, which may temporarily supply the want of religion." [3] Thus the utility of a religion depended not on whether its doctrines were true but on the kind of ethic which it promoted. Machiavelli criticized Christianity for making its adherents too submissive; and the great examples of patriotic virtue which he held up for imitation were mostly pagan. Higher values, going beyond the need for order and for military strength, Machiavelli did not recognize. The conviction that freedom and order were ultimately harmonious and that this harmony could be realized by following the guidance of nature, which has inspired the Western world in all its periods of major creativity and had been implicit in the more important artistic achievements of the Renaissance, had no place at all in his thinking.

For Machiavelli, history was essentially meaningless because it was repetitive rather than progressive. Peoples retained the same general qualities—the Germans and the French, for example, remained "full of avarice, pride, cruelty and bad faith," whether they were destroying the Roman Empire or invading contemporary Italy; and social processes were generally cyclic. States "pass from order into confusion, and afterwards recur to a state of order again." "The nature of mundane affairs not allowing them to continue in an even course, when they have arrived at their greatest perfection, they soon begin to decline. In the same manner, having been reduced to disorder, and sunk to their utmost state of depression, unable to descend lower, they of necessity reascend." [4] Military valor produced repose, and this

---

[3] Machiavelli: *Discourses,* 1–12; 1–11.
[4] Machiavelli: *Discourses,* 3–43; 5–1.

led to disorder; but from disorder there developed a new order leading to virtue and military glory. This is a good example of Machiavelli's propensity for *a priori* argument unsupported by any factual evidence. The notion that states moved through cyclic processes was of Greek origin and was an example of the main deficiency of Greek thought: its inability to envisage the possibility of progress in time and its consequent view of the human condition as essentially unchanging. In the history of the Greek city-states, cyclic hypotheses may have had a little factual corroboration, though not very much. In Western history, both medieval and modern, they have had none at all. One cannot name a single Western state which may be regarded as reverting from good to evil and then, "of necessity," returning to good. Processes of growth and decline are much too complicated and prolonged to be explained in such simple terms. Here, as often, Machiavelli displayed none of the capacity for realistic observation with which his admirers have credited him.

Machiavelli regarded the Italy of his own time as at the bottom of the cycle. "The present," he declared, "has nothing that compensates for all the extreme misery, infamy and degradation of a period where there is neither observance of religion, law, or military discipline, and which is stained by every species of the lowest brutality." [5] Whence could salvation come? This is the problem confronting every thinker who depicts human beings as wholly evil, lacking in the capacity for spontaneous moral affirmation and for disinterested social and political loyalties; and the problem is, of course, insoluble. If all men were motivated simply by the drive for power, then civilization could never have begun.

Like other pessimists before and since, Machiavelli was compelled to postulate a *deus ex machina* in the form of some beneficent lawgiver free from the normal human vices. A state could be regenerated by the advent of "a good wise and powerful

---

[5] Machiavelli: *Discourses,* 2, Introduction.

citizen" who could make good laws. The most notable example in history of the effectiveness of good legislation was the early Roman republic, which had prospered under the guidance of a series of lawgivers, the results being manifested in "the prodigies of virtue and wisdom displayed by the kings, captains, citizens and legislators who sacrificed themselves for their country." [6]

Contemporary Italy, however, offered no opportunity for a lawgiver. A new state, preferably covering the whole nation, had first to be created; and because of the lack of appropriate loyalties and institutions, Machiavelli believed that it could be created only by a strong individual seeking power for himself and wholly unscrupulous in the methods he employed. This is the theme of *The Prince.* In order to understand this explosive little book, it is essential to recognize that Machiavelli, as he explained very clearly at the outset, was not concerned with established states, monarchical or republican. His subject was the formation of a new monarchy which was not supported by long-established traditions and institutions and had no claim to be considered as legitimate. Thus *The Prince* was not concerned with power in general, only with how it could be won and held where there were no religious beliefs and ethical ideals strong enough to give it support. Machiavelli's main example of the pursuit of power was the career of Cesare Borgia. He had apparently hoped that this vigorous, talented, and completely amoral adventurer could become the ruler of all Italy. But Cesare had disappeared into obscurity after the death of his father, and Machiavelli then transferred his hopes to the Medici family, writing *The Prince* largely for their edification.

Dealing with a situation that is relatively rare in human history, *The Prince* is by no means a major contribution to political thought. Most governments are normally accepted by their subjects as legitimate, their authority being supported by well-established moral and religious values. Changes in the con-

---

[6] Machiavelli: *Discourses,* 14, 1; 1, Introduction.

cept of legitimacy (from monarchy to democracy, for example) bring about major revolutions. The political condition of Renaissance Italy was highly unusual in that the traditional rules of legitimacy had lost their appeal and no new ones had won general acceptance. The city-states no longer recognized the authority of the empire; with the exception of Venice, they had failed to find a new focus for loyalty in republicanism, either oligarchical or democratic; and only a few of the despotic dynasties had held power long enough to make obedience habitual. But the only solution for Italy's political difficulties was a new legitimacy, and this could not be created by the rationalistic methods advocated by Machiavelli. All history has demonstrated that power can be lastingly effective only when it is exercised in accord with generally accepted ideals and beliefs. Power alone is necessarily self-defeating. But Italy had reached an impasse in which a recognition of this truth was impossible without a total change of intellectual attitudes. Machiavelli could conceive of moral and religious ideals only as subordinate to the welfare of the state, not as setting standards to which the state must conform and by which it established claims to loyalty.

For northern Europeans, both attracted and repelled by the Italy of the Renaissance, Machiavelli became a monstrous figure, symbolizing all that they found alarming in the growth of rationalism and the decline of traditional standards. In the literature of Elizabethan England, for example, he appears as a wholly destructive force, almost diabolical in quality, whose doctrines threatened to destroy all the values of the traditional order as expounded by such conservative-minded writers as Shakespeare. The Machiavelli of legend is far more significant than the Machiavelli of reality. It is true that Machiavelli found a mischievous pleasure in shocking his readers by praising Cesare Borgia's murders and deceptions, but his amoralism should not be overestimated. The real Machiavelli is important chiefly because of his awareness of the erosion of objective standards of truth and morality which was bringing the Renaissance to an end. There appeared to be nothing outside the individual to guide and direct him, so that he was left to invent his own subjective views of reality. Standards had degenerated into the arbitrary whims of individuals. The belief in objective principles was partially reinstated by the Counter Reformation; but before this became effective, Machiavellianism found its artistic equivalent in the movement known as mannerism.

The word "mannerism" has only recently come into general use among art historians. In its original Italian form (derived from *maniera,* usually translated "style") it was applied to a small group of mid-sixteenth-century artists, sometimes descriptively because they sought to achieve a strongly marked personal manner of painting, sometimes with the derogatory connotation that they were too deeply influenced by the styles of Raphael and Michelangelo. The original mannerists included Parmigianino, Pontormo, and Bronzino, all of whom were born in northern Italy close to the turn of the century. In recent years, however, art historians have given mannerism a much broader meaning and have extended it to a wide variety of artists, in northern and western Europe as well as in Italy and including at least two major figures, Tintoretto and El Greco. According to some historians, mannerism constitutes an important and distinctive epoch in the development of the arts, filling the gap between the decline of the Renaissance and the rise of the baroque.

The most obvious feature of Italian mannerism was that artists no longer considered it necessary to be convincingly realistic in their presentation of space. Earlier artists had, of course, departed from spatial realism, as can be seen in Leonardo's *Last Supper* and in Raphael's *Miraculous Draft of Fishes;* but they had continued to give the illusion of actuality, the spectator being deceived unless he analyzed the picture in detail. But the mannerists openly distorted the presentation of space, asserting their independence of the rules of perspective which had been carefully worked out in order to render space convincingly. In mannerist paintings, different groups of figures often occupy different spaces, and figures in the background may be almost as large as those in the foreground. The figures, moreover, tend to be lacking in the sense of material solidity and tactility and are often unnaturally elongated and portrayed from unusual and sometimes puzzling angles. Another departure from realistic observation is the emphasis on sharp clear-cut lines, especially on lines that are "serpentine." Thus, instead of striving to copy nature and to show all objects as existing in the same infinite three-dimensional space, painters now gave expression to an inner subjective design that visibly departed from nature. Mannerism was, therefore, a denial of the main principles that had animated the development of Italian art ever since Giotto. It was often regarded as originating with Michelangelo; but whereas Michelangelo's departures from realism were the products of a compelling inner vision comparable to that of a religious prophet, the mannerists gave the impression of seeking novelty for its own sake.

The new movement was defended on the basis of beliefs that had been implicit in the work of the High Renaissance but had never been fully expressed. Leonardo and Michelangelo had affirmed their own powers of independent creation, though they had always claimed to be guided by nature, or at least by laws that were somehow implicit in nature though not always visible and fully realized. But the mannerists openly claimed divine inspiration. According to Vasari, himself a mannerist painter as well as the first great art historian, "the artist's object was to make things not as nature makes them but as she *would* make them." [7] The arts originated in nature, but their master was "that divine light infused into us by special grace, which has made us not only superior to all other animals, but has exalted us, if it be permitted to speak, to the similitude of God himself." [8] Thus the mannerists claimed that the inner form (*desegno interno*) which guided the work of art was a reflection of the mind of God and was revealed to the artist by divine grace. But despite these

---

[7] Giorgio Vasari: *Lives of the Artists,* translated by A. B. Hinds (London, 1927), I, 350.

[8] Erwin Panofsky: *Renaissance and Renascences in Western Art,* p. 140.

claims to divine guidance, the sense of inner compulsion was lacking. The mannerists were inventing rather than discovering.

Mannerism may have been partly caused by a feeling that the High Renaissance had exhausted all the possibilities of the line of development which Giotto had originated, so that artists could avoid becoming mere imitators only by taking some new direction. The unsurpassable achievements of Leonardo and Michelangelo must have been burdensome to disciples who failed to assert their independence. But the most obvious feature of mannerism was that it was the product of a society which no longer retained any deep or convincing belief in order, and in which individuals, lacking the guidance of accepted values, were likely to feel insecure and alienated. Mannerist painting does not actually give the impression of being inspired by divine grace. Its values are much too uncertain.

The insecurity of the Italian mannerists is curiously conveyed by their portraits, especially those of Bronzino. They emphasize the aristocratic status of their sitters, as reflected in their appearance of decorum and refinement (Pontormo's *Lady and Her Dog* has been described by Bernard Berenson as the first portrait to stress the social position of the sitter); yet at the same time the poses seem a little strained and uneasy, as though these noble personages had to cling to external forms to prevent an inner collapse and the onset of chaos. A mask of self-discipline, isolating the sitter from other people, seems to cover a barely repressed inner self-consciousness and insecurity. The exuberant vitality and confidence of earlier Renaissance portraits have disappeared.

Much of the French and German art of the same period shows similar tendencies. In part, these were a continuation of trends that had become established during the medieval decadence, but they were also owing to Italian influences. The Italian mannerists could be copied much more easily than the masters of the High Renaissance. As had happened earlier with International Gothic, there was, in fact, a considerable interplay of mutual influences between Italy and the north, made possible by the similarity of artistic methods and objectives. If mannerism is given its recent extended meaning, as covering most of European art during the last three quarters of the sixteenth century, then it can be described as rich, varied, and technically skillful; but all of it was slightly offbeat, resorting to shock effects by choosing subjects that were bizarre and perverse. And if one excludes painters who gave expression to definite religious beliefs, then mannerism does not include any major master. It should perhaps be regarded not as a style, but rather as the lack of one. This was a period in which individual artists went their own way, looking for novel subjects and techniques instead of working within the limits of some established tradition.

In spite of their claims to be guided by divine grace, the Italian mannerists emphasized sexuality much more strongly than their predecessors had, while appearing to deny it. Their half-clothed figures were much more provocative than the nudes of which Michelangelo was so fond. Parmigianino described his own aesthetic objective as the creation of *venusta* (loveliness) and *grazia*. S. J. Freedberg speaks of him as displaying "a swift, almost volatile mellifluousness rather than the serene and simply comprehensible balance of the High Renaissance." His elongated figures suggested a dematerialization of the female body; yet at the same time, by portraying flesh sensuously and emphasizing the body by half concealing it, he aroused erotic feelings with a somewhat perverse flavor. Other mannerist painters tended to suggest homosexual or sadistic attitudes. What is one to make of Bronzino's *John the Baptist,* in which the saint is portrayed as a beautiful boy, naked except for a flimsy cloth loosely covering his loins?

Both in Italy and in the north, mannerist painting sought to titillate or horrify its viewers, and could make no central and controlling affirmation. Painters liked to portray scenes from unfamiliar and unexpected angles and were fond of unusual effects of light and darkness, the treatment of which owed much to Leonardo. They could represent an elegance and preciosity which seemed a little effete, and could also revel in scenes of gross coarseness and sensuality. They loved the female body;

never before or since has painting produced so many sensuous and provocative nymphs and goddesses. But this love was always a little perverse, arousing pornographic attitudes, and was often combined with sadistic or homosexual suggestions. Much of mannerist art consisted of representations of strange monsters and other dream figures which evoked feelings of horror. These tendencies spread to France in the 1530's, when Italian artists were brought to decorate the royal palaces. Sensuality, coarseness, and horror were carried further by German and Flemish artists of the same period. No nudes could exhibit a more perverse sensuality than those of Lucas Cranach; no exhibitions of human grossness could combine exuberance and horror more effectively than those of Hieronymus Bosch and of the elder Pieter Breughel.

The final phase in the history of Renaissance painting belongs to Venice. This uniquely beautiful city is a visible refutation of the notion that high artistic achievement must always be associated with noble political and ethical ideals, faith in human beings, and generosity of spirit. From its foundation by refugees from the mainland early in the Dark Ages, Venice had been controlled by an oligarchy of wealthy merchants whose primary concern was the enrichment of themselves and their city and who sternly repressed any democratic tendencies among the lower orders of society. It was much the most stable of the Italian states; but its policy was always determined by narrowly materialistic motivations, unilluminated by any respect for Christian or feudal ideals and incapable of self-sacrifice. When Western noblemen had gone crusading, the Venetian merchants had shown no compunction in taking advantage of their financial innocence. The only element of altruism in the mentality of the Venetians was their loyalty to their city, which took precedence over all broader obligations; and their city meant chiefly tangible wealth in the form of houses, banquets, festivities, and money. It was typical of Venice that the excellence of her prostitutes became famous all over Europe.

Yet the Venetian merchants, despite their devotion to money

and pleasure, created a city which was in itself a work of art; and
they had enough aesthetic sense to support a school of painters
whose work was surpassed only by the Florentines. It was to be
expected that Venetian art would be concerned primarily with
giving sensuous pleasure and that its subject matter would be
more secular and less religious than that of other regions of Italy.
The Venetians tended to emphasize color rather than linear design; and while religious themes were not lacking, artists found a
readier market for paintings which glorified the city and its pag-
eantry, presented the portraits of doges and other prominent
citizens, or reveled in beautiful landscapes or in nude Venuses.
Yet despite the lack of spiritual content, Venetian art was never
cheaply meretricious. Devotion to the city seemed somehow to
take the place of religious faith. And during the period when the
rest of Italy was succumbing to Spanish rule and the Counter
Reformation, Venice was still independent, though the main
sources of her wealth were drying up. Hence the Renaissance
lasted longer in Venice, by perhaps half a century, though it
could not exist permanently in this one city without support from
elsewhere. A sense of harmony and of relaxed enjoyment of the
sensuous world was the hallmark of the Venetian spirit, as displayed in the work of the two Bellinis, of Giorgione, and of
Titian. This is genuinely humanistic art, omitting every element
of transcendentalism and affirming the glory of man and the
beauty of the sensuous world.

The last major figure of Renaissance art, on the other hand,
introduced new elements. Tintoretto shared in the sense of easy
mastery and of material splendor which characterized his Venetian predecessors. It is impossible to contemplate the innumerable vast canvases and frescoes which he produced over a
period of fifty years without being awed by his fecundity and self-
confident power. His figures are vigorous, handsome, self-
assured, and richly varied. But, like the later Michelangelo, he
gave expression to attitudes which denied the basic faith of the
Renaissance and marked the end of the whole movement that had
originated with Giotto. He was no longer content to present fig-

ures in three-dimensional space as the ultimate reality. His art was a search for a new reality, composed of human figures but presenting paradoxes and conflicts which only religious belief could interpret and make meaningful. Like his mannerist predecessors, he took liberties with space and perspective. He presented his figures from unexpected angles, thus implying that reality varied according to the spectator's point of view. He presented many scenes of wild and frenetic movement; he liked to emphasize light and darkness, his skies usually being stormy and filled with lurid and murky cloud shapes; and his paintings were crowded with figures, many of them in strange postures and presented from unusual angles. A typical Tintoretto painting presents a swirling mass of figures in motion, shown in twilight under clouds about to be dissolved in a thunderstorm. His work is profoundly religious in spirit, but it is the sophisticated religion of the Counter Reformation, recognizing that there can be no easy harmony of faith and reason and that religion can be vital only if it accepts and transcends the paradoxical elements in human life. Truth is to be found not in direct contemplation of material things but in light; and light illuminates things not in the steady and even glow of daylight but in flashes of vision and inspiration illuminating fragments of the dark. Truth thus varies with the observer, yet it has a transcendental validity.

How far art had traveled since the High Renaissance can be seen in such a painting as Tintoretto's *The Last Supper,* in the church of San Giorgio, painted near the end of his life.[9] This

---

[9] In the course of an astonishingly long and productive career Tintoretto painted six versions of the last supper in different Venetian churches: in San Marcuolo in 1547; in San Trovaso about 1560; in San Paolo between 1565 and 1570; in San Stefano in 1580; in San Rocco between 1576 and 1581; and in San Giorgio between 1592 and 1594. The variations between these different versions of the gospel narrative illustrate Tintoretto's spiritual development. In the first picture in the series Christ is portrayed in the center and the disciples are clearly subordinated to him, as in all previous last suppers. In the later pictures Christ becomes progressively less conspicuous and more difficult to identify, and the disciples become involved in various activities unrelated to

differs far more sharply from Leonardo's version than Leonardo's from Ghirlandaio's. The room is dimly lit, and most of it is left in darkness, thus emphasizing a few bright objects. The angle from which the painting is focused is unclear, but apparently the scene is observed from a corner of the room, the table at which Christ and his disciples are eating being placed diagonally across the left side of the picture. The room is crowded with figures, nearly thirty altogether, including half a dozen angels and (apparently) God the Father descending from the ceiling, and most of them are in convulsive movement. The two figures placed most prominently in the foreground, a couple of waitresses, are the least important for the theme of the painting. But none of the figures is clearly marked out from the others, and Christ, seated near the far end of the table, is difficult to identify. None of the figures seems to have an independent life, the painting being carefully organized to convey one total effect. This was the religion of the Counter Reformation, in which truth was to be found in transcendental visions, not in the daylight world of realistic space and time.

---

the central theme. The San Giorgio version is the last and most meaningful of the series. It exhibits divine grace as manifested not in the ordinary processes of nature but in special manifestations which man must search for and which run counter to realistic expectations.

20

Humanists and Protestants

Meanwhile the aims and attitudes of the Renaissance had been spreading to other parts of Europe, and the dominant groups, lay and clerical, had been acquiring some of its faith in human power, its passionate enthusiasm for humanistic studies, and its easy sensuality. Yet until the later decades of the sixteenth century there was notably less creativity elsewhere than in Italy; and only in literature, not in any of the visual arts, did the northern achievement eventually surpass that of the Italians. In the north, and also in Spain, the whole Renaissance view of life remained highly controversial. In Italy it had evolved without serious opposition; and when finally the preservation of some kind of social order made different values necessary, the Italians could turn back with little sense of strain to the authoritarianism represented by the Catholic Reformation. But in the northern countries, traditional beliefs and attitudes had retained more vitality and could not easily be reconciled with those of the Renaissance. To most educated northerners the rationalism and sensuousness of Italians like Machiavelli appeared as destructive and anarchical forces which could lead only to the dissolution of all social order.

Most Europeans still accepted monarchy as the only natural and effective form of government, ordained by God and symbolizing the unity of the divine order of the universe. Kingship, it must be admitted, was criticized more sharply than in earlier centuries, but the major challenge to all forms of authority, clerical and secular, came not from the growth of rationalism, but from the mystical individualism based on religious belief which had been developing in the Netherlands and the Rhineland during the later Middle Ages and which—incidentally—was largely hostile to the Renaissance. This movement, combined with various political and economic factors, led in the early sixteenth century to the Protestant Reformation. Although the movement was quickly politicalized, its sources were to be found in the belief of the mystics that the individual who was inspired by divine grace had a direct communion with God and did not need the mediation of priests and religious institutions.

Humanism began to develop in northern Europe in the late fifteenth century. In its northern form it was closely allied with movements for the reform of religion and remained sharply opposed to all manifestations of paganism. Its ideal was a Christianity which would stress ethics rather than theology and would restore the simple beliefs and ways of living that had been displayed by the early Church before it had been perverted by Constantine. Its most famous spokesman was Erasmus, who was both the most learned scholar of his time and a firm opponent of almost every aspect of the Italian Renaissance. Apart from his devotion to classical scholarship, he should perhaps be defined not as a spokesman of the Renaissance, but as the representative of a northern reaction against it. "I brought it about," he declared, "that humanism, which among the Italians and especially among the Romans, savored of nothing but pure paganism, began nobly to celebrate Christ." [1] It is significant that this individualistic mysticism and moralism had developed in areas of Europe where kingship had never established deep roots or inspired any deep respect and where government was exercised chiefly by local noblemen and merchants. This was important not only as a matter of practical politics. The individual could not allay his insecurities by thinking of himself as a member of a visible

---

[1] Quoted in Hiram Haydn: *The Counter-Renaissance*, p. 66.

God-created order. He had therefore to develop a sense of spiritual independence, giving allegiance directly to God rather than to God's representatives on earth, whether lay or clerical.

In the three major states of western Europe (France, Spain, and England), on the other hand, power now belonged to strong monarchies which worked through centralized and well-established institutions. In the early years of the sixteenth century the kings of the three countries appeared to have relatively enlightened attitudes, displaying a sympathetic interest in the growth of learning and promising to support religious reforms as long as they did not become heretical. But in spite of their professed adhesion to Erasmean values, they continued to cherish medieval ideals of chivalry, regarding military glory as a nobler and more necessary source of fame than cultural achievement. Intermittent warfare among the three states therefore continued, though the wars were on a minor scale and generally had no serious consequences.

Erasmus and his disciples deplored this addiction to military glory and hoped that their royal patrons would recognize the supremacy of learning and no longer waste their substance on death and destruction. The Christian humanism of northern Europe was associated with a rational attitude to political and ethical values. But Erasmean ideals had little practical influence; and if one examines the literature and art of northern Europe in the sixteenth century for their deeper significance and implications, one finds that much gives expression to very different attitudes. Despite the attractions of the Italian Renaissance, many writers and artists felt a stronger sympathy for the traditional views of man and man's society. Most northern European scholars and writers continued to regard human society as an ordered unity, expressing suspicion and dislike for the growing strength of individualism, both in politics and in economic developments. And they continued to glorify the chivalric code, regarding the warrior as the noblest specimen of humanity and as morally far superior to the merchant and the politician. Chivalry was still regarded as an essential part of the social order.

This conflict of views and values was a main underlying theme of much of the literature of the northern Renaissance; and while its authors may have delighted in the physical beauties of Italian art, they were alarmed by the lack of political and moral standards among the Italians and the consequent Machiavellianism. The ideals and practices of chivalry had come to be regarded as symbolic of the whole medieval viewpoint. Spain was the country where this glorification of chivalry was most deeply rooted and lasted longest; and the greatest work of Spanish literature presented its ideals, expressed by Don Quixote, as no longer valid in realistic terms but as essentially nobler than the attitudes that had replaced them. This nostalgia for an idealized feudalism can be found in much of the writing of the sixteenth century, though it does not often achieve fully overt and conscious expression.[2]

Yet in spite of the continuing glorification of royal authority and the idealization of the feudal past, the earlier years of the sixteenth century were a relatively optimistic period. Humanist scholarship and a recognition of its importance were gaining

---

[2] Consider, for example, the wording of a passage in Shakespeare's *Othello*, a play which was primarily concerned with the private lives of the principal characters, without presenting any political implications. When Othello becomes convinced of Desdemona's violation of her marriage vows, he immediately sees this as a threat to all ordered society, and the aspect of society which he chooses for emphasis is the glory of chivalric warfare. "Chaos has come again," he exclaims, and he must bid farewell to all "the pride, pomp and circumstance of glorious war." We may suppose that Shakespeare was not fully aware of the implications of Othello's remarks, but the wording makes it inescapably plain that an act of unchastity meant a denial of the whole social order, and that the most important part of that order was the code of chivalric warfare. This was Othello's view, and it seems probable that it was also Shakespeare's. Such an interpretation of the play also explains the role played by Iago. Most readers feel that Iago's combination of rationalism and destructive malice does not make a plausible character and that he seems inadequately motivated toward the acts of villainy that he performs. But Iago represents the Italian Renaissance as it appeared to a northern European who still cherished medieval values. This interpretation does not make him a plausible character within the limits of the play, but it explains Shakespeare's intentions.

398

ground; and there were hopes of a new era of peace and order based on confidence in human nature. The new spirit that was spreading through the West was exemplified in Thomas More's *Utopia* (published in 1516). Before the 1530's it was not necessary for individuals to choose sides in a conflict of beliefs, and humanist reformers could work for general agreement as to the need for a more spiritual religion which would give less emphasis to mechanical details of ritual and dogma.

Thus for a brief period cultural tolerance and trust in human reason seemed to be increasing, and there were hopes of a social transformation that might lead to a new world order. While humanism in its northern religious form was the main source of the new spirit—in the northern Renaissance there was very little of the frank paganism of Italy—a number of extraneous developments contributed to it. Especially important were the inventions of paper and printing (the former was probably the more important), which made possible the spread of literacy over wide segments of the population. Important in a different way was the discovery of America and of sea routes to the East, which stimulated human self-confidence and the human imagination, in addition to promoting economic growth. This period in Western history, lasting for all too brief an interval, may be known as the Erasmean moment.

· · ·

Born out of wedlock, of middle-class parents, in the Dutch city of Gouda in or about the year 1469, Erasmus imbibed at the school of the Brethren of the Common Life at Deventer both classical scholarship and a religion which stressed ethics and mysticism. Subsequently his guardians confined him in a monastery, where he spent six miserable years, acquiring a hatred of monasticism to which he gave frequent and bitter expression in later years. Finally he secured permission to move to Paris to study theology, and thereafter was able to support himself as a private tutor to young noblemen and as a literary hack. At home wherever there were classical scholars, Erasmus never settled anywhere permanently. During his earlier life, a visit to England in 1499 and another from 1509 to 1514 were especially important because he encountered humanist scholars, notably John Colet and Thomas More, who confirmed his conception of religion as primarily a simple and enlightened ethical code. His later life was spent mostly at Louvain, Basel, and Freiburg. Writing books addressed largely to general readers, not only to scholars, he was perhaps too concerned with denouncing and ridiculing contemporary abuses to take rank as a writer of lasting importance, though his eloquence and wit would certainly have been better remembered if he had written in one of the major vernaculars rather than in Ciceronian Latin. Probably his most important achievement was his Latin translation of the New Testament, which showed how deeply the Christianity of the Renaissance Popes differed from that of the gospels. In letters and shorter pieces he was outspoken in attacking clerical corruption; and despising the passion for military glory which continued to animate most Renaissance kings, he denounced war as always evil. The obsequiousness (at least by modern standards) with which he wrote to kings and noblemen may disturb some twentieth-century readers, but it must be remembered that any critic of the Church incurred real dangers. Kings and bishops, even those who had given patronage to scholars, easily changed their minds with little warning; and scholars who expressed radical views with too much frankness were sometimes convicted of heresy and sentenced with an appalling casualness to be burned alive.

Erasmus had little interest in any of the arts, and the essence of his teaching was that "to be a philosopher and to be a Christian is synonymous in fact. The only difference is the nomenclature." [3] His basic beliefs probably owed more to late medieval mysticism than to the humanist movement. Despite a lack of all hereditary advantages and a career devoted mainly to

---

[3] Quoted in Haydn: op. cit., p. 46.

classical and Christian scholarship, Erasmus, like Petrarch two centuries earlier, became the most widely known man in Europe. By his own account (he was probably telling the truth, though modesty was not one of his more conspicuous virtues), his admirers included the emperor and the kings of England, France, and Denmark, "along with more princes, more bishops, more learned and honorable men than I can name, not only in England, France, Flanders and Germany, but even in Poland and Hungary." [4] Erasmus's extraordinary career was made possible by the invention of the printing press and by the continued use of classical Latin as a lingua franca among men of learning. All this was accomplished by a man in poor health (he had the stone from a relatively early age), with no powerful protector, little animal vitality, and nothing to support him except his humanistic learning and his capacity for pungent criticism of anything that interfered with the ethics of the gospels.

Although the Christian humanism represented by Erasmus and his disciples won the enthusiastic support of many men of learning who looked forward to a general reformation brought about by peaceful persuasion, it never became an organized movement or acquired any appreciable popular support. It was an attitude that was necessarily restricted to students of the classics and that considerably exaggerated the resemblances between classicism and the gospels. The morality of Greek and Roman paganism, even in its most enlightened forms, was much further from Christianity than Erasmus was willing to recognize. Yet Christian humanism continued to appeal to scholars and poets for several generations. And in spite of its inner contradictions and its unrealistic hopefulness about human nature, its influence was widespread and mostly beneficial. It promoted a spirit of tolerance and of confidence in man's capacity to civilize himself

---

[4] Quoted in Trevor-Roper: *Men and Events: Historical Essays* (London, 1957), p. 36. Erasmus should have included Spain, where there was a strong Erasmean movement among the clergy, though it was eventually suppressed by the monarchy.

which is rare in any period of history and was especially necessary in an age of acute religious conflicts. Erasmus left little behind him but a name; his books soon ceased to be read. But his memory has continued, long after his death, to support civilization.

. . .

The religious revolution which many people hoped that Erasmus would lead was started in the year 1517 by Martin Luther. Luther was a man of learning and of undeniable intellectual ability, but what was more important was his emotional quality. Major social changes are never brought about by appeals to reason. Much more powerful and compelling forces are necessary. Men who change the course of history present views of life which may appear to be rational, but which actually are projections of intense emotional experience. What gives cogency to the work of the great innovators is not any appearance of logic, but the intensity of the emotional responses which they express and elicit. Luther appeared at first to be a disciple of Erasmus; but his beliefs were determined not by any general interest in theological reform, but by cataclysmic emotional experiences which drove him to search for a personal salvation. Like Erasmus, Luther acquired an individualistic view of religion, believing in direct contact between the human soul and the divine spirit, without intermediaries. But in place of Erasmus's gentle humanism, he insisted on the universality of sin and believed that man could be saved only by emotional experiences which transcended reason.

The son of a middle-class mine owner in Saxony, Luther was educated by parents who expected him to have a distinguished worldly career. But his fear of damnation outweighed all other considerations; and in 1505, at the age of twenty-two, he fled from the world and sought relief from his anxieties by becoming a monk. His fears had been sharpened by the death of a friend who was struck by lightning. Thenceforth his career was determined by his fear of damnation. Unable to find any authority, either clerical or secular, from which he could gather moral guidance and support, he could only search for some inner source of reassurance. This was, of course, in accord with traditional Christianity (though not with the corrupt Church of the Renaissance), which had always affirmed that salvation was to be obtained only by the union of the individual with the divine spirit. Where Luther deviated from the traditional experience was in the hypertension of his sense of guilt. He regarded the natural man as so wholly drenched in sin that he could do nothing to save himself from God's just anger. Luther's experience can, of course, be made intelligible to modern readers only by presenting it in the vocabulary of psychiatry.

For seven years Luther struggled to overcome his anxiety by complying with all the rules of monastic life and by the practice of asceticism. "I wore myself out in self-sacrifice," he declared afterward, "tormenting myself with fastings, vigils, prayers, and other burdensome tasks, with the idea of attaining to righteousness by my works. I observed the rule of my order so strictly that I venture to say that if ever a monk could have attained heaven through monkery, I should certainly have got there." "I have known a man," he declared, speaking of himself, "who asserted that he had often suffered these pains of hell at a very brief interval of time, so grave and so infernal that neither tongue could speak nor pen describe them, nor one who has not experienced them can believe so that if they were completed or lasted half an hour, yea six minutes, he would utterly perish and all his bones would be reduced to ashes. Then God appears fearfully angry and along with him the whole creation. There is no flight, then, no consolation either within or without, but accusation on all sides. . . . At such a moment the soul cannot believe that it can be redeemed." [5]

The great illumination by which Luther ceased to fear divine punishment was associated with a rediscovery of the theology of

---

[5] Quoted in James Mackinnon: *Luther and the Reformation,* I, 93, 114.

St. Paul, and more particularly of the Epistle to the Romans. Man's works, he realized, must always be inadequate and tainted with sin and hence could never earn salvation. As long as one trusted in the efficacy of works, one was among the damned. Salvation was the fruit of faith. This was the free gift of divine grace to those human beings who had been elected, and man became assured of it by recognizing his sinfulness and turning to communion with God, knowing that the penalty for the sins of humanity had been paid by Christ on the cross. Good works would be one of the consequences of salvation, but could never be its cause.

How far can Luther's spiritual experience be attributed to social factors as well as to his personal development? After his break with the papacy, when he began to speak frankly and openly about the essence of Christian experience as he knew it, he quickly won mass support. Are we to suppose that the German people were passing through a phase of economic and social development which sharpened their anxieties and sense of insecurity and made them ready to respond to a teacher who promised them salvation by a more direct way than had been customary in the Roman Church? [6] All societies engender anxiety, the causes of which are both internal and external. It is unlikely that the degree of anxiety in early sixteenth-century Germany was

---

[6] There was never a German school of painting, as there was a French and an Italian school; but from time to time there have been Germans who painted, particularly during the Renaissance, and some of them have given expression to attitudes bearing some relation to the religious development of Germany. Two of them, who were older contemporaries of Luther, did work excelled only by the greatest of the Italians: Albrecht Dürer and Matthias Grünewald. Grünewald is remembered chiefly for the painting of a large altarpiece in a monastic house at Isenheim in Alsace. Dürer, on the other hand, was immensely productive, though he apparently preferred woodcuts to paintings. During a visit to Italy he acquired a deep interest in the theory of art, about which he wrote extensively. The work of both men displays intense and complex feelings, verging on hysteria, and presents a view of life that is visibly lacking in the self-confident sense of mastery which characterizes most of the Italians.

conspicuously stronger than at other periods or that one can trace any elements in Luther's teaching which had a direct relevance to contemporary social problems. Insofar as Luther's doctrines differed from those of other Christian prophets, the causes are to be found in his personal development rather than in social trends. Luther felt and expressed the Christian experience with such intensity that he would have been capable of making converts in any kind of Christian society. His teaching began as a cry from the abyss, not as a social program; and by demonstrating in his own development how anxiety was overcome by Christian belief, he inaugurated a new phase in the history of religion.

Man's self-surrender to the spirit of God and his consequent sense of freedom from sin and guilt had always been the essence of Christian experience, though there had been variations in interpretation. Luther's version of it displayed some significant differences from that prevalent in the Middle Ages. In the first place, it was much closer to the original Pauline version and less affected by Platonism. The love which it sought to promote was *agape* rather than *eros*. In the second place, it combined a strong individualism in the interpretation of Christian experience with a strong authoritarianism in all secular matters. Luther's sole concern was the relationship of God and the individual soul, and he had virtually nothing to say about social organization, the laws of nature, and other important questions which had normally formed a part of Christian teaching. His view of human nature was far blacker than that of orthodox Christian doctrine, and this meant that he regarded worldly society as incapable of redemption and of little concern to theology.

Thus Luther, while still (in his own opinion) a loyal member of the Catholic Church, had been led by personal experience to a view of religion fundamentally different from that of Renaissance Christianity. Given his volcanic temperament and disregard for considerations of personal safety, an open schism could scarcely be prevented. It began in 1517, when Luther made public protest against the sale of indulgences. This sale was authorized by the Pope to cover certain expenses incurred by the Church, and contributors were led to believe that their stay in purgatory would be substantially reduced. This was therefore an especially glaring example of the belief (repudiated by Luther) that human sins could be partially canceled by what the Church affirmed to be good works. Luther's protests met only with clerical antagonism, and within the next few years he broke completely with papal authority. This marked the beginning of Protestantism. Its rapid spread through most of northern Europe was largely the result of materialistic motivations which had no connection with theology. Kings and noblemen for many generations had been resentful of papal demands for money and envious of the wealth and estates of bishops and monastic orders. The adoption of Protestantism enabled them to expropriate church lands and other properties, most of which became the property either of the monarch or of the secular nobility. Also of importance was the growth of nationalistic sentiment. The new Protestant churches were controlled by secular authorities who had long resented the supremacy claimed by papal officials whose headquarters were in Italy. Once Luther had provided religious justifications for Protestantism, the authority of the Roman Church was quickly ended in most of northern Germany and in Scandinavia and England; and groups of Protestant believers made considerable headway in southern Germany, France, and the Netherlands. It was not until the practices of the Roman Church had been radically purified by the Catholic Reformation that the growth of Protestantism was halted.

Rediscovering Pauline theology, with its belief that by making a total surrender of the self the individual could achieve union with God and freedom from all his anxieties, Protestantism gave its adherents a new sense of liberation, but its individualism was restricted to the realm of spiritual experience and had few positive political or social implications. The most obvious political result of the Lutheran revolt was the strengthening of the secular state. According to Luther, only a small minority of the human race was capable of redemption, and the unredeemed could be controlled only by the naked and brutal exercise of power. Luther regarded all attempts at reforming society as necessarily futile, and was therefore an extreme conservative in his political views. On a few occasions he expressed a more democratic attitude. "The spiritual man judges all things," he affirmed. "The Christian congregation or community has the right and power to judge of doctrine and appoint and depose its teachers." [7] But he never extended such affirmations to secular affairs.

Some of his supporters were not content with the reform of religion and believed that the Christian Church should promote social revolution in this world as well as personal salvation in the next. These ideas spread to the exploited peasants of southern Germany, leading to a large-scale rebellion in 1524, and brought about a resurgence of the belief in the rapid approach of the millennium, preached by a radical sect known as Anabaptists. But for Luther man was too deeply tainted with sin for social revolution to be possible. Always giving voice to extremist opinions, Luther bitterly denounced the rebellious peasants and called for wholesale slaughter, a panacea which the upper classes were only too ready to adopt. Luther's attitude toward worldly affairs had a lasting and deleterious effect on the political development of northern Germany.

Luther's main and lasting political importance, however, was in initiating processes which led to the total separation of church and state. The Catholic Church, despite its emphasis on the mystical experience of individuals, had never fully transcended the primeval conception of religious ritual and belief as designed to affirm the submission to God of the community as a whole and thereby to win divine protection against earthly enemies. The notion of a church divorced from society and consisting only of its own members had ceased to be tenable in the fourth century of our era, when Constantine made Christianity the official religion of the Roman Empire. It was now revived in the Protestant

---

[7] Mackinnon: op. cit., III, 93, 114.

movement, though several generations passed before it achieved fully explicit acceptance.

If Protestantism was to survive, it needed more convincing logic and more effective organization than Luther was able to establish. These were supplied by the Frenchman John Calvin, who completed the first edition of his comprehensive *Institutes of the Christian Religion* in 1536 and subsequently sought security in the Swiss city-state of Geneva, where he became a leading figure until his death in 1564. In Calvin's writings there is no trace of the emotional drives that had determined Luther's revolt against Rome. The *Institutes* accepted Luther's experience of redemption as valid, regarding divine inspiration and the words of the Bible as the two ultimate authorities by which all Christians should be guided and judged. But Calvin was more interested in presenting Protestant doctrine as comprehensive and coherent and in working out the details of a new kind of organization. Church and state, though closely connected, were to become two separate organizations; and the Church, no longer to be regarded as all-inclusive, should consist only of those persons who seemed to be among the redeemed. This meant that the Church was superior to the state, and its spokesmen, being endowed with divine knowledge, should formulate the policies to be followed by the secular authorities. In practice, Calvinist church membership came mostly from the middle class, both urban and rural; and although Calvin was careful to insist that the king must be obeyed and that there was no right of rebellion, the adoption of his doctrines would have deprived monarchy of effective authority and made it subordinate to middle-class believers. In practice the spread of Calvinism was partially responsible for civil wars in France, the Netherlands, Scotland, England, and southern Germany.

For those persons who could no longer accept either the Catholic Church or the monarchical state as authoritative expressions of the will of God, there were strong reasons for the adoption of Calvinism. It gave the individual the assurance of belonging to a divinely guided organization which would protect him in this life and reward him with eternal happiness in the next and would take the place of secular authority. By teaching him the virtues of hard work and thrift, it generally enabled him to win economic success. Repudiating monasticism, it taught an asceticism of daily life which was represented as enjoying divine approval; but it also inculcated the doctrine that the rich man should consider himself the trustee of the wealth that he had accumulated, not as its absolute owner. Its ethic was comprehensive, but not unduly severe, though later generations of Calvinists, for reasons that are not easy to define, gradually adopted much stricter attitudes. But Calvin himself declared that men should be capable of enjoyment in this world no less than in the next. "Ivory and gold and riches are the good creatures of God," Calvin declared, "permitted, nay destined by divine power, for the use of man; nor was it ever forbidden to laugh, or to be full, or to add new to old and hereditary possessions, or to be delighted with music or to drink wine." [8]

Calvinism was one of the major influences in the transition from medieval to modern society, especially in leading to the separation of church and state; and though Calvin could resort to extreme penalties for men whom he regarded as dangerously heretical (understandably, posterity has never forgiven him for the burning of Servetus), his ethical standards retained some of the mildness of Renaissance humanism. Calvin has often been blamed for restrictions which actually were adopted by the Protestant churches in the nineteenth century. Paradoxically, the long-term result of the growth of Calvinism was to separate church and state and hence to make it possible for the individual to choose freely his own brand of religion. This was an important aspect of the breakdown of the medieval belief in unity.

The concept of religious freedom, however, won support very slowly. In the sixteenth century it remained unknown except among small mystical groups whose doctrines were regarded by persons in authority as self-evidently absurd.

---

[8] John Calvin: *Institutes of the Christian Religion,* III, 19.

21

France and Spain

Among the transalpine countries it was France that was most friendly to the influences of the Renaissance and where the conflict between northern and Italian attitudes was mildest and least overt. But France did not maintain the cultural leadership that she had exercised during the early Middle Ages, and her contributions to the Renaissance included little that was new or deeply original. Her main role during the sixteenth century was that of intermediary, transmitting Italian attitudes and artistic techniques to her northern neighbors.

The center of Renaissance influence was the royal court, and this gave it a somewhat esoteric quality. Popular art forms, especially those connected with religion, mostly continued to be largely medieval in attitude. But the tone and subject matter of the more elevated forms of art depended largely on the tastes of the reigning monarch and the leading noblemen of his court. Art patrons connected with the court favored imitation of the Italians and were interested, in general, in arts that could be enjoyed, especially those that emphasized sexuality and that were secular in tone and subject matter. The lack of popular appeal was regarded as a proof of excellence. And although there were no artistic creations of the highest quality, the poets and artists of this period developed new techniques borrowed from the Italians which prepared the way for the high achievements of French literature during the seventeenth century.

The transportation from Italy to France of masses of art objects, accompanied by appropriate craftsmen, began with Charles VIII's invasion of 1494. But it was not until the accession of Francis I (1515–47) that the French court began to be hospitable to Italian artists on a higher level. A glamorous figure, eager to dominate every part of his government and brimming with energy, sensuous enjoyment, and self-esteem, Francis seemed to humanist observers to be capable of giving intelligent and enlightened patronage to writers and artists. In actuality his taste for the arts was quite superficial. He preferred the thrills and sensations of hand-to-hand conflict in battle (the invention of gunpowder had so far made very little difference to warfare), and this preference had the enthusiastic support of most of the young noblemen of the country. When decisions had to be made, it became obvious that Francis's view of life was largely medieval and that his humanist admirers had been misled in supposing that he would accept new values.

In painting the record of Renaissance France was not impressive, largely because the Italians whom the French considered as masters belonged to the decadent mannerist school. At the instigation of King Francis, several Italian mannerists, the most important being Giovanni Battista Rosso and Francesco Primaticcio, moved to France early in the sixteenth century, settling in the royal palace of Fontainebleau, where they established a school. This set the standards for French official and aristocratic art for the next half-century. The most obvious characteristic of the Fontainebleau group was their love for depicting femininity, a commodity with which they decorated vast stretches of the palace walls. Not until the following century did France produce any artist of major importance (Nicolas Poussin was born in 1594). Much more interesting work was being done in Flanders by men like Pieter Breughel and Hieronymus Bosch, but their popular subject matter and their Flemish origins prevented their recognition by the French court.

In architecture there was a similar dichotomy of styles. The tastes of the court promoted the adoption of Italian classicism;

but this did not extend to church buildings, in which the court probably had no interest and which continued until near the end of the sixteenth century to conform to Gothic traditions. This late Gothic was faithful to its name "flamboyant," being often extravagantly decorated; but it retained the basic characteristics which had been established in the earlier Middle Ages. This was an art form which continued to evoke popular support. The new Renaissance art styles, on the other hand, were adopted mostly by the court and the nobility.

In the field of secular building there were pressing reasons for stylistic innovation. During the Middle Ages the upper classes had been impelled to live in castles, which provided security at the price of acute discomfort. The spread of peace and the end of private warfare made it possible for them to build themselves palaces, which were not intended to provide security but which supplied their owners with both beauty and comfort. From the Renaissance down to the rise of industry and the growth of cities in the nineteenth century, palaces, both for the kings and for the nobility, remained the most important of architectural forms. Palace-building was a favorite occupation of Francis I. He was responsible for several immense structures in the Loire valley and also on the outskirts of Paris. These were designed to glorify the king and to provide accommodation for the hundreds of aristocratic courtiers who were expected to accompany him when he went hunting or engaged in some other form of large-scale royal entertainment.

The architects and craftsmen who built the palaces appear to have been mostly French, though to please the king they did their best to adopt Italian styles. The imitation of the Italians became closer and more accurate in the 1540's when Sebastiano Serlio, an Italian connoisseur of architecture and author of books setting forth the essentials of the classical style, settled in France, bringing his books with him. This fusion of styles (most clearly exemplified by the palace of Chambord) recalled the combination of northern and Mediterranean influences in the art of Carolingian France. In general, the ground-floor plans tended to conform

412

with the ordered harmony and simplicity of Italian classicism, while the upper stories retained a Gothic exuberance illustrated especially in the proliferation of turrets and spires.[1]

Most of the literature of this period was written by authors who were close to the court, their main importance in literary history being the introduction of Italian styles. This applied to poets like Clément Marot and Pierre Ronsard and to the king's sister, Margaret, whose *Heptameron* was an imitation of Boccaccio's *Decameron,* and (in spite of its author's professed Protestantism) almost as frankly sexual as the original. But one major figure had no connection with the court and gave expression to the Erasmean attitude with complete frankness, though in an utterly different style and form. This was François Rabelais, who published four books about Gargantua and Pantagruel between 1534 and 1546. In Rabelais, France produced her first major writer whose values (despite the medieval form in which they were expressed) were recognizably modern. Rabelais's optimistic point of view reflected the French spirit in the early years of the sixteenth century, and could not have developed in the same way at any other period of French history.

Gargantua owed almost nothing to Italy, being an independent expression of the northern Renaissance. The tone of the book is tolerant and positive, with little sense of conflict. The popular literature of medieval France had included as one of its genres tall stories about giants, and Rabelais himself had actually pro-

---

[1] In the late Middle Ages various different factors tended to make castles obsolete. In particular, the adoption of new kinds of weapons (gunpowder being the most important) caused them to be less defensible, while the growth of wealth and of a sense of security (owing largely to the abolition of private warfare) caused the wealthier members of the upper class to seek more domestic comfort. There was, in fact, a continuing revolution in ways of living, with lasting and far-reaching consequences, the most significant being perhaps the growth of privacy and the recognition of its advantages. Where earlier generations had built castles (in which almost all human needs were satisfied in one big central hall), the rich men of the sixteenth century, headed by the king, built palaces which provided adequate space and comfort for their inmates, including, in particular, numerous rooms equipped with doors.

duced a specimen before it occurred to him that this could be used as a vehicle for presenting his views on more serious subjects. Thus his work marked no sharp break with the past. Otherwise the main influence which Rabelais acknowledged was that of Erasmus, to whom he had written a most admiring letter in the year 1532. In subject matter and style nothing could be more different than Erasmus's restrained and intellectual essays about Christian morality and Rabelais's exuberant indecency and delighted acceptance of every aspect of human nature, including especially those which polite society chooses to regard as unmentionable. Yet both men were optimistic about human potentialities, both of them simplified Christianity, seeing no value in the involved theological argumentation of the scholastics, and both of them communicated tolerance and optimism, suggesting that human potentialities were limitless.

In form, *Gargantua and Pantagruel* is a collection of tall stories about giants. Nothing could be more free-flowing and uninhibited, and apparently the promotion of laughter is the only objective. But throughout the whole narrative Rabelais is concerned with the promotion of humanistic values. His two central characters, the two giants after whom the book is named, evoke almost constant laughter by their giant performances; but both Gargantua and Pantagruel are champions of humanism, and the whole tone of the book promotes a warm support of its values. This is exemplified with special clarity in Rabelais's account of the ideal education which his main characters received, in his hostile references to monasticism, and in his advocacy of peace and his caustic accounts of the military ambitions of kings. The most explicit statement of his values is his account of Gargantua's Abbey of Thélème, which is the direct opposite of a medieval abbey, since women are admitted (if they are sufficiently beautiful), the inmates are free to come and go as they please, may marry, are expected to be rich, and may all live in utter freedom, the general motto being "Do what you will." The most important of the rooms of the abbey are the six libraries for books in the six languages of most use to humanists (Greek, Latin, Hebrew, French, Italian, and Spanish). From Rabelais's description of this ideal abbey it is apparent that he trusted human beings to be virtuous if conditions were favorable, and felt that they were entitled to complete moral freedom.

The Protestant Reformation quickly put an end to the optimism of the early sixteenth century and inaugurated a gloomy period of religious warfare, which began in France in the 1560's.

The Catholic Church responded to the Protestant revolt by reforming its practices but refused to make any change in its beliefs. Derived from divine revelation, they were not considered subject to rational investigation and revision, acceptance being based on the authority of the Church, which transcended reason. This uncompromising response to Lutheranism was affirmed by the Council of Trent, which held its first meetings in 1545. The Protestant movement was equally insistent on obedience to authority, as represented not by the Church but by the Bible, and had an equal lack of confidence in human reason. Thus the two religious groups confronted each other, and both of them claimed the support of supernatural powers. As long as they denied the validity of reason, peace was impossible. Catholic and Protestant, both of them claiming divine support, had more in common with each other than either of them had with Erasmean humanists.

Francis had encouraged French Protestants by his apparent tolerance, but when the lines were drawn more clearly, he began to resort to persecution, presumably in fear for his own salvation. By the 1540's the French government was committed to a policy of killing Protestants or driving them into exile. In 1546 Étienne Dolet, a humanist scholar with a distinguished record of scholarly achievement, was burned at the stake because of his heretical views. He was followed by others. Individuals with Protestant sympathies now had to choose between professing full adherence to the dogmas of the Catholic Church and the risk of death by publicly suffering the most revolting form of capital punishment.

Francis continued to maintain Catholic beliefs by force until his death in 1547. He was followed by his son, Henry II. Dying prematurely in 1559, Henry left four sons, all of whom were weak and corrupt. Three of these Valois princes occupied the throne in turn, without leaving offspring. This situation enabled the widow of Henry II, Catherine de' Medici, to seek to make herself *de facto* ruler of France, though she was never in full control of the government. Catherine was unable to cope effectively with the religious conflicts, and the result was a series of civil wars over a period of more than thirty years. Catherine and her sons alternated between stern support for the Catholic Church and attempts to end the conflict by compromise. The Protestant forces were strengthened by the adhesion of many small noblemen from the provinces who wanted to remain independent of the central government and to preserve laws and customs surviving from the Middle Ages.

As long as both parties claimed divine aid, armed conflict was inevitable. The episode which posterity best remembers is the slaughter of fifty thousand leading Protestants in the St. Bartholomew's Day massacre of 1572, though it appears relatively mild when compared with twentieth-century achievements in genocide. Eventually the last of the Valois kings died, and his legitimate successor (a distant cousin of the Bourbon family) was Henry of Navarre, who was professedly a Protestant and—what was more important—a man of refreshing tolerance and warm energy. Becoming King of France as Henry IV in 1589, he adopted Catholicism for political reasons which everybody understood and most Frenchmen approved. In 1598 he granted a limited (though effective) religious freedom to Protestants, thus bringing the wars to an end in a compromise settlement.

The wars had no significant material effects. Neither party could claim victory, and their relative strengths remained almost unchanged. The restoration of peace and order was brought about by factors which can fairly be called accidental, the most obvious being Henry IV's accession to the throne. Nevertheless, the wars had important and mostly beneficial effects on French modes of thinking. During the conflict it became increasingly apparent that order could be restored only if men adopted a rational attitude toward political conflicts, basing their opinions not on mystical interpretations of the supposed will of God but on pragmatic considerations of expediency.

The Italians, especially Machiavelli and his friend the Florentine historian Francesco Guicciardini, have generally been credited with inaugurating the rational study of politics, free from religious assumptions; but they applied their political rationalism within a very narrow sphere, dealing only with the Italian city-states. For the first comprehensive application of rationalism to political problems, one must turn to French writers of the late sixteenth century, and particularly to Jean Bodin. Born of a bourgeois provincial family and pursuing a career as a lawyer, Bodin wrote several books; the most important, *Six Books of the Commonwealth,* was published in 1576. Bodin's central affirmation was that the main criterion of political values was not the will of God but historical experience. Man rather than God was the central figure in political theory, and human welfare was its main purpose, the test of its validity being essentially pragmatic rather than authoritarian. Lacking the incisiveness and the vigorous radicalism of Machiavelli, Bodin was not a very lively writer, particularly since his readers had to wade through masses of factual material derived from all the societies, past and present, with which Bodin could become acquainted; but he can fairly be regarded as the founder of modern political science. And despite the general objectivity of his approach, he was animated not only by a scientific love of truth but also by the hope that its diffusion would contribute to ending the religious wars. Fearing anarchy, he insisted that in every state there must be some authority, preferably the king, endowed with sovereign power. He is remembered chiefly for his analysis of sovereignty.

Bodin did not wholly succeed in separating politics from religion. God, he declared, was still the ruler of the universe, and he had established moral laws which human beings must continue to obey. Monarchy, moreover, was in accord with natural law, as was proved by the consensus of human and animal groups. Thus far Bodin's thinking was still medieval.[2] But he did

---

[2] See Jean Bodin: *Six Books of the Commonwealth,* translated by M. J. Tooley (New York, 1955), especially pp. 29, 154, 199.

not support the belief in a divine oneness which had been the main component of the religious view of life and of political conservatism. And although Bodin did not repudiate religious doctrines, his acceptance of them was casual and perfunctory.

Much more vigorous was Bodin's assertion that monarchy was the most prevalent form of government because its merits had been demonstrated throughout human history. Thus, by an apparent paradox, he used skepticism about religious beliefs in order to promote generally conservative conclusions. France needed a government which could enforce peace and order and would not become involved in conflicts about religion; and this could be achieved only by one that did not try to enforce any particular system of beliefs but was willing to accept whatever had popular support, absolute truths being unknown and unknowable. Bodin denounced any form of religious intolerance, and defended the right of individuals to choose their own beliefs.[3]

The most important service that men like Bodin could render to France was not the advocacy of new ideas but the relaxation of emotional tensions. As long as the country was split into two hostile groups, each of them claiming divine guidance and exclusive rights to salvation, peace and toleration were impossible. Individuals remaining in doubt about the right way to win divine favor could not rest in tranquillity. But peace of mind was dependent on the acceptance of uncertainty. The necessary repudiation of all dogmas was the essential doctrine of a greater man than Bodin: Michel Eyquem, lord of Montaigne.

A member of the lesser nobility with a home in southwestern France, Montaigne witnessed and deplored the wars of religion without participating in them. He was on friendly terms with

---

[3] Bodin: op. cit., pp. 114, 141, 142. Rejecting the traditional belief in divine oneness, Bodin was able to dispense with some of its earthly exemplifications. He was probably the first political theorist who was able to deny as mythical the universality of the Roman Empire. "Rome itself," he calmly remarks, "never ruled more than a thirtieth part of the globe," adding that he had been accused of heresy for making this statement (p. 38).

418

most of the leading figures of his time. Inspiring liking and confidence among all his associates, he might have played a leading role in French politics as an advocate of tolerance and moderation if he had been so inclined. His *Essays,* in which he sought to explore the essential qualities of human nature, were of immense importance in the history of Western thought; more than any other figure of his time, Montaigne formulated the differences between medieval man and the man of the coming Enlightenment. He jettisoned the whole moral and intellectual heritage of the Middle Ages, substituting adherence to nature for the moral laws that had been imposed upon human beings by the Church. Yet his radicalism did not extend to his political views. Skeptical about the values of social change, he deduced conservative conclusions from his revolutionary premises. But he remains a living force among Western thinkers, chiefly because of the honesty of his self-revelation and his warmth of personality.

Montaigne's nature was very different from the nature of the philosophers, having no connections either with the conservative view of authority as based on natural law or with the liberal conception of natural rights. Nature—for Montaigne—was something to be discovered, for which reason he devoted his life to an analysis of human behavior. In the beginning he took notes of all human peculiarities, mostly derived from classical sources, but he gradually became concerned with himself as his chief subject, though with no element of self-condemnation, simply regarding himself as a typical specimen. The apparent formlessness of his *Essays,* their lack of structure and tendency to wander, contributed to this self-examination. His purpose was moral discovery, and too much formal organization would have inhibited it. Refusing to believe that nature consisted of any neat patterns, he chose to write with a corresponding lack of order, seeking to give expression to every idiosyncrasy.

By "nature" Montaigne meant chiefly "instinct"; and his basic affirmation was that instinct could always be trusted, whereas mind generally led men astray. And since to follow instinct was generally pleasurable, it should be accepted as good.

Montaigne repudiated the whole Christian tradition of ascetic practices and belief in the sinfulness of the body. "Nature," he declared, "has with motherly tenderness observed this principle: that the actions she has enjoined for our need should also be pleasurable to us; and she incites us to them not only through reason but also through appetite. It is wrong to infringe her laws." "Nature always gives us laws that are more successful than those we give ourselves." [4]

While Montaigne's approach to ethics was revolutionary—if anything so quiet and unpretentious can be so described—his politics were conservative, though for radical reasons. It was better, he believed, to conform with established laws and customs, not because they were in accord with truth and justice but because any possible alternatives would be equally false. "The laws maintain their credit, not because they are just but because they are laws. This is the mystic foundation of their authority; they have no other." "The most plausible counsel that our reason gives us is generally for everyone to obey the laws of his own country." And if one sought to avoid the dangers of intellectualism and did not aspire to become a sage, one should generally follow the example of the common man. "He who cannot attain the noble impassibility of the Stoics, let him seek shelter in the bosom of that insensibility which I admire in the common man." "The middle region harbors the tempests; the two extremes, those of the philosophers and the rustics, concur in tranquillity and happiness." And with an implicit dismissal of the hope of immortality in the Christian heaven, Montaigne insists that "life ought to be an aim to itself, its own purpose; its true study is to regulate itself, guide itself, suffer itself." [5]

Thus Montaigne's response to the problem of the northern Renaissance—the problem of conflicting views of life and different standards of truth—was a general skepticism that denied the

---

[4] Michel de Montaigne: *Essays,* translated by Jacob Zeitlin (New York, 1934–6), II, 222; III, 308.

[5] Montaigne: op. cit.

validity of any kind of truth. He revealed himself more fully than any other figure prior to the Enlightenment—his frankness was much bolder and more comprehensive than that of Petrarch—and left an attractive impression of humanity, tolerance, and common sense. And his work may be regarded as registering the farthest point that Western man had reached in repudiating the attitudes of the Middle Ages. In spite of his conception of nature as somehow supporting his revolt against the beliefs of medieval man, what Montaigne essentially contributed to Western development was nothing positive, but a *tabula rasa* making room for new views of life. Most human beings demand a faith to live by and cannot remain content with the uncertainties that were recommended by Montaigne. French thought of the seventeenth century looked for positive convictions, but it was largely owing to Montaigne that it had to start afresh from new beginnings. The two most significant thinkers of the period were Descartes and Pascal, and each of them was steeped in Montaigne and regarded himself as engaged in finding an answer to Montaigne's skepticism, Descartes in a rationalism which began in universal doubt, and Pascal in religious beliefs which transcended reason.

· · ·

It is difficult for moderns to remember that in the sixteenth century Spain was the strongest European power. The unification of Aragon and Castile by the marriage of Ferdinand and Isabella, followed by the completion of the reconquest of the Moorish provinces in 1492 and by the discovery and settlement of the Americas, gave Spain great material resources and a self-confidence which found expression in imperialist expansion. From the Italian wars at the beginning of the sixteenth century until the defeat of the Armada by English seamen in 1588, Spain seemed invincible. Material achievement was accompanied by cultural efflorescence, though this was briefer and more limited than the equivalent movements elsewhere. One of the main reasons for this brevity, no doubt, was that religious intolerance was institutionalized earlier and more fully in Spain than in other Western countries. Spain had its Erasmean moment early in the sixteenth century, when scholars like Francisco de Vittoria gave expression to liberal interpretations of religious and philosophical doctrine, but the interlude was quickly ended by the hostility of the crown and the Church hierarchy. Spaniards were forbidden to express attitudes that might endanger the political supremacy of the king and the doctrines of the Church.

Spanish attitudes and ways of living were generally similar to those of other Western nations, but there were always subtle differences of emphasis and interpretation which gave a distinctive quality to Spanish development and which have led some Spanish historians to suggest (half seriously) that Spain did not really belong to the West and that Europe ended at the Pyrenees. The main affirmations of Western civilization—the belief that nature is fundamentally good and that man should be guided by its laws—and the consequent confidence in the ultimate union of freedom and order have never been fully accepted in Spain. For Spaniards the basic reality is conflict rather than harmony. Christian belief is regarded as the main defining and unifying force in the making of the Spanish nation, and this is affirmed rather than proved, validation being established by warriors in battle rather than by theologians.

This view of life was presumably a result of the long conflict with the Mohammedans, beginning in the eighth century when these infidels first invaded the peninsula and not ended until their final expulsion in 1492. This historical experience established for Spaniards the supremacy of the warrior and the mystic over the peace-loving and comfort-loving citizen, and demonstrated the importance of beliefs that transcended reason.

Thus Christian Spain had come to believe that nations were built by the affirmation of beliefs and that any realities which conflicted with such beliefs must be suppressed. Denial of the myths upon which the Spanish nation had been built would endanger the whole structure. According to the official interpretations, Spanish medieval history had been one long crusade directed toward the expulsion of the Moors back to Africa. Yet in reality there had been long intervals of peace, with much fraternization between the adherents of the two religions; and whenever war began again, it was largely fought by feudalistic warriors hoping to conquer land and make themselves into a leisured aristocracy. Thus there was an element of falsification about the whole story of the reconquest; but the Spaniards preferred to affirm the truth of the idealized version. They chose to obliterate the fact that even the famous Cid, the greatest hero of the reconquest, had sometimes fought against fellow Christians and lent his services to Mohammedan chieftains. And in order to make a suitable myth out of the earliest and most famous of the events of the war, they joined the French in falsifying the death of Roland, attributing it to the Mohammedans and forgetting that it was actually the work of Christian Basques resisting the threat of French domination. It is Don Quixote's insistence on— so to speak—choosing his own reality in defiance of all factual evidence which makes him seem typical of the deeper levels of the Spanish character. Don Quixote found his own reality in knight-errantry and maintained that chivalric fictions represented a higher form of truth.

Since every Spaniard had his own version of reality, Spanish political life was frequently turbulent, and conflicts—even those between groups of Christians—could be settled only by force. Other Western countries believed that they could be ended by an appeal to natural law, but for Spain nothing (except God) was higher than the individual. The only effective method of maintaining peace and order was, therefore, the rule of an individual, either king or dictator. Throughout the history of Spain periods of one-man government have alternated with periods of civil war and temporary anarchy. Spaniards have never found it easy to cooperate with each other and have failed to develop institutions providing effectively for communal decision and action.

Believing that his moral and political values were derived not from nature (as the West has generally affirmed) but from transcendental sources, the Spaniard has combined a realistic view of the sensuous world with a devotion to religious beliefs that has frequently passed all normal and rational limits. On the one hand, Spanish literature has been singularly realistic in its treatment of human crimes and weaknesses. Not sharing in the utopian hope of Western man that everything natural is capable of perfection, the Spanish writer has dealt with evils with a singular frankness and without illusions. It is significant that it was Spain which developed the picaresque novel, the first example of what became a popular trend in the literature of all Western countries being the anonymous *Lazarillo de Tormes* (published in 1554). On the other hand, the Spanish temperament had found direct expression in saints who pursued holiness with a fervor unsurpassed among other Western peoples. Perhaps the most typical Spaniards of the great age of the sixteenth century were St. Teresa and the founder of the Jesuit Order, St. Ignatius Loyola, both of whom displayed, combined with an intense spirituality, a most realistic understanding of the human beings with whom they had dealings. It is significant that both of them, in adolescence, were avid readers of the romances of chivalry that turned the brains of poor Don Quixote. The values to be found in the romances were congenial to the Spanish temperament; the error of Don Quixote was his failure to apply them realistically.

Spain was influenced by the Renaissance, but took from it only what she could absorb, which was, perhaps, not of major significance. In general, she may be said to have preferred the exuberant anarchism of medieval art forms to the tidy and well-organized structures, exemplifying human creativity, which were introduced by the Renaissance.

Medieval Spain had developed her own form of Gothic, characterized by relatively small window space (this was to be expected in a country of such intense sunlight) and by elaborate ornamentation. The Renaissance brought some modifications but could not change the basic tradition. A new royal palace, Philip II's Escorial outside Madrid, marked an attempt by the Spanish monarchy to introduce classical designs from Renaissance Italy. An immense structure, it had an orderliness and an inner logic which were new to Spanish architecture, but it could not change popular tastes. The monarchy could impose an alien style on its own buildings, but most Spaniards apparently preferred elaborate ornamentation to the neat and tidy structures preferred by the Italians. Spanish Gothic changed by slow degrees, with little overt conflict, into the equally ornamented style of the seventeenth-century baroque.

Meanwhile the special qualities of Spanish culture had attracted a painter who had come from Crete and whose earlier work combined what still survived of Byzantinism with the mannerism of the later Italian schools. Although he did not come from Italy to Spain until after the age of thirty, probably about the year 1575, El Greco seemed from his arrival to have a special affinity for Spanish culture. He never gained any wide popularity or strong official approval, but he continued to work in Toledo, the most medieval of Spanish cities, until his death in 1614.

El Greco's painting is primarily a statement of the belief that transcendental ideas and values are more real than the natural world of the flesh and the senses. He distorts sensuous appearances, elongating his figures, portraying them from unfamiliar angles, and illuminating them with splashes of dazzling color, wholly unrealistic and mostly white and red. Many of his figures seem not only to be weirdly shaped but also to have a lack of normal vitality. But they derive their being from the ideal world, which is usually left to be inferred, thought it is sometimes presented directly. One of the most effective renderings of the two worlds is the *Burial of the Count of Orgaz*. The world below, covering the bottom half of the picture, presents a group of noblemen performing the burial service. They display a lack of vitality and of relationship with each other, and most of them are not even paying attention to the ceremony honoring their former colleague, though two saints have miraculously descended from heaven to perform it. The upper half of the picture, however, which consists also of between twenty and thirty human figures, is vibrant with spiritual activity. The figures have an energy which is communicated to them by Christ, St. Peter, and the Virgin Mary. Thus the world of material forces which human beings inhabit is subordinate to the world of the spirit. El Greco must have treasured the approval of St. Teresa, who declared: "I see a white and a red of a quality as one finds nowhere in nature; for they shine more brightly than the colors we perceive; and I see pictures, as no painter has yet painted, whose models one finds nowhere in nature; and yet they are nature itself, and life itself, and the most perfect beauty imaginable." [6]

Very different aspects of Spanish culture were portrayed in prose fiction and the drama, which began to flourish in the later sixteenth century. Having abandoned the assumption that nature was the source of values and standards, Spanish writers were free to present it realistically, without feeling obliged to present any idealistic view of human nature and society. Spanish literature of the so-called Golden Age had an immense and varied vitality and anticipated the literatures of other countries in its freedom from inhibitions. The first realistic novel, *La Celestina* by Fernando de Rojas, was published in 1499. Later writers cultivated the picaresque, having no feeling that novels about rogues should be condemned as falsifications of human realities. But it was the drama which most fully represented Spanish secular literature. Its most prolific author, Lope de Vega, is remembered for his immense productivity rather than for any specific invention. But one character presented by another author is remembered as achieving the symbolic status which ensures the attention of posterity. Tirsa de Molina presented the story of Don Juan, who has continued to represent certain aspects of masculine sexuality. Less popular but more significantly Spanish is the masterpiece of the seventeenth-century dramatist Calderón, *Life Is a Dream*. This presents a man who is made to live in two different styles, one luxurious and the other miserable, and who must decide for himself which of them is real and which is imaginary.

---

[6] See *Encyclopaedia Britannica*, 15th edn., XXII, 70.

The whole Spanish character is affirmed in the greatest of Spanish books, *Don Quixote,* of which the first part was published in 1605 and the second in 1615. Like all great books, it gives expression to the main underlying tendencies both of its society and of its time, thereby making its readers conscious of the psychic forces motivating them. The central problem of *Don Quixote* is characteristic of the Renaissance. Two different conceptions of reality are presented, one spiritual and transcendental, the other materialistic; the materialistic view of life is presented as true. It is, in fact, fully exemplified in Sancho Panza, who speaks with a naturalness and a freedom that were new in literature. But Don Quixote rejects this truth and affirms the reality of an imaginary world based on medieval values. There is no doubt at all that Don Quixote's chivalric view of life is entirely illusory; yet the reader gradually comes to feel that it has a nobility and an idealism which are in some way superior to the realistic views of other people.

To chivalric views of human life Don Quixote, after awakening from his delusion, says farewell, but solely for himself, by no means for all his fellow countrymen. This is Spain and not England, and values do not have to be realistically corroborated to be accepted as guides to behavior. In Spain the Middle Ages have continued to exist down to modern times, not from any necessity or any illusion but simply because most Spaniards have preferred it that way.

22

The English Renaissance

The nature of spiritual and intellectual changes is sometimes displayed most clearly on the periphery of a culture area, in provincial countries which have not previously exhibited any continuous creativity. In the main cultural centers, changes often come about by slow evolutionary processes, so that there is never any sharp confrontation of old and new attitudes. In peripheral areas, on the other hand, beliefs and attitudes may remain largely undisturbed until they are abruptly challenged by the advent of a whole new view of life which has developed in the main centers. The meaning of Romanticism, for example, was in some ways more clearly visible in the American writers of the 1840's than it was in the literature of Europe, where it remained entangled with a variety of traditional forms and attitudes. Similarly, it was in Elizabethan England that the meaning of the Renaissance was most sharply expressed, for—to a larger degree than elsewhere—it appeared there as an alien force threatening to subvert earlier views of life that were still well established. In fact, the general tendency of many Elizabethans, both men of letters and men of affairs, was to view the late medieval development of scientific thinking and the rationalism and individualism associated with the Italian Renaissance as destructive of all social order. It was this awareness of a fundamental conflict of values that made Elizabethan England so abruptly and powerfully creative.

The official beliefs of sixteenth-century England can be described as still largely medieval and even feudal. Yet these beliefs had never fully corresponded to social realities and had little concrete effect on ways of living. They were reiterated because they gave support to a social order which was, in actual fact, much less feudal and much more individualistic than anybody recognized.

The development of England since the early Middle Ages had been significantly different from that of the continental countries, although its importance was not generally recognized until the late eighteenth and nineteenth centuries, when the English parliamentary system began to be considered as a model for all countries seeking effective self-government. The English monarchy, unlike those of France and Spain, never acquired any absolute authority; and English citizens always retained certain rights and liberties. The English were more successful than other peoples in retaining the limitations on royal power that had characterized the government of the Germanic tribesmen. The Roman belief in the absolute power of the emperor had never struck roots in English institutions, which were shaped by the traditional English "common law" rather than by Roman law.

The kings of the Germanic tribes had been expected to consult with the more important of their subjects before making important new decisions. Alone among the Western peoples, the English had succeeded in retaining this principle and building it into their form of government. The feudal Great Council, which had originally consisted solely of the higher nobility and which gradually disappeared in other Western countries, was in England expanded to include a House of Commons as well as a House of Lords, and by the end of the thirteenth century this "Parliament" was recognized as an established part of the English government. Its powers remained uncertain and severely restricted, and often seemed more verbal than real. But before the end of the fourteenth century it was recognized that any new laws and new collections of taxes should be of concern to Parliament, though the main authority continued to be the king. Important political changes were made not by the king alone but by the king in Parliament, though it was a long time before Parliament acquired enough power to oppose his wishes. Popular rebellions continued to occur when misgovernment invited them, but they were almost always directed not against the king himself but against the king's counselors, who were supposed to have misled him; such rebellions usually ended tragically in the slaughter of most of the participants. However, they demonstrated the political independence of the English peoples. Possibly more important than this popular interest in national policy was the limitation of royal power over individuals. The concept of individual right, maintained by an independent judiciary, was traced by later generations back to the signing of the Magna Carta by King John in 1215. In actuality the Magna Carta was primarily concerned with the privileges of the nobility, not with the rights of the common people, but it is true that it established an important precedent for the limitation of royal power. By the later Middle Ages, the English had become well aware of these unique features of their form of government and regarded themselves, unlike the French, as a free people.

It should be added that the monarchy was allowed considerable leeway in dealing with powerful individuals. Under Henry VIII, for example, officials who lost favor with the king were so regularly beheaded that one wonders why anybody should have chosen so hazardous an occupation as the royal service. But Henry's capricious severity undoubtedly increased his popularity with the mass of the population, who were in no danger of losing their own heads.

What were the causes of this unique political development— a development which in later centuries was to have a profound influence on the institutions of the whole Western world? This question has no simple answer. It was important that England was an island and hence secure against foreign invasions except under very unusual conditions (the Norman conquest was possible only because it coincided with an invasion from Norway; the English King Harold had to crush the Norwegians before moving, with badly depleted forces, against Duke William). The English, therefore, did not normally need strong government for defense against foreign enemies. The Norman conquest, moreover, was of great importance because it made it possible for William to organize English institutions in such a way as to limit the powers of the feudal ruling class and check the growth of great magnates controlling whole provinces, like those in France and Germany. There were no sharp separations in England between noblemen and commoners, and in the later Middle Ages wealthy commoner families of bourgeois origin could often buy land and achieve aristocratic status, though it might be several generations before their origin was forgotten. These and other factors caused English politics to become an interplay among kings, nobility, and commons. In France the power of the magnates was so great that the bourgeoisie was compelled always to turn to the monarchy for protection. In England the bourgeoisie supported the monarchy only when support was deserved, and it expected protection in return. It frequently happened that a strong king (like Henry II and Edward I) who could claim popular support against the magnates had a weak or tyrannical successor whose policies led to an alliance of nobility and bourgeoisie demanding better government. Thus royal power always remained limited, and the limits gradually became accepted and institutionalized.

These geographical and historical accidents provide partial explanations for the unique features of English development, but they do not wholly account for it. English political history during the Middle Ages was frequently turbulent and bloody, and several English kings suffered ignominious and violent deaths at the hands of rebellious subjects. But there was less indiscriminate brutality than in other Western countries and a stronger sense of national unity as taking precedence over private interests. English nationalism was always strongly xenophobic; contempt for foreigners was already an English attitude in the early Middle Ages. But nationalism was associated with individual rights and liberties and with limitations on the powers of government, and was mainly therefore a progressive force in spite of its ethnic exclusiveness. The kind of private war which so often disrupted medieval France was a rare occurrence in England, and the sense of national loyalty as paramount extended to beliefs and ideas. The English have rarely been tempted to suppose that any set of beliefs had a universal scope and authority. For the Englishman, ultimate reality is itself illogical and disorderly and cannot be defined by any of the neat generalizations preferred by non-English philosophers. On the few occasions when Englishmen have succumbed to the temptation to suppose that their ideas were absolute truth—most notably in the civil wars of the seventeenth century—they have quickly become disillusioned and returned to the national faith in compromise.

During the later Middle Ages, the English government was frequently ineffectual in maintaining order, largely because through much of the period there was a lack of firm royal leadership. In consequence, England suffered through a dreary series of conflicts among the ruling classes, known as the Wars of the Roses and caused mainly by disputes about the succession to the monarchy. After most of the important participants had killed each other, order was restored by the seizure of power in 1485 by Henry Tudor, who could claim a somewhat tenuous hereditary right to the throne through his mother, and was able to strengthen it by marrying the daughter of a previous king. This inaugurated a new Tudor dynasty which lasted until the death of Elizabeth I in 1603 and which had both more real power and more enthusiastic popular support than any other dynasty in English history. This was perhaps not wholly true of its founder, who became Henry VII and reigned until 1509. But his son, Henry VIII, despite his fondness for beheading wives and officials who had disappointed him (or possibly because of this propensity), always retained his personal popularity with the mass of his subjects. His immediate successors, his son Edward VI (1547–53) and his older daughter Mary (1553–8), aroused less enthusiasm; Edward died young and Mary tried to impose Catholic beliefs by the burning of three hundred Protestants. But Elizabeth throughout her long reign of forty-five years displayed all Henry's capacity for arousing popular enthusiasm and relatively little of his brutality.

According to accepted political theory, the Tudors were solely responsible for the government of England and—as the legitimate heirs of previous kings—owed their appointment to God. But the monarch had duties as well as powers, and if he failed to perform them, the whole realm would suffer. Could an erring king be removed from office by a successful rebellion of his subjects? This perennial question was never satisfactorily answered. The most usual reply was that he could be removed only by God, though God might act through human agencies. But it was generally agreed that the king was primarily responsible for the welfare of his subjects, and that royal misgovernment might have catastrophic effects. Order was always based on royal authority, and if the king failed to enforce it, the result would be mob riots and uprisings and general anarchy. Any attempt to shift the responsibilities of government from the king to the people would have most unhappy results. This view of English institutions was stated by Tudor propagandists and supported by official authorities. It was the subject of "homilies" which clergymen were required to read to their congregations and of historical chronicles, particularly that of Edward Hall. Near the end of the Tudor period it became the central theme of the historical plays of Shakespeare. Yet although virtually every Englishman spoke as though this view of kingship was self-evident, it is very plain that the Tudors could appear to be absolute only because they were popular. They maintained no standing army and had to rely on calling out the militia when the kingdom was in danger. They were frequently short of money, even for the ordinary expenses of government, and did not employ any large bureaucracy. The tasks of local government were performed by country gentlemen who served as justices of the peace and were not paid or otherwise rewarded for their services. Occasional rebellions, caused either by the economic grievances of some part of the population or by religious dissensions, were crushed with some difficulty owing to the lack of a professional army. They demonstrated the continued existence of an independent spirit among the mass of the population.

In reality, the Tudors were able to govern only because their policies were in accord with the wishes of most of their subjects. The most important event of the Tudor period was the establishment of religious independence, which was accomplished by Henry VIII in a series of acts of Parliament, the most far-reaching being the Act of Supremacy of 1534. But in becoming Protestant, England did not cease to be Catholic, and Henry gave no encouragement whatever to the spiritual individualism that had characterized continental Protestantism. This was primarily a political and economic rather than a theological change, its most significant results being the increase in royal power and the confiscation of church properties, most of which were acquired by royal officials of middle-class origins. It was significant that the king acted through Parliament, which passed the necessary legislation to make the English Church independent of Rome. There can be little doubt that most Englishmen applauded Henry's break with the Roman Church and approved at the same time of his theological authoritarianism and his antagonism to religious radicalism.[1]

The relationship between Henry and his subjects was subtle and complex, resembling effective political leadership in a mod-

---

[1] Mystical and radical views of religion could be found in England. The most important of such movements was the Lollard movement, founded in the 1370's by an Oxford theologian, John Wyclif. Denouncing the wealth and powers of the clergy and insisting that the Bible was the only true source of religious belief, Wyclif anticipated much of the doctrine of seventeenth-century Puritanism. He was allowed to die peacefully in his bed in 1384, but the authorities were less tolerant toward his followers, who were known as Lollards and who spread the doctrine by underground methods. In 1401 Parliament imposed the death sentence upon heretics, several of whom were burned. But despite this horrifying penalty, Lollardy survived among peasants and craftsmen in rural areas such as the Chiltern Hills. Its contribution to the growth of Puritanism has probably been underestimated by historians.

434

ern democracy more than the absolutism of France and Spain. The last of the Tudors, Elizabeth I, had all of Henry's political sophistication, along with a capacity to make use of her femininity for political purposes. Inheriting the crown at a time when England was in danger of both religious civil wars and foreign invasions, Elizabeth displayed a freedom from any form of religious fanaticism and a political insight which led to the glories of her later years, when the Spanish Armada had been defeated. Assuming the role of mother of her people and refusing to dilute her leadership by sharing it with a husband, she convinced her subjects that what she felt for them was love and what she expected was that her love be returned. Both a virgin and—symbolically—a mother, Elizabeth may be regarded as a successor of the Virgin Mary, though it must be added that her relations with male courtiers had a sexual flavor recalling the attitudes of troubadour poetry. But in an age of religious warfare, with all its horrors, Elizabeth had the great virtue of perceiving that religious belief was a man's private affair and that as long as he did not try to impose his beliefs on other people he should not be interfered with. Elizabeth could use force with all the customary barbarity in crushing political revolts, but the motivation was always political, not religious. She was, moreover, an intellectually gifted woman who had received a Renaissance education. The fragments of her speeches that have been preserved are magnificent. These qualities far outweigh the vanity and the ingratitude for which she has been blamed; and she may perhaps be permitted to keep in death the privacy about her sexual attitudes which she guarded so strictly in her lifetime.

In actuality, of course, English society was becoming steadily more money-minded, by processes that long antedated the rule of the Tudors. Throughout the sixteenth century, large-scale industry and commerce continued to grow, and the urban population became more numerous and more influential. The voyages of discovery and the consequent importation of silver by Spain from her American mines brought about a steady price inflation, which stimulated economic enterprise in all Western countries.

435

England was peculiarly able to take advantage of these developments both because of her geographical position and because of her relative freedom from the religious conflicts which disturbed other countries. Large-scale foreign trade began to be handled by commercial companies, no longer by individual merchants, and the investors often included noblemen as well as members of the middle class. Where profit was to be expected, the English aristocracy were not inhibited by traditional conceptions of their role in society.

Similar changes were taking place in rural England, where class lines were becoming more fluid. New families, often of bourgeois origin, were acquiring large estates, much of them formerly the property of the Church, and were buying patents of nobility from the College of Heralds. The yeoman class, generally regarded as the backbone of the nation, was becoming more differentiated, some of its members rising into the gentry and others sinking to wage labor. Serfdom no longer existed, but beggars and vagabonds had become a major social problem. All these changes were regarded by public officials and social commentators with strong disapproval, the feudal past being quite unrealistically glorified. Much of the blame was attributed to the growth of sheep-rearing in place of agriculture. The growth of the textile industry both in the Netherlands and in England made sheep-rearing profitable, but unfortunately it required little labor and led to the enclosure of lands which had formerly been used for agriculture. The enclosure movement was vigorously denounced by everybody who mentioned it, and both its extent and its harmful effects were generally exaggerated. It was blamed, in particular, for the proliferation of vagabonds unable to find work.

Tudor statesmen did much to promote economic growth and displayed a concern for all aspects of national life far more detailed and comprehensive than is shown by any modern government. But their official values (as distinct from their actual policies) remained strongly medieval. "In every aspect of its economic policy," it has been said, "the government pursued the

436

consistent aim of protecting the social fabric from the dissolving forces of the new commercialism." [2] Its attempts to maintain medieval economic values by regulating wages and conditions of labor were wholly ineffectual; and its denunciation of enclosures, though vigorous and frequent, had little visible result.

By a curious paradox the Protestant Reformation, in spite of its individualistic implications, had at first the effect in England of strengthening medieval conceptions of social unity, at least as long as the Tudors ruled. England, it was affirmed in the Act of Supremacy of 1534, was an "empire," by which it was meant that it was wholly independent of any foreign power and its ruler was responsible to God alone. Thenceforth church and state were closely connected, and the monarch was the master (or mistress) of both. Seeking to minimize doctrinal differences, whether emphasized by Catholics or by Puritans, Elizabeth regarded the Church of England as the spiritual expression of national unity and the support of royal authority. In the words of her favorite Archbishop of Canterbury, Thomas Whitgift, there was "no such distinction of the Commonwealth and the Church that they should be counted, as it were, two separate bodies." And as long as political conflicts were avoided, Elizabeth was willing to allow a wide divergence of beliefs and to leave doctrinal definitions vague and ambiguous. She set an excellent example of this policy when she became queen, by omitting the phrase "head of the Church" from her list of titles and substituting a vague and tantalizing "etc.," the meaning of which could only be guessed at. Many conflicts throughout history could have been prevented by a similarly discreet use of an "etc."

In spite of her devotion to peace and national unity, Elizabeth did not find it possible to avoid all religious intolerance, but her motivations were political and not religious. Catholics were forbidden by a papal bull of 1571 to accept Elizabeth as queen; and though most English Catholics contrived to ignore papal

---

[2] E. Lipson: *Economic History of England*, III, 292.

demands for armed rebellion and remained loyal to the established order, a small minority began to engage in plots and conspiracies for the murder of their queen. Obviously it was necessary to take precautions against them. More important for the future was the growth of Puritanism, which inculcated a religious individualism hostile to the concept of social unity that Elizabeth sought above all things to maintain. The Puritans were disciples of John Calvin, but they went further than their master in open opposition to royal authority, making public affirmation of political attitudes which had remained implicit in the writings of Calvin himself. The essence of Puritanism was its belief in the direct communication of the individual believer with the divine spirit. The Church was no longer to be considered as the nation in its religious aspects, but was to consist only of those who seemed to be among the elect. State and Church were therefore to be considered as two distinct bodies; and since the Church could pronounce the divine will, it was superior to the state. The magistrates were expected to follow the instructions of the ministers. Puritanism appealed especially to citizens of the middle class, both urban and rural, and would have made the monarchy subordinate to middle-class believers. The original Puritans wanted to transform the Church of England in accord with their own beliefs, and had no intention of allowing freedom of speech to their opponents, but more radical groups soon began to emerge which believed in freedom for everybody. But during Elizabeth's reign, despite much religious controversy, Puritanism did not have a very wide appeal, and though Elizabeth resorted to repression, there was no serious persecution. Under her incompetent Stuart successors, on the other hand, Puritanism developed into a force capable of temporarily destroying the monarchy. More clearly than any other aspect of sixteenth-century England, it represented the individualism of the future as against the medieval belief in the divine order of society.

In historical retrospect it is easy to see in Tudor England, and in some measure as a result of Tudor policies, the dissolution of traditional concepts of order and the growth of a new kind of society. It is therefore surprising how little public awareness of these changes can be found. Almost all the literature of Elizabethan England was permeated with traditional concepts, and the new individualism was regarded by almost every Elizabethan writer with profound antagonism. If one is to judge English society by its literary expressions, it appears to have accepted almost unanimously the traditional belief in royal supremacy as in accord with the will of God, the concept of a social hierarchy in which everybody had his appointed hereditary place, and even much of the theology of the Catholic Church. Official Elizabethan values were profoundly conservative and profoundly unrealistic, continuing to affirm early medieval views of society. The myth of a divinely created order had even less justification under Elizabeth than in the Middle Ages, for it was now limited to the national state, and there was not even any attempt to envisage any larger union, the relations among different states being determined solely by material power.[3] Yet Elizabethan writers still used the argument from analogy in a thoroughly medieval manner. The best-known and the most elaborate statements of this argument are to be found in the writings of Shakespeare: the argument from astronomy, royal power being compared to the role of the sun in the universe, as stated by Ulysses in *Troilus and Cressida,* and the argument from the human body, every social group having its appointed functions in an organic society, as

---

[3] Established mainly for political reasons, lacking in any coherent philosophy or point of view, and staffed by men whose most obvious qualification was their capacity for survival, the Church of England during the early years of Elizabeth's reign seemed scarcely respectable. But it gradually acquired a character of its own. Of decisive importance was the publication during the 1590's of Richard Hooker's *Of the Laws of Ecclesiastical Polity,* which described the beliefs and institutions of the English Church, in opposition to those advocated by the Puritans. In refreshing contrast with almost all other theologians of almost all other churches, Hooker minimized the roles of inspiration and of authority and emphasized the power of human reason. Taking much from the more liberal of the scholastics, Hooker gave the Church of England a theology which inspired respect for its intellectual quality and its warm humanity.

stated by Menenius Agrippa in *Coriolanus*. In view of the placing and tone of these passages, there can be little doubt that they represented Shakespeare's personal beliefs.[4]

This organic view of society remained essentially feudal in its values. Each social group was supposed to have its own special functions, and the rank of the individual was fixed by birth. In reality, class lines were partially fluid, and most prominent Englishmen were of middle-class origin and not entitled to the noble ancestry to which they made claim. But according to popular opinion, leadership belonged to a hereditary nobility displaying the traditional chivalric qualities of courage and generosity. Other classes, such as the yeoman farmers and the agricultural laborers, were expected to perform their own tasks under the leadership and guidance of the aristocracy. In all Elizabethan literature the social climber and the merchant who is too intent on moneymaking are presented with stern disapproval. This is especially obvious in the realistic type of drama developed after 1600 by Ben Jonson and Philip Massinger and other later dramatists. So deeply ingrained was this type of thinking that in descriptions of the class hierarchy the bourgeoisie (who repre-

---

[4] This traditional mode of thought was still so firmly established in the England of the Tudors and early Stuarts that it seems desirable to quote some more illustrations. John Hayward, writing in 1603, declared: "The whole world is nothing but a great state; a state is no other than a great family; and a family no other than a great body. As one God ruleth the world, one master the family, as all the members of one body receive both sense and motion from one head, which is the seat and tower both of understanding and of will, so it seemeth no less natural, that one state should be governed by one commander." In 1606 E. Forset wrote: "The Commonweale with all her parts, order, qualities and requisites whatsoever is (for better understanding and illustration) set forth by sundry fit resemblances, as by the architecture of a house, by the swarming and cohabitation of bees in a hive, by a ship floating over the sea, and such like; but by none more properly than either by the universal mass of the whole world . . . or else by the body of man, being the lesser world, even the diminutive and model of that wide extending universal." Hayward and Forset quoted in J. E. Phillips: *The State in Shakespearean Greek and Roman Plays* (New York, 1940).

440

sented an individualism not easy to reconcile with the myth) is sometimes not even mentioned.[5]

The Elizabethan stage was not only politically conservative; it also presented a view of life which was largely Catholic.[6] Catholic beliefs and institutions are normally presented sympathetically, obviously under the assumption that the audience would both understand them and approve of them. The higher members of the Catholic hierarchy may be shown as corrupt, but this had been true of much medieval literature written long before the advent of Protestantism. Monks and friars, on the other hand, frequently appear as good characters (as in all Shakespeare's Italian comedies), and such Catholic doctrines as the belief in purgatory (which was not accepted by the Church of England) are stated without criticism, in the apparent expectation that the audience will not be puzzled or antagonized. It is clearly stated, for example, that Hamlet's father has to return to purgatory after his ghostly visit to Elsinore. In the whole range of Elizabethan and Jacobean drama, the Church of England, official church of the English people, is virtually nonexistent,

---

[5] See, for example, the statement of Sir Philip Sidney, quoted in the biography written by his friend Fulke Greville: *Life of Sir Philip Sidney* (London, 1907), XVI, 189. Sidney himself, who became—not unjustifiably—the beau ideal of the Elizabethan nobleman, is a typical example of the results of social mobility. On his mother's side he was a Dudley. The original Dudley, of middle-class origin, was a notoriously severe tax-collector under Henry VII. Henry VIII, in a move for popular approval, had him beheaded. The next-generation Dudley rose to be Duke of Northumberland, sought power as greedily as his father had sought money, and was beheaded under Mary. The duke's son was Elizabeth's not very prepossessing would-be lover, the Earl of Leicester. Leicester's sister married Sir Henry Sidney, the father of Sir Philip. In spite of this inglorious record, Sir Philip, according to Fulke Greville, declared that his "chiefest honor is to be a Dudley," and was glad "to have causes to set forth the nobility of that blood whereof I am descended."

[6] A statistical detail mentioned casually in A. L. Rowse: *The England of Elizabeth,* p. 348, is a startling reminder that English society was still largely barbaric. In the year 1598, in the county of Devon, seventy-four persons were hanged as criminals. Devon is only one out of fifty-two counties in England and Wales, and there is no indication that this was an untypical year.

except possibly in the form of a few rural clergymen who appear more or less as comic characters. For the average play-going Englishman, it would appear, the Reformation meant simply a nationalistic revolt against the power and the monetary demands of Rome, with no essential change in beliefs and practices.

In style (including everything to which this word can be applied) Elizabethan England was deeply and pervasively influenced by the Italian Renaissance. Among the nobility, both old and new, the pursuit of worldly glory had become more important than eternal salvation. The physical world, no longer dismissed as tainted with sin, offered manifold opportunities both for glory and for enjoyment. Manners, costumes, and ways of living reflected a new appreciation of the sensuous world. Especially characteristic of the new era was the building of enormous country houses by the wealthier members of the nobility. This was made possible by the peace and prosperity maintained by the Tudor dynasty, and reflected the desire of the aristocracy for visible expressions of their worldly glory.

Elizabethan literature—at least in its more serious and less popular forms—borrowed extensively from that of Italy, in both its techniques and its subject matter. And, like the Italians, the Elizabethans celebrated human love, and they adopted the Platonic theory of not sublimating earthly love into the love of God but—reversing the process—finding a religious justification for the love of the senses. Yet the doctrines affirmed by most Elizabethans, especially by those writers who affirmed popular attitudes, remained uncompromisingly medieval. A popular saying that the Italianate Englishman was the devil incarnate expressed the conviction of most literate Englishmen. In the drama, which was produced for popular entertainment and reflected popular attitudes, traditional values were barely questioned. Rationalism and individualism were strongly condemned and regarded as dangerous to the social organism. Shakespeare's Edmund and his Iago, both of whom presented explicitly rationalistic views of life, appeared as villains with no redeeming features.

As elsewhere, the herald of the Renaissance in England was

442

the humanist movement. In the late fifteenth century, English scholars were beginning to study the classics, to introduce new educational ideals, and to preach a simpler version of Christianity, with an emphasis on ethical values. English humanism was distinctly Christian and did not at first lead to any conflict between religious and classical attitudes. Erasmus found groups of scholars in London and Cambridge who made congenial and stimulating companions, the most notable being Thomas More. More's *Utopia,* written in Latin, showed a boldly speculative spirit, presenting moral ideals which seemed to have little connection with those of the Church. Paradoxically, he refused to support the Reformation, and was put to death by Henry VIII not for heresy but for upholding the Church in the matter of the king's divorce.

Under the stress of religious conflict there was little further cultural development for nearly half a century; [7] but when a new creativity began to show itself, it developed quickly. Its beginnings can be almost precisely dated about the year 1580, with the emergence of a group of young writers and scholars, whose acknowledged leader was Sir Philip Sidney, while their most productive member was Edmund Spenser. Their emphasis was wholly positive. They welcomed the introduction from France and Italy of new ideas and new literary techniques with a sense of excitement that can happen only once in the history of a literature. Confident of the truth and the comprehensive scope of Christian humanism, they apparently felt capable of anglicizing and assimilating the whole of the literary heritage of the continental Renaissance (the lack of any development of the visual

---

[7] As a result of the Norman Conquest, English literature had been slow in developing. French and not English was the official language of government and of the upper classes from 1066 until the fourteenth century. The first important writer to use English was Geoffrey Chaucer, whose *Canterbury Tales* was written near the end of the fourteenth century. Most English critics have regarded Chaucer as typically English because of his pleasure in all the varieties of human nature, his bluff common sense, and his realistic values.

arts in this period in England is difficult to explain). Awareness and analysis of the deep conflicts of values between Christianity and the Renaissance came only with the next generation.

What the Renaissance meant to these fortunate young men was principally the love of beauty, including the beauty of women, and they saw no incongruity between sexual desire, provided it was purged of lasciviousness and directed toward virtuous women, and Christian belief. They differed from their Mediterranean predecessors in regarding marriage as the proper end and consummation of desire, but beauty was considered the work of God and identified with virtue. An attractive woman, in fact, was necessarily virtuous (this bizarre justification of sexuality remained a commonplace of Elizabethan literature until it was denied by the dramatists).

Of all the figures of the English Renaissance, none was more attractive or more variously gifted than Sir Philip Sidney, who combined all the graces of Castiglione's courtier with a moral seriousness and sobriety that could develop more easily in northern Europe than in the Mediterranean countries. He had a personal charm which captivated everybody he met (with the single exception of Queen Elizabeth, who was offended when Sidney protested too vigorously against suggestions that she marry a French prince). In his lifetime he was regarded by his friends both in England and on the continent as primarily a potential statesman, the coming leader of Protestant Europe. His death by battle in Flanders in 1586 at the age of thirty-two seemed an irreparable loss. He survives in history as the first major figure in Elizabethan literature, author of a Petrarchan sonnet sequence addressed to "Stella," of a pastoral romance, *Arcadia,* and of a discerning and well-argued *Defense of Poesie.* Posterity remembers especially the call for emotional reality early in his sonnet sequence, "look in thy heart, and write," and his chivalric gesture, when on the point of death, in giving a drink of water to a soldier who appeared to be more in need of it. No doubt his early death was fortunate for his reputation. No human being could have fulfilled the expectations he had aroused by his extraordinary gifts. And only at this particular juncture in English history, when a whole new world of culture had suddenly become open and the conflicts between irreconcilable attitudes had not yet become overt, could there have appeared a figure so harmonious and versatile and so little inhibited by inner conflicts.

Both in his *Defense of Poesie* and in his *Arcadia,* Sidney insists that the poet "makes things even better than Nature bringeth forth, or quite anew forms such as never were in Nature," and thus inspires the reader to embody this ideal world in his own living. Thus he accepted the exalted view of the artist's creativity which had become current in Renaissance Italy and the optimistic identification of beauty with virtue. Imaginative literature provided "moral images, and examples (as directing threads) to guide every man through the confused labyrinth of his own desires and life." [8] This view of literature was exemplified in the *Arcadia,* which was regarded for the next century as a classic work, with twenty reprintings in English and thirty in various foreign languages, though it did not retain its significance for later generations. Any modern reader with enough patience to grapple with Sidney's artificial style and with the rather tiring conventions of pastoralism will gradually discover that he is in a familiar atmosphere. The idealization of a simple and natural life, the preposterously complicated plot with men disguised as women and vice versa (transvestism seems to have fascinated the Elizabethans), the glorification of chastity, the element of supernaturalism, chiefly in the form of oracles, the serenity of the conclusion—this strongly resembles the Shakespeare of the last plays. And the obvious indebtedness of Shakespeare to Sidney suggests that the *Arcadia* may have more merits than the modern reader has been willing to recognize. Pastoralism was used to convey certain views of life which were characteristic of the Renaissance, particularly the sense of the goodness of nature and the innocence of those who lived close to it.

---

[8] Fulke Greville: op. cit., XVIII, 223.

The sense of happy discovery and the absense of inner conflicts and tensions are equally marked in the work of Sidney's friend and protégé Edmund Spenser. All the positive elements of the Elizabethan spirit are to be found in *The Faerie Queene,* which remains a work of great charm, pictorial rather than analytical. The earlier sections are overweighted with allegory, which refers both to contemporary political events and to moral and spiritual forces. Thus the Faerie Queene herself is at the same time Queen Elizabeth and heavenly beauty, while Duessa signifies false religious belief and also has qualities of Mary Queen of Scots. But in the later books Spenser mostly forgets about the allegory and concentrates on the narrative and on its pictorial qualities.

The work is permeated with the Tudor sense of political order. The knights go forth not, as in most medieval romances, to rescue the unfortunate and the oppressed, but to enforce justice. And in spite of Spenser's obviously gentle temperament, he could be quite ruthless in his attitude to evildoers, or those he regarded as such. A whole book, the fifth, is devoted specifically to justice, personified by Sir Artegall; and numerous scenes make it plain that justice includes the preservation of class differences and property rights. Spenser had no use for the "raskall rabble" (I, xii, 19) or for proposals for the redistribution of property. He spent much of his later life in Ireland, where a series of officials was attempting to enforce English rule by slaughtering all who rebelled against it; and both in *The Faerie Queene* and in prose writings he made it quite plain that he approved of this savage policy. Sir Artegall is, in fact, modeled after the most severe of the English rulers of Ireland, Lord Grey de Wilton.

The most striking feature of the poem, however, is Spenser's ability to set side by side religious and Renaissance attitudes with no apparent awareness of their incompatibility. He was himself a deeply religious man, inclined toward Puritanism, and *The Faerie Queene* is, among several other things, an allegorical presentation of the Christian virtues. Yet the poem is pervaded with a delight in physical beauty equal to that displayed by any Renais-

446

sance painter, and in a number of passages Spenser writes glow-
ingly of the pleasures of sexual love. Particularly explicit is the
account of the Gardens of Adonis in canto vi of Book III:

> For here all plenty and all pleasure flowes,
> And sweet Love gentle fitts emongst them throwes,
> Without fell rancor or fond gealosy:
> Franckly each paramor his leman knowes,
> Each bird his mate, ne any does envy
> Their goodly meriment and gay felicity.

Almost as lightheartedly sensuous are accounts of the Bower of
Bliss and of the abode of the lascivious Phaedria in Book II,
though in these passages Spenser does in the end remember that
sensuality is to be condemned.

The inconsistency is flagrant and cannot be transcended. Yet
Spenser believed that unifying principles could be found in Platonic love. This conception is set forth in his *Hymne in Honour
of Love*. The love of beauty is the main formative and ordering
principle of the universe, ending the primeval chaos and elevating human beings above baseness and making them heroic. There
is a pattern of perfect beauty in heaven; and the more beautiful a
material object is, the closer it is to heaven. Beauty of the body is
derived from beauty of the soul, and is always imperfect and
subject to decay; but the lover recreates a finer beauty than is
apparent to the naked eye in the beloved object, seeing the inner
beauty that is not wholly realized in the flesh.

Thus the love of sensuous beauty was imbued with religious
values, forming the lower rungs of a spiritual ladder which culminated in the love of God. In many of his shorter poems, and
particularly in the *Epithalamion* with which he celebrated his
own marriage, Spenser composed the most ecstatic glorifications
of physical love in all English literature.

This state of euphoria could not last, and the later Elizabethans found themselves confronted by a conflict of values and
views of life which they were incapable of resolving. One world
—the world of the Middle Ages, with its sense of unity and order

and its values derived from religious revelation—was rapidly disappearing, and a new world of which matter and energy were the ultimate components was taking its place. The spokesman of one world thought of causation as formal and final and maintained a teleological view of the universe. What was of decisive importance was the end which all creation sought to achieve. But now a new world was taking shape in which causation was primarily material and efficient, and the end could not be known. Which of these two worlds was the reality and which was the illusion? This basic question was implicit in much of the writing of the 1590's and early 1600's. It was expressed in the drama, giving it a depth and a tension possible only in an age of unusually rapid transition.

Possibly the highest of literary genres, first-class poetic drama is also one of the rarest. It can flourish only in a period when human beings are seen as individuals, not merely as representatives of classes, but when society is still felt to be permeated with religious values, so that the deeds and sufferings of individuals can be presented as having a universal significance. The Elizabethan age was an almost perfect example of such a situation. Man could not yet be separated from the society to which he belonged, and the social structure was legitimized by conformity to divine law. The dramatists were therefore constantly aware of the political and religious implications of the actions which they described. They saw their characters in relation always to social and cosmic wholes.

Originating in religious ceremonials and gradually achieving independence, the drama had become a popular art form during the Middle Ages, but relatively little of the medieval drama had much aesthetic value. With the coming of the Renaissance to England, scholars began to write plays that conformed to classical standards, the tragedies of Seneca being considered the most appropriate models; but such works had little popular appeal and were presented only before upper-class or learned audiences. There were thus two different dramatic traditions, and the great age of the Elizabethan theater began when these traditions were

448

brought together. In the 1580's, university-trained "wits" found that it was possible to support themselves by writing plays for the popular theater.[9]

Yet despite the work of the "wits," much of the drama of the 1590's and early 1600's was written solely for popular entertainment and was totally devoid of literary or intellectual value. With implausible characters and plots filled with violence and horror, frequently featuring patriotic appeals to the "groundlings," it resembled the popular literature of all other periods and has survived only by accident. Nothing could be cheaper or more absurdly melodramatic than some of the works of Thomas Heywood, for example. Even the best of the drama was partially vitiated by the demands of the audience for blood-curdling scenes of horror interspersed with slapstick humor. Although the court and many of the nobility gave their support to the popular drama, academic intellectuals continued to regard it with some degree of scorn because of its failure to conform to classical standards. Seneca remained the model dramatist, and Fulke Greville and others wrote Senecan tragedies, though they do not

---

[9] The economic motivation should not be overlooked. In the Middle Ages, scholars and intellectuals could normally expect appointments in the service of the Church. The establishment of the Church of England, accompanied as it was by the secularization of much church property, had vastly reduced the number of available positions, so that one of its unexpected by-products was the appearance of an intelligentsia in need of economic support. Patronage by rich noblemen became an established procedure, and remained so until the eighteenth century; but the supply of "wits" looking for patrons was always larger than the demand. Most of the Elizabethan poets and dramatists lived bohemian lives, were often close to starvation, and died relatively young. Those who survived often did so by finally taking holy orders and becoming Anglican clergymen, despite youthful records of debauchery. Similar factors were operative in other Western countries. Therefore, the independent (though usually poverty-stricken) intellectual was to remain an important feature of Western society, not clearly paralleled in the history of any earlier civilization. Shakespeare was apparently unique among Elizabethan writers in making a good living from the popular stage and using it to achieve higher social status in his native town.

seem to have ever been acted in public. The play which Hamlet described as caviar to the general appears to have been of the Senecan type, and in praising it Hamlet was conforming to the usual literary standards of the educated Elizabethan nobleman. (This, incidentally, is an indication that Hamlet was not a self-portrait. It is most unlikely that Shakespeare would have shared his character's theatrical preferences.)

The first Elizabethan play of major importance was the *Tamburlaine* of Christopher Marlowe, apparently produced in the winter of 1587–8. Much of the action was crudely melodramatic; but it was written in resonant and soaring verse, with simple iambic rhythms which captivated popular audiences; and above all it had a theme which, in spite of the lack of all subtlety and sophistication, gave expression to some of the deepest emotions of the age. Tamburlaine was the lawless individualist who made himself the most powerful emperor on earth and was finally vanquished only by death. No other dramatist of the age expressed so much sympathy for the new forces that were threatening to revolutionize society or showed so little reverence for traditional values. That constant awareness of man's membership in a complex social order which is conspicuous in Shakespeare was totally lacking in Marlowe. Even his imagery was derived almost wholly from astronomy and other forms of learning, not from ordinary human living.[1] Of Marlowe's later plays (he lived only to the age of twenty-nine) *Doctor Faustus* deals most directly with man's desire for power and pleasure and with the death which brings it to an end. Marlowe seems to have been regarded by his contemporaries as an atheist and a libertine, but his view of human life is profoundly ambiguous, for while he glorifies individualistic values, he recognizes that they must end in the defeat of death. Faustus's last speeches show a kind of total disintegration, with no hope of salvation.

---

[1] Though he had a vivid sense of color, it was almost restricted to black, scarlet, and yellow, none of which are colors suggestive of human life.

Later dramatists were profoundly influenced by Marlowe's individualism, but they regarded it, in general, as a subversive force. Only George Chapman (better known as translator of Homer) can be regarded as a disciple of Marlowe. Other dramatists mostly affirmed traditional beliefs in the divine order which Marlowe had repudiated. Yet there was always an uneasy awareness of two kinds of truth, the religious and the naturalistic, with no apparent relationship between them. And if man could not rely on any external guidance or protection, he could only seek within himself for some source of inner strength. The later dramatists were strongly influenced by Stoicism, which they found in the plays and essays of Seneca; but they mostly ignored the Stoic belief in natural law and the equality of man, and took from Stoicism chiefly its morality of individual endurance. There was no repetition of the terror and disintegration of the last scene in *Doctor Faustus*. Man could find within himself an inner strength which offered no explanation for the predicament in which he found himself, but which enabled him to endure suffering and annihilation without cringing. As T. S. Eliot has pointed out, this assertion of the self is displayed by most of Shakespeare's heroes at the moment of death. The words of Flamineo in the last scene of Webster's *The White Devil* sum up the whole mood:

> At my self I will begin and end.
> While we look up to heaven we confound
> Knowledge with knowledge. O, I am in a mist.

This note of desperation represented a kind of *ne plus ultra* of the Elizabethan mind.

Dramatists did not begin any serious exploration of the Marlowean universe until after 1600. The 1590's, at least as represented in the theater, seem to have been a relatively happy period, marked by a sense of national greatness resulting from the defeat of the Spanish Armada in 1588 and by a loyal warmth of feeling for the queen whose policies had been so fully vindicated. It was during this period that Shakespeare established himself as the most popular living dramatist, and his early work fully reflects the optimism of the time.

Of Shakespeare we know that he was generally liked by his associates and competitors—references to him show an unmistakably genuine affection—that he made a good deal of money out of the theater, and that although born into a middle-class family, he ended his life as a gentleman. His view of life, though perhaps not specifically religious (at least in his writings), was certainly conservative. His historical plays are definitely sympathetic to the belief in the traditional order, especially when one considers what he added to his sources or omitted from them. The most obvious elements in his greatness as a writer are his mastery of language and the comprehensiveness of his sympathies and sensibilities. He could empathize with a vast range of characters, though with a definite preference for those who displayed courtesy and gentleness, while his imagery was drawn from the whole of human experience, but more especially from the daily living of the household and the garden (in this fondness for homely parallels he resembled Jesus of Nazareth). He seems to have been a supreme example of what Keats called "negative capability"—the capacity of the imaginative writer to enter into other people's experiences and attitudes without making them his own. He was apparently not a pioneer in the development of new attitudes and techniques. When he turned from comedy to tragedy, he was following a general theatrical trend, not responding to any personal change of mood. But although his themes were determined by the preferences of his audience, he could explore their implications to an extraordinary depth. All this implies that he was not a self-conscious artist of the type which the Renaissance had produced in Italy. Except in a few of his sonnets he displayed none of Michelangelo's conviction of creative genius, and thought of himself as a theatrical craftsman rather than an artist. It is in keeping with this conception of his character that he seems to have given no thought to the publication or preservation of his plays.

Of the early comedies little need be said. Their purpose was entertainment, which they have never ceased to provide. There is no questioning of the conventional values of the time, and the main theme is love, which is presented in wholly positive terms. The characters engage in much of that playful dialectic or scholasticism of love which began with the troubadours and which modern readers often find a little tiresome. The hero is always a young nobleman, and his character is normally presented as without any serious faults, at least according to the mores of his time and class. It is noticeable that he is usually careful to make sure that the heroine has a substantial dowry before he permits himself to pay court to her (Bassanio and the Claudio of *Much Ado About Nothing* are obvious examples), but this display of common sense is accepted by Shakespeare as normal and not presented critically. In the last scene all the younger characters are married off to each other, often with no verisimilitude and little likelihood of subsequent harmony, but such questions, of course, are not raised. It is one of the conventions of this kind of entertainment that all the characters will live happily ever after.

In the histories, Shakespeare continues to be interested primarily in individuals and to be capable of a wide range of sympathetic portrayals, but in these plays a general view of society is always implied and sometimes stated in detail, and the behavior of individuals thereby acquires a social significance that is absent from the comedies. Shakespeare's eight-play interpretation of English history from the fall of Richard II in 1399 to the final ending of the civil wars with the victory of Henry Tudor in 1485 was original in no significant way. A series of historical chroniclers, the most important being Edward Hall, had presented the official Tudor view, restating the traditional concepts of the social order and of the divine origins of royal authority and telling the story of the civil wars in terms wholly favorable to the new dynasty. In finding the same principles of order embodied in the universe, in society, and in the human body, Shakespeare was displaying a way of thinking which had been a commonplace for a thousand years. More typically Shakespearean, perhaps, was the comparison of society to a garden which the gardener must keep in order. Order for Shakespeare always implies collaboration between man and nature. Throughout the plays, the monarch is represented as ruling by divine right, though it is also insisted that he must perform his duties effectively and that any failure on his part is the main cause of disorder in society. There is nowhere any sympathy for popular government, or indeed any suggestion that such government is even possible. Throughout the whole sequence of plays, Parliament is barely mentioned, and with no understanding of its functions and potential importance.[2] In all these political attitudes Shakespeare was, of course, conforming to the expectations of his audience, but one can fairly suppose that they also represented his own conscious convictions. He went beyond his sources in insisting on the doctrine of divine right (as, for example, in the Bishop of Carlisle's speech in *Richard II*) and in emphasizing the lawlessness and destructiveness of mob behavior, such as the Cade rebellion in *Henry VI*.

In describing the behavior of his upper-class characters Shakespeare emphasizes the pursuit of honor. This is a key value in the histories, as is love in the comedies; and it is generally presented without overt criticism. It meant primarily a reputation for warlike valor, and was to be achieved (to borrow a word from the French *chansons*) by showing oneself *preux*. That an Elizabethan audience would accept unquestioningly this essentially feudal value is another illustration of the persistence of the medieval tradition. Elizabethan drama is, in fact, full of young noblemen lusting after chances to win honor in war (Bertram in *All's Well That Ends Well* is a good example), and Elizabethan life no doubt offered many concrete opportunities, despite the fact that feudalism had long since disappeared. Henry V's war with France is described by Shakespeare approvingly as motivated by a desire for honor, and Henry believes that it has legal

---

[2] Marlowe showed a clearer understanding of the importance of Parliament, as he showed in two references in *Edward II* (ll. 1825, 2073). Possibly this may reflect differences of political attitude between the two playwrights.

justification. Yet the play opens with a scene in which two clerical dignitaries express consternation at a threat to confiscate half
the properties of the Church and decide to counter it by encouraging Henry to assert his claims to France. All Henry's warlike
activities, including the killing of the French prisoners at Agincourt, are presented sympathetically and no doubt were received
by the play's audience with full approval. This is an extraordinary example of the early Shakespeare's ability to be aware of
disillusioning realities without being emotionally concerned
about them.

In two of the three Roman plays, Shakespeare's subject matter was again largely political, though even more than in the
histories his primary concern was to present the effects of political responsibilities on the lives and characters of individuals. It is
remarkable how fully he was able to think in Roman terms,
imaginatively reconstructing a whole society from the somewhat
meager evidence supplied by Plutarch. The Elizabethan concept
of legitimacy is wholly absent; there is no suggestion whatever
that society needs a single divinely appointed ruler. It is the
Roman republic that represents legitimate authority. Thus
Shakespeare's interpretation of Roman history is a Renaissance
rather than a medieval view; and it is astonishing that a loyal
citizen of Tudor England could have adopted this view so completely.

In the first of the Roman plays, Caesar is plainly a usurper, in
no way comparable to a medieval king; and Shakespeare goes
beyond Plutarch in emphasizing his human weaknesses, both
physical and emotional. The conspirators are, on the whole,
presented sympathetically, and the main purpose of the play is to
show how Brutus, though a wholly honorable man, brings ruin
upon himself and his associates through errors of judgment and a
foolish excess of idealism. In *Coriolanus,* the subject is more
narrowly political, and the republic—even more fully than in
Julius Caesar—represents the legitimate authority. Both Coriolanus himself and the leaders of the plebs are at fault, the former
in displaying an aristocratic arrogance and brutality, and the

455

latter in trying to subvert the republic for the benefit of the masses. The play is essentially a plea for moderation, and its central spokesman, Menenius Agrippa, who stands for legitimacy, recognizes that errors have been committed by both sides.

At about the turn of the century, the mood of the London theater began to change. Dramatists no longer accepted love and the pursuit of honor as positive values not to be questioned. They now began to express doubts about the whole social order. They continued to believe in traditional ideals, but could no longer see these ideals as effectively embodied in existing society. As Miss Ellis-Fermor has remarked, they were obsessed by "the sense of the loss of a spiritual significance from within the revealed world of fact and event." They displayed a "growing sense of the futility of man's endeavor, of the doom which waited not upon him alone, but upon the civilization he had built." [3] This new mood was rationalistic, and its effect on the traditional order was wholly negative and destructive. Instead of love, men saw a wholly sensual lust, and instead of the pursuit of honor, they saw the vulgar and egotistical ambition of the social climber. This view of life was shared by a number of dramatists, among them Ben Jonson, John Marston, George Chapman, Cyril Tourneur, John Webster, Thomas Middleton, and Shakespeare. The mood dominated the stage for about a decade and was then followed by a revival of romantic comedy.

It is tempting to suppose that Shakespeare's change from comedy to tragedy was a product of his own psychological evolution, especially as the mood of the earlier tragedies is similar to that of the later sonnets, and that he initiated the new vogue for pessimism and bitter social satire. But it is plain that one man, however gifted, could not so decisively have changed the whole tone of the London stage; and while the chronological evidence is uncertain, it would appear that the change was initiated by Jonson, Marston, and Chapman, and that Shakespeare followed

---

[3] Una Ellis-Fermor: *The Jacobean Drama,* pp. 8, 21.

their example only after it had become apparent that this was what audiences had come to enjoy. Thus Shakespeare was impelled to explore the deeper levels of the human psyche only after such explorations had become popular with London theatergoers. He was always a craftsman rather than a self-conscious artist.

Although the new mood was expressed in Shakespeare's tragedies, its more typical manifestations were in bitter and satirical comedies, in which a series of "malcontents" indulged in railing against the established order. The malcontent was already a well-established psychological type, having been defined by a writer named William Rankins in his *English Ape,* published in 1588. Having failed to achieve worldly success, the malcontent felt a deep sense of frustration; he was, moreover, either a melancholiac or given to manic-depressive alternations. In the new drama, a long series of malcontents gave expression to doubts about the values of the social order and to the reduction of love, especially in women, to mere animal sensuality. Such, for example, were Marston's Malevole, Jonson's Macilente, and Chapman's Dowsecer. Their complaints were echoed in a number of Shakespearean plays, especially in *Hamlet* and *Lear.* The same attitude was expressed in satirical verse, which suddenly became popular, notable examples being the writings of Joseph Hall and John Donne.

Most of the dramatists continued to accept traditional values. The only important exception was George Chapman, the most philosophical of the group, who in several of his tragedies, especially *Bussy d'Ambois* and *The Conspiracy and Tragedy of Byron,* glorified the ambitious superman as an individual who lived in accordance with nature and was therefore above the law. But the dramatists were no longer confident that their values were embodied in existing society, though they paid their respects to the expectations of their audience by vindicating traditional notions of good and evil in their finales. In the new commercialized society which was taking shape, what seemed to the dramatists to be a reprehensible greed for money would be judged by different standards, and the medieval emphasis on the duty of generosity would seem like a justification of wastefulness. Similarly, the ambitious individualism which the Elizabethans identified with Machiavellianism would soon be viewed with approval rather than as a threat to society.

The dramatists were especially concerned with the destructiveness of sexual desire. The Platonic view of love which had satisfied Sidney and Spenser now seemed naïve. Some men of the new generation explicitly repudiated it and glorified a love that was frankly physical. John Donne must have appealed to many of his associates when he affirmed that love must have sensuous expression, "Else a great Prince in prison lies" ("The Extasie"). But in the drama physical desire was mostly presented in tones of revulsion, and descriptions of the secret thoughts of innocent-seeming women became almost obsessive.[4] A series of women was shown as carried to death by sexual passion, among the most poignant being the heroines of Middleton's *The Changeling* and of the two somber tragedies of John Webster.

Thus the mood which pervades the plays of Shakespeare's early tragic period was shared by a number of contemporary dramatists. In giving expression to this state of mind, Shakespeare explored more deeply the sensibility which he shared with his contemporaries. The railing speeches which characterize the

---

[4] A typical example, in Marston's *Malcontent* (I, iii), is the following speech describing a girl's thoughts at her wedding banquet:

> And yet even then, the thew of her delight
> Flowes from lewde heat of apprehension,
> Only from strange imagination rankeness,
> That formes the adulterer's presence in her soule,
> And makes her thinke she clips the foule knave's loins.

Lodovico, in Webster's *The White Devil*, speaks similarly (IV, ii):

> Like brides at wedding-dinners, with their looks turned
> From the least wanton jest, their puling stomach
> Sick of the modesty, when their thoughts are loose,
> Even acting of those hot and lustful sports
> Are to ensue about midnight.

malcontent appear in several of his plays, and are sometimes put into the mouths of characters who would not be expected to express such sentiments—what would a prince of Denmark know of "the oppressor's wrong, the proud man's contumely, the pangs of dispriz'd love, the law's delay, the insolence of office" (*Hamlet*, III, i)? Another theme appearing in the plays of this period is the problem of truth. The central character may be confronted by two opposite interpretations of a situation and remain uncertain which of them is correct. One of these interpretations can roughly be identified as according with traditional values, the other as representing the destructive aspects of rationalism.

The Shakespearean play that most fully represents the new attitudes is *Troilus and Cressida*. Probably written not for the general public, but for an intellectual audience (the lawyers of the Inns of Court have been suggested), it contains more philosophical argument than any of the other plays, and the mood is wholly cynical, the observations of the railing Thersites being confirmed by the actions of all the leading characters. We are never allowed to forget that the whole Trojan war has been provoked by a cuckold and a whore; Helen is portrayed as a simpering idiot; and romantic love, as felt by Troilus, is a naïve illusion. Nor does the pursuit of honor fare better than that of love. Having explained in detail that it is wrong for the Trojans to keep the stolen Helen, Hector decides that honor requires them to keep her, the ultimate result being, as the audience knows, the destruction of the city. Achilles, the great exemplar of honor among the Greeks, is a boorish lout, and he eventually kills Hector not in fair combat but after finding him unarmed. Thus all the values of the old order are very thoroughly denied, and no new values are presented to replace them.

Hamlet is Shakespeare's major work of this period, and it remains the greatest product of the English Renaissance and the only product that penetrates to what may be described as a mythical level. The overt theme of the play reflects the Elizabethan view of life; but in its presentation Shakespeare includes material the full significance of which he cannot have consciously understood but which is accessible to psychological analysis. On a superficial reading the meaning of the play remains an enigma; yet few critics have agreed with the verdict of T. S. Eliot (in an early essay) that this obscurity makes *Hamlet* unsuccessful. Audiences normally find its performance to be a deeply moving experience, and there can be no doubt that they respond to the play's hidden meanings, even though, like the author, they are normally unable to make these meanings explicit.

On the manifest level *Hamlet* presents the problem of truth. The court of Denmark appears on the surface to be a specimen of the everyday world. All the characters (except Hamlet himself) appear to be shallow and commonplace to an extent unequaled in any other Shakespearean play. At the same time the King and Queen can obviously perform their duties with the necessary minimum of competence; Polonius is a typical counselor, though somewhat long-winded and of mediocre ability; Ophelia is a girl who obeys her parents and has little strength of character. Yet this apparently innocent society is deeply corrupt, being founded on an unavenged murder and adultery; and this is known only to Hamlet and to the guilty persons. Hamlet is presented as a typical Renaissance nobleman, cultured, talented, and attractive. He is capable of acting vigorously and decisively, as for example in his treatment of Rosencrantz and Guildenstern, and the hesitation that overcomes him in dealing with his uncle is by no means characteristic of him in other situations. Along with his friend Horatio, he represents, in general, the forces of virtue; while the world around him is basically evil. The most obvious reason for his hesitation is the uncertainty of the truth. Can his insight into the hidden evils of the social order be regarded as trustworthy when they do not seem to be shared by anybody else?

When one begins to examine the play more closely, however, one immediately discovers that Hamlet's doubts are due to deeper factors. Why actually does he hesitate? This is, of course, the central probelm of the play, and none of the more rational explanations is satisfactory. There can be no doubt that he does hesitate: he tells us so himself. He continues to do so after the play scene has ended all doubt about his uncle's guilt, and actually, of course, he had no genuine doubts earlier, the play scene being largely an excuse for delaying action. Nor are the practical difficulties to be regarded as serious obstacles. He has plenty of opportunities for killing Claudius, and in case there is any doubt on this point, Shakespeare shows Laertes breaking into the king's chamber with almost ludicrous ease and threatening to kill him. There are, in fact, two other characters in the play with dead fathers to avenge—Laertes and Fortinbras—and both of them show a vigor and decisiveness which is in sharp contrast to Hamlet's hesitations. Nor is Hamlet shown as a character who is normally incapable of action. He can do anything except kill Claudius.

Thus none of the rational interpretations of Hamlet's delay carries conviction; and as Shakespeare does not explain it, it is likely that he did not himself know the true answer. To state Hamlet's psychic situation as briefly as possible, he is inhibited from action because of his complicated emotions toward his father, and these work in two different ways. Claudius, as the husband of his mother, has taken his father's place, and hence has become the focus of all the inhibitions that prevent Hamlet from expressing his deep hostility toward the father. At the same time Claudius has killed the father, and having committed the crime that Hamlet would himself have wished to commit, has thereby become identified with Hamlet himself. Thus for two different but closely allied reasons Claudius is the one male character in the play against whom Hamlet cannot act directly. The truth of this explanation can be supported by reference to Hamlet's attitude toward his mother, as displayed when he urges her to restrain her sexual desires. In this scene Hamlet's own sexual feelings toward Gertrude are evident and almost reach overt expression.

This psychological explanation, however, does not take us to the deepest level of the play, though it points in that direction. Below the psychic level is the mythical; and it is this that especially constitutes the greatness of the play and is responsible for its lasting and almost universal appeal. A work of art may be described as myth-creating when it gives form and shape to some universal human experience which has a profound spiritual significance. Hamlet's task is not only to kill the father-symbol represented by Claudius, but also, and more meaningfully, to identify himself with his own father by assuming the task of avenging his death. He must, in fact, become his father. Thus the real subject of *Hamlet* is the obligation of the young man to achieve maturity by taking his father's place instead of continuing to feel fear and hatred toward his father while identifying himself with his mother. *Hamlet* is a response to the puberty experience, which is one of the universal experiences of the whole human race. And this links it with the greatest dramatic masterpiece of the classical civilization, the *Oresteia* of Aeschylus, which has a parallel theme. In the *Oresteia,* as in *Hamlet,* the son is faced with the task of avenging his father, though he is required to kill not only the mother's paramour, but also the mother herself; and this task fills him with acute pangs of conscience, represented by the Furies. He wins acquittal and release when, after being put on trial before the highest Athenian law court, he is told by the goddess Pallas Athene that the identification with the father takes precedence over that with the mother. Thus *Hamlet* and the *Oresteia* have essentially the same subject: the emotional struggle of the young man to achieve psychic maturity. And it is significant that each of them was written during a period of rapid cultural change when the young man could not simply model himself after his parents, but was required to assume the full responsibilities of independence.

The next of the major tragedies, *Othello,* appears on a superficial reading to be solely concerned with individual characters without deeper meanings. Presenting a single line of action which leads directly and almost inevitably to the final catastrophe, it is the smoothest and most objective of the tragedies. Iago alone plays the role of malcontent, and the good characters do not engage in the confused but powerful diatribes against corrupt societies that disturb the surface of *Hamlet* and *Lear*. Yet the theme of the play is—once more—the problem of truth; and this leads Shakespeare—perhaps unconsciously—to give a deeper significance to the leading characters which is not wholly in harmony with their places in the play. As suggested in the previous chapter, conflict between the two views of life is the real subject, though it remains implicit and is never fully explained. Iago, in particular, lacks adequate motivation, and the reason for this is that he is not only a villain in a play; he represents the whole new rationalistic view of life. Desdemona, on the other hand, is not merely a slandered wife. She is the embodiment of traditional values of love and fidelity. Why otherwise does Othello declare that if Desdemona is unfaithful, then "chaos is come again"? And why does he go on to see in his wife's misbehavior the destruction of a whole society:

> Farewell the plumed troop, and the big wars,
> That make ambition virtue! O, farewell!
> Farewell the neighing steed, and the shrill trump,
> The spirit-stirring drum, the ear-piercing fife,
> The royal banner, and all quality,
> Pride, pomp and circumstance of glorious war.

Othello is saying farewell to the whole medieval view of life, which is being destroyed by an unmotivated rationalism.

The third and fourth of the major tragedies, *Lear* and *Macbeth,* mark a progression toward more positive values. Although Shakespeare seems to have begun his exploration of tragic themes in response to new theatrical trends, we may suppose that he found it personally necessary to work through the new modes of thought and sensibility in order to arrive at new positive affirmations. The view of life presented in these later tragedies no longer corroborates the cynicism of the malcontent and the Machiavellian, and is not paralleled in the work of Shakespeare's contemporaries.

Lear has the largest scope and the most comprehensive range of characters of any of the plays. One is constantly aware not only of the wide varieties of human attitudes and experience, but also of the whole world of animate and inanimate nature. Much of the material parallels that of the earlier tragedies. Lear and Gloucester belong to the old feudal order, while the younger generation, Cordelia and Edgar excepted, represent the new destructive rationalism. Edmund, with his wholly amoral ambition and the blithe self-assurance with which he puts it into action, is the perfect Machiavellian, while the railing of the malcontent appears in some of Edmund's speeches and—with more violence and passion—in the diatribes of Lear on the heath. But the play ends with positive affirmations, which can fairly be described as close to the Christian ethic, although this is not made explicit. Lear's sufferings have a purgative effect, and he learns a humility and a sympathy for all human suffering which make him a very different man from the domineering and egotistical king of the first act.

The new emphasis on the positive is even more marked in *Macbeth*. This is the antithesis of *Hamlet* in that it presents a single center of evil in a society otherwise good. Except for Macbeth and his wife, all the leading characters are conspicuously noble and virtuous; and the abnormal quality of evil is suggested by the appearance of the witches and by the occurrence of unnatural portents. The night of the murder, as described by several of the characters, is marked by a long series of prodigies, as though Macbeth's action was so contrary to nature that it had disturbed the whole natural order. Macbeth himself, moreover, is presented in terms wholly without precedent on the Elizabethan stage. Judged by his actions, he is a typical exemplar of the Machiavellian; but Shakespeare shows him to us from the inside and makes him human. All previous Elizabethan Machiavellians had been symbols of the new rationalistic individualism, portrayed with no human weaknesses or doubts and deriving a positive pleasure from their contempt for all moral scruples; and they had generally died as unrepentently as they had lived. Macbeth, on the other hand, undertakes the murder of Duncan with many misgivings, recognizing its criminal quality; and though one crime leads to a series of others and his character steadily deteriorates, he takes no pleasure in his rise to kingship and by the end of the play is a quivering mass of nerves. He is the one Machiavellian character for whom the audience can feel only a pity which overrides all moral condemnation.

Thus Shakespeare had stated the dilemma presented by the conflict of values and had then moved beyond it. In *Lear* and *Macbeth* he affirms the natural and universal quality of good and evil, condemning individualistic ambition in terms not of the traditional social order, but of simple humanity. This recovery of faith in the essential goodness of nature led to the matured optimism of his final period.

Once again changes in the mood of Shakespearean drama ran parallel with new theatrical developments, although the correspondence was less close, and the chronological evidence makes it possible that Shakespeare himself was the main innovator. Around the year 1610, romantic comedy began to have a new vogue, represented especially in the work of John Fletcher and his sometime collaborator Francis Beaumont. This was connected not only with changes of taste among popular audiences, but also with a growing fondness among the aristocracy for theatrical entertainments featuring elaborate staging, romantic plots, and no serious intellectual content. Fletcher was the favorite dramatist of the court and the nobility, and for a long period was regarded as superior to Shakespeare. Yet his whole work was essentially escapist, turning away from all serious discussion of moral and political values. His plots mostly presented imaginary kingdoms with a strong pastoral flavor; and his characters would —so to speak—sing arias on the traditional themes of love and honor in all their possible ramifications. Of genuine emotion and real human problems there was never a trace. This marked the beginning of the decadence of the drama, though a series of increasingly mediocre playwrights kept it alive in some form until the closing of the theaters at the outbreak of civil war in 1642.

There are certain superficial parallels between the plays of Shakespeare's last period and the work of Fletcher, but Shakespeare has an underlying seriousness lacking in his younger contemporaries. The four late romances—*Pericles, Cymbeline, The Winter's Tale,* and *The Tempest*—all have a pastoral flavor apparently derived from Sir Philip Sidney's *Arcadia* and are all far removed from realism; Shakespeare appears to be presenting, in symbolic terms, a whole new view of life.

Evil is abundantly present in these last plays, but it is not a fundamental element in human life. It is often inadequately motivated (as with Leontes in *The Winter's Tale*), and is overcome in the course of time with relative ease and without leaving any permanently bad results. The main emphasis is on the ultimate beneficence of nature, the healing effects of time, and the innocence of youth, particularly if it has grown up in a natural environment, free from the corrupting effects of a sophisticated civilization. All four plays have recognition scenes; somebody who has been lost is found again, and found under conditions which wipe out the misdeeds responsible for the original disappearance. In all four plays a young woman is portrayed as possessing a natural innocence which is stronger than the forces of evil. Nature is fundamentally good, and the natural processes of growth can be relied upon to ensure the continuance of virtue. There is, moreover, an element of the supernatural, not identified with any particular formal religious belief, which suggests that the goodness of human life is supported by forces transcending nature. The tone of the plays is generally idyllic; and though evil is real, it does not have such shattering effects as in the tragedies. The young women—Marina, Perdita, Imogen, and Miranda—are strong because they are innocent; and they represent the beneficence of a nature with which human art can cooperate.

Apparently without the aid of any formal theology, Shakespeare had arrived at affirmations corresponding to those of Dante. Like Dante he had passed through hell in the four great tragedies. And like Dante he had found an earthly paradise, free from emotional conflict and tension, where virtue was symbolized in the figure of a young woman. The mood expressed in the romances of his final period resembles that of the last section of the *Purgatorio*.

Shakespeare's vision of goodness, however, was wholly personal and not shared by his contemporaries. Through the early decades of the seventeenth century the conflicts that had been explored by the dramatists continued with increasing intensity, and the moral and intellectual forces which the dramatists had felt to be essentially destructive steadily gained in strength. Gradually English society became polarized around two opposite tendencies, and the conflict of values assumed political forms. Elizabeth had maintained the sense of national unity by making herself the focus of all loyalties, and spokesmen both of the old sense of cosmic order and unity and of the new rationalistic individualism had been included among her advisers. But after her death in 1603 her Stuart successors, James I and Charles I, lacked her political insight, appealing too exclusively to the supporters of the traditional view and governing incompetently and corruptly.

Two movements in particular represented the future: the growth of science and Puritanism.

The Renaissance had done little to promote science, but toward the end of the sixteenth century, scientific progress was resumed with a new awareness of its revolutionary implications. Its main English spokesman was Francis Bacon, though he was important chiefly in emphasizing the implications of the scientific method rather than in making any new discoveries. And what Bacon especially affirmed in his *Novum Organum* and other writings was that science must become independent of religion. Men, he declared, should "soberly render unto faith the things that are faith's"; and having thus paid his respects to religion and quickly dismissed it, Bacon went on to enlarge on what might be expected from science after it had been liberated from theology. What a liberated science might accomplish was nothing less than "the empire of man over things." Thus by abandoning the medieval belief in a divinely created order, man could become the master of nature.[4]

---

[4] Francis Bacon: *Novum Organum,* translated by T. Fowler (Oxford, 1889), I, 65, 129.

The cultural implications of the new scientific world-view, including in particular its relationship to individualism, were given expression in the well-known lines of John Donne, which summarize so exactly the cultural situation that it is impossible not to quote them. In his "An Anatomie of the World: First Anniversary," referring to the work of Copernicus and Kepler, Donne complained that the "new Philosophy calls all in doubt." The planets, it appeared, did not move in circles and the earth was no longer the center of the universe. And Donne immediately concludes that chaos in the heavens will produce chaos in human society:

> 'Tis all in peeces, all cohaerence gone
> All just supply, and all Relation:
> Prince, Subject, Father, Sonne, are things forgot,
> For every man alone thinkes he hath got
> To be a Phoenix, and that there can bee
> None of that kinde, of which he is, but hee.

To the believers in a cosmic order it did indeed seem that the new world meant total chaos and that all traditional notions of authority were being dissolved. The new sciences, with their emphasis on material and efficient causes and their repudiation of formal and final causes, seemed to be incompatible with the whole Christian and classical view of society. But there was one rapidly growing group—the Puritans—which found its authority not in any external power, but in the words of the Bible and in the secret witness of the Holy Spirit in the hearts of true believers. There were many different forms of Puritanism, but all of them, in varying degrees, represented a new form of individualism and regarded the Church as composed only of the elect and not of the nation as a whole. And as a result of the incompetence of the early Stuart kings, Puritanism became identified with opposition to the monarchy and attracted many individuals whose motivations were primarily political rather than religious.

There was no single cause for the gradual dissolution of the

British people into two opposing groups which eventually—in 1642—came to war with each other. Individual motivations varied, and the choice of sides seemed often to be illogical. Members of the nobility, the gentry, and the middle class were to be found on both sides of the conflict, which cannot be interpreted as a class war. Economic and other material factors carried much weight, but what seemed to be chiefly at stake was something much deeper. Fundamentally, the war was a conflict between the medieval belief in the organic unity of society and post-medieval individualism. Loyalty to the monarchy was associated with medieval social ideals, such as the belief in rigid class distinctions, a paternalistic supervision of economic activities in the interests not of the upper class but of the nation as a whole, and a suspicion of new economic enterprises. Its opponents, including some of the nobility as well as the urban merchants, were disposed to invest in new enterprises and to dislike government regulation. Puritanism was associated with laissez-faire attitudes, leaving each individual free to make or mar his own fortune, and promoting economic expansion both at home and overseas. This ambitious spirit, combined with hostility toward the Roman Church, made the Puritans eager for a war with Spain that would enable them to plunder the Spanish overseas empire.

These differences had begun to show themselves under Elizabeth. While some of her advisers were conservative both at home and abroad, other members of her council, notably Leicester and (in the next generation) Sir Walter Raleigh and the ill-fated Earl of Essex, were for offensive action against Spain; and although their own lives were far from realizing Puritan ideals, they supported Puritanism politically. But Elizabeth was much too shrewd to allow such differences to become dangerous. Under her Stuart successors, on the other hand, English society split into two hostile groups. And while the two sides were probably fairly matched in numbers and material resources, the opponents of the king were decisively superior in vigor, skill, and determination. They knew that they were fighting for new beliefs and a new way of life. There was much that was valuable in the traditional attitudes; but those who fought for them were deficient in skill, energy, and honesty. And though the monarchy, after being overthrown in the civil war of the forties, was restored in 1659, there was no attempt to re-establish the social and economic ideals of the Middle Ages.

The Middle Ages had begun in the British Isles, earlier than on the continent, in the fusion of barbaric and Mediterranean traditions. Political and economic institutions, literary and artistic styles, and general views of life all showed both classical and Celto-Teutonic influences. What was most characteristically medieval was the emphasis on cultural and political unity. The ending of the Middle Ages, marked by the dissolution of this sense of unity and the effective triumph of individualism, can less easily be dated, since developments in different countries varied in speed and intensity. But 1642 would be one possible date—it is appropriate to choose an event in the history of England, since this country was moving toward cultural leadership in political ideals and institutions and in the sciences. The next major movement in the cultural history of the West, the Enlightenment, was largely based on ideas and attitudes that had originated with Isaac Newton, John Locke, and other English intellectuals.

LIST OF BOOKS

A comprehensive bibliography would obviously be impossible. This list is restricted to secondary authorities to which I have made some direct reference or which I have found especially useful. With a few exceptions, they are available in English.

GENERAL AND CULTURAL HISTORY: THE MIDDLE AGES.

Artz, Frederick: *The Mind of the Middle Ages* (New York, 1954).

Bloch, Marc: *Feudal Society* (London, 1961). A definitive study, written by one of the greatest of modern historians. Bloch was killed by the Nazis during the Occupation.

Clark, Sir George, ed.: *Oxford History of England,* 15 vols. (Oxford, 1937–50).

Haskins, Charles Homer: *The Renaissance of the Twelfth Century* (Cambridge, Mass., 1927).

Huizinga, Johan: *The Waning of the Middle Ages* (London, 1924). Written by a Dutch historian, this study of social and cultural trends during the fourteenth and fifteenth centuries in western Europe, especially in Burgundy and the Netherlands, is always lively and sometimes profound.

Kilgour, Raymond L.: *The Decline of Chivalry* (New York, 1937). Based on French literature of the fourteenth and fifteenth centuries.

Lipson, E.: *Economic History of England,* 3 vols. (London, 1926–62).

Muller, Herbert J.: *Freedom in the Western World* (New York, 1963). A historical account, both lively and learned.

Painter, Sidney: *French Chivalry* (Baltimore, 1940).

Pirenne, Henri: *Medieval Cities* (London, 1925).

————: *Economic and Social History of Medieval Europe*

(London, 1937). Pirenne, a Belgian historian, was perhaps the best of twentieth-century medievalists.

Southern, R. W.: *The Making of the Middle Ages* (London,
1953). Early medieval history, chiefly French. Delightful to read, and based on solid scholarship.

Taylor, Henry Osborn: *The Medieval Mind,* 2 vols. (Cambridge, Mass, 1927). Useful summaries of medieval
writings, but Taylor's comments are generally superficial.

GENERAL AND CULTURAL HISTORY: THE RENAISSANCE.

Baron, Hans: *The Crisis of the Early Italian Renaissance*
(Princeton, 1955). An analysis of the growth of republican ideals in fourteenth-century Florence, which has
modified the traditional emphasis on the role of the despots in Renaissance Italy.

Burckhardt, Jacob: *The Civilization of the Renaissance in Italy*
(first English translation in London in 1878; frequently
reprinted). Still a great book, though its emphasis on the
individualism of the Renaissance has undergone considerable revisions.

Ferguson, Wallace K.: *Europe in Transition, 1300–1520* (Boston, 1962). An authoritative account of all aspects of
European civilization during the period covered.

Hay, Denys: *The Italian Renaissance in Its Historical Background* (Cambridge, England, 1961). A short but authoritative description.

Haydn, Hiram: *The Counter-Renaissance* (New York, 1950).
An account of the pessimistic and irrational elements in
the Renaissance mind.

Mazzeo, J. A.: *Renaissance and Revolution* (New York, 1965).
A stimulating collection of essays.

Rowse, A. L.: *The England of Elizabeth* (London, 1951). Perhaps the most useful of Mr. Rowse's books on Elizabethan themes. His writings are both lively and based on
solid research, though he is too inclined to claim mo-

nopolistic rights over the whole field of Elizabethan historiography.

RELIGION

Cohn, Norman: *The Pursuit of the Millennium* (New York, 1951). A lively, though superficial, account of medieval mystical cults.

Coulton, G. G.: *Five Centuries of Religion* (Cambridge, England, 1925).

————: *Life in the Middle Ages* (Cambridge, England, 1930). In these and other books Mr. Coulton gives a lively picture of medieval society, and disagrees vigorously with Roman Catholic views of medieval culture.

Erikson, Erik: *Young Man Luther* (New York, 1958). Probably the only psychoanalytic study of a historical character that can be regarded as convincing.

Jones, Rufus: *Studies in Mystical Religion* (New York, 1909).

————: *The Flowering of Mysticism* (New York, 1939). Useful surveys of mysticism in the Western world, written by a Quaker sympathizer.

Mackinnon, James: *Luther and the Reformation,* 4 vols. (London, 1962).

Nygren, Anders: *Agape and Eros* (London, 1953). A history of Christian interpretations of love, which shows convincingly that from the time of Constantine to the time of Luther they owed more to Plotinus than to the gospels.

Otto, Rudolf: *Mysticism, East and West,* translated by B. Bracey and R. Payne (London, 1932). A convincing analysis of the parallelisms between Eckhart and Indian mysticism.

PHILOSOPHY AND SCIENCE

Allen, John William: *History of Political Thought in the Sixteenth Century* (London, 1957).

Brehier, Emile: *The Philosophy of the Middle Ages* (New York, 1963).

Butterfield, H.: *The Origins of Modern Science 1300–1800* (London, 1951). A first-rate account, written by a leading historian for the general reader.

Carlyle, R. W. and A. J.: *History of Medieval Political Theory in the West,* 6 vols. (London, 1903–36).

Cassirer, Ernst et al.: *The Renaissance Philosophy of Man* (Chicago, 1948). Short but illuminating essays.

Crombie, A. C.: *Medieval and Early Modern Science,* 2 vols. (New York, 1959). An excellent survey, based on solid scholarship and intelligible to the general reader.

Gilby, Thomas H.: *Principality and Polity* (London, 1967). A liberal interpretation of St. Thomas Aquinas, written by a Catholic priest.

Gilson, Etienne: *The Spirit of Medieval Philosophy* (New York, 1936).

————: *Reason and Revelation in the Middle Ages* (New York, 1938).

————: *History of Christian Philosophy in the Middle Ages* (New York, 1955). Gilson has an immense knowledge of medieval thought, and his viewpoint is that of a liberal Catholic.

Kocher, Paul H.: *Science and Philosophy in Tudor England* (New York, 1935).

Kristeller, P. O.: *The Philosophy of Marsilio Ficino* (New York, 1943).

————: *Eight Philosophers of the Italian Renaissance* (Stanford, 1964). Short but authoritative discussions.

Kuhn, Thomas S.: *The Copernican Revolution* (New York, 1957). A discussion of its social implications.

Lewis, Ewart: *Medieval Political Ideas* (New York, 1954).

Pieper, J.: *Scholasticism* (New York, 1960).

Rice, Eugene F.: *The Renaissance Idea of Wisdom* (New York, 1958).

Vignaux, Paul: *Philosophy in the Middle Ages,* translated by E. C. Hall (New York: Meridian Books; 1959).

Wulf, Maurice de: *History of Medieval Philosophy* (Edinburgh, 1952).

LITERATURE

Auerbach, Erich: *Mimesis* (New York: Anchor Books; 1953). A fascinating analysis of stylistic changes in European literature, showing how they reflected the development of society.

————: *The Literary Language and Its Public in Late Latin Antiquity and the Middle Ages* (Princeton, 1965). Shows how the development of literature during the Dark Ages was impeded by the lack of appropriate languages.

Bolgar, R. R.: *The Classical Heritage* (Cambridge, England, 1954). Shows how classical literature survived during the Dark and Middle Ages.

Bush, Douglas: *Mythology and the Renaissance Tradition in English Poetry* (Cambridge, Mass., 1957).

Castro, Amerigo: *El Pensamiento de Cervantes* (Madrid, 1925). Finds more evidences of thought in Cervantes than the general reader would have expected.

Crossland, Jessie: *The Old French Epic* (London, 1951).

————: *Medieval French Literature* (London, 1956).

Curtius, Ernst R.: *European Literature and the Latin Middle Ages* (New York, 1953).

Ellis-Fermor, Una: *The Jacobean Drama* (London, 1936). An interpretation which stresses pessimistic aspects.

Fergusson, Francis: *Dante's Drama of the Mind* (Princeton, 1953). A brief but penetrating analysis.

Frappier, Jean: *Les Chansons de Geste du Cycle de Guillaume d'Orange.* (Paris, 1955).

Greg, W. W.: *Pastoral Poetry and Pastoral Drama* (London, 1906).

Grierson, Sir Herbert J. C.: *Cross Currents in English Literature of the Seventeenth Century* (Baltimore, 1966).

Jackson, K. H.: *A Celtic Miscellany* (Cambridge, Mass., 1951). Contains some early poetry from Wales and Ireland.

Jeanroy, Alfred: *La Poésie Lyrique des Troubadours,* 2 vols. (Paris, 1934). French scholarship at its best.

Ker, W. P.: *The Dark Ages* (London, 1923). A well-written survey of Dark Age literature.

Knights, L. C.: *Drama and Society in the Age of Jonson* (London, 1937). Stresses the conservatism, both economic and political, of the Jacobean theatre.

Laistner, M. L. W.: *Thought and Letters in Western Europe, A.D. 500–900.* (Ithaca, 1958). Gives more detail than Ker, but lacks Ker's graceful style.

Lewis, C. S.: *The Allegory of Love: A Study in Medieval Tradition* (Oxford, 1936). An excellent account of a literary genre which meant more to medieval minds than it does to us.

Raby, Frederick J. E.: *A History of Christian Latin Poetry from the Beginnings to the Close of the Middle Ages* (Oxford, 1934).

————: *A History of Secular Latin Poetry from the Beginnings to the Close of the Middle Ages* (Oxford, 1954). Comprehensive, authoritative, and easy to read.

Tilley, Arthur: *Literature of the French Renaissance,* 2 vols. (New York, 1959).

Tillyard, Eustace Mandeville: *The Elizabethan World Picture* (Cambridge, England, 1934).

THE VISUAL ARTS

Benesch, Otto: *Art of the Renaissance in Northern Europe* (Cambridge, Mass., 1945).

Berenson, Bernard: *Italian Painters of the Renaissance* (New York, 1948). The most useful general survey of the field, concentrating on what each painter produced, with little interpretation.

Bunin, M. S.: *Space in Medieval Art* (New York, 1940).

Clements, Robert J.: *Michelangelo's Theory of Art* (New York, 1961). Contains all of Michelangelo's recorded utterances, written and spoken, on this subject.

Evans, Joan: *Art in Medieval France, 987–1498* (Cambridge, Mass., 1948).

List of Books

————: *Church Art of the Medieval Period* (Cambridge, England, 1950).

Freedberg, Sidney J.: *Painting of the High Renaissance in Rome and Florence* (New York, 1961).

Hauser, Arnold: *A Social History of Art,* 2 vols. (New York, 1951). A comprehensive history of the arts in the Western world, with emphasis on sociological aspects.

Henry, Françoise: *Irish Art in the Early Christian Period, to 800 A.D.* (London, 1966).

Hinks, Roger: *Carolingian Art* (London, 1935).

Holt, Elizabeth: *A Documentary History of Art,* 2 vols. (New York, 1951). What artists and art critics have said about artistic theory and practice. Extremely useful for anybody interested in art history.

Larousse Encyclopedia of Byzantine and Medieval Art: and of *Renaissance and Baroque Art,* ed. René Huyghe (London, 1963, 1961). Of the innumerable art books that have been published in the last decade, these are the most comprehensive and the most useful to students.

Lavedan, Pierre: *French Architecture* (London, 1956).

Morey, Charles Rufus: *Mediaeval Art* (Princeton, 1942).

Panofsky, Erwin: *Gothic Art and Scholasticism* (Lancaster, Penn., 1951).

————: *Early Netherlandish Painting* (New York, 1953).

————: *Meaning in the Visual Arts* (New York: Anchor Books; 1955).

————: *Renaissance and Renascences in Western Art* (Copenhagen, 1960). An art historian who sees the relations of art to social and cultural backgrounds.

Pevsner, Nikolaus: *Outline of European Architecture* (London, 1963).

Simson, Otto von: *The Gothic Cathedral* (New York, 1956). Contains a detailed analysis of Chartres, emphasizing its symbolic meanings.

Sypher, Wylie: *Four Stages of Renaissance Style* (New York, 1956). A suggestive interpretation which emphasizes mannerism.

Wolfflin, Heinrich: *Art of the Italian Renaissance* (New York, 1913).

———: *Principles of Art History* (New York, 1932).

———: *Classic Art* (New York, 1952).

——— *Renaissance and Baroque* (London, 1964). Wölfflin, whose dates were 1864–1945, may be regarded as the principal founder of art history. He was apparently the first art historian who recognized that his functions were to analyze style and to interpret its relations to the general history of culture.

Worringer, Wilhelm: *Form in Gothic* (the first English edition appeared in London in 1927). In this little book Worringer applies to medieval architecture his famous distinction in art history between abstractionism and emotional identification.

MUSIC

Lang, Paul: *Music in Western Civilization* (New York, 1941).

Reese, Gustave: *Music in the Middle Ages* (New York, 1940).

———: *Music in the Renaissance* (New York, 1954).

Stevens, Denis, and Alec Robertson: *Penguin History of Music,* 2 vols. (London, 1960).

Index

i

Index

Index

Index

main bequest of, 99; *see also*
Holy Roman Empire
Roman law, 66, 248
Roman Saturnalia, 56
romance: origins of, 210; themes of,
210–12, 213–14; Celtic
mythology in, 212–13; as
forerunner of novel, 213, 215
Romance of the Rose, The, 171,
276–7
Romanesque style: characterized,
159, 219; origin of, 217–18,
222; examples of, 218–19, 229,
303; basilica form of, 219–20;
sculpture of, 220, 226
Romantic movement, 343–4 *n.,*
351, 428
Rome, 137, 301–2, 371, 380;
see also Roman Empire
Romuald, St., 58
Ronsard, Pierre de, 413
Roscelin of Compiègne, 183
Rosso, Giovanni Battista, 411
Ruthwell, stone crosses of, 85
Ruysbroek, Jan van, 285

Sadoleto, Jacopo, 343
St. Bartholomew's Day massacre,
416
St. Denis, abbey of, 157, 223–4, 229
St. Mark, cathedral of, 329
St. Martin of Tours, church of, 218
St. Peter, church of, 347
Saint-Victor, abbey of, 181
Sainte Chapelle, 236
Saladin, 145–6
Salimbene, 237
Salutati, Coluccio, 338
Sankara, 283
Santa Maria degli Angeli, 347
Santa Maria del Carmine, 350
Santa Maria del Fiore, 348
Sassanid kingdom, 107, 111
Saxon dynasty, 95, 125
Saxons, 26, 96
Scandinavia, 96, 121–2

scenici, 191
Schism, Great, 244–5
scholasticism, 42, 115, 123, 156,
176–7, 180, 182, 250–65, 286,
288; *see also* faith; rationalism;
realism; Aristotle; Thomism
science: Roman, 36; Dark Age,
59–61; and doctrine of natural
law, 174; impact of nominalist
philosophy on, 280, 286–94;
16th-century progress in, 311,
467–8; *see also* technology
scientific method, 289–90, 467
Scotland, 76, 81, 85
Seneca, 448–9, 451
Sens, cathedral of, 223
Serlio, Sebastiano, 412
Servetus, 409
Sforza, Ludovico, 369
Shakespeare, William, 368, 433,
441, 442, 445, 450, 451–67;
Troilus and Cressida, 60, 439,
459; *Othello,* 398 *n.,* 462–3;
Coriolanus, 440, 455–6; *Hamlet,*
450, 457, 459–62; elements of
greatness of, 452; comedies of,
452–3; sonnets of, 452, 456;
Much Ado About Nothing, 453;
histories of, 453–5; *Richard II,*
453–4; *Henry VI,* 454; *All's Well
That Ends Well,* 454; Roman plays
of, 455–6; *Julius Caesar,* 455;
tragedies of, 456–7; *King Lear,*
365, 457, 463–4; *Macbeth,*
463–5; late romances of, 466;
The Winter's Tale, 466
Shiism, 112–14
Sicily, 125, 145, 302, 303, 307–8
Sidney, Philip, 411*n.,* 443;
Arcadia, 444–5, 466;
Defense of Poesie, 444
Siena, 278, 306, 332–3
Sigebert I (King of Franks), 71
Siger of Brabant, 251
sirventes, 208–9
Sistine Chapel, 353 *n.,* 373–7

Index

A NOTE ABOUT THE AUTHOR

Henry Bamford Parkes was born in Sheffield, England, in 1904. After earning his B.A. at Oxford, he came to the United States and did his graduate work at the University of Michigan, where he received his Ph.D. in 1929. Since 1930 he has been on the faculty of New York University. Mr. Parkes has also taught at Barnard College, the University of Wyoming, and the University of Washington, has lectured at the New School (New York), and has been an editorial writer for the Baltimore Sun. *He has contributed widely to periodicals. During the 1956–7 academic year he was Fulbright professor in Greece, at the University of Athens. His published books include* Jonathan Edwards (*1930*), A History of Mexico (*1938*), Marxism: An Autopsy (*1939*), The Pragmatic Test (*1942*), Recent Americana (*1942*), The World After War (*1942*), The American Experience (*1947*), The United States of America (*1953*), *and* Gods and Men (*1959*). *Mr. Parkes is married and has two daughters.*

A NOTE ON THE TYPE

The text of this book was set on the Linotype in a face called TIMES ROMAN, *designed by* STANLEY MORISON *for* The Times (*London*), *and first introduced by that newspaper in 1932.*

Among typographers and designers of the twentieth century, Stanley Morison has been a strong forming influence, as typographical adviser to the English Monotype Corporation, as a director of two distinguished English publishing houses, and as a writer of sensibility, erudition, and keen practical sense.

In 1930 Morison wrote: "Type design moves at the pace of the most conservative reader. The good type-designer therefore realises that, for a new fount to be successful, it has to be so good that only very few recognise its novelty. If readers do not notice the consummate reticence and rare discipline of a new type, it is probably a good letter." It is now generally recognized that in the creation of Times Roman *Morison successfully met the qualifications of this theoretical doctrine.*

Composed, printed, and bound by Kingsport Press, Inc., Kingsport, Tennessee. Typography and binding design based on originals by Warren Chappell.

WARREN  CHAPPELL